The Telegraph

Guide to Commuterland
Finding a home within reach of London

The Telegraph
Guide to Commuterland

Finding a home within reach of London

Caroline McGhie

This revised and extended edition first published in 2009 by
Aurum Press Ltd, 7 Greenland Avenue, London NW1 0ND.

Copyright © 1992, 1997, 2000, 2004, 2009 by Caroline McGhie.

The original edition of this book was first published in 1992
by Good Books.
First published by Aurum in 2004.

Caroline McGhie has exerted her moral right to be identified
as the author of this work in accordance with the Copyright,
Designs and Patent Act 1998.

All rights reserved. No part of this book may be reproduced
or utilised in any form or by any means, electronic or mechanical,
including photocopying, recording or by any information
storage and retrieval system, without prior permission from
Aurum Press Ltd.

A catalogue record of this book is available from the
British Library.

ISBN 978 1 84513 479 2

10 9 8 7 6 5 4 3 2 1

2013   2012   2011   2010   2009

Edited by Jane Hutchings
Line drawings by Vincent Design
Rail travel information by Barry Doe
Book designed by Blue Gum
Typeset by M Rules

Printed and bound by MPG Books, Bodmin, Cornwall

CONTENTS

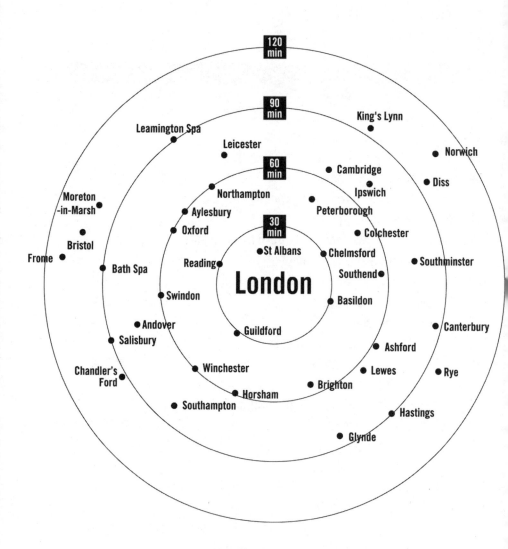

INTRODUCTION

It might seem cynical to present the English countryside as one huge emporium from which we can pick a lifestyle, calculate a journey, choose a school for our children and buy a house. But the truth is that in the 21st century we are rich in choice and there are many different lives we could lead, in many different places. The force for change is usually a house move – the biggest financial decision any of us ever makes.

What gathering of friends, especially in London, is complete without its stock-in-trade conversation about the quality of life? The questions are always the same. What point is there in slaving round-the-clock at the office if our precious leisure hours have to be spent in urban parks and shopping malls? What point is there in sitting daily in traffic jams if the local schools are inadequate, the air quality too poor and the garden too small for the lifestyle we feel we deserve? How can we inject more pleasure into our lives and reduce the stress?

Repeated property booms created the economic lever to make it happen. If we decide that the good things in life – the things that really matter – are walks from the back door, views over the hills, awareness of the changing seasons, shopkeepers who know your name, then selling up and moving out is often the answer. For years the price of a Victorian semi in London has paid for the pretty country cottage, the old vicarage, even the pony paddock.

Now the huge price hikes of the noughties are over and house values have been dropping fast – by around 20 per cent in 2008, with an expected further drop of perhaps 10 per cent in 2009. In some areas – parts of Hertfordshire, Northamptonshire and Kent – prices have risen and fallen back to where they were when the 2004 edition was published. This isn't all bad news, because suddenly the rural dream becomes more affordable again. People priced out of the market may now be able to return. Those who have lost their jobs in the recession may decide to start again in a new place, yet maintain their links with London.

Commuterland's magic carpet appeals to many. Couples who have reached pivotal points in their lives are especially prone to restlessness. Older couples whose children have left home inevitably feel tempted. Perhaps a flat in town and a cottage in the country might be the answer? Younger couples with new babies wonder if they want children who are hip and streetwise, or ruddy-cheeked and nature-loving. First-time buyers these days leave the decision to purchase until later (often not until their early 30s) and want to look out of London for areas they can afford.

We are often more able to uproot than we think. The computer age has dramatically loosened the chains of the workplace since the first *Guide to Commuterland* appeared in 1992. With mobile phones and laptops we can work on the train, prepare for meetings, sort domestic hiccups. More people can now work from home, or part-time commute by travelling to the office only two or three days a week. Back in the 1990s the optimum commute was 60 minutes. Now the circle has widened and people routinely take the 90-minute option.

Preparing this edition, we found that life outside London was full of energy. People are joining their amateur dramatics societies and singing in choirs. Farmers' markets are flowering in towns everywhere. Campaigns are being fought against the march of the big supermarkets and thoughtless new housing.

Wherever your chosen place, don't make an ill-considered, badly researched plunge. The reality is that a manageable commute coupled with a genuinely enhanced lifestyle is possible only after careful consideration of a wide range of factors. You may never find *exactly* what you want, but you need to be happy with the compromise.

For full-time commuters the first consideration is the length and convenience of the rail journey. Decide which London terminus you want to arrive at. If you work in the City, for instance, then London Bridge and Liverpool Street win hands down over Paddington or Victoria. The conventional wisdom is that the journeys which sandwich the main commute (home to station, London terminus to place of work) are best kept down to 15 minutes each. The maximum sensible number of changes en route is two. Each extra change increases the likelihood of missed connections or other unplanned delays. Most people find that 90 minutes is the maximum tolerable limit for a journey – a time-band that has an inevitable influence on property prices.

It is no good consulting a map to estimate your likely journey time, because the rail networks make a nonsense of geography. You will find throughout this book that stopping services from stations closer to London take longer than faster trains from places further out. Frequency of service is just as important. If you miss your train, how long will you have to wait for the next? This matters especially if you need to work flexible hours and you don't want to turn into an office clock-watcher.

The purpose of this book is to do as much of the initial homework for you as possible. It follows the railway lines out of London in all directions and describes villages within reach of each station. It tries to encapsulate the character of each town and village, the landscape that surrounds it, the quality of schools and communications, journey times to London, the range of available property and what it costs. The detail is not comprehensive, but it should be enough to give you a clear idea of where to look – and where to avoid.

What to watch for

- Be quite certain about whether you want to live in the country, or whether you would be happier living in a town with the country a short drive away. If you want people close by, shops within walking distance, roads that are well lit at night, then the deep countryside is not for you. Good country towns, which offer cafés and bistros, have become fashionable.
- What are your primary needs? Proximity to a good school, supermarket, fashion and foodie shops? Isolation, great walks, big views, village life?
- If village life is what you want, find out how the village of your choice works socially. Are you prepared to put time into keeping the cogs of the village turning? Will you shop locally and support the local farmers' market?
- Make sure you have allowed for inflation, fluctuating petrol prices and interest rate rises in your house-price-plus-season-ticket calculation, and mounting school fees if

they are part of the package (though the credit crunch is putting extra pressure on children to get into grammar schools and good comprehensives).

- Remember that villages with cohesive centres, period houses and charm, will have the highest prices. You can be quite sure that wherever a modern developer has been too heavy-handed the prices will be more vulnerable in times of slump.
- Beware taking on too much land unless you really have the time to garden it or can afford to hire help.

Caroline McGhie,
North Norfolk,
February 2009

ACKNOWLEDGEMENTS

This book is the result of team effort. It has been put together by dedicated researchers – Amanda Houchen, Rachel Jenkins, Emily Jenkinson, Claire Newing, Honor Peter, Amy Quirke, Jo Renshaw and Elizabeth Tyzack – who have talked to estate agents, parish clerks, town and county councils up and down the country in order to gather up-to-date information. Book editor Jane Hutchings has performed a magnificent role in assembling the pieces of the *Commuterland* patchwork and sewing them invisibly together.

Crucial information about season tickets, journey times and frequency of trains has been prepared by the public transport travel consultant Barry Doe, who sifted all the timetables and fares manuals of all the rail companies crossed by the guide. His knowledge is encyclopedic. See www.barrydoe.co.uk for his own on-line annual National Rail Passenger Operators' Map.

The School League Tables provided invaluable help in finding schools that produced the best results, though there are more than we had space to mention. Useful sources of further information include local government websites, the *Shire County Guides* (Shire Publications Ltd) and *The Villages of Britain* series (Countryside Books), which are marvellous repositories of oral history prepared by the Women's Institute.

Supreme efforts have been made to achieve factual accuracy in a world where perceptions of people and places vary, and where the pace of physical change in our towns and villages is now extremely rapid. We are grateful to all those people who have shared their local knowledge with us to make this book as useful as it is.

NOTES ON RAIL TRAVEL INFORMATION

Journey time

The journey time is the time taken by the fastest train to London in a normal off-peak hour.

Peak trains

Peak trains are the number of through trains per hour arriving at the London Terminal in a two-hour period measured roughly between 0730 and 0930. Where there is a significant advantage in changing en route, either to increase the frequency or cut down the journey time, this is mentioned.

Season tickets

- Season ticket prices quoted are Standard Class annuals. The *weekly season* price (any seven consecutive days) can be found by dividing the annual by 40; the *monthly season* price (valid for a calendar month and starting any day) by dividing the annual by 10.41.
- First class seasons are 60 per cent more than Standard out of Liverpool Street, Kings Cross and St Pancras International into Essex, East Anglia and towards Bedford and Cambridge; 70 per cent more on inter-city services to Peterborough, Wellingborough and beyond and on services out of Waterloo; and 100 per cent more out of Paddington to Reading and beyond. In all other cases they are 50 per cent more.
- Travelcards are available, adding all trains, tubes, light railways, trams and buses in Greater London. These are in the order of £650 extra per annum (or £1,000 for first class), but vary from line to line and can be a lot cheaper.
- Any *annual season* or *Travelcard* is automatically a Gold Card and offers users a 34 per cent discount on off-peak fares for any journey in London and the South-east.

Rail maps

The maps are schematic diagrams only and are not drawn to scale.

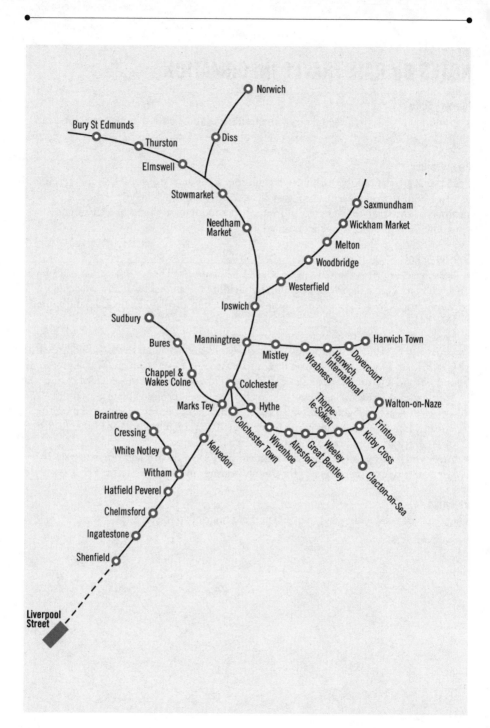

Liverpool Street
> **Norwich**

Journey: 23 min
Season: £2460
Peak: 12 per hr
Off-peak: 6 per hr

SHENFIELD is a mutated village but nonetheless the greengrocer and butcher know you by name. There are three parts to it: the village itself, with bread-and-butter Victorian and Thirties' streets; Hutton Mount, where avenues of huge double-garaged detached houses priced at £750,000 to £2m peep out from between the trees; and Hutton proper, which is strictly Sixties, congested but more affordable. It is on London's doorstep, just outside the M25, with the result that the station car park has been extended and is considered expensive.

Journey: 30 min
Season: £2760
Peak: 3 per hr
Off-peak: 1 per hr

INGATESTONE This is a village with small town pretensions and well over 4,000 inhabitants, many of them East Enders who have moved up and out. Its best features are a collection of 19th-century almshouses and the High Street, which is on a reassuringly human scale. A three-bedroom semi-detached will cost up to £380,000; a five-bedroom house in a smart address like Chantry Drive, £950,000. One of its greatest attractions is the Anglo-European School, to which parents send their children from all over Essex. Many of the passengers drive south to avoid the parking problems at Chelmsford, though they lose with one hand what they gain with the other because it is more difficult to get a seat at Ingatestone.

Journey: 34 min
Season: £3140
Peak: 8 per hr
Off-peak: 5 per hr

CHELMSFORD has just billowed with new developments. Broomfield and Links Drive are the right side of the railway tracks, Boarded Barns the wrong side. A lot of investment has been made in shopping. There are several out-of-town superstores including Tesco, Sainsbury's, Asda, and two malls – High Chelmer and The Meadows – while the Thursday antiques and secondhand market continues to draw the bargain-hunters. Essex County Cricket Club, in the centre, is due to be redeveloped to provide even better sports facilities and 300 new homes. Chelmsford's grammar schools are a magnet to those disillusioned with London state schools. A family house in a leafy street will cost £340,000 to £400,000. The town is due

to sprout a further 40,000 homes in the next few years around
Boreham Airfield, Broomfield, North Springfield and Beaulieu Park.
The surrounding countryside, despite its savaging from developers,
still contains some wonderful surprises.

The station is one of the busiest in the country for morning
commuters. Extra trains start here, in an attempt to provide more
seats. A second station has been proposed on the north-eastern
fringes at Springfield, but has yet to become reality.

On the east flank of the town is **Sandon**, with a pretty village green.
A three-bedroom cottage on the green will cost around £200,000,
while a four-bedroom property with two acres would fetch £925,000.
Modern four-bedroom houses are £600,000 to £700,000. The village
is very much a dormitory, protected by the A12 bypass, and the roar
of the traffic is still audible in some of the houses. The well-liked
comprehensive school has a large sixth form and draws children from
further afield, including Maldon and South Woodham Ferrers. A
monthly farmers' market is held in the village hall.

'Danbury is a
commuter village,
but not posh. It's
not a don't-touch-
me place.
Everyone and his
grandmother goes
there on Sundays
for a walk'

A little further out is **Danbury**, larger than most people's concept of
the archetypal village and on the busy A414. It has its own shops and
pubs, some of them 16th-century, and the Common, woods and lakes
are big attractions. A period house with four bedrooms would cost
£695,000 at least. 'It's a commuter village, but not posh. It's not a
don't-touch-me place. Everyone and his grandmother goes there on
Sundays for a walk,' was how one local pundit described it. Others,
however, consider it very smart. The heather and bracken of Danbury
and Lingwood Commons (National Trust) provide one of the few
known breeding grounds for the Rosy Marbled Moth. Blake's Wood
offers 100 acres of hornbeam and chestnut coppice carpeted with
bluebells in the spring. **Little Baddow**, scarcely separated from Danbury,
has more airs and graces. It has a lovely cricket pitch in the woods
and huge five-bedroom houses in the quiet Rysley cul-de-sac that sell
for up to £750,000.

Another classic commuter village is **Stock**, with its cluttered narrow
streets, pond and village green, though it suffers from the traffic on
the B1007. It has its own wine store, post office, general store,
newsagent, fish shop, florist, hairdresser, and Italian restaurant, and a
wealth of societies from flower arranging to drama and the British
Legion. The local church is worth a visit in order to admire its
intricately constructed timber belfry. The village also has a brick
tower windmill with two sails attached, which is tucked down the
aptly named Mill Lane. This is one of several surviving mills that are a
feature of the Essex countryside. A Grade Two listed 18th-century
refurbished former farmhouse would cost £685,000; a three-bedroom
end-of-terrace with gardens and parking around £350,000.

House style in East Anglia

This is a region where stonelessness has led to resourcefulness. Without stone for building, early residents turned to timber and plaster, and later brought in the first Flemish bricks as ballast in returning wool boats. Hand-made bricks can still be bought at Bulmer in Suffolk.

It was to timber that the early builders on the Essex marshes turned, around the horizontal mudflats and sea wall walks of the Blackwater estuary. Here you find modest white weatherboarded cottages looking like land-locked boats or beach huts that have strayed on to solid ground. The cleft oak boards are laid with the seasoned bark-edge to the outside of the building in order to give the walls maximum protection from the elements.

Once the lovely pastoral landscape of Suffolk unfolds, it reveals some of the best medieval houses in the country, built upon the early profits of the wool trade at a time when this was one of the richest and most densely populated regions of the country. Streets full of drunken timbered houses with first-floor jetties projecting over the road, built long before the chimney or the water closet had even been thought of, are the survivors of a veritable building boom. They are now fiercely guarded by the Suffolk Preservation Society, whose headquarters is among the silvery timbered buildings of Lavenham.

Suffolk also offers a wonderful architectural palette of colours – distinctive buffs, creams, yellows and pinks. Old manor houses with many gables have often had their wattle and daub walls plastered and colour-washed. Others have distinctive pargeting where the plaster is raised into patterns of foliage or figures to make the walls resemble skilfully iced cakes.

To the west of Chelmsford is a clutch of picturesque villages. **Writtle** is close in enough to be a suburb, with a five-bedroom detached house near the village green costing £725,000. The green and duck pond are the envy of the county. Hylands Park is a Grade Two Star neo-classical wonder with its grounds open to the public. It provides the setting for the annual V Festival of music.

Nearby is a collection of hamlets, linked to Chelmsford by an intermittent bus service, where four-to-five-bedroom houses cost anything from £330,000 to £950,000. **Mashbury** is without a pub or shop or jumble sales, but remarkable for its togetherness. **Good Easter** has one of the oldest barns in the country and a village green with a pump on it, where a three-bedroom semi will cost £300,000. **High Easter** is the prettiest, with a café and a restaurant. A four-bedroom timber-framed detached house will cost around £500,000. **Chignall Smealy** and **Chignall St James** have some timbered houses and a pub called the Three Elms. **Pleshey** is particularly sought after because of its thatched cottages, church and motte-and-bailey castle. A four-bedroom house with outbuildings and four acres of land could cost £750,000.

Journey: 43 min
Season: £3320
Peak: 2 per hr
Off-peak: 1 per hr

HATFIELD PEVEREL Commuterland in the lee of the A12. Good-neighbourliness shows itself in the form of Neighbourhood Watch and a wine club set up by bibulous incomers. A cottage on the green in Hatfield Peverel would start at £250,000 for two bedrooms though a small two-bedroom house elsewhere in the village could cost £175,000. New home lovers should look at Beaulieu Park, between Hatfield Peverel and Chelmsford, for an interesting mix of mock Victorian and New England style weatherboarded houses, where a four-bedroom house would cost £325,000. A three-bedroom Grade Two listed house with large garden at Great Leighs, a good six-mile drive from the station, might cost around £450,000.

Journey: 43 min
Season: £3480
Peak: 7 per hr
Off-peak: 4 per hr

WITHAM The smart set don't live in **Witham** itself, which has become a town that people go to for shopping or pass through on their way to the station. Dorothy L. Sayers was not so proud, however. She lived and wrote in Newland Street and a little plaque is there to prove it. The town still serves as the social hub for the surrounding villages, which feed commuters on to the fast main line train services to Liverpool Street. Car parking spaces are plentiful.

The conservationist lobby is strong, with old stalwarts belonging to the Witham and Countryside Society and culture vultures joining the Witham Amateur Operatic Society and Witham Dramatic Club. The entire 18th- and 19th-century High Street has been designated a conservation area. Apart from the Bramston Sports Centre, there is little for the young; the nearest cinemas are in Colchester, Chelmsford and Braintree. In the Seventies the town was identified as a London overspill, which is why it now contains an array of modern estates. A two-bedroom cottage might be bought for £150,000; a four-bedroom, two-bathroom detached house might cost around £355,000.

All the surrounding villages are significantly more expensive. Scarcely separated from Witham itself is **Chipping Hill**, with the Woolpack Inn, a triangular green and a manor house. The view from here was described by Horace Walpole in 1749 as 'sweet meadows falling down a hill and rising again on the other side of the prettiest winding stream you ever saw'. **Wickham Bishops**, set on a hill a couple of miles out, looks down its nose at the others. A five-bedroom mock-Georgian house with a generous garden will command £480,000 here. **Great Braxted** is slightly cheaper, as is **Great Totham**, which is further from the station. The yachting fraternity flock to **Tollesbury**, 12 miles away, where there is a large modern marina on a creek of the Blackwater.

> Branch line to **Braintree** via **White Notley** and **Cressing**

Through trains:	
2 per hr (peak)	
1 per hr (off-peak)	
Journey time (from	
Braintree): 63 min	
Season ticket from	
Braintree: £3580	

The through train service to Liverpool Street on this line was introduced in 1990 as a result of vigorous lobbying by the Witham and Braintree Rail Users Association. People still take the shuttle into Witham and wait five minutes for a fast connection.

Few commuters use **White Notley**. The station is kept open because there is a level crossing here, manned by human hand until recently, but now automatic. **Cressing** is another walk-to-the-station village. The station is no more than a country halt with a platform and shelter. The village has 1,700 inhabitants, two pubs and a post office. It also has its own primary school, though the nearest secondary schools are in Braintree. A three-bedroom semi could be bought for at least £275,000. Old Cressing, part of which is a conservation area, is scissored from new Cressing by the main road. As one parish councillor put it, 'Nobody would ever describe it as quaint, or even picturesque, but it is a good working village.' **Braintree** is the birthplace of the Crittall window and about as pretty – but it has improved hugely in recent years. There are entire estates built on the outskirts which are full of former Londoners, happy to swap the East End for a slower pace of life, better schools and no traffic jams. It also now has the Freeport shopping village and Great Notley Village, a development of 2,000 homes with some smart detailing. Many thousands more new homes are planned in this area. Property prices in Braintree vary from £140,000 for a three-bedroom semi to £300,000 for a four-bedroom detached house, and £700,000 for a five-bedroom cottage with equestrian facilities and substantial grounds.

Traditional Essex weatherboarded house

> Continuation of main line

Journey: 49 min
Season: £3580
Peak: 4 per hr
Off-peak: 1 per hr

KELVEDON is sought-after for its strong village heartbeat. The local church and the Kelvedon Players organise a variety of activities between them, including children's groups and an annual pantomime. Once people have settled here they rarely move out. A Grade Two listed three-bedroom cottage with inglenook fireplace will cost £370,000. An 18th-century, six-bedroom Georgian town house within walking distance of the station will cost £700,000. **Feering**, less than two miles away, is almost umbilically linked. It has a community centre and village school, an art club, choir, WI, bowls, football, Scouts and Guides. The villages share a cricket club. On May Day the pubs throw their doors open while the village green throbs with dancers. Newcomers quickly become assimilated. A five-bedroom cottage with studio, garage, gardens and orchard would cost £575,000.

Journey: 53 min
Season: £3660
Peak: 3 per hr
Off-peak: 2 per hr

MARKS TEY All the Teys, **Marks Tey**, **Little Tey** and **Great Tey**, are within a 10-minute drive of this or Colchester station. Marks Tey has large Seventies' estates where you can buy a three-bedroom semi for £185,000 or a four-bedroom detached for £230,000 to £260,000. Little Tey, next door, is also a grazing ground for first- and second-time buyers. Great Tey is a little more remote, with its own village shop, post office and village hall. **Coggeshall**, a couple of miles from Marks Tey and Kelvedon stations, is more seductive, wonderfully medieval, with old lace-making traditions and a much-loved inn called The Woolpack. It has a regular Thursday market, which sells everything from buttons and WI jam to fruit and veg. Another feather in its cap is Paycocke's House (National Trust), one of the most famous Tudor houses in the country. A period four-bedroom house might cost from £375,000 to £625,000.

> Branch line to Sudbury via Chappel and Wakes Colne and Bures

No through trains.
Change at Marks
Tey: 1 per hr (peak
and off-peak)
Journey time (from
Sudbury): 76 min
Season ticket (from
Sudbury): £3920

Villagers living along this branch line would be just as likely to drive into Colchester to catch one of the more frequent trains. **Chappel** and **Wakes Colne** are two villages sewn together by a vast and spectacular Victorian viaduct. The River Stour, crossed by a small bridge, marks the line which slices **Bures** between Essex and Suffolk. As a result it has two of everything, from parish clerks downwards. The cricket club and green are picturesque. There is conspicuous wealth here, and some weekend cottages. The odd pop musician sweeps through in his Rolls Royce. A little two-bedroom Victorian cottage costs £170,000; a four-bedroom semi with views will fetch £250,000, while a modern five-bedroom house in a quiet country lane will cost £400,000.

Sudbury's irresistible charms compensate for the inconvenience of the journey for the brave who commute from here. The jumble of historic cottages, churches and grander gabled houses, Gainsborough's birthplace among them, sit in the arm of the River Stour, cushioned by water meadows. Stalls fill the market square on Thursdays and Saturdays. The Sudbury Dramatic Theatre raised the money to build The Quay Theatre, and down towards the water meadows there are tennis, rowing and cricket clubs. The Kingfisher Leisure Pool provides a dash of Disneyland with flume rides and wave machine, and has a state-of-the-art gym.

> *The jumble of historic cottages, churches and grander gabled houses sit in the arm of the River Stour*

A few commuters choose to live in the town and walk to the station, or even drive to Marks Tey or Colchester. You might get a two-bedroom flat for around £75,000 to £90,000, or a three-bedroom house standing in its own garden for £239,000. A Grade Two listed, five-bedroom town house with garden can be bought for £400,000. Great Cornard was originally a London overspill zone and somewhat stigmatised as such, but people have bought their council houses and the area has lifted.

Most people opt for the villages. **Long Melford**, three-and-a-half miles out, is one of the most admired in the county with an achingly lovely long main street (hence the name of the village), which eventually erupts on to the green and a cathedral-sized church. No wonder it is loved by film location hunters. Charming Melford Hall, now owned by the National Trust, is where Beatrix Potter first drew Jemima Puddleduck. The Green is one of *the* addresses. A double-fronted four-bedroom house with games room and cellar would cost

Thatched cricket pavilion, Bures

£540,000; though you can get a two-bedroom Victorian terraced cottage for £150,000. The village has its own school, post office, grocery stores, butcher and baker. It crawls with antiques dealers and American tourists in the summer.

Lavenham, four miles from Sudbury, is another film-set medieval village, with restaurants, dried flower and teddy bear shops, 300 listed buildings and the home of the Suffolk Preservation Society. A four-bedroom period cottage would cost £315,000. 'A place caught in time' is how one resident describes it – but unfortunately it is beyond the 10-mile belt round Colchester and hard for regular commuters to reach at the end of a long day. **Cavendish** on the River Stour is another with a village green, antiques shops and restaurants, but think hard about the journey before you look at it. A three-bedroom house with studio and pond will cost £315,000.

> Continuation of main line

Journey: 51 min
Season: £3960
Peak: 8 per hr
Off- peak: 5 per hr

COLCHESTER People have time for **Colchester**, the oldest town in Britain, with a show-stopping Norman castle built on the foundations of a Roman Temple. The medieval alleyways in the old quarter harbour specialist shops such as a doll's house emporium, while the two pedestrianised shopping centres serve up all the usual chain stores. A farmers' market is held once a month. Three-bedroom terraced houses in town cost £130,000 to £280,000. A five-bedroom period semi in one of the best areas such as Lexden will cost £340,000 to £570,000. There are any number of societies, including archaeological, jazz and folk, and choral. The town has two theatres – the Mercury repertory company and the Headgate Theatre for amateur productions – and the Colchester Arts Centre and an eight-screen cinema. Colchester Leisure World is an impressive multi-sports stadium. Annual events include summer concerts in the park and the Oyster Feast in October, at which assorted media figures are invited to gorge themselves. The Company Shed is meant to be one of the best places to eat oysters in the area.

The Colchester bag is brimming with goodies. The Colnes (see Chappel and Wakes Colne, page 20) are handsome but not glamorous and all have a gas supply – no dreaded oil tank lurking in the garden. **Earls Colne**, two miles away, is the biggest and is self-contained, with a supermarket, restaurants and individual shops in the period High Street. A 16th-century, Grade Two listed, four-bedroom town house will cost from £385,000, a three-bedroom cottage will fetch £200,000. **White Colne** is merely a ribbon settlement along the main A604 to Earls Colne, with a mobile shop three times a week. Properties along the main road cost about 10 per cent less than those on quieter roads. **Colne Engaine** is the most desirable of this group. It has a classic village green framed with period houses, a shop, pub, church and primary school. You need £210,000 for a two-bedroom terraced house and over £270,000 to start looking for a family house here.

Eight Ash Green is also highly prized. The A1124 cuts through the centre, skirting the green and the little houses that circle it. It has a village store, primary school, church, petrol station and a gas supply. There is a mix of houses, from ex-local authority selling from £175,000, to small peg-tiled timber cottages, or new four-bedroom detached houses for £265,000 within reach of Marks Tey station.

Fordham, on the River Colne, is rather more dislocated. It does a kind of vanishing act half way along the main street, then gives you a second helping as you turn the bend. Children travel up to 20 miles to Colchester Royal Grammar School (boys) or The County High (girls) if they can get a place.

The Horkesleys will give you more for your money – you could pick up a cottage in **Great Horkesley** for £200,000. **Stoke-by-Nayland**, however, eight miles from Colchester, is where the poetry begins and drunken timber-framed houses splashed with Suffolk pink-wash colour the landscape. It is set high on a ridge over the Stour, with a church that commands a giddy view of Constable country in all directions. **Boxford**, a couple of miles further out, is as pretty and quieter.

> Branch line to Clacton-on-Sea or Walton-on-Naze via Colchester Town, Hythe, Wivenhoe, Alresford, Great Bentley, Weeley, Thorpe-le-Soken, Kirby Cross and Frinton

For train information, see overleaf

WIVENHOE is a little quayside town that is subject to commuter clotting by those who want to avoid the stressful drive into Colchester (which can take 45 minutes). Parking space is so precious that the public car park has introduced a maximum stay of three hours, Monday to Saturday.

The town is gradually metamorphosing from a working port where the oyster catch was all-important, to a boating place with craft shops, attracting local artists and writers. At certain times of year the pubs bulge with students from Essex University, based in the tower blocks in Wivenhoe Park. It is distinct from Colchester five miles away and is cushioned by green fields which are fiercely defended from development. Old shipyards are being turned into new houses and

Journey: 86 min
(from Clacton)

Season: £4300 (from
Clacton)

Through trains
from Clacton:

3 per hr (peak)

1 per hr (off-peak)

This service is
from Clacton,
Thorpe-le-Soken
and Wivenhoe only.
Other stations:
change at
Colchester

*Weed your front
garden in Kirby-
le-Soken and you
could spend all
day talking to
passers-by*

prices vary from £150,000 for a two-bedroom flat to £285,000 for a five-bedroom town house. The ferry to Rowhedge (once used to take the doctor to Fingringhoe and bring men to work in the shipyards) is operated by volunteers from April to October. Detached period houses on the quay cost over £285,000. Smaller three-bedroom Victorian terraced houses come in under £150,000. Wivenhoe has an infant and primary school, and local societies including the Gilbert and Sullivan Society, the Mercury Youth Theatre and the Pantomime Group. There is also an annual regatta. The Colne Barrier controls the tidal flow south of town in order to protect homes from flooding during surges.

Great Bentley is chiefly notable for having what is reputed to be the largest village green in England. At 43 acres it swallows the cricket green, two football pitches and the annual gymkhana – and the houses on it are the ones to aim for. Something with three bedrooms off the green might cost £200,000. There is a pharmacy, a Tesco and a farm shop, a primary school and allotments for local residents.

Clacton-on-Sea may one day find itself a conservation area. It epitomises the pre-war seaside resort, where those with fond memories of holidays in bed-and-breakfasts and days on the pier might choose to buy their final bungalow and take up a round of golf on Sundays. The average three-bedroom semi costs £125,000; a two-up-two-down £115,000. It is described by some as being full of 'East Enders-made-good driving their Range Rovers'.

My dear, if you live in **Frinton**, you have arrived. That is to say that you have certainly distanced yourself from that frightful candyfloss and razmatazz in Clacton. The old railway level-crossing gates are the heavenly portals to Frinton. Outside is where the modern estates are put, and it isn't Frinton proper. For Frinton is *very* proper. There was a huge fight to stop the arrival of a pub (nicknamed locally The Stick and Zimmer), a fish-and-chip shop and even the first ice-cream shop is back from the beach in a discreet position on Connaught Avenue. It also has its commuters who use the direct trains to Liverpool Street. Solicitors, doctors, dentists and accountants are attracted to the cavernous houses – servants' quarters and tennis courts included – worth over £470,000, that sit in swathes of garden in The Avenues. There is no problem buying virgin olive oil here. Connaught Avenue, with its designer clothes shops, jewellers and delicatessens, is known as the Bond Street of Essex. The local clubs and societies cover three foolscap pages, but it is bridge evenings that make the world go round, coupled with the Frinton Summer Theatre, the annual tennis tournament and the 18-hole links.

You get sand as fine, but house prices considerably cheaper in **Walton-on-Naze**. A three-bedroom semi on the outskirts could take

£185,000 off you. There are regulation seaside resort chip shops, safe bathing, fresh lobster to be bought in the summertime and a pier, but the main attractions are the sheltered inlets behind The Naze where the yacht club is located. The saltings and mudflats, designated as a Site of Special Scientific Interest, are a staging post for flocks of migrating birds and there are monthly guided walks.

Kirby-le-Soken, two miles away, is sought-after because of its proximity to Frinton. It was originally threaded on to a single long main street, in the Essex tradition, but has since sprung bungaloid growths around it. One village shop has closed, leaving a post office stores and two pubs. Everybody knows everybody in this village. Cottage windows are papered with posters flagging local events, and gardens are regularly thrown open to the public for good causes. Weed your front garden here and you could spend all day talking to passers-by.

> Continuation of main line

Journey: 62 min
Season: £4400
Peak: 5 per hr
Off-peak: 3 per hr

MANNINGTREE This station is often preferred to Colchester because it is marginally easier to park the car (though nothing is free) and easier to get a seat. **Manningtree** town itself has a charming frontage on to the Stour, known as the Walls, where homeowners have houses worth from £250,000 to £800,000. Legoland-style executive houses have leeched on to it. Visitors to the port are struck by the swans and sailing barges. The social life is mixed – old skippers and commuters drink together in the pubs – and the Stour Choral Society adds a cultural note.

East Bergholt is one of the set-piece villages in this area, sprawly but prime commuter territory, where houses go for up to 25 per cent more than similar ones nearby. Constable wrote of it in 1776: 'I even love every stile and stump and every lane in the village.' He painted it enough times, and the cottage he used as a studio is still there, as is Willy Lott's cottage, which he made famous by painting. It doesn't seethe with tourists quite as much as other local sightseeing spots. A three-bedroom detached cottage might sell for £240,000. A modern four- or five-bedroom detached house that would sell for £430,000 in Ipswich would fetch at least £150,000 more here. Houses at **Flatford Mill**, the hamlet nearby, are similarly fought over. The mill, which was owned by Constable's father and painted by the man himself, attracts so many visitors that there are now one-way lanes.

Dedham is positively stockbroker now. Despite the tourist influx in the summer, it is a place that people still dream of moving to. Sir Alfred Munnings's home, Castle House, where his paintings are on display, lies just to the south. Those who live in the High Street are martyrs to the tourists who make parking and shopping impossible. Even a little two-bedroom flat here will cost £235,000 and most properties cost around 25 per cent more than those in other villages. One resident of many years remembers how quiet it used to be. 'It looks beautiful at eight o'clock at night when nobody is here.' Her commuting husband used to park in a field to catch the train at Manningtree. Now he will wait three hours to get on a train that allows him a seat. There is a farmers' market once a month at the Parish Church.

> Branch line to Harwich Town via Mistley, Wrabness, Harwich International and Dovercourt

Journey: 93 min (from Harwich Town)

Season: £4400 (from Harwich Town)

Peak: 1 through train per hr plus 2 per hr changing at Manningtree

Off-peak: 1 per hr changing at Manningtree

While Manningtree benefits from the stops made by fast trains coming through from Harwich and Norwich, the small stops out along the tidal estuary towards Harwich do not. Properties are scattered and isolated along this out-of-the-way stretch of coastline, and the journey, which usually involves a change at Manningtree, is slow but spectacular.

> Continuation of main line

Journey: 72 min

Season: £5060

Peak: 4 per hr

Off peak: 3 per hr

IPSWICH is described as a town of convenience – good for shopping. It's also a centre for entertainment, with cinemas, two venues for stage productions, the Regent Theatre and The New Wolsey Theatre, and The Railway in Foxhall Road for live music gigs. To the east, near the well-respected Northgate comprehensive, two-bedroom terraced houses in need of refurbishment can be bought from £75,000; a four-bedroom Victorian terrace for £187,000; detached houses for £250,000 to £500,000. A £350m development has transformed the waterfront into a hip venue where a one-bedroom penthouse might cost £300,000. The prices rise when you get close to a park, especially Christchurch Park where there are private schools.

Schools in Suffolk

One of the honeypots is Ipswich which has two star private schools, Ipswich School for both sexes and Ipswich High for girls. Another is Bury St Edmunds (now more accessible by train), which has Culford independent school, and two comprehensives, King Edward VI and St Benedict's Catholic co-educational school.

Woodbridge (also more accessible) has a pair of independent schools – Framlingham College and Woodbridge – as well as the comprehensives Thomas Mills High and Farlingaye High. Another independent mixed school with good results is St Felix at Southwold, overlooking the Blyth estuary.

Here a substantial family house will cost £600,000. A restored farmhouse with 100 acres and barns with planning permission on the outskirts could fetch £1.25m. The Shotley Peninsula, in the tongue of land south of Ipswich, is where the naturalists and yachting types gather. It has the River Orwell to one side, the Stour to the other and oozing mudflats between that attract wildfowl and waders. **Stutton** is the popular village here, on the Alton Reservoir which is a sailing centre. **Shotley Gate**, at the tip, provides a vantage point from which to watch the ships ploughing in and out of Harwich.

To the west of Ipswich is **Hadleigh**, a classic period market town untouched by the deadening hand of the vast supermarkets – Tesco's repeated planning applications have met with strong opposition. Eight miles from Ipswich, Hadleigh is a model collection of medieval and Georgian houses, and provides everything that a small town should, from wine bars and interior designers to banks and solicitors. A three-bedroom end-of-terrace period cottage here would cost £170,000 to £200,000; a large Georgian town house £665,000.

'The price of the houses in Kersey depends on how desperate people are to buy their fantasy'

Just two miles beyond it is **Kersey**, where the price of the houses depends on how desperate people are to buy their fantasy. The hillside, running steeply down to a watersplash, is stacked with remarkable lichen-cloaked half-timbered houses, built 500 years ago on the profits of the cloth industry. A three-bedroom, Grade Two listed cottage would sell for £440,000.

To the east is **Woodbridge**, one of the most loved towns in this part of Suffolk. It has its own station and a direct service into Liverpool Street. High-ranking, high-salaried types buy up the 16th-century houses round this old port on the Deben estuary. It is serious boating and foody country. The Loaves and Fishes is a wonderful deli and there is a farmers' market twice a month. You can buy a three-bedroom, three-storey, Grade Two listed terraced cottage a few minutes' stroll from the River Deben from £200,000. Or you could spend £3.5m on a Georgian country house with six bedrooms, woodland and grounds on the banks of the River Ore. It also has its own highly respected co-educational state and private schools, including a prep.

> Branch line to Saxmundham via Westerfield, Woodbridge, Melton and Wickham Market

Journey: 119 min (from Saxmundham)

Season: £5840

1 per hr (peak) plus 1 changing at Ipswich;

1 every 2 hrs (off-peak)

Much of this remarkable coast had been off limit for daily commuters because there were so few direct services, but accessibility has improved with the addition of more through trains. Beyond Saxmundham the line continues to Lowestoft.

Those who can't afford **Woodbridge** (see Ipswich) might consider **Little** and **Great Bealings**, or **Grundisburgh** (pronounced Grundsbra), which is cheaper and popular with families because it has a good primary school. A three-bedroom house overlooking the green in Grundisburgh can be bought for £250,000. **Ufford** is very pretty and unspoilt, and **Wickham Market** is also an unpretentious little town with a market square fringed with white-fronted Georgian houses. A three-bedroom cottage here would cost around £170,000. The station is a mile out of town.

Or you could journey on to **Saxmundham** and head for **Aldeburgh**, now hugely fashionable with North Londoners who keep weekend homes here. Most people find it enchanting (fresh fish to be bought off the boats on the beach every morning) and many like to retire here. Prices vary from £300,000 for a three-bedroom cottage in the town centre to £395,000 and more for a four-bedroom detached house near the beach. The internationally renowned music festival is staged down the road at **Snape**, where long-held plans are being implemented for Benjamin Britten's and Peter Pears's vision to create an entire campus for musicians, with new housing on site which is already coming on stream. Or there are four- and five-bedroom detached houses in the Edwardian seaside model village of **Thorpeness** that sell for £450,000 to £650,000.

Beyond the eerie sight of the now decommissioned Sizewell power station you come to the villages of **Westleton** and **Middleton**. These are hugely popular with escapees from the City who want to don Barbours, wellies and tweed hats and visit those wonderful vanishing cliffs at Dunwich (National Trust) or the Royal Society for the Protection of Birds reserve at Minsmere. Westleton has a village green and duck pond to go with its Suffolk thatch, colour wash and wattle-and-daub cottages. You could

Suffolk half-timbered and thatched cottage

get a three-bedroom bungalow with quarter of an acre of land for £265,000. **Yoxford** is worth thinking about too. **Peasenhall** is pretty, and **Framlingham** provides the nearest classic country town, with a market square and old castle at its heart, and a good independent school, Framlingham College. Though it is rather too far for hardened commuters.

> Continuation of main line

Journey: 93 min
Season: £5160
Peak: 2 per hr
changing at Ipswich
Off-peak: 1 per hr
changing at Ipswich
No through trains

NEEDHAM MARKET has plenty of old houses, some with Georgian façades, and a wondrous 15th-century chapel with a double hammerbeam roof that sent Pevsner into orbit. He described it as 'a whole church with nave, aisles and clerestory seemingly in the air'. A farmers' market takes place once a month. Buyers are drawn to the villages to the west that bask in the reflected glow of nearby Lavenham. A shock to the system is an application to construct a £25m indoor ski centre called SnOasis, attracting 200,000 visitors each month. Approval has already been granted for part of the development, which includes housing and a new station. Nearby **Hitcham** has a post office and general store, and a densely-packed parish calendar. **Bildeston** has all the black and cream wickerwork architecture of a village built on the profits of the medieval clothing industry. It also has restaurants and a doctor's surgery. To the east of Needham Market the houses have much humbler origins.

Journey: 85 min
Season: £5160
Peak: 3 per hr
Off-peak: 3 every
2 hrs

STOWMARKET has a strategic position just on the lip of the Suffolk prairie. Beyond the A45 all the last dimples in the countryside have been ironed flat, and the trees and hedges unpicked from a landscape that blazes yellow with rape in the summer. Little two-up-two-downs cost £110,000; modern, three-bedroom detached houses £160,000 to £175,000. **Haughley** is pretty enough to have been colonised by commuters to Bury or Ipswich. It combines new developments on the outskirts with an intimate old village street and a green with a 60-ton parish coal-house on it, built in 1861. It also has shops, restaurants, and a strong interest in organic farming (this is where the Soil Association experiments with pesticide-free crops). **Wetherden** has not been developed quite so much, and its preoccupations are firmly agricultural and horsey – point-to-points are well attended. Newmarket is not that far away. A four-bedroom detached house in either village could be expected to cost around £380,000.

> Branch line to Bury St Edmunds via Elmswell and Thurston

Few through trains
Journey time (from Bury St Edmunds): 98 min
Season ticket from Bury St Edmunds: £5360 (also valid Kings Cross via Cambridge)
Peak: 2 per hr from Bury St Edmunds changing at Ipswich or Cambridge
Off-peak: 1 per hr (1 through train every 2 hrs and the other hour by changing at Ipswich or Cambridge)

This area is not nearly as popular with London commuters as that served by the fast electric trains to Diss. Both **Elmswell** and **Thurston** have grown hugely in recent years, swallowing new houses like packets of sweets.

Bury St Edmunds could be forgiven for regarding itself as the capital of East Anglia. As atmospheric as Norwich, Cambridge or King's Lynn, it sits right at the heart of the region on the conjunction of the A14, A143 and A134. On the rail network it stands on the watershed, suspended 28 miles from Cambridge and Ipswich. People travel west via Cambridge, east via Ipswich. Georgian and medieval houses crowd the centre, and in summer the tourists flock in to see the abbey ruins. The street market opens on Wednesdays and Saturdays. British Sugar has made it the base for one of its major production plants. West Suffolk Hospital is also there, and so is the Greene King brewery. Victorian terraced houses stand in appropriately named streets – Queens Road, Kings Road, Albert Crescent and so on. Two-bedroom versions start at around £150,000. Something more lavish at an address like Home Farm Lane will cost over £395,000.

Three miles to the north is **Culford**, best known for its mixed day and boarding public school. Four-bedroom modern estate houses sell at £280,000. To the north-west you rapidly enter the Fens, and most people tend to prefer the more undulating landscape to the south. **Fornham St Martin**, on the northern edge, has recently been relieved with a bypass. Four-bedroom houses skirting the Fornham Park golf course sell at over £335,000. **Fornham All Saints** is an older village, centred around the church and village green – it also has the Swallow Suffolk Golf and Country Club with a spa and beauty centre. A three-bedroom cottage here might fetch £300,000.

To the south is **Horringer** (once known as Horningsheath) with a set-piece church and green beside the entrance to Ickworth House (National Trust). The green is framed by neat cottages in plastered timber, flintwork and white brick that sell in an instant. Or there is **Cockfield**, an extraordinary cluster of hamlets, each with its own green, where a five-bedroom period cottage with three reception rooms might sell for £350,000. A mile away is **Great Green**, where they have village cricket on summer Sunday afternoons and four-bedroom modern houses costing around £320,000.

> Continuation of main line

Journey: 97 min
Season: £5780
Peak: 3 per hr
Off-peak: 2 per hr

DISS is extremely popular with commuters because the trains whistle through to London. During the property boom of the late Eighties the town expanded, a few computer companies moved in and prices went up. It currently has a population of around 7,500, and still has a weekly Friday market, though it no longer includes livestock. It has an indoor swimming pool, squash and tennis courts, and an 18-hole golf course. In the town itself (which has mains gas) the most desirable streets include Mount Street, but also Denmark Street and Friends Road, where older Georgian houses mix with Fifties' properties. A period semi with three bedrooms might sell for up to £185,000; a four-bedroom detached with large garden £225,000; an unfinished barn conversion with three bedrooms £295,000.

Dickleburgh, three miles to the north, has its own village stores, post office, doctor's surgery and primary school, and a bypass. Or you could look west to **Redgrave**, which has a village green and pub. Much closer to Diss is **Palgrave**, which has a preponderance of artists, including a cartoonist, who live in the plastered and thatched cottages and regularly show their work. There is a green and a primary school. Locals complain that the school is cramped Victorian, but it cannot expand because it is built on common land. The pub closed several years ago and the bar in the village hall is open only occasionally. Houses in The Haven, a small development by Hopkins and Moore, sell at around £250,000 for three to four bedrooms.

Georgian farmhouse, south Norfolk

Schools in Norfolk

In Norfolk the widest choice is in Norwich. Schools here include the two strong independents, Norwich School for boys and girls and Norwich High for girls, as well as the Roman Catholic comprehensive Notre Dame High School. A particularly interesting school in Norfolk is Wymondham College, probably Europe's largest mixed state boarding school, where tuition is free and the cost of boarding lower than at any comparable private school. It is not to be confused with Wymondham High comprehensive, which also does very well. Gresham's, at Holt near the North Norfolk coast, is the co-educational independent school in the area for day pupils and boarders.

South-west is **Mellis**, a tiny scattered village with the largest common in Suffolk (237 acres). The Suffolk Wildlife Trust likes to delay hay-cutting until high summer to allow the wild flowers to reseed. The common is bisected by the main railway line, which can be noisy depending which way the wind is blowing. There is a pub, but no post office or shop. Children attend the primary school here, then go to secondary school in Eye which also has a sixth-form college.

For a lively village life it would be better to look east to **Hoxne** (rhymes with oxen), which is set around the village green with an outstanding half-timbered priory with herringbone brickwork. It has its share of modern ribbon development. The village has a primary school, one pub, a shop and a service station. Morris dancers visit in the summer and the harvest breakfast on the green in the autumn is a must. This comes a fortnight after the rousing harvest festival and harvest lunch. A small terraced house here with two bedrooms could be had for around £155,000. Something bigger with three bedrooms would start at £180,000.

Eye, four miles south, is a typical Suffolk town on the River Dove, with two banks, a florist, butcher and baker, an old castle and a new business park on the former airfield. Though it is no longer a borough, it still has its mayor and deputy mayor. It attracts lots of London commuters and buzzes with societies. These include the High Suffolk Flower Club, the Eye Theatre and the Eye Bach Choir. It has a primary school and a small hospital that caters mainly for the elderly. Gardening is competitive – residents throw their gardens open to the public. Church fund-raising activities are frequent and impressive. A four-bedroom detached house with garden and paddock at **Yaxley**, two miles away, would hit the market with a price tag of around £350,000. A restored mid-terrace cottage with two bedrooms would cost £160,000.

Journey: 114 min

Season: £6240

Peak: 3 per hr

Off-peak: 2 per hr

NORWICH Few people commute this far, although the more frequent service to London makes the journey easier. The attractions of **Norwich** are strong, especially with the Broads and the Norfolk beaches just a car drive away. The hospital and the University of East Anglia swell the ranks of middle-class professionals. The city retains a strong sense of history with the old castle, huge tented market and vibrant shopping centre at its heart, where street buskers, students and wealthy shoppers mix. The Riverside area around the railway station and Carrow Road football ground (home turf for Delia Smith) has been transformed into a lively modern shopping and leisure complex, with a cinema, bars and restaurants, swimming pool and bowling. House of Fraser can be found in the recently opened Chapelfield Centre on the former Nestlé site. A farmers' market is held once a month on the Norfolk Showground. To be near enough to the station you need to look to the south-west, in an area known as The Golden Triangle, where you could pay £285,000 for a Victorian, three-bedroom detached house. On a modern estate you could buy a detached four-bedroom house for £270,000.

'The attractions of Norwich are strong, especially with the Broads and the Norfolk beaches just a car drive away'

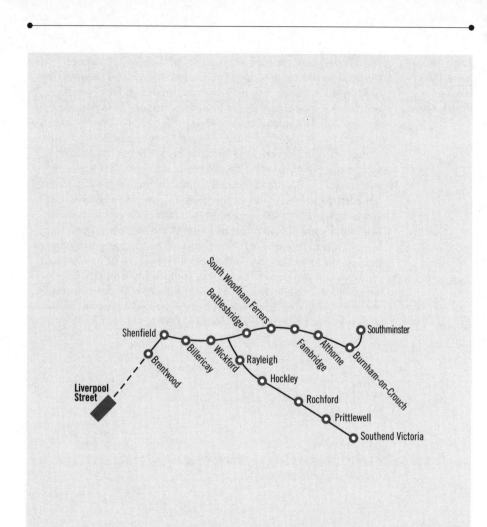

Liverpool Street
> **Southend**

Journey: 40 min	**BRENTWOOD** People are fond of Brentwood because of its
Season: £2120	traditional high street with independent shops, monthly farmers' and
Peak: 7 per hr	craft markets and its convenient position. It is on Junction 28 of the
Off-peak: 6 per hr	M25, yet within walking distance of fields, woods and the lakes of

Thorndon Park. It exudes a sense of wealth, even among the young.
Ford and British Telecom have a strong presence as employers; Ford
once owned a lot of property, which has now been sold off. Modern
estates have been grafted on to gracious Victorian terraces and
Thirties' cul-de-sacs. In The Homesteads, for instance, mansion-sized
houses are packed as tight as country cottages to create a feeling of
village intimacy. A four-bedroom property here would cost £700,000 to
£975,000. Brentwood's adult population empties into London every
weekday, though many of them opt to catch the train at Shenfield.

Journey: 23 min	**SHENFIELD**
Season: £2460	See **Liverpool Street to Norwich** line (page 15).
Peak: 12 per hr	
Off-peak: 6 per hr	

Journey: 30 min	**BILLERICAY** is bustling, respectable and genteel. House prices are
Season: £2760	not as high as at Shenfield, but are similar to those in Brentwood and
Peak: 7 per hr	Chelmsford. The town is close enough to the open countryside to
Off-peak: 3 per hr	attract a steady drift of people from London's East End. A private golf

course has been built on the Chelmsford side, and at Barleylands Craft
Village and Farm Centre a farmers' market is held twice a month. Car
parking spaces in the station car park are scarce as hens' teeth during
peak times and a mobile clamping unit picks off illegal parkers. There
is a year long wait for season ticket parking and remember, there are
between 3,000 and 4,000 season ticket holders to compete with.

For train	**WICKFORD** People who live in **Wickford** consider themselves
information, see	superior to those who live in Basildon, but inferior to those from
overleaf	Rayleigh. Commuters pour in from the Dengie peninsula to catch the

Journey: 36 min
Season: £2820
Peak: 7 per hr
Off-peak: 3 per hr

fast trains here, rather than take the slower service on the Southminster branch line. Some of the trains stop at Stratford, where people can switch painlessly to the London Underground or Docklands Light Railway. The town is a tumour of Sixties' estates built on to the village of Shotgate, with green belt on three sides. You could spend £215,000 on a new three-bedroom semi, or well over £230,000 on a house with four bedrooms. Housing estates are popular. On the Wick housing development a whole new settlement has emerged with houses selling from £155,000 for two bedrooms to £210,000 for two to three bedrooms.

> Branch line to Southminster via Battlesbridge, South Woodham Ferrers, Fambridge, Althorne and Burnham-on-Crouch

Journey time (from Southminster): 96 min (69 min peak)
Season ticket from Southminster: £3400
Peak: 2 per hr
Off-peak: 1 per hr changing at Shenfield

SOUTH WOODHAM FERRERS is almost other-worldly, epitomising all that the *Essex Design Guide* had to say about the use of traditional materials and regional styles. Building began in 1976, which makes it one of the more recent attempts to create a planned new town instead of a rash of new developments. Everything has steep pitched roofs and eaves, and banks resemble barns. The William de Ferrers school doubles as a public library, and a new community centre, Champion Manor Hall, is home to a variety of clubs and societies. Planning regulations are tough; you are not allowed to park a caravan outside the front of your house. The Round Table and other similar organisations are strong in a place where people were once all newcomers together, forging links for the first time. The town has grown up, and the place that was once inhabited entirely by thirty-somethings who were all relatively well-off and wrinkle-free, now has much more of a mix of ages and income brackets. One-bedroom houses start at £115,000, four-bedroom detached houses at £215,000 to £475,000. The Marsh Farm Country Park provides 350 acres of reclaimed marshland in which to walk the dog and the shopping development offers retail therapy.

At **North Fambridge** you enter yachting country. It has a post office and a general store and is encircled by small new estates. A typical large four-bedroom detached house will cost £260,000 to £595,000. **Althorne** is a tiny hamlet, one-and-a-half miles from its station on the river. It is mostly modern, with a post office-cum-shop, a pub, the Ferryboat Inn, and home-produced beef available from Althorne Beef. A semi here costs £165,000 upwards, a bungalow £190,000 and a detached house £375,000 to £595,000. **Burnham-on-Crouch** is the yachting capital of the

Dengie peninsula, known as the pearl or the Cowes of the east coast. There are four yacht clubs. Burnham Week has been the highlight of the local sailing calendar for more than a century and attracts hundreds of yachts and thousands of visitors every year. The town has a mix of Victorian, Georgian and classic Essex weatherboarded cottages, and a huge modern complex of flats built on the quay, popular with weekenders who want long lonely walks. Overlooking the river you could expect to spend £315,000 for four bedrooms; a studio will go for £120,000. An older two-bedroom cottage could be had for £125,000.

Southminster suddenly seems remote at the end of the line, and house prices dip accordingly. It is a close farming community on the very edge of the marshes that stretch timelessly into the North Sea. A three-bedroom semi here would cost £160,000. A Grade Two listed farmhouse on over an acre of land would be upwards of £450,000. Southminster has its own primary school, cricket and football teams, and operatic and choral society. Local delicacies which can be bought from Thorogood & Sons farm include hand-picked asparagus, or home reared lamb and beef from Steeple Gate family farm. **Tillingham**, to the north, is the archetypal Essex village with weatherboarded cottages, a green, a church, a pub and a farm which has a weekly box scheme supplying organic vegetables to the residents of the Dengie Peninsular. A two-bedroom cottage in a terrace starts at £130,000; a detached house in mature gardens would cost £350,000. Still within reach of Southminster station is **Bradwell-on-Sea**. It has a good collection of cottages. Bradwell Lodge, a Georgian house near the Blackwater with internal decorations by Robert Adam, is where Erskine Childers wrote *The Riddle of the Sands*. The ancient chapel of St-Peter's-on-the-Wall, built in 654, is the focus of the annual Bradwell Pilgrimage in July. You can walk 12 miles along the sea wall from here without meeting a soul. Close by is a marina and bird reserve. The nuclear power station has been decommissioned, but there are plans for a wind farm of ten turbines.

'Burnham-on-Crouch, the yachting capital of the Dengie peninsula, is known as the pearl or the Cowes of the east coast'

Riverside apartments, Burnham-on-Crouch

> Continuation of main line

Journey: 41 min
Season: £3000
Peak: 6 per hr
Off-peak: 3 per hr

RAYLEIGH mushroomed in the Thirties, and considers itself upmarket of Basildon and Wickford. The large windmill at one end of the High Street adds a gracious note, and since its refurbishment has become a local tourist attraction. A modern three-bedroom semi costs £225,000. The nearby village of **Hullbridge** once had the dubious honour of being dubbed by *The Sun* as the sexiest place in England. The reasons given were no more exciting than its high per capita birthrate and a local councillor's claim that the place is so boring that people have nothing better to do than stay at home and make babies. The village should be valued more for the fact that it sits on the Crouch Estuary. You can walk along the sea wall to Battlesbridge, where you can enjoy one of the slivers of Essex landscape that has remained unsullied by modern pressures. It is less expensive than other areas.

Journey: 45 min
Season: £3000
Peak: 6 per hr
Off-peak: 3 per hr

HOCKLEY The Southend area was developed in the 1890s, and the further you come inland from the tip, the more modern it becomes. Hockley and **Hawkwell**, about six miles inland, have mostly Sixties' and Seventies' houses. Hockley Woods is the largest remaining area of the wild wood that covered Essex after the Ice Age. This is the place for Sunday walks along the bridleways, with drinks at The Bull afterwards. Lakeside and Bluewater provide the all-singing, all-dancing shopping experiences in this part of the world.

Journey: 49 min
Season: £3000
Peak: 6 per hr
Off-peak: 3 per hr

ROCHFORD is a plain town with a square surrounded by banks and specialist shops, including gift shops, a tea and coffee shop, and a watch repairer. The market is held here every Tuesday. Hall Road is the smart address. The houses here have huge gardens running down to the golf course, and you'll need over £1.2m to buy one. The town tends to feel overshadowed by Southend. It has a reservoir popular with anglers on Sundays. The choice of shops has improved with the opening of the Lakeside shopping centre off the M25 at Thurrock. **Ashingdon**, three miles away, has higher property prices. A modern one-bedroom flat can be had for £175,000, while four-bedroom houses can cost over £290,000. It has a pub, a few shops, and sits in a patch of rural Essex that is attempting to keep urbanisation at bay. Builders are, however, trying to fill the gaps with new houses.

I'll tell you how bad Prittlewell used to be,' says one commuter. 'I sent a bottle of wine to the station manager just because my train was on time. Then 77 consecutive journeys were 10 minutes late*'*

Journey: 53 min
Season: £3000
Peak: 6 per hr
Off-peak: 3 per hr

PRITTLEWELL is a restrained northern suburb of Southend where two- to three-bedroom semis cost around £160,000. People who travel this line have seen the service improve dramatically. 'I'll tell you how bad it used to be,' says one commuter. 'I sent a bottle of wine to the station manager just because my train was on time. Then 77 consecutive journeys were 10 minutes late.'

Journey: 55 min
Season: £3000
Peak: 6 per hr
Off- peak: 3 per hr

SOUTHEND VICTORIA See Southend on the **Fenchurch Street to Shoeburyness** line (page 43). Most people prefer to use that line because the journey is quicker.

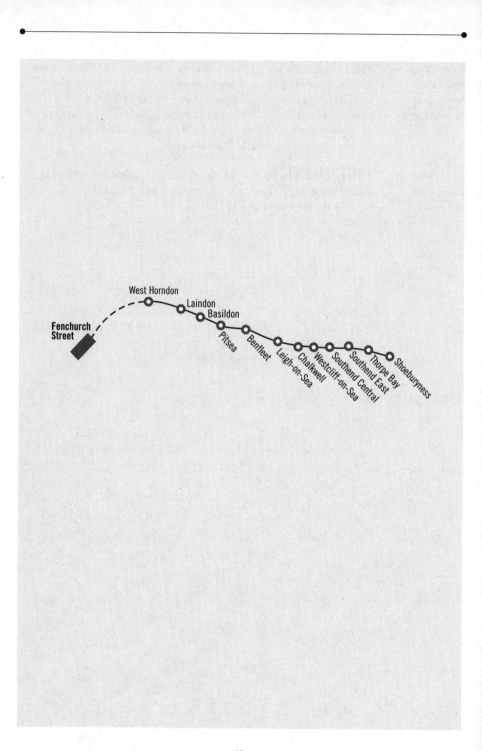

West Horndon

Laindon

Basildon

Fenchurch
Street

Pitsea

Benfleet

Leigh-on-Sea

Chalkwell

Westcliff-on-Sea

Southend Central

Southend East

Thorpe Bay

Shoeburyness

Fenchurch Street
> Shoeburyness

Journey: 29 min
Season: £1824
Peak: 4 per hr
Off-peak: 2 per hr

WEST HORNDON Classic between-the-wars and post-war suburbia has sprouted at West Horndon because of the sheer convenience of the rail service, though it somehow remains rural and most of the Thirties' bungalows have 150ft gardens, many of them backing on to fields. The station attracts commuters along the A128 from Brentwood, who find it easier to drive south and catch the train here rather than tangle with the traffic in Brentwood or Basildon. A three-bedroom bungalow sells for around £300,000; a detached five-bedroom house for around £330,000.

Journey: 32 min
Season: £2188
Peak: 7 per hr
Off-peak: 4 per hr

LAINDON station has the advantage of an extra platform. A number of services start from here, and its commuters are guaranteed a seat. The less expensive area, known locally as Alcatraz, is subject to urban renewal and three-bedroom terraced houses here now cost around £130,000. The better area is Langdon Hills, within a few minutes' walk of the station, where modern detached houses sell for about £230,000 to £280,000.

Journey: 35 min
Season: £2188
Peak: 5 per hr
Off-peak: 4 per hr

BASILDON has virtually swallowed up **Laindon** and **Pitsea**. As one of a clutch of new towns planned after the Second World War to absorb people and industry from London, it exists as a kind of joke to people who once thought we could be weaned away from commuting. The planners believed people could live and work in the same place – industrial development was zoned to the north of the town – and for this reason it was built without a station, but they finally had to bow to pressure and build one in the Seventies. Now 60 years old, Basildon is no longer a 'new' town. Its phenomenal rate of growth has not been without its problems; older residents have felt increasingly

'West Horndon somehow remains rural and most of the Thirties' bungalows have 150ft gardens, many of them backing on to fields'

uneasy about walking alone at night, and sometimes the town has had to be heavily policed. To counter that, the centre was given a multi-million-pound makeover, together with a millennium glass bell tower opened by the Queen. The town is poised to benefit from being part of the proposed regeneration of the Thames Gateway area, which should pull in new businesses. Around 1,310 new homes are planned for the Craylands and Fryern estate with improved public transport. You could buy a four-bedroom executive house with garage for £230,000 to £400,000.

Journey: 41 min

Season: £2300

Peak: 4 per hr

Off-peak: 4 per hr

PITSEA is rather more friendly than Basildon proper, with a defined centre and an open-air market in the sea of ex-council housing. Estate agents say it is one of the few affordable areas around. A three-bedroom terraced house can be found for £140,000, a two-bedroom flat for £130,000. Pitsea Mount offers some of the best private housing very close to the station, with four-bedroom detached houses costing £280,000.

Journey: 42 min

Season: £2608

Peak: 8 per hr

Off-peak: 4 per hr

BENFLEET The Southend Rail Travellers Association says this is one of the busiest stations on the entire line, serving a huge catchment area swollen with Sixties' development. **Benfleet** itself is little more than ribbon development along the A130, and it is hard to find anything you could define as a centre. A three-bedroom terraced house would cost between £160,000 and £215,000, detached executive houses with four or five bedrooms from £320,000 to £400,000.

The station also attracts commuters from **Canvey Island**, which is really the scrag end of Essex. So much of it lies below sea level that houses tend to offer views of the sea wall or the oil refineries. You can get a little one-bedroom bungalow for £130,000, or a three-bedroom semi for around £170,000. Traffic in and out of the island strangles the only two roads linking it to the mainland, although there is talk of road improvements and better access. Peter de Savary once had plans to build 4,300 houses, accompanied by a new station just south of Benfleet, but these were shelved and now Wilson Connolly have built a large development instead.

'Leigh blends a certain eccentricity (of the take-the-tricycle-rather-than-the-bus kind) with airs and graces'

Journey: 47 min

Season: £2608

Peak: 8 per hr

Off-peak: 4 per hr

LEIGH-ON-SEA blends a certain eccentricity (of the take-the-tricycle-rather-than-the-bus kind) with airs and graces, and is more sought-after than its neighbours. The old town in particular is worth going to see, since it retains its historical integrity as a working fishing village. You can watch the boats landing their catches, and the cockle sheds are well stocked. The two- or three-bedroom terraced cottages rarely come on the market and are quickly snapped up when they do, for £230,000 or more.

Birdwatchers are treated to endless sightings of migratory birds that stop off at Two Tree Island, a stretch of saltmarsh that was once a refuse dump. Hadleigh Country Park offers 387 acres of marsh, sea wall and grassland, loved by visiting geese, and woodpeckers and dragonflies in summer. Many of the larger houses have been filleted into flats. Something with one bedroom might sell at £110,000, two bedrooms at £120,000. Unconverted Twenties' and Thirties' houses up on the cliffs go for over £250,000 to £400,000. There is pressure on car owners within a walk of The Broadway and the station because parking is impossible.

Journey: 50 min
Season: £2608
Peak: 8 per hr
Off-peak: 4 per hr

CHALKWELL The Chalkwell Hall estate is extremely popular, being south of the London Road, close to the Fenchurch Street line and the bracing breezes from the sea front. A detached house with three bedrooms and a garage will cost around £400,000.

Journey: 52 min
Season: £2700
Peak: 8 per hr
Off-peak: 4 per hr

WESTCLIFF-ON-SEA is a dignified old Victorian lady of a town, which is failing to fend off the encroaching seaside tat. Sadly, her densely layered streets of 19th-century houses, many of them now converted into flats, tend to be jammed with cars that can't find anywhere to park. She has a more cosmopolitan air these days, thanks to her appeal to asylum seekers. Average prices of flats range from around £95,000 for one bedroom to £125,000 for two, and up to £400,000 for something along the front. The Cliff Gardens run all the way along the cliffs to Southend.

Journey: 54 min
Season: £2700
Peak: 8 per hr
Off-peak: 4 per hr

Westcliff is a dignified old Victorian lady of a town, which is failing to fend off the encroaching seaside tat

SOUTHEND CENTRAL Southend has spent the last few decades adjusting to the death of the Great British Holiday, while simultaneously adapting itself as a London dormitory. A huge injection of European regeneration money has helped, as will the arrival of a new campus for the University of Essex and a Further Education College, which is promising to bring 20,000 students. A £22m renovation of the Victoria Shopping Centre is underway to draw out-of-town shoppers back to the town, and a farmers' market is held twice a month. The Royal Bank of Scotland and the administrators of VAT are both large local employers.

Southend remains popular with day-trippers and bank holiday weekenders, and has not lost the kiss-me-quick feel of the Fifties. Strolling along the Prom is still a popular Sunday morning pastime. Its efforts in the late 18th and 19th centuries to rival the elegance of other seaside resorts such as Brighton have endowed it with some fine buildings, including the Royal Terrace. The 1¼-mile-long pier, which has miraculously survived various disasters, including a fire in 2005, is now cherished and restored and complemented by the theme park

Adventure Island, where thrills are supplied by The Vortex and The Scorpion. The sailing fraternity is strong here: there are five yacht clubs either side of Southend, in the stretch between **Thorpe Bay** and **Leigh Old Town**. Average house prices run from £150,000 for a two-bedroom house, £230,000 for a three-bedroom semi and well over £280,000 for one in a better area such as Leigh-on-Sea (see page 42).

Southend Airport, to the north of the town, is undergoing a multi-million pound expansion, which will include a new £12m railway station, terminal building, control tower and hotel in preparation for the London Olympics in 2012.

Journey: 57 min
Season: £2700
Peak: 8 per hr
Off-peak: 4 per hr

SOUTHEND EAST
This is the area known as **Southchurch**. A great web of residential streets extends from Southend Central to Thorpe Bay, stitched together by a long main road of shops and offices. A three-bedroom semi on one of the nicest roads – Southchurch Boulevard or Arlington Road, for example – will cost around £350,000. In less popular streets the price drops to around £225,000. Two- or three-bedroom terraced houses sell for around £175,000 to £220,000.

'Thorpe Bay is the most expensive part of Southend, and even those who live on the fringe-of-the-fringe say they live here'

Seafront property, Southend

Schools in Essex

The choice of high-performing grammars, ex-grammars and comprehensives in Essex makes it attractive to ambitious parents with young families who cannot afford to use the private sector. Be warned, however, that some of the best schools have five times too many applicants for the number of places. Entrance requirements are stiff.

Many of the schools appear in clusters. Southend, for instance, has Southend Boys' High, Southend Girls' High, both traditional grammar schools, as well as two good state schools, Westcliff High for boys and Westcliff High for girls.

Brentwood independent schools are Brentwood and Peniel Academy (non-selective), the good comprehensives include St Martin's and the Ursuline, ex-grammar, comprehensive girls' convent. There is also Shenfield High (mixed) at Shenfield. Not far away is the Anglo-European at Ingatestone,

a comprehensive that promotes the International Baccalaureate

Chelmsford has the County High School for Girls and the boys' equivalent, King Edward VI Grammar School, which has choral links with the cathedral. New Hall is the nearby girls' day and boarding school.

Colchester has the grammar County High School for Girls, and the Colchester Royal Grammar for boys – a descendant of the ancient town school established in 1206.

Other places with strong schools are Hornchurch, which has The Campion boys' Catholic comprehensive; Loughton, which has the Davenant Foundation co-eduational school; Saffron Walden with its County High; Hockley with Greensward College comprehensive; and Woodford Green, which has the girls' grammar Woodford County High.

Journey: 60 min
Season: £2820
Peak: 8 per hr
Off-peak: 4 per hr

THORPE BAY is the most expensive part of Southend, and even those who live on the fringe-of-the-fringe say they live here. Detached houses with four to five bedrooms, built early this century, sell for £475,000 to £600,000. Those on the sea front might go for anything up to £1m. The private golf club and Conservative politics feature large on the social circuit, which is fuelled with new money and is anxious to dissociate itself from anything too downmarket. There is a wine bar, but no pub. The place excites envy in its neighbours, as described by one local cricketer with typical Essex bluntness: 'When you played against Thorpe Bay, you bowled at the batsman, not the wicket.'

Journey: 64 min
Season: £2820
Peak: 8 per hr
Off-peak: 4 per hr

SHOEBURYNESS With its sprawling council estates and industrial zones, Shoeburyness has little to offer other than cheapness. It has a beach, which is good for windsurfing, sailing and jet skiing. There are a few one-bedroom flats near the station that sell for around £115,000; a three-bedroom house can be had for around £150,000. On the Grade Two listed Shoebury Garrison development a substantial family home with four bedrooms and original features may cost around £580,000. To the north it becomes a little more sedate and a good house can be bought in the £350,000 range.

Barling, nearby, offers a profound contrast with one foot still firmly planted in the past. Among the 300-year old cottages, it is also possible to buy a five-bedroom detached house for £430,000. A Grade Two listed, five-bedroom farmhouse with equestrian facilities would cost at least £1.9m. Alternatively there is **Great Wakering**, with its church, pubs and shops. A three-bedroom mid-terrace here would cost from £165,000; a three-bedroom semi with a long rear garden around £200,000.

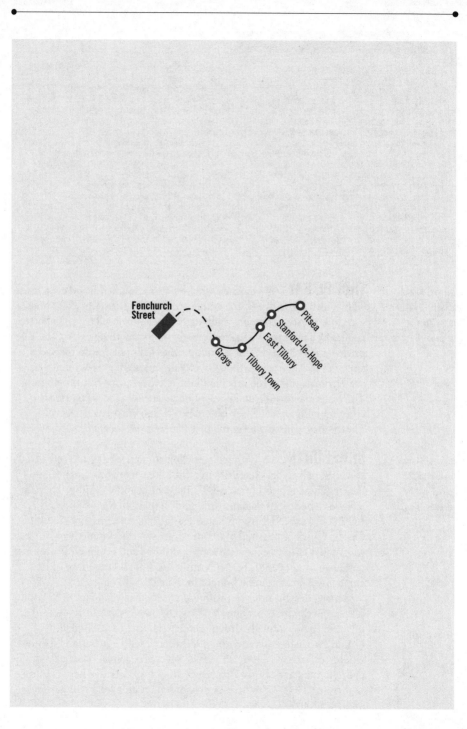

Fenchurch Street
> Pitsea (via Tilbury)

Journey: 35 min

Season: £1824

Peak: 7 per hr

Off-peak: 4 per hr

GRAYS was built in two surges – the first in the late 19th century and the second in the Thirties – and is now one of the busiest commercial centres in this part of Essex. Cheaper homes in the £130,000 range are snapped up here. The most comfortable area to live is **North Grays**, where the roads are filled with large Thirties' houses. The four-bedroom detached variety would cost between £300,000 and £400,000.

North Stifford is another popular part, with the remnants of the old village still intact (blink and you miss it). A one-bedroom terraced cottage could cost from £150,000 upwards, a three-bedroom detached house in a semi-rural location around £480,000.

The vast Lakeside shopping centre at Thurrock, two or three miles away, offering one of the largest concentrations of shopping in Europe and a nine-screen cinema, has had a huge impact. It has also spawned the new Bannatynes Leisure Centre. Grays itself is a good shopping centre with small outlets of the big chains.

Nearby is **Chafford Hundred**, where an entire new town of 5,500 houses has been built on the old chalk pits beside the M25 and the Dartford Tunnel. It has a rich mix of one-bedroom flats for £135,000, two bedrooms at £160,000, up to four-bedroom houses selling from £250,000 to £350,000, with maisonettes, semis and terraced housing between. It also has its own main line railway station (on a link between Grays and Upminster), and schools are in place.

At Chafford Hundred, an entire new town of 5,500 houses has been built on the old chalk pits beside the M25 and the Dartford Tunnel

Journey: 41 min	
Season: £1824	
Peak: 5 per hr	
Off-peak: 2 per hr	

TILBURY TOWN Tilbury itself bears all the warts and eyesores that the 20th century could have thrown at it. When the ships coming up the Thames got so big that they couldn't squeeze up to London any more, Tilbury developed a dock complex so huge that it can be seen for miles around. Housing is very council-orientated and cheap. Many former council tenants have bought their properties and an ex-council house with three bedrooms now costs around £125,000. **Tilbury Riverside** burgeoned on the back of the boat-trains to Europe in the 1850s, but it long ago lost its station and now the only ferry that ploughs in and out is for Gravesend.

Journey: 47 min	
Season: £2188	
Peak: 5 per hr	
Off-peak: 2 per hr	

EAST TILBURY There are strangely rural, long-forgotten pockets in this town. Around quiet corners you come suddenly upon dirt tracks that open up long walks beside the Thames. The Bata shoe company was started here by Czechoslovakians, who built their own distinctive 1930s flat-roofed houses, schools and cinema, now much admired and designated a conservation area. The factory has closed, but is preserved, and many of the houses have been sold on the open market. The old Bata office block has been converted into flats. A three-bedroom terraced house here costs about £150,000, but you can also buy a four-bedroom detached house from about £240,000. The Lakeside shopping centre at Thurrock has sucked much of the retail energy from these nearby areas. Modernisation came late to this line, the old timber platform in the station has been replaced, the manually operated level-crossing gates now work automatically, and there has been a £300m investment in carriages.

Commuters used to call it the Misery Line but a great deal of money has been spent on track and signalling improvements. Meanwhile, overcrowding has eased as more people work from home for one or two days a week or opt to travel by car.

‘Commuters used to call it the Misery Line, but a great deal of money has been spent on track and signalling improvements. Meanwhile, overcrowding has eased’

Journey: 51 min
Season: £2188
Peak: 6 per hr
Off-peak: 2 per hr

STANFORD-LE-HOPE There are a few late 19th-century streets near the station but otherwise most of **Stanford-Le-Hope** is an eruption of low-cost Sixties' housing that gathered around **Corringham** and **Coryton** as far as the big oil refineries on the edge of the Thames. Plans have been approved for a container port near Coryton and the area is expected to swallow a lot of new Thames Gateway housing. Three-bedroom semis are priced at about £180,000 to £220,000, standard four-bedroom detached houses at £300,000, with the most expensive in the range selling for about £380,000 to £480,000. From here people might prefer to travel by rail up to **Pitsea** and change to the main line into Fenchurch Street, rather than take the slow and indirect route through **Tilbury**.

Journey: 41 min
Season: £2300
Peak: 4 per hr
Off-peak: 4 per hr

PITSEA See **Fenchurch Street to Shoeburyness** line (page 42).

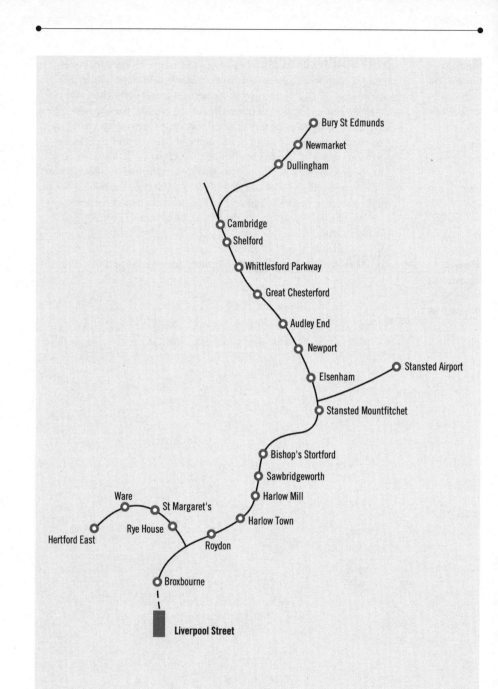

Bury St Edmunds
Newmarket
Dullingham
Cambridge
Shelford
Whittlesford Parkway
Great Chesterford
Audley End
Newport
Stansted Airport
Elsenham
Stansted Mountfitchet
Bishop's Stortford
Sawbridgeworth
Harlow Mill
Ware
St Margaret's
Harlow Town
Rye House
Hertford East
Roydon
Broxbourne

Liverpool Street

Liverpool Street
> Cambridge

Journey: 27 min
Season: £2180
Peak: 7 per hr
Off-peak: 4 per hr

BROXBOURNE The railway came to Broxbourne in 1840. Victorian houses immediately started going up around the station, and it has been commuter country ever since. To the south of it is a soothing pocket of countryside where the New River lazes across the meadows. Other relics of the rural past, including Broxbourne Woods, have been retained by conversion into parkland. The Lea Valley Regional Park runs for 23 miles from Bromley-by-Bow through Broxbourne to Ware, making Broxbourne a handy resort for boating and holiday chalets. Plans are in hand to transform the Lea Valley Leisure Pool, and perhaps add an adventure playground and athletics track. Detached houses on the more residential western side of the town can sell for up to £630,000. Smaller three-bedroom houses to the east fetch up to £350,000. Large amounts of new housing are planned at Canada Fields. There is the vast out-of-town Brookfield Retail Park at Cheshunt to the south, where there is also a golf course.

Broxbourne doesn't stop before **Hoddesdon** begins, though the atmosphere becomes rather more industrial. Hoddesdon is tightly bound by the green belt and it has a proper town centre with 17th-century buildings set around the old clock tower – an area busy with stalls on market day. The two good state schools attract large numbers of families. Houses on the west and south sides are more desirable, being removed from the more industrial east. In the mix of Victorian, Thirties' and Sixties' houses you could buy a three-bedroom semi for up to £320,000. Larger houses, such as those in the privacy of College Road, sell for £400,000 to £520,000.

Hoddesdon has a proper town centre with 17th-century buildings set around an old clock tower – an area busy with stalls on market day

> Fork to Hertford East via Rye House, St Margaret's and Ware

Journey: 39 min
Season: £2180
Peak: 2 per hr
Off-peak: 2 per hr

RYE HOUSE sits on the northern edge of Hoddesdon, on the finger of the Lea Valley Regional Park where the remains of the old Rye House gatehouse still stand. There was once a thriving nursery garden industry here. In the Thirties, says the local council, the Lea Valley had 'the world's largest accumulation of glasshouses'. Between 1968 and 1971 much of the old nursery land was surrendered to housing, thus creating what is now known as the Hundred Acre Estate, attached to the north side of Hoddesdon. Here you can buy a basic terraced house for £200,000; a three-bedroom semi for £240,000. The 1999 version is Rye House Village, 140 houses built beside the station, where a two-bedroom flat can cost £160,000 and a three-bedroom detached house £250,000. Elsewhere in Rye House, property tends to be fairly cheap. The relative modesty of the houses here is ironic considering that there was once a plan to make Rye House into a kind of genteel pleasure garden. The plans were buried when Sir Giles Gilbert Scott's huge power station arrived. Today a combined cycle gas turbine power station does the job. Entertainments at Rye House Stadium include go-kart, speedway and greyhound racing.

Journey: 41 min
Season: £2220
Peak: 2 per hr
Off-peak: 2 per hr

ST MARGARET'S The village here is **Stanstead St Margaret's**, divided from **Stanstead Abbotts** by the River Lea, though sharing a vicar. A bypass has reduced the amount of through-traffic from 19,000 vehicles a day to 9,000. It is a fast-growing village with new houses going up all the time. There is one pub remaining, The Jolly Fisherman. The old malt industry lingers like a ghost. Disused cowls and chutes litter the skyline, and the occasional whiff of it wafts over the terraced cottages and modern estates in Stanstead Abbotts. There are some small shops and a post office on this side of the river, with playing fields and sports club just outside at St Margaretsbury. Stanstead Abbotts has a primary school attached to the church. Most of the older children attend secondary schools in Hertford or North Hoddesdon. The Stansteads have a marina with narrowboats and cruisers for hire. Property prices are slightly higher than those in Hoddesdon.

Journey: 45 min

Season: £2220

Peak: 2 per hr

Off-peak: 2 per hr

WARE People say that this is where the chimneypots stop and the countryside begins. **Ware** is a good old market town, which hasn't been spoilt, and beyond it lies what the estate agents like to call the golden box – a group of handsome villages in a landscape that, despite its proximity to London, preserves a feeling of remoteness. The town has a strong sense of history. In developing new sites, Roman remains have been unearthed, as well as bodies from the time of the Black Death, shipped along the River Lea for burial outside London. What Hertfordshire sent in return was water – channelled to London's East End by way of the New River, a canal built in the early 17th century. Much of the town's wealth was created by the malt industry, and many of the old maltings have been converted into flats, mini-Docklands style. The main local employer is SmithKlineGlaxo, whose factory is set in parkland by the river. You can buy a one-bedroom flat on the water for £220,000; a three-bedroom apartment with parking for £250,000. It is a charming place to live. The narrowboats still come past and there are some pretty walks along the riverbank from where you can view the extraordinarily delicate old gazebos behind the houses in the High Street, where the gardens run down to the river.

The town centre also contains quite a few mews houses, developed from the old stables and courtyards behind the High Street. Four-bedroom town houses with paved courtyards at the back cost £435,000. There are some smart modern houses closer to the golf course on the south side of the town, where something with four bedrooms and a double garage would fetch up to £575,000. There are specialist shops – including Victoria Beckham's sister's clothes shop – restaurants and a farmers' market. The town has lots of clubs and societies, which show themselves off every July during Ware Festival. There are indoor and outdoor heated swimming pools and, for team sports, Ware Football Club, Hertford Rugby Club at Hoe Lane, and cricket on the Old Hertfordians ground.

18th-century riverfront gazebos, Ware

The villages are in a very different price zone. Footballers, pop stars and television personalities lurk down these country lanes, and you could easily pay up to £1.5m for an ex-farmhouse with acreage. **Great Amwell** is both the most expensive and the prettiest, with the New River draped in willows. Here it widens to a pool with two islands. These hold monuments to the New River's creator, the engineer Sir Hugh Myddleton. Two miles away are the imposing buildings of Haileybury College. A period house with five bedrooms and two acres in Great Amwell could easily cost £1.8m, though you

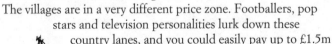

might find a little two-up-two-down for £190,000. The village has an annual flower show and every so often it opens its gardens to the public.

To the east is **Hunsdon**. Its timbered and weatherboarded cottages, village school and friendly atmosphere all contribute to its great appeal. Saturday coffee mornings are a regular event in the village hall, and there are societies for toddlers, tennis players and the elderly, and an enthusiastic amateur dramatics group. Small Victorian cottages cost around £240,000. Three-bedroom cottages can be expected to cost at least £320,000, and farmhouse-sized properties up to £950,000. New houses have been built in small handfuls for those at managing director level, priced at over £450,000 for five bedrooms.

In the precious northern belt are villages such as **Standon** and **Puckeridge** in the Rib Valley. Standon is favourite, with its wide curving High Street, timber-framed houses and village school. St Edmund's Roman Catholic College is a few miles to the west. Property prices are slightly higher than those in Hunsdon. Puckeridge has a twisting High Street and more the feel of a small town about it, with Sixties and Seventies developments tacked on. More new development has followed as a result of the expansion of Stansted Airport. An older two-bedroom terrace here would cost £220,000; a new four-bedroom house £360,000. The Thurlow hunt rides out from Brent Pelham nearby.

Braughing is a film-set village built at the confluence of the River Quin with the Rib. The approach to it is by way of a ford known as The Splash that occasionally floods. It has an aviation society, local history society and fiercely active bell-ringing group. There is drama and tennis too. The family-run butcher's, The Braughing Sausage Company, is renowned for its meat and famous Braughing sausages. The colour-washed cottages have often been used as backdrops to television feature films, and some have superb pargeting. The smallest cottage here would cost around £220,000, with prices rising to about £800,000 for the larger period houses.

Journey: 49 min
Season: £2220 (also valid from Hertford North)
Peak: 2 per hr
Off-peak: 2 per hr

HERTFORD EAST See **Moorgate to Stevenage** line (page 92).

> Continuation of main line

Journey: 30 min
Season: £2284
Peak: 2 per hr
Off-peak: 1 per hr

ROYDON is quite a commuter haven, being handsome enough to have a conservation booklet written about it, but not chocolate boxy. Some of the houses are genuinely Georgian; others have false Georgian fronts. The village revolves around the church, the green and the High Street, which has many listed buildings. The school still thrives and, though the butcher has gone, there is a bakery, chemist, part-time doctor's surgery, an Italian restaurant and a hairdresser. Historical relics include village stocks and lock-up. Roydon has a flower festival every other year; the tennis court is well-used, the Roydon Players can be relied upon for local drama and there are three conservation societies ready to see off the Government's plans for thousands of new homes. There are some five-bedroom houses with large gardens that sell for £550,000 but they can top £1m; a period house will cost £950,000 at the very least.

Journey: 31 min
Season: £2760
Peak: 6 per hr
Off-peak: 4 per hr

HARLOW TOWN It has to be said that many people hate **Harlow** in spite of its parks and Henry Moore sculptures (most of which are now so valuable that they have had to be put away in museums). The New Town was created in 1947, to the masterplan of Sir Frederick Gibberd, as a series of four large residential zones in a rural setting, each with its own infrastructure. The population jumped from 4,000 to over 80,000, mostly as a result of London overspill. A two-bedroom terraced house at Church Langley will cost over £180,000 and a five-bedroom detached £475,000. Harlow has two good shopping complexes, Broad Walk and the newly-opened Harvey Shopping Centre, a nightclub, bingo hall and the Playhouse theatre. A new leisure centre is due to open in late 2009, featuring two swimming pools, badminton and tennis courts and a gym, as well as a Science Alive hands-on learning centre.

Journey: 37 min
Season: £2760
Peak: 2 per hr
Off-peak: 1 per hr

HARLOW MILL This is the station for some of Harlow's smarter parts – Mark Hall North, for instance, where a three-bedroom house costs £235,000. **Harlow Old Town** is very popular because of the older period properties it contains, together with good little shops, including two bakers. A house here is likely to cost 10–20 per cent more than its nearest equivalent in the New Town. There are many pretty villages to the east. At **Fyfield** or **Moreton**, for example, you could buy a three-bedroom cottage for £365,000, or a country house with six bedrooms and paddocks for £1.4m. People who live in this area are not famous for their liking of Harlow and are more likely to nip south and use the Central Line from Epping.

Journey: 38 min
Season: £3060
Peak: 3 per hr
Off-peak: 2 per hr

SAWBRIDGEWORTH is a low-rise town set in the fields and woods between Harlow and Bishop's Stortford, and – though at this point you are in Hertfordshire – this is where you begin to see the distinct local building styles of Essex: steep tiled gables and dormers, overhanging upper storeys, timber and weatherboarding. The town has two primary schools, enough shops for day-to-day needs, including bakers and butchers, and a farmers' market. There are all the usual societies, plus a lacemakers' group. In a strange reversal of trends, the old cinema has been turned into a Catholic Church. Horse-riding is popular with local children. Flats by the river overlooking the marina attract commuters, who also benefit from being little more than five miles from Stansted Airport. Famous nearby residents include Posh and Becks who keep their English base here. Two bedrooms cost £180,000, three bedrooms £260,000. Older three-bedroom semis can be bought for £250,000.

Journey: 37 min
Season: £3232
Peak: 7 per hr
Off-peak: 4 per hr

BISHOP'S STORTFORD is a wealthy little market town surrounded by pretty villages. Aircraft coming in and out of Stansted Airport fly around it to avoid causing any distress to those who live here. It has a good shopping centre, with a newly extended mall and branches of Sainsbury's, Waitrose and Marks & Spencer. A market is held on most Thursdays along the twisting main street. The town buzzes with activities, including both operatic and amateur dramatic societies. The H20 nightclub and a couple of wine bars cater for ravers.

The older, more attractive buildings are in North Street, Windhill and the Old High Street. It is possible to buy a two-bedroom house in Bishop's Stortford for as little as £190,000, but a three-bedroom semi would take you to £260,000 and you should expect to pay £370,000 for a four-bedroom detached. A new two-bedroom apartment in the heart of town would cost around £200,000. The better side of town is the north-west corner where Stortford College, the private boys' school, is situated, and the houses are large and secluded. Prices here range between £585,000 and £825,000. There is an equestrian centre at Hallingbury Hall, Little Hallingbury. A substantial country house with nine bedrooms and land on the edge of town might cost £1.7m.

To the west, on the Hertfordshire-Essex borders, are the Hadhams. **Much Hadham** is probably the smartest village in the area. Its fashionable status derives from the fact that the Bishop of London once took up residence here, and subsequent bishops kept the palace going for centuries. It has a charming mix of Elizabethan cottages, 18th-century town houses and Victorian almshouses, and the blacksmith's forge has become part of a crafts museum. As in any village, the sizes and prices of the houses span a wide range. The

18th-century four-bedroom town houses with walled gardens can be bought for £670,000. A five-bedroom barn conversion at **Little Hadham** would cost £750,000.

Further north are the Pelhams. **Stocking Pelham** is a particularly pretty village where a good country house with three acres could easily reach £1.2m.

To the south-east is **Hatfield Broad Oak**, built on the edge of Hatfield Forest – more than 1,000 acres of National Trust woodland donated by the Puckeridge and Essex hunts. It is a handsome village full of Georgian buildings. There is some post-war development south and east of the High Street. Hatfield Broad Oak has a post-office-cum-general store, a butcher, beauty salon and florist. The influx of commuters and working wives who are out of the village during the day,.and so shop elsewhere, is making life difficult for the shopkeepers. Barrington Hall, a grand country house set in parkland, is now the office of a perfume company. You do get the occasional stray aircraft overhead, but for the most part they disturb other villages such as Great Hallingbury.

Journey: 51 min
Season: £3384
Peak: 3 per hr
Off-peak: 1 per hr

STANSTED MOUNTFITCHET The proposed expansion of Stansted Airport cannot but have a huge effect on the area surrounding it, particularly as long-term plans include the building of a second runway and an increase in passenger numbers from 25 million to 35 million a year. There is, however, a fast train service from the airport on a spur line from here with trains dashing into London four times an hour in under 45 minutes (see below). A four-bedroom converted barn in the area will cost £585,000. One of the nicest places within striking distance of the railway station is **Manuden** – a tiny one-and-a-half street village on the River Stort with some pretty, jettied timber-framed houses. A three-bedroom end-of-terrace might cost around £350,000; a four-bedroom house with garage and mature garden could fetch £600,000.

> Branch line to Stansted Airport

Journey: 46 min
Season: £3520
Peak: 4 per hr
Off-peak: 4 per hr

STANSTED AIRPORT As parking is plentiful beside architect Norman Foster's impressive **Stansted Airport** terminal, and trains into London are swift, commuters are increasingly tempted to use the station. Both the rail link and the M11 bring the land of windmills within easy reach.

> Continuation of main line

Journey: 54 min
Season: £3384
Peak: 2 per hr
Off-peak: 1 per hr

ELSENHAM offers a good view of the air traffic in and out of Stansted but is little affected by the noise, although the proposed expansion of the airport could bring new road links within the village boundaries. Its two most prominent features are a village pump in a domed octagonal well-house, and Elsenham Hall, a late Georgian red-brick mansion by the church. The village has seen a lot of new development in the last two decades and the range of property is large, with prices from £180,000 for a three-bedroom house to over £425,000 for a modern estate house and £750,000 for a six-bedroom Grade Two listed home. Shops include a post office, newsagent and supermarket, and there is a pub, hairdresser and garage. Bishop's Stortford is nearby for major shopping. It is a very horsey kind of a village, with plenty of activities: WI, gardening club, allotment association, cricket, football and keep-fit clubs. One of the Government's much-vaunted eco towns is planned for land to the north-east and opposition to it is strong.

Ugley, just to the north, does not deserve its name. Incidentally, the Women's Institute here refers to itself as the Women's Institute of Ugley, rather than the Ugley Women's Institute. And **Quendon**, too, is very pretty. The big house, Quendon Park, is surrounded by a wooded deer-park and has a good William and Mary south front. A six-bedroom Georgian farmhouse with 3½ acres is likely to cost £1m.

To the north-east on the young River Chelmer is **Thaxted**, an impressive old town with a guildhall that broods over the open market place and an old windmill at the end of Fishmarket Street, which has been restored as a museum. The church, with 181ft spire and medieval roofs, is one of the finest in Essex. Thaxted's problem is that it lies beneath the flight path to Stansted Airport, though people are so attached to the town that they don't seem to mind. Many of them move house within the village, and some Londoners have second homes here. A two-bedroom semi will cost around £200,000; a four-bedroom detached modern house £260,000.

Journey: 60 min
Season: £3460
Peak: 2 per hr
Off-peak: 1 per hr

NEWPORT has always been more expensive than the neighbouring town of Saffron Walden, to which it long ago lost its market. It has a fine main street of gracious houses, all within easy reach of the station and the M11. An added attraction is Newport Free School for boys – an ex-grammar but still highly respected. Three-bedroom houses in the centre of Newport cost from £215,000.

Essex begins to get pricey here, with a collection of very pretty villages. South-west of the station are **Clavering**, with its cluster of cottages around the church, and **Rickling Green**. The latter has a picture-book green with a cricket pitch appropriately overlooked by a pub called The Cricketers (owned by the parents of chef Jamie Oliver). Two-bedroom thatched cottages sell for £190,000 to £300,000, large country houses with land for £1m to £1.2m.

Only a mile from the station to the west is **Wicken Bonhunt**, very small and exclusive, where an ordinary four-bedroom house will cost around £330,000. Another mile brings you to **Arkesden**, by a little stream called Wicken Water. Thatched cottages spread themselves around a green, with a 16th-century hall and 13th–14th-century church. An 18th-century house with five bedrooms and five reception rooms would cost over £750,000.

On the east side is **Widdington**, also very small and expensive. This hilltop village has cottages around a green and larger houses hidden in the lanes. A four-bedroom detached house would cost around £515,000; a detached three-bedroom cottage around £435,000. **Debden** is another thatched village on the way to nowhere, but it does have two pubs and a heroic community shop that has been going for more than 20 years. A four-bedroom cottage in the centre of the village will cost £425,000.

> *Rickling Green has a picture-book green with a cricket pitch appropriately overlooked by a pub called The Cricketers*

AUDLEY END There is little more at **Audley End** than the station itself. The town it serves is **Saffron Walden**. It has a handsome market place with narrow medieval rows running off it, small specialist shops, a Waitrose and a branch of Eaden Lilley department store. It is a stronghold of conservationists who want to protect the charming streets of timber-framed houses. The huge common, once used for grazing cattle and medieval tournaments, now serves as a fairground and recreation area. Its most puzzling feature is a rare turf maze – archaeologists still don't understand its purpose. Friends co-educational private school is a draw for many of the families who come to live here.

Journey: 56 min
Season: £3620
Peak: 4 per hr
Off-peak: 2 per hr

There are quite a few inexpensive modern estates. A one-bedroom flat will cost around £90,000; a five-bedroom semi up to £380,000. The town can be rather touristy in summer.

The villages nearby are beyond the reach of most local young couples. At **Wendens Ambo** a five-bedroom barn conversion with landscaped gardens would cost around £775,000. The lane to the church has some particularly appealing cottages. Nearby **Littlebury** is also expensive, with a good collection of lath-and-plaster cottages beside the miniature River Cam, near the site of an Iron Age camp. A refurbished end-of-terrace cottage will cost £200,000; a Grade Two listed brick barn conversion would be likely to fetch £570,000.

On the east side of Audley End is **Wimbish** – little more than a smattering of houses through the lanes. The presence of an army barracks pulls the prices down. **Hempstead**, Dick Turpin's birthplace, is very popular, though the road to it is winding and slow. **Finchingfield** is much photographed because of the beautiful juxtaposition of church, pond and cottages, not to mention its windmill and Elizabethan big house. A four-bedroom period house with a garden could be bought for around £475,000.

Journey: 69 min
Season: £3620
Peak: 2 per hr
Off-peak: 1 per hr

GREAT CHESTERFORD and Little Chesterford are both extremely

prestigious, having a very popular primary school and being close enough to Cambridge to attract people who work there. The River Cam tiptoes through both, and in Great Chesterford it is overlooked by a large watermill converted into flats. The village has a thriving post-office/shop, two pubs and a hotel, and a small industrial sector providing employment. A four-bedroom Grade Two listed cottage will cost £500,000. **Hadstock**, to the east, is a pretty village with thatched cottages around a green, but it is less expensive.

Journey: 64 min
Season: £3700
Peak: 4 per hr
Off-peak: 2 per hr

WHITTLESFORD PARKWAY Ideally situated close to Cambridge

and the M11, the village of **Whittlesford** is quite sizeable and prices can be higher than neighbouring **Duxford**. Most people know Duxford for its airfield (well to the west), which houses part of the collection of the Imperial War Museum. In addition to the permanent display of historic aircraft there are flying displays and pleasure flights in the summer. There are some nice old pubs and some thatched cottages, though these have been rather swamped by the new estates and bungalows. A two-bedroom detached bungalow will cost around £210,000; a three-bedroom detached house £235,000.

Sawston has an image-problem caused by the large council estates by which it is surrounded, and the fact that it is being expanded to meet Cambridgeshire's ever-growing housing needs. What draws many people to it is the presence of a Cambridge Village College (see Comberton, page 62). Small one-bedroom houses cost around £160,000; three-bedroom semis £200,000; new three- and four-bedroom houses £270,000.

Journey: 77 min
Season: £3740
Peak: 2 per hr
Off-peak: 1 per hr

SHELFORD Great Shelford and Little Shelford, with Stapleford into

which they merge at the base of the Gog Magog hills, all ooze prosperity. This is where the Cambridge wealthy – businessmen and London commuters and academics – choose to make their homes. The houses are large and secluded, with parks and other green open spaces to enhance the feeling of spaciousness. There are plenty of shops, including a delicatessen. Period houses in Great Shelford's Mingle Lane and Gog Magog Way, which leads to the Gog Magog Golf Club, are thought to have particular appeal. A six-bedroom house with mature gardens would cost £1.4m. You don't *have* to be rich to live here: there is a development close to the station with three-bedroom starter homes at £170,000. Sawston Village College, one of the much-admired Cambridge Village Colleges (see Comberton, page 62) is the local secondary school.

To Liverpool Street
Journey: 71 min
Season: £3780
(also valid into Kings Cross)
Peak: 4 per hr
Off-peak: 2 per hr

To Kings Cross
Journey: 48 min
Season: £3780
Peak: 2 per hr
Off-peak: 3 per hr

CAMBRIDGE The line beyond here goes to **King's Lynn**. For villages close to stations on the **Kings Cross to King's Lynn** line via Cambridge and Ely see pages 72–79.

The property market in **Cambridge** has a mind of its own, being heavily influenced by the constant comings and goings of university academics and the staff of the high-tech industries that have thrived in the university's shadow. During the Eighties the explosion of scientific, medical and agricultural companies based on university research became known as the Cambridge Phenomenon – and predictably it delivered an upward thrust to local house prices. People continue to pour into the area to work and so tight is the green belt girth of this beautiful but tiny city, that an entirely new settlement called **Cambourne** has been built to the west. Prairie fields have been turned into 3,000 houses, with a 50-acre business park, two primary schools and a heavy environmental spin (ponds, trees and walks are high on the agenda). Plans have been submitted for an additional 950 homes. Small three-bedroom houses sell at £190,000; five-bedroom executive homes start at £400,000.

'The Cambridge Phenomenon predictably delivered an upward thrust to local house prices'

To the north of Cambridge lie the Science Park, with more than 90 high-tech companies, and the stark flat landscape of the Fens. It is the south that most people prefer to live. The station is here, and so are the better schools, including The Perse co-educational private school. Planning applications have been submitted to modernise the station itself and redevelop the immediate area to provide student accommodation and 330 new dwellings. The area near the station, around Tenison Road, is popular with professional couples; two-bedroom Victorian terraces here cost £250,000. On the other side of the tracks they cost £230,000. Larger four-bedroom Victorian houses in the station area will cost around £600,000. Alternatively, to the west there is Newnham, an old-established residential area where a typical bay-fronted, three-bedroom Victorian house would cost £350,000. The higher prices in Cambridge are around the £1m mark.

The most expensive, exclusive and attractive village in the area has to be **Grantchester**, two miles to the south. Rupert Brooke lived here as a student at the Old Vicarage, now occupied by Jeffrey Archer. Brooke's best-remembered lines, 'Stands the Church clock at ten to three?/And is there honey still for tea?', are a reference to his time in Grantchester. The village's many attractions include walks along the

61

Cam, the old tea-rooms, which students punt to, and pretty cottages that sell for enormous sums. You could possibly get a small two-bedroom Victorian terrace for £275,000; but a favoured four-bedroom house with a large garden is likely to fetch £625,000 and upwards.

To the west of Cambridge is **Comberton**. This is a good village for families since it contains one of the highly-regarded Cambridge Village Colleges. A handful of these were built to embody the ideas of Henry Morris, chief education officer at Cambridge from 1922 to 1954. He believed that secondary schools could be run like small colleges, serving several villages while at the same time fulfilling their cultural needs and providing adult education. Property and prices in the villages (excluding Grantchester) tend to be more family-friendly than in Cambridge itself.

'**Madingley has stunning views to the spires and towers of Cambridge**'

Due west of Cambridge is **Madingley** – worth looking at because of the stunning views to the spires and towers of Cambridge, seen against the backdrop of the Gog Magog hills. Much of the village is owned by the university, and the hall is now a hostel for graduates. Prices are probably up to 10 per cent lower than in Grantchester.

The countryside to the north looks markedly less friendly but lower prices attract those who want big roomy houses. **Histon**, previously the base of the Chivers jam-making enterprise, is almost a small town now, with shops, sub-branches of banks, building societies and garages. Its main attraction is its proximity to **Impington**, which has a Village College designed in the early Thirties by Walter Gropius and Max Fry. It is also close to **Girton**, home not only of Girton College but also of Girton Golf Club. A two-bedroom house here will cost £190,000.

To the east, on the edge of the Fens, which can sometimes look like the edge of the world, are **Swaffham Bulbeck** and **Swaffham Prior**. They are eight miles from Cambridge, but worth considering if you want to escape the academic atmosphere affecting some of the other villages. Both are remarkably unspoiled and have some charming period cottages. At Swaffham Prior (where the poet Edwin Muir once lived) you could buy a two-bedroom terraced cottage for £180,000; a four-bedroom property with stables and grazing for £550,000.

Schools in Cambridgeshire

Educational excellence in Cambridgeshire is centred on Cambridge itself. High-flying state schools include the Village College comprehensives such as Bottisham, Swavesey, Cottenham, Sawston, Comberton, Impington, Linton, and Melbourn, from which children can go on to sixth-form centres. In the private sector there is The Leys for both sexes,

The Perse independent school for boys (girls in the sixth and fully co-educational from 2010), Perse Girls', and St Mary's Roman Catholic day and boarding school for girls. Those who live at St Ives or St Neots often look to Kimbolton in Huntingdon, a co-educational independent day school (with some boarding), which was once a grammar.

The A14 is an important dividing line in the east. Anything to the south of it, where the countryside starts to ripple again, will command a higher price. **Fulbourn** serves as a Cambridge suburb, with new developments encroaching on the older houses and thatched cottages, though proposals for additional housing are being vigorously opposed by the parish council. There is a primary school, a post office and a range of shops, including a butcher, greengrocer and flower shop. Two pubs remain of the original 20-plus that once served coach travellers en route to Newmarket. A three-bedroom semi on a new estate will cost £225,000; an older style three-bedroom semi around £295,000; a detached house around £300,000.

> Branch line to Bury St Edmunds via Dullingham and Newmarket

No through trains

Trains to
Cambridge: 1 per hr
Journey: 76 min
(from Newmarket)

Season (from
Newmarket:) £4140

DULLINGHAM is quite remote and therefore suited to two-car families. It has become very popular because of its proximity to Cambridge and its pretty thatch-and-clunch cottages, old farm and stables and village green. A two-bedroom cottage with an outbuilding will cost £260,000. **Newmarket** is the place to live if you are a fancier of horseflesh – it is home to 4,200 horses and there are more swimming pools here for horses than for humans. The town lives and breathes racing. The chalk downland is peppered with stud farms, shelter belts and exercise areas, with the National Stud at Newmarket Heath. Strings of horses can be seen each day trailing through the town to the horsewalks on to the gallops. There are two racecourses – the Rowley Mile and the July. A large house with stabling and acreage could cost more than £3m. **Kennett** again is rather remote – a quiet Fenside village that feels a little stranded between Cambridge and Suffolk. It shares its post office and village hall with neighbouring **Kentford**. There is a primary school and secondary-age children take the bus to Soham Village College, eight miles away. The single street has some period houses, flint and half-timbering. At the end of it is the grave of a gypsy boy who was hanged 200 years ago for stealing sheep. The grave always has flowers on it – rumour has it that the flowers laid on Derby Day foretell the colours of the winner. A family-sized house here could be bought for £290,000. For **Bury St Edmunds**, see **Liverpool Street to Norwich** line, page 30.

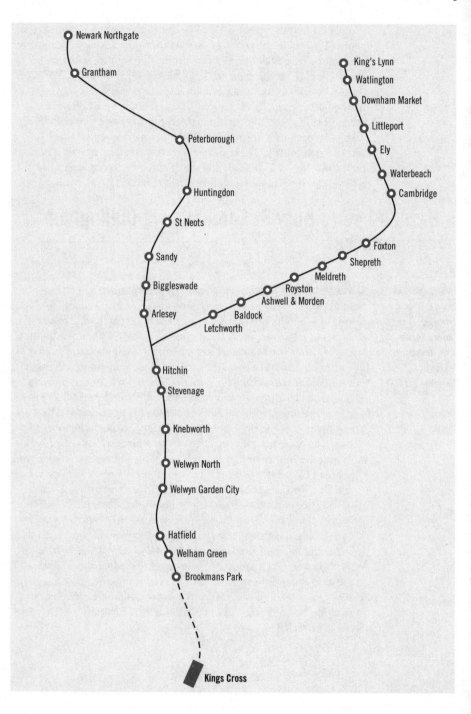

> Newark Northgate and King's Lynn

To Moorgate
Journey: 37 min
Season: £1680
Peak: 4 per hr
Off-peak: 3 per hr

BROOKMANS PARK This is the world of personalised number plates and golf courses, the playground to **Potters Bar**. Large expensive houses, some of them sealed behind tall hedges, have been built between lakes and woodlands in the grounds of two long-demolished country houses, called Brookmans and Gobions. The railway arrived in 1926, and suburbia gradually ate up the surrounding fields. A four-bedroom house in more exclusive **Brookmans Park** can be bought for £500,000, though prices run into millions with ease. Moffats Farm is thought once to have been the home of Dr Thomas Muffett, author of the nursery rhyme *Little Miss Muffet*.

To Moorgate
Journey: 39 min
Season: £1880
Peak: 4 per hr
Off-peak: 3 per hr

WELHAM GREEN is a step down from Brookmans Park. The village offers a mix of private developments and council estates built around a centre with a green, shops, pubs, restaurants and a garage. A three-bedroom detached house could be bought for £350,000 – possibly 30 per cent cheaper than an equivalent house in Brookmans Park. There is a commemorative stone to the Italian balloonist Vincenzo Lunardi, who made the first balloon ascent outside France in 1784. He landed here to let his cat out of the basket because it was feeling sick.

For train information, see overleaf

HATFIELD was built in four stages. There was the Old Town, then the New Town and the arrival of the railway – when it became known as 'California' because it was 'out west and bit rough'. Then came the post-war stage of the New Town, and now the old British Aerospace site has sprouted a major shopping mall – The Galleria – multiplex cinema and David Lloyd leisure centre. The University of Hertfordshire's de Havilland campus contains the Hertfordshire Sports Village, built to Sport England standards, which is open to local residents. Hatfield may be dreary but has a brilliant strategic position – being close to the A1,

To Kings Cross
Journey: 26 min
Season: £2080
Peak: 3 per hr
Off-peak: 2 per hr

To Moorgate
Journey: 43 min
Season: £2080
Peak: 4 per hr
Off-peak: 3 per hr

the M25, and only a wingbeat from Kings Cross by train – and it offers lower house prices than surrounding areas. Its greatest public attraction is Hatfield House, built by Robert Cecil. Among its many distinctions is the fact that it was one of the first houses to be lit by 'Edison-Swan electric incandescent light bulbs', patented in 1879.

Most people prefer the red-brick houses of Old Hatfield to the Thirties-style houses and shopping parades of the 1948 New Town. A cottage with two bedrooms in Old Hatfield will cost around £220,000, though a flat of similar size would be slightly cheaper at £160,000. A three- or four-bedroom detached house will cost from £260,000 upwards. Two of the best areas are The Ryde, which has detached houses and bungalows, and Ellenbrook, where there is a mix of Thirties' semis and detached houses. The lowest price for something with three bedrooms here would be £280,000; £500,000 for five bedrooms. In New Hatfield the starting price for a four-bedroom detached house is around £250,000.

To Kings Cross
Journey: 29 min
Season: £2240
Peak: 4 per hr
Off-peak: 2 per hr

To Moorgate
Journey: 47 min
Season: £2240
Peak: 4 per hr
Off-peak: 3 per hr

WELWYN GARDEN CITY

Ebenezer Howard, with his chief architect Louis de Soissons, designed **Welwyn Garden City** as a sustainable town with its own employment zones, but the lure of the commute was not resisted for long. Early residents in the Twenties had to wade through the builders' mud in their wellington boots to get to the station, and changed into their city shoes on the train. The fusion of garden and city still remains very attractive, and the original cottagey houses behind perfectly clipped hedges are much sought after. Many have been kept on a ball-and-chain by 99-year or 999-year council leases (inherited from the Welwyn Garden Company), but freeholds are now available. The utilitarian planning means that there is very little sense of one street being more up-market than any other. The wide main shopping boulevards now look strangely dated, and local shops and businesses tend to feel they have lost out to the bustle and variety of St Albans and Stevenage. There is a John Lewis department store, a Debenhams and a Waitrose, and the Howard Centre close to the station has added greatly to the shopping scene. Sports enthusiasts are catered for by the impressive Gosling Sports Park and two 18-hole golf courses.

The best side of the town is the west, where a three-bedroom semi with a garage in a quiet tree-lined road could cost £280,000 to £320,000. It is possible to buy a two-bedroom terraced house for around £175,000. The town is still evolving – large private estates have gone up to the east at the Panshanger aerodrome. A three-bedroom semi on a new private estate will cost around £225,000.

There is some very pretty, rolling wooded countryside around Welwyn Garden City, and those who prefer an older village could

'Executive home', Wheathampstead

look at **Wheathampstead** to the west. As you approach the charming High Street from the direction of St Albans you pass a small quay on the River Lea, where people stop to chat or sit and fish. On one side of the road is a 400-year-old pub, The Bull. On the other is a converted water mill, which now contains a butcher, patisserie and jeweller. The village has three primary schools, from which children move on to secondary schools in Harpenden and St Albans. There is a library, three churches of different denominations, and lots of clubs and societies, including wine-making and archery clubs, cricket and tennis. You could pay over £210,000 for a Victorian cottage, or £500,000 for a five-bedroom house. Nearby is Brocket Hall, where Lady Caroline Lamb once emerged naked from a soup tureen and where more recently Lord Brocket ran a glitzy hotel and conference centre. He sold it on a 60-year lease in 1996 when he was imprisoned for insurance fraud and it is still a favourite for conferences.

Old Welwyn, just to the north of Welwyn Garden City, is so much more refined and mature than its neighbour. It has a mix of houses from one-bedroom cottages with small courtyard gardens, priced at around £180,000, to larger three-bedroom cottages fronting the road at £300,000. On the edge, away from the shops in the main street, is the executive development of Danesbury Park where a four-bedroom house will cost £450,000.

To Kings Cross
Journey: 31 min
Season: £2340
Peak: 3 per hr
Off-peak: 2 per hr

WELWYN NORTH The village best served by this station is **Digswell**, which consists of large detached houses with secluded gardens sewn into the lanes behind high hedges – some of them dominated by the huge viaduct built to carry the Great Northern Railway over the valley. It has the advantage of being close to a main line station yet only two miles from Welwyn Garden City. Houses tend to be sold very discreetly, and are not cheap. You would need to spend £500,000 for a four-bedroom bungalow. A small but pretty lake is maintained by the Digswell Lake Society.

Tewin is another wooded dormitory, but the sale of the village by the Cowper estate in 1919 led to its rapid expansion, with large new estates leeching on. The Upper Green is still used for tennis, cricket and football matches and there are badminton and bowls clubs. The village shop and post office is run by the community. A three-bedroom cottage on the green would cost £350,000; four- and five-bedroom detached houses fetch around £750,000. The tomb of Lady Anne Grimston in the parish church fascinates visitors and locals alike. Before her death in 1713 she had scoffed that the after-life was as likely as a tree growing through her grave. The tomb is now a macabre tangle of root and branch.

The Ayots to the west, like Digswell, are very exclusive: **Ayot St Peter**, perched on a hilltop, and **Ayot St Lawrence**, with its narrow lanes enclosed between hedgebanks. The latter has a popular pub, the Brocket Arms, and George Bernard Shaw's house, the late-Victorian Shaw's Corner, where he lived until his death in 1950. The house, which has Shaw's writing hut at the bottom of the garden, is in the hands of the National Trust. The village's most prominent landmark is the extraordinary neo-classical parish church, seen like an 18th-century folly across a meadow. House prices are higher than those in Tewin. Little cottages are few on the ground as most of the houses come large and expensive, starting at £800,000 and running into millions.

To Kings Cross
Journey: 35 min
Season: £2520
Peak: 3 per hr
Off-peak: 2 per hr

KNEBWORTH As is the case with most towns and villages in this area, there is an old and a new **Knebworth**. Old Knebworth grew up around the big house and parkland. The newer part was built around the railway station, which arrived at the turn of the century. Lutyens tried his hand with some cottages in Deards End Lane and Park Lane, and he also produced a golf clubhouse and the remarkable church of St Martin. Knebworth retains a village atmosphere and has a library and village school as well as a Co-op store and family butcher. It is hugely popular with commuters, many of whom never escape from the sound of the trains, because the railway line runs right through the middle and many of the older, quainter cottages back straight on to it. A two-bedroom cottage in this position will cost £220,000 to £240,000. In Deards End Lane, a Lutyens house will cost upwards of £1.5m. There are plenty of local activities and clubs, from cricket to amateur dramatics and old-time dancing, and there is an annual summer fête. This is aside from the country shows, concerts and car rallies at Knebworth House.

Commuters at Knebworth nurture a huge grapevine, planted when the station opened, with its roots in the platform. At one time the station master harvested up to 55lb of grapes from it and made five or six gallons of wine.

Many people prefer the atmosphere of the smaller, more rural villages such as **Datchworth** to the east, where the community spirit remains strong and anyone who falls ill, or who can't fetch the children from school, soon finds their needs catered for. Pony paddocks and riding stables abound. It has a post office and two general stores, a village museum in the old blacksmith's forge, and a sports pavilion with a rugby field behind it. There is a mix of property, from three-bedroom cottages needing a bit of work which sell at around £250,000 to the kind of place that comes with an acre of ground, tennis court and price-tag of around £1.5m. The village is spread between a web of greens. The harsher realities of life in the past are recalled at Datchworth Green in the centre, where the children's swings, summer tennis and cricket matches and annual fête are overlooked by the old whipping post.

To Kings Cross
Journey: 27 min
Season: £2840
Peak: 6 per hr
Off-peak: 4 per hr

To Moorgate
Journey: 61 min
Season: £2840
Peak: 2 per hr
Off-peak: 1 per hr

Distinctive late-Victorian cottage, Old Stevenage

STEVENAGE offers something like safety-net housing for people who can't afford Hertfordshire's plusher towns and villages. Huge new estates are now zoned west of the A1 and in the north-east of town. It isn't attractive, but the prices are low by comparison and the train service is excellent. The station is served not only by the Cambridge and Peterborough commuter services but also by the Inter-City high speed trains on the East Coast main line into Kings Cross, and Moorgate trains on the Cuffley route (see page 91). The New Town developments, colour-coded on old maps, have streets fancifully named after famous explorers, cathedrals, inventors, cricketers and so on, but in reality they offer little more than the uniformity of the three-bedroom mid- and end-of-terrace. Most are designed according to the Radburn principle, which means that motorists and pedestrians are kept well apart.

The beauty of the large modern shopping centre is that it is genuinely traffic-free. The various neighbourhoods, including the industrial area, are joined to each other, and to the centre, by a cycleway, a cleverly designed miniature road network which at peak periods takes up to 1,100 people per hour on their way to and from school or work. The shopping centre offers excellent choice, with all the major chain stores as well as a large range of retail warehouses, such as B&Q and Homebase, and the Forum shopping centre. Massive town centre redevelopment is in the pipeline and the area is one of those zoned for growth by the Government. At Poplars, where there is a Sainsbury's superstore, starter homes can be bought for £130,000. The covered market under the town centre multi-storey car park is open Wednesday to Saturday, and the stalls for the outdoor market go up on Wednesdays and Saturdays.

Stevenage is very strong on computers and technology, both in the businesses it attracts to its huge industrial parks – including GlaxoSmithKline – and in its educational facilities. North Herts College opened in 2003 with spanking new science laboratories and the Gordon Craig Theatre. Leisure facilities are lavish, too, with a huge leisure centre-cum-theatre for sports, conferences and exhibitions. There are three 18-hole golf courses – a municipal one in Stevenage itself, and one each at Knebworth and Graveley. The place for Sunday walks is Fairlands Valley Park, where there is a sailing and fishing lake, a boating lake and a bandstand for open-air concerts.

The Old Town, 'Hilton' in E.M. Forster's *Howards End*, is greatly cherished, and property prices are proportionately higher. A two-bedroom cottage would cost around £180,000; a three-bedroom cottage more than £200,000. On Stevenage's margins are some sedate, tree-lined roads that attract the middle-class professionals – Rectory Lane and Granby Road, for example, where a detached house with four or five bedrooms and a large garden may cost upwards of £350,000.

There is also a leap in house prices between the New Town and the villages that surround it. **Benington** in the east, for example, has a picture-postcard village green and timbered cottages, and is very sought-after – though it does also have its share of new developments and local authority housing. An older house with four bedrooms would take you into the £400,000 range.

Walkern is much busier, with a main street that takes quite a lot of traffic. Estates have sprung up around the old dovecote and pond, and by the chequer-brick Manor Farm. A two-bedroom period cottage will cost around £200,000.

Aston is also popular and much closer to Stevenage, though it is a little hemmed in by Stevenage and has had its own struggle to restrict development – the field in the village centre (with cricket pitch and pavilion) has been fiercely defended. Most of the new housing is kept to small developments in cul-de-sacs. A large four-bedroom detached would cost £450,000.

House style in Hertfordshire

In Hertfordshire you find an essentially modest county, now marbled with stockbroker enclaves and new towns. The prettiest cottages tend to be small and unassuming. Geologically the county sits on the rim of a saucer of chalk filled with clay and knuckles of flint. Without stone, early builders used timber from the forests.

Every town has a handful of timber-framed buildings, though in Hitchin these were hidden behind brick façades when brick superseded timber as the fashionable material to use.

There are charming cottages built of clunch, a type of chalk stone, some of the best of which can be seen at Ashwell.

The county has also borrowed from its neighbours – some weatherboarding from Essex, some yellowy brick from Cambridgeshire.

Journey: 32 min
Season: £3000
Peak: 6 per hr
Off-peak: 4 per hr

HITCHIN has managed to retain its character better than some of the surrounding towns. Parts of the centre still remain in a medieval time-warp – the Market Place, the lanes leading off it to the cathedral-sized St Mary's church and the River Hiz. Tilehouse Street, now relieved of all its through traffic, remains just as medieval England must have known it; and Bancroft was once admired as one of the best urban streets in England. It is a classic small market town, once famous for straw-plaiting, surrounded by popular commuter villages. The shopping centre is good enough with a large traditional market (three times a week), bars and restaurants. In the town itself four- to five-bedroom houses sell for £450,000 to £550,000. Large three-bedroom semis on the south side of the town can be bought for around £250,000. The Avenue, Wymondley Road and Benslow Lane are quiet leafy roads only 15 minutes' walk from the station, and contain some rather grand houses. Large Victorian and Edwardian houses in The Avenue tend to sell for up to £800,000.

Pirton has a compact rounded shape, which affects the social dynamics and makes it a more convivial place to live

The villages of **Gosmore** and **Charlton** to the south are close to Hitchin and therefore desirable. Gosmore has a green and some very pretty period houses. You could spend anything from £225,000 for a tiny two-bedroom cottage to over £350,000 for a three-bedroom period house. **Pirton** also scores because it isn't linear like many of the other villages in the area, but has a compact rounded shape, which affects the social dynamics and makes it a more convivial place to live. A Victorian three-bedroom semi will cost around £350,000.

Great Wymondley and **Little Wymondley** also loom in the Hitchin firmament, the irony being that Little Wymondley is by far the larger of the two. Great Wymondley is little more than an untidy crossroads with a few cottages, a pub, and the humps of a medieval castle. A bypass has relieved Little Wymondley of traffic, causing house prices to rise. A two-bedroom period cottage will now cost £250,000.

St Ippollits (sometimes just called Ippollits, and spelled in a variety of different ways) is a pretty hilltop village with smartly painted timbered houses and a dominating church, which gives the village its name. New four-bedroom executive homes cost £400,000. Commuters from St Ippollitts and the Wymondleys also have the option of travelling from Stevenage, where car-parking is easier.

> Fork to Cambridge and King's Lynn

Journey: 36 min
Season: £3200
Peak: 4 per hr
Off-peak: 2 per hr

LETCHWORTH You need to make sure your face fits in Letchworth. This was the first garden city, and the dream is still intact, as wholesome as a Hovis advertisement. To those who come from elsewhere to live – and to the groups of Japanese architects who come to gawp at it in summer – it can seem strange indeed. In the past, Ebenezer Howard's social experiment attracted a distinct type of middle-class teetaller, full of good intentions and disposed to vegetarianism. Today it is more liberal, but it was an almost dry town and until recently had only one pub. Once upon a time there was just the Skittles Inn, which sold only lemonade and ginger beer, but this has been turned into The Settlement community centre. The beauty of all this is that it is generally safe to roam the streets at night. The town's 1936 art deco cinema is now a four-screen complex. There is a supermarket, sports and leisure centre and, like Hitchin, the town has retained its 1930s' open-air swimming pool. Letchworth Museum & Art Gallery, housed in an attractive Edwardian building designed by Barry Parker, offers an insight into the local history.

'Letchworth was the first garden city, and the dream is still intact, as wholesome as a Hovis advertisement'

The sought-after properties are the original garden city houses, which have a rural calm about them. The cottages in Nevells Road, Icknield Way and Wilbury Road are worth just going to look at. An original garden city house with four bedrooms would cost around £400,000 (Sollershott West and East, and The Broadway have good examples), while a two-bedroom Edwardian terraced cottage could be bought for £200,000.

The town can afford to be particularly proud of its schools. Not only does it have two well-known public schools, St Francis' College for Girls and St Christopher's (progressive, vegetarian, boarding for boys and girls), but it also has two reasonable comprehensives, Highfield and Fernhill. The town is still growing, and properties on the newish estates tend to be cheaper than in the Garden City proper. A three-bedroom detached house on the Lordship Farm estate, for instance, will cost £275,000. An old asylum building in parkland is in the final stages of development to provide 900 new homes with garden city credentials at Fairfield Park.

Of the villages close by, **Norton** has a haphazard charm, a primary school, two pubs and a common that offers 63 acres of woodland with deer. **Willian** is little more than a hamlet, made endearing by its duck pond and some very old houses, but property in both these villages rarely comes on the market.

Journey: 39 min

Season: £3280

Peak: 4 per hr

Off-peak: 2 per hr

BALDOCK is a classic small market town, with pubs from its coaching days and a much admired wide main street. People enjoy living here. After years of wrangling a bypass has been built to siphon traffic out of the centre. The main asset for shoppers is a vast Tesco superstore in a converted neo-classical hosiery factory, which once also enjoyed a brief life as a film studio. The traditional High Street has to compete with the shopping centres in Stevenage and Cambridge, but the ancient tradition of the Wednesday market has kept it alive. The town musters a butcher and a baker, plus plenty of solicitors and estate agents, antiques shops and restaurants.

Almost anywhere in Baldock is nice to live. There are streets of timber-frame and colour-wash, Georgian and Victorian houses and some modest modern estates. Even the council estates are arranged in well-kept, tree-lined avenues. A two-bedroom, mid-terrace Victorian cottage will cost around £200,000; a Georgian house with four bedrooms from £350,000. Baldock is just within range of people who work in Cambridge (20 miles), and this is reflected in the property prices. It is also attractive for its secondary school. Knight's Templar Comprehensive has a good reputation for academic achievement and is the preferred choice of many parents who could afford to have their children educated privately.

Journey: 59 min

(42 min peak)

Season: £3380

Peak: 3 per hr

Off-peak: 1 per hr

ASHWELL & MORDEN The station is too far outside the village to walk, so parking spaces are keenly contested. Waiting to be picked up is no great hardship, though, since there is a country pub right opposite the station. **Ashwell** is a commuter dormitory that manages to retain a ferociously active village social life. There is a playgroup, a day nursery, a stage school and a dance school, and every year the Ashwell Show grows less like a village flower show and more like a county horse show. It really is *the* chic village to live on this prairie. The attraction lies in its sense of complete self-containment and in the preservation of its architecture. Timber-framed cottages, some cob, are followed by dignified Georgian town houses. It has a pretty church in clunch and flint, and a primary school that is not only highly thought of educationally, but is also a social engine to the village. It has a bakery, three pubs, an award-winning butcher, a pharmacy, a doctor's surgery, a dentist, a weaver and a potter. There is also the Ashwell Village Museum, housed in an ancient timber-framed cottage and run entirely by volunteers. People expect their houses to sell at a premium in Ashwell, so you have to be ready for this when you go house-hunting. A two-up-two-down here might cost £250,000 – considerably more than it would fetch a few miles away in Royston. A four-bedroom cottage will cost £500,000. **Kelshall** sits in the foothills of the Chilterns, with views right across Bedfordshire and

Cambridgeshire. It is an extremely well-kept and close-knit village. A four-bedroom detached house costs around £400,000. **Therfield** is another proud old Chilterns village whose agricultural heritage goes back a very long way, as the long barrows on Therfield Heath testify. A two-bedroom ex-local authority home will cost £250,000; a four-bedroom house around £400,000.

Journey: 47 min
Season: £3640
Peak: 4 per hr
Off-peak: 2 per hr

ROYSTON sits on the borders of Hertfordshire and Cambridgeshire, so residents have the choice of two education systems. It offers cheap housing and convenience. In addition to the railway line it also has easy access to the A10, M25, A1 and M11. There is a new leisure centre and a monthly farmers' market. Traditionally the south side of town is thought to be better than the north, where some of the housing estates have been built at a very high density, close to the huge Tesco. Property prices start at £150,000 for a two-bedroom Victorian cottage and £190,000 for a three-bedroom semi. The modern houses tend to be cheaper than the older Victorian/Edwardian ones which offer more room. The heath, which has a golf course on it, is the place to walk and ride.

The surrounding countryside offers a wide choice of villages. **Barley**, to the south-east, is a pretty village with a strong local community, good walks and an all-purpose village shop. There is a riding school, doctor's surgery with dispensary, two pubs and a primary school. Its greatest assets are a Grade Two Star, restored Tudor town house, used for village activities, weddings and harvest suppers, and a small village cage or lock-up, which remains as a curiosity. A two-bedroom cottage will cost £215,000 or more. Barley's position on the chalk toes of the Chilterns accounts for the villagers' historic nickname, 'the little men from the hills'.

Three-bedroom period cottage, near Royston

Barkway is rather more elegant, with a wonderful array of timber-framed and Georgian brick houses. One of these with four bedrooms and parking on the main street will cost over £500,000. A two-bedroom cottage will cost over £250,000, but these are few and far between. Barkway still has a good village school where the numbers are increasing. **Bassingbourn**, to the north, also has an impressive main street lined with period houses. The nearby army barracks does not affect house prices. A five-bedroom detached house with four reception rooms will cost from £550,000 to £750,000.

Journey: 69 min	
Season: £3640	
Peak: 2 per hr	
Off-peak: 1 per hr	

MELDRETH This was once serious fruit-growing country, but

Meldreth now has only one commercial orchard left with a farm shop attached. It has a recreation ground, and beneath a spreading chestnut tree are the old village stocks and a whipping post. It is an enormously welcoming village, though it is rather scattered. The primary school is well regarded, as is the Melbourn College for 11–16-year-olds nearby. Leisure opportunities include tennis, croquet, and football. Village people may also use the riding stables attached to the Meldreth Manor School, which is run by Scope. The village contains a mix of old thatched cottages and new developments, though much of the newer housing seems very uniform. Semis sell for around £170,000; four-bedroom detached houses for £399,000.

Melbourn is across the fields. Its attractions include several restaurants and pubs and a very strong community spirit. Property prices are similar to those in Meldreth.

Journey: 72 min	
Season: £3640	
Peak: 2 per hr	
Off-peak: 1 per hr	

SHEPRETH The feature of **Shepreth** village centre is a stream with

two old mills on its banks. There are some pretty thatched cottages and several modern closes built in the late Sixties and Seventies. The village has a shop-cum-post-office, a Montessori school, two trout farms and the Shepreth Wildlife Park nature reserve. The houses tend to be larger than those in Meldreth – those backing on to open fields in Frog End are probably the best for views though worst for being close to the shops. Two-bedroom cottages start at around £170,000 while four-bedroom detached houses cost from £310,000 upwards. Annual village events include a horticultural show, harvest festival and the Shepreth festival of arts and crafts. Several artists live in the locality. It is a horsey area and you may even spot the odd pony and trap clipping along.

Journey: 74 min	
Season: £3640	
Peak: 2 per hr	
Off-peak: 1 per hr	

FOXTON is attractive and quiet, with a pretty, but tiny green and

some good timber-framed houses in the long main street. The village has two churches, a shop-cum-post-office, pub, primary school and village hall. There are all the usual societies for women, toddlers and the elderly, plus the formidable Foxton Gardeners Association which organises a regular September show. The village is best known to outsiders for being the subject of a highly-praised historical book, *The Common Stream*, by local author Rowland Parker, published in 1975. Foxton tends to be rather sought-after because of the railway station and its proximity to Cambridge. A Grade Two listed, two-bedroom semi in need of work costs around £200,000.

Barrington nearby has a huge set-piece green with thatched cottages on one side and a fine church on the other. The Cambridge factor is a significant influence on prices. A four- to five-bedroom house on the green cannot be bought for less than £440,000. There are some modern developments discreetly tucked away in cul-de-sacs, where four-bedroom detached houses sell for around £325,000 to £400,000. An acre or two of land, however, could put the price up. Clunch, the chalk-stone used so extensively in local building, was quarried nearby.

Journey: 48 min

CAMBRIDGE See **Liverpool Street to Cambridge** (page 61).

Season: £3780

Peak: 2 per hr

Off-peak: 3 per hr

Most London services from the following stations go to Kings Cross. At peak times there is a limited direct service to Liverpool Street, otherwise passengers for Liverpool Street must change at Cambridge.

Journey: 58 min

(66 min peak)

Season: £3860

Peak: 2 per hr

(plus 1 per hr to Liverpool St)

Off-peak: 1 per hr

WATERBEACH The trains out of **Waterbeach** in the morning are full of children on their way to school in Cambridge or Ely. The village does have its own primary school, which doubles as a community centre. Here you can also take evening classes, or join the Waterbeach Players or the brass band. Waterbeach has an army barracks, a post office, Chinese takeaway, three grocery shops, fish-and-chip shop, butchers and bakers, and several pubs. There is a Tesco three miles away at **Milton**. The Waterbeach Feast, a procession of floats and stalls, is held every June, when the local women traditionally have always made frumenty – boiled wheat in a thick, sweet milk-and-sugar sauce with raisins. The best houses are the Cambridge brick houses in the conservation area around the village green. A two-bedroom version will cost from £150,000. A three-bedroom semi in Waterbeach is likely to cost around £185,000. New housing has been going up fast.

Cottenham, also on the edge of the Fens close to Waterbeach station, has a Village College (see Comberton, page 62) and some useful shops in its favour, but it has expanded rather brutally. Its population doubled in only 20 years. A three-bedroom cottage will cost around £185,000, better value than in nearby Histon, while a four-bedroom modern detached house will cost £240,000 to £340,000.

Journey: 67 min

Season: £3940

Peak: 2 per hr

(plus 1 per hr to

Liverpool St)

Off-peak: 1 per hr

ELY had remained aloof, cut off from Cambridge by the Fens for so long that the last property boom arrived as something of a shock. Now, however, it has become an immensely popular alternative to the hothouse of Cambridge and new housing using old styles is springing up around the edges with price tags of £300,000 for four bedrooms. A house with a view of Ely's remarkable 11th-century cathedral is usually thought more desirable than a home in one of the villages. It is a small, compact city with shops in and around the tiny High Street, a Tesco and a Waitrose. A farmers' market is held twice a month in Market Square. Georgian houses sit happily alongside Thirties' semis, and there are no distinct up-market areas. A renovated Grade Two listed town house with four bedrooms can be expected to cost £325,000. There are dramatic and choral societies for those inspired by the theatrical Fen landscapes. King's School is situated close to the cathedral.

Some people are also attracted to the area by thoughts of the *Good Life* – the cottage with a productive vegetable garden, a few ducks and a goat. Villages to the south, such as **Witchford**, **Sutton**, **Haddenham** and **Stretham**, are the most sought-after. You should expect to pay around £140,000 for a two-bedroom semi; between £200,000 and £235,000 for a four-bedroom detached.

Journey: 75 min

(84 min peak)

Season: £3980

Peak: 2 per hr

(plus I per hr to

Liverpool St)

Off-peak: 1 per hr

LITTLEPORT is a thriving little town on this huge horizontal landscape, with some beautiful old houses as well as plenty of new estates. There are three thatched properties in the town centre (adding a touch of cosiness) and to commemorate the fact that the Harleys of the Harley-Davidson Motor Company originally came from here, a motorbike statue was unveiled in 2003 to mark the 100th anniversary of the business. Littleport is also known for its textiles industry, producing shirts for Paul Smith, gowns for the Royal Family and scarves for Hogwarts students in the Harry Potter films. Building is in progress to provide 660 houses on the western side of the town. A four-bedroom period cottage will cost around £210,000. Littleport has a leisure and sports centre and Littleport Village College provides evening classes. There is a post office and plenty of day-to-day shops, including a wonderful bakery, a butcher and an ironmonger. A small market is held on Tuesdays. 'The best thing about living here is that there are such beautiful sunsets, flooding across acres and acres of open sky,' says one local resident.

'The best thing about living in Littleport is that there are such beautiful sunsets, flooding across acres and acres of open sky'

Journey: 84 min
(93 min peak)
Season: £4160
Peak: 2 per hr
(plus 1 per hr to
Liverpool St)
Off-peak: 1 per hr

DOWNHAM MARKET is popular with people who are taking early retirement – over 40 per cent of the population is aged over 60 – but families are being courted with hundreds of modern four-bedroom houses. It is a pleasant Norfolk town with plenty of shops, good high school, a floodlit football ground, a swimming pool, and two small industrial estates on the outskirts. It used to be an inland port but today the river, contained in its high banks, is a thing to walk beside rather than a busy thoroughfare for imports and exports. The station waiting room is an experience. It has an open fire, comfy armchairs, quirky books to read, and serves breakfasts to order – even porridge. A two-bedroom terraced house will cost between £110,000 and £155,000; a three-bedroom semi with a garage £140,000.

Journey: 90 min
(99 min peak)
Season: £4240
Peak: 2 per hr
(plus 1 per hr to
Liverpool St)
Off-peak: 1 per hr

WATLINGTON This village has expanded rapidly in recent years with new developments. It has a couple of shops, a primary school, a doctor's surgery and a village 'office' with IT, Internet and photocopying facilities. Houses here are slightly cheaper than Downham Market – a two-bedroom terraced house would cost around £100,000 to £120,000. A five-bedroom property with stables and orchard could be bought for £300,000.

Journey: 97 min
(106 min peak)
Season: £4380
Peak: 2 per hr
(plus 1 per hr to
Liverpool St)
Off-peak: 1 per hr

KING'S LYNN The old port of **King's Lynn** has a definite appeal for birdwatchers, who can be seen in their anoraks and wellington boots scanning the sky with their binoculars. The marshes and mudflats of The Wash are a great attraction for waterfowl and waders, and the riverside is a favourite spot for watching the boats come in. Architecturally, King's Lynn lost much of its dignity in the 20th century and its sense of prosperity at the same time. The conservationists now have a firm grip on what is left – a historic legacy that includes the merchants' houses of Nelson Street, Queen Street and King Street, most of which are now used as offices

A 200-year-old
brick-and-flint
farmhouse,
Downham Market

and occasionally as locations in television costume dramas. The Corn Exchange Theatre attracts big musical and theatrical names, and in the summer it plays host to the King's Lynn Festival, usually attended by one of the Royals (Sandringham is only eight miles away). It has the biggest shopping centre for miles around. Among the older properties you could pick up a three-bedroom cottage for £125,000. Even a good period three-bedroom town house will probably not exceed £200,000. The new Nar development to the south of the town is underway to provide contemporary apartments along the river, housing, a business park, school and shops, followed by a marina.

> Continuation of main line from Hitchin

Journey: 38 min
Season: £3160
Peak: 2 per hr
Off-peak: 1 or
2 per hr

ARLESEY You are on to the Bedfordshire plains here, where the low, sprawling, yellow-brick villages can seem monotonous and unimaginative after the variety of Hertfordshire. Arlesey itself might be short on charm, but lays claim to being the longest linear village in the country, with a High Street of Victorian brick houses, many of which have been extended at the back to provide bathrooms and kitchens. A three-bedroom detached house will cost around £190,000. Its immediate neighbour, **Stotfold**, is a similar large village, dominated by the local yellow brick, and has a comparable mix of Victorian and modern housing at similar prices. Stotfold has the additional advantage of having a secondary school, being close to the A1M, and offering the choice of whisking down the motorway for the better train service from Stevenage. Letchworth and Baldock are also nearby.

Shillington is another large, though rather more rural, village of yellow brick with the occasional timber-framed house and an intimate gathering of 17th-century houses around the hilltop church of All Saints, an impressive local landmark. Closer to Arlesey is **Henlow**, where prices are slightly increased by the proximity of RAF Henlow. This is the village where sports and showbiz personalities come to revitalise at Champneys Henlow Grange Health Farm. Henlow has a few shops and pubs and good sports facilities. County cricket is played at The Pyghtles. Other villages worth looking at in this catchment are **Meppershall**, **Lower Stondon** and **Clifton**.

Journey: 45 min
(35 min peak)
Season: £3440
Peak: 3 per hr
Off-peak: 2 per hr

BIGGLESWADE is a town of yellow brick houses and market-gardening set on the River Ivel, which was once just navigable from the sea. Greene King had a brewery here, which may explain why there are so many pubs. There is a busy market on Saturdays. The shops have enjoyed a town centre makeover, yet people still tend to go to Cambridge for major purchases. Proximity to the A1 (where there is a Sainsbury's) means that Stevenage is also easily accessible. One of the more highly regarded streets is London Road, where large four-bedroom houses can be bought for £269,000 upwards. It is a busy road and seems to have less appeal for incomers than it does for people moving locally.

Those in search of the rural idyll must go west to **Ickwell Green**, whose village green has a cricket club and a maypole on it and is fringed with colour-washed, brick and tiled cottages. Houses for sale here are as rare as hen's teeth and agents are wary about quoting prices because they are all so individual. **Old Warden** is even more picturesque, having been preserved by the Shuttleworth Estate. The cottages are thatched, with gingerbread trimmings and chimneypots, and very few of them ever reach the open market. But its very presence is a magnet to the area, attracting people to the neighbouring villages. The Shuttleworth Collection of historic aircraft is a major attraction to visitors, especially on flying days. **Northill**, the third village in the cluster, is not quite so rarefied. The occasional modern house has crept in beside the older cottages around the pub and the duck pond. A two-bedroom thatched semi will cost around £200,000. There are stables in the area and it is fairly horsey.

Potton, to the north-east, is the size of a small town, with a population of over 5,000. Its market square is much admired, though the only way to live in it would be to buy a flat over one of the shops. The likely price for a two-bedroom cottage is £135,000. Otherwise property in the town tends to be cheaper than Biggleswade or Sandy (see below). It is the headquarters of the eponymous Potton company, makers of neo-Tudor self-build home kits.

'In picturesque Old Warden the cottages are thatched, with gingerbread trimmings and chimneypots'

Journey: 45 min
Season: £3560
Peak: 2 per hr
Off-peak: 2 per hr

SANDY is as plain as can be – an old Bedfordshire village that acquired a station and then sponged up overspilling Londoners into its large council estates and yellow-brick streets. It is perhaps a shade cheaper than Biggleswade. The Royal Society for the Protection of Birds has its headquarters outside the town at Sandy Lodge, and there are some pleasant woodland walks. Two of the more expensive places to live are the large Victorian houses along Bedford Road, which can be a little noisy because of proximity to the A1, and the modern houses on the riverfront at Mill Lane. The average price of a two-bedroom house in Sandy is £130,000. Two huge housing estates, Ivel Park and Fallow Field, offer five-bedroom homes which cost £290,000.

Beeston, on the southern edge of Sandy, is divided by the A1, and quite a few properties are blighted by it. Nevertheless, the conservation area with the green, old thatched cottages and blacksmith's forge offers pleasant relief from some of the other, drearier villages in the area. **Tempsford**, to the north, is also spliced by the A1. Its wartime aerodrome was used by the Special Operations Executive to drop secret agents into occupied France, and it was from here that the bandleader Glenn Miller took off on his fatal flight in 1944. The new Salford Meadow development has three-, four-, and five-bedroom houses from between £190,000 and £300,000.

Journey: 53 min
(39 min peak)
Season: £3840
Peak: 4 per hr
Off-peak: 2 per hr

ST NEOTS is prettier than many of the towns in the area and larger, with a population of 30,000 or more. The market square, surrounded by fine Georgian buildings, is alive with gastro-pubs and cafés and al fresco eating in the summer. The farmer's market appears on the second and fourth Sunday of each month, complete with live entertainment. Cricket and rugby are played on the huge 160-acre common, and there is a choice of three golf courses. The operatic society, the St Neots Players, stages productions at the Priory Centre. Huntingdon Regional College has an annexe in the town.

The River Great Ouse contributes both colour and charm, and offers the opportunity to fish, or to walk the Ouse Valley Way. For the people who come to St Neots to mess about in boats, there is a rowing club and two marinas. Unsurprisingly, some of the nicest places to live are close to the river. **Eaton Ford**, for example, was once a riverside village in its own right, but has now been absorbed by the town. The period architecture, combined with St Neots Golf Club and the river meadows, have pushed the price of a four-bedroom detached house to around £260,000.

Semi-detached thatched
cottage, Bedfordshire

Also popular is Old St Neots, in the area around the market square and shops, with walks in the woods of Priory Park. A two-bedroom house with a garden will cost about £145,000. Slightly cheaper is **Eaton Socon**, another former village drawn into the St Neots fold, where houses tend to be arranged in terraces. A four-bedroom detached house could cost around £230,000. It has the advantage of being on the A1, convenient for commuting to Stevenage or Hatfield. Less popular is **Eynesbury**, where the council estates have mushroomed through the period houses, prices are low and new private estates have appeared at £225,000 to £400,000 for four bedrooms. More housing is being built to the east of the railway.

People looking for a village home tend to head eastwards, where the countryside starts to undulate a little – though property prices begin to rise as you get closer to Cambridge. **Great Gransden**, **Little Gransden** and **Waresley** have pretty Elizabethan thatched cottages and are particularly popular with professional couples. A three-bedroom semi in one of these villages would fetch around £195,000. **Eltisley** is slightly cheaper, with an extraordinarily large village green and a lovely thatched cricket pavilion that is used for meetings as well as cricket matches. The village has a pub and a popular primary school that also serves the villages nearby. There are some small new housing estates, popular with young families, and some bungalows for the elderly. A three-bedroom detached house would cost more than the equivalent in St Neots, but less than in the Gransdens.

To the north-west is Grafham Water, a huge man-made reservoir that draws people from miles around for walking, water skiing, windsurfing and other watersports. **Perry** was a village that had little to say for itself before Grafham Water was made, but prices are now similar to those in Eaton Ford. One possible drawback of living near open water is that midges can be a problem in the summer.

Journey: 60 min
(45 min peak)

Season: £4020

Peak: 4 per hr

Off-peak: 2 per hr

HUNTINGDON Most people will probably prefer the neighbouring villages to **Huntingdon** itself, though the old county town is not unattractive. Oliver Cromwell lived here, and the old school, which both he and Samuel Pepys once attended, has been turned into a Cromwell Museum. Previous house-price booms brought Londoners in search of cheaper housing, so there is a well-established body of commuters. Builders have been keeping pace with demand and the town centre has been pedestrianised. The truth is that people tend to spend their lives trying to move out of this area rather than in. The cheapest housing is found among the ex-council houses. Better addresses include Hartford and Sapley, where the period properties add a touch of class to the newer developments and bungalows. A modern house with four bedrooms in either area will cost from £220,000 to £280,000.

Across the 14th-century bridge in **Godmanchester**, the tone is raised by some pretty, pastel-coloured 16th–18th-century houses, and by pleasant walks along the Great Ouse to Portholme Great Meadow, which is ablaze with wild flowers in spring. Much of Godmanchester is a designated conservation area, and there are some particularly fine houses in Post Street, Earning Street and the Causeway, often with gardens running down to the river. A modern five-bedroom house here is likely to fetch between £300,000 and £400,000, while a five-bedroom period house with a garden on the river will push the price towards the £800,000 mark. Not far to the west is **Brampton**, where Pepys lived for a time and where the Brampton racecourse can be found. It retains its village green, though there have been a lot of new developments. The RAF station here is nothing to worry about – its function is purely administrative. The proximity of Grafham Water makes it a popular village for watersports enthusiasts.

St Ives, five miles to the east, also has more charm than Huntingdon, with a pot-pourri of building styles along the quay and a smattering of pubs and restaurants. The centre is a conservation area, and the threadwork of alleyways between Market Hill and the riverside is particularly intriguing. It grew up on the site of a large Easter Fair, and is the St Ives of the nursery rhyme.

Close to it, nudging the Fens, are some of the most desirable villages in the area. **Hemingford Abbots**, formerly part of the Ramsey Abbey estate, seduces everyone with its thatched cottages and lovely walks. It is full of successful local businessmen and young couples attracted like moths to the Cambridge lamplight – all waxed jackets, Land Rovers and labradors. 'There is a lot of pride in the village. If there is an art exhibition in the area, it will always be held in Hemingford Abbots,' says one local resident. There are two-up-two-down Victorian terraces selling for £175,000. The wealthier aim for the small urban palaces in Common Lane. Some of these have river frontages and might sell for around £1m. The walks are idyllic, along footpaths that cross the meadows to Houghton Mill, an early Ouse watermill in a beautiful setting that attracts visitors in search of tea in the summer. Those with less money might look next door in **Hemingford Grey**, which is the poor relation living off the Hemingford name. There are many more family-sized houses here. A four-bedroom modern house would cost around £300,000.

Houghton and **Wyton**, pronounced 'Hooton' and 'Witton', are also cheaper because they are that much further from the A1. The High Street linking the two villages is punctuated by a green and has a

'Hemingford Abbots is full of successful local businessmen and young couples attracted like moths to the Cambridge lamplight'

supermarket with a deli. The housing market offers a mix of old and new. A four-bedroom modern estate house will cost around £325,000; a five-bedroom period house up to £600,000. To the north is **Woodhurst**, a perfect example of a ring village. Some of the four-bedroom houses on new developments will cost £400,000.

Due north of Huntingdon are **Little** and **Great Stukeley** (where the former prime minister John Major lives), which offer a reasonable mix of old and new houses, council estates and chalet bungalows. A modern house with four bedrooms and a plot of land in Great Stukeley is likely to cost around £275,000. A four-bedroom period family house can be bought for £325,000.

Journey: 50 min with dual season; 62 min peak, 76 min off-peak with First Capital Connect (FCC) season

Season: £5892 (all), £5000 (FCC only)

Peak: 4 per hr using either option

Off peak: 3 per hr (fast), 2 per hr (FCC)

PETERBOROUGH The tower of the Norman cathedral, which contains the tomb of Catherine of Aragon, is just about the only thing of beauty in **Peterborough**. It is visible from almost anywhere in the city and is illuminated at night. What the city lacks in aesthetics, it gains in purpose-built leisure facilities – cathedrals of contemporary life. The Queensgate shopping centre's malls and squares, in marble, glass and steel, are air-conditioned, American-style. There is a 13-screen cinema, an ice-rink, a rowing and canoeing centre, an indoor cricket stadium and three golf courses. The city is ringed with fast roads and bypasses, making life easy for drivers and pedestrians alike. The Key Theatre, opened in 1973, keeps the culture vultures happy, with everything from opera and ballet to Christmas panto. The Lady Lodge Arts Centre, in an old farmhouse at Orton Goldhay, puts a crafty-vegetarian spin on photography, music and the theatre.

Those interested in new housing should trawl the streets of **Hampton**, the new £500m satellite town to the south, with homes for more than 13,000 people and a separate shopping centre, where four-bedroom houses cost £185,000 to £250,000. Otherwise, househunting becomes a question of working your way around the various Ortons. **Orton Goldhay** has shoals of ex-council terraced properties. At **Orton Malborne** there are more private houses in the mix, but prices remain similar. A three-bedroom semi will cost around £120,000; a three-bedroom detached £145,000. Prices rise sharply in the sumptuous estates of **Orton Wistow**, where a modern three-bedroom house can start at £170,000, or from £200,000 for four bedrooms. Similar properties can also be found in **Werrington** and **Gunthorpe**, both of which retain a core of older housing. Much of central Peterborough is to be avoided, especially the repetitive drabness of the older terraces. **Westown** is a preferred area, where three-bedroom semis with gardens sell at around £130,000. For real one-upmanship, there are the houses in Thorpe Park Road, Thorpe Road and Westwood Road, where Thirties' homes in voluminous gardens sell at anything over £300,000 to the city's doctors, dentists and solicitors. The less wealthy middle-classes find themselves in **Longthorpe** and **Netherton**, where there is a range of older houses. A three-bedroom thatched cottage could cost £250,000.

To the east of Peterborough is stark Fenland. Most people find it too glum and head determinedly for the undulating landscape and stone villages to the west. For those who are undeterred, **Whittlesey** in the east is set right in the Fens. Just to the south of it is King's Dyke, designed to introduce a sharp kink into the network of navigable waterways and so limit the size of vessels passing between the Rivers Nene and Ouse. The village has a brickworks, but is still dwarfed by the surrounding flat expanse. A two-bedroom detached bungalow might cost £120,000; an older three-bedroom bay-fronted semi £130,000. **Thorney**, slightly further north, was kept intact as an estate village throughout the 19th century and so has a greater sense of history. The mock-Jacobean water tower adds a flourish to the skyline. An older three-bedroom semi here will cost £130,000.

The villages to the south of Peterborough are also somewhat lacking in visual appeal. **Yaxley**, being so close to the A1, offers the convenience of an easy commute to the towns both north and south. Technically it is a village, though it has all the amenities and proliferating housing estates of a small town. On the Ferndale estate a two-bedroom house costs from £130,000, rising to around £200,000 for four bedrooms. The old part of Yaxley is the most sought after – particularly the thatched cottages that skirt the village green with the old village pump in the centre. Run-of-the-mill three-bedroom semis fetch around £140,000; two-bedroom period cottages £115,000. The countryside around is not for those who want conventional beauty. 'There are no hedgerows, no trees and no hills. But it grows on you,' said one resident who had been converted. Large tracts between Yaxley and Fletton, including an old brick pit, are being swallowed by the new Hampton township. The villages west of the A1(M) such as **Folksworth**, **Haddon** and **Stilton** hear the growl of the motorway.

North and west of Peterborough are the best areas to look. **Market Deeping** and its satellites **Deeping St James** and **Deeping Gate** ('Deeping' refers to the deep meadows on the banks of the River Welland), are a major attraction. Market Deeping is an attractive old town with wide streets, some old stone houses and pubs, and with good old-fashioned butchers and bakers mixed in between the antiques shops. It has its own library and health centre, and an industrial zone, including such light industries as fireplace manufacturers and double-glazing specialists. There are two primary schools in addition to a good comprehensive and a leisure centre at Deeping St James. The eight-mile drive to Peterborough station is only a matter of minutes along

'The tower of the Norman cathedral is just about the only thing of beauty in Peterborough'

the A15. An older stone house with three bedrooms will cost £170,000 upwards depending on how much land comes with it. A three-bedroom semi will fetch considerably more than its counterpart in Peterborough. A four-bedroom detached house with a garage on a modern estate would cost around £180,000.

The stone villages in the Deepings corridor are all desirable and have been protected from over-development. They include **Maxey**, **Barnack**, **Ufford** and **Helpston**, the last being where the poet John Clare lived in the 19th century, and where he wrote his poems about the agricultural changes he saw going on around him. He is buried in the churchyard and there is a memorial to him at the crossroads. A large cottage with four bedrooms might cost £250,000 in any of these villages, or slightly more if it is thatched.

Due west of Peterborough you find a similar kind of charm in places such as **Wansford**. The village combines with Stibbington, which has a post office/shop serving a population of about 450 between the two communities. A beautiful stone packhorse bridge links the two halves across the River Nene. The Fitzwilliam Hunt meets outside the Haycock Hotel, an old coaching inn, on New Year's Day. Close by is **Elton**, which is regarded as an aspirational village and carries a premium. It has some good 17th-century houses, with Elton Hall to the south and a lock on the Nene to the west. A three-bedroom stone cottage in Elton might cost £300,000. All these villages benefit from being close to Stamford, an attractive medieval town and a good antidote to Peterborough.

All these villages benefit from being close to Stamford, an attractive medieval town and a good antidote to Peterborough

Journey: 64 min
Season: £6692
Peak: 3 per hr
Off-peak: 1 or
2 per hr

GRANTHAM A solid band of commuters have arrived in **Grantham** on the crest of the various housing booms, as high prices rippled out from London. Today's residents also include 'virtual commuters', who make only occasional visits to London, or former commuters who set up local companies in the area in order to work nearer to home.

'Everyone knows that Lady Thatcher was born here, but not many people remember that Sir Isaac Newton was born here, too**'**

What everyone knows about Grantham is that Lady Thatcher was born here, in North Parade. Not quite so many people remember that Sir Isaac Newton was born here, too. Thatcher was educated at Kesteven and Grantham Girls' School, which is still doing for girls

Early 20th-century farmhouse, Grantham area

what Kings does for boys. The town also has an associated college of Nottingham Trent University offering courses in building, business studies and engineering. Leisure is high on the agenda, in the form of the Meres Leisure Centre and athletics and football stadium. There are golf courses at Belton Park, Belton Woods and Stoke Rochford, and good fishing on the River Witham.

Grantham has a smattering of ancient houses in Castlegate and Church Street, as well as the celebrated Angel and Royal Hotel, but much of it now consists of new development. At the lower end of the market, two-bedroom period town houses start at £85,000. Four-bedroom detached houses cost between £170,000 and £300,000. The best roads to live in are probably those leading out towards the villages of Manthorpe and Belton. Large detached houses, set well back from the road, can be bought for around £300,000.

The limestone hills around Grantham contain some pretty stone villages, particularly in the west. **Barrowby**, for instance, stands high enough to afford good views across the Vale of Belvoir. A four-bedroom family-sized stone house here might cost £350,000. **Denton** is another handsome stone village, which used to be part of the Welby estate. Denton Reservoir nearby is popular with anglers, and has some attractive pathways along its banks. There is some Sixties' housing in the mix, and a small council estate. You could expect to pay £350,000 for a three-bedroom period house with a garage; £110,000 for a semi.

Closer to Grantham, **Harlaxton** is sufficiently attractive to have been designated a conservation area and has not been abused by unimaginative modern development. It owes much of its style to the Gregory family, who built the eye-catching manor house in the early 19th century as well as some of the Regency-style houses in the village. A country cottage with three bedrooms might cost £300,000.

Perhaps two of the most exclusive villages are **Manthorpe** and **Belton** to the north, sandwiched by Belton Hall and its magnificent park, now in the hands of the National Trust. Little ever comes up for sale in Belton, but if you were lucky you could expect to pay £450,000 for something with four bedrooms.

Journey: 82 min
Season: £7460
Peak: 3 per hr
Off-peak: 1 or
2 per hr

NEWARK NORTHGATE A Royalist stronghold in the Civil War, this

proud town does its best to ignore the great snake of the River Trent that slithers past, encased inside high banks to prevent it from flooding. The lovely cobblestone market place is a major feature, though the 14th-century former draper's shop, which is supposed to be one of the oldest domestic buildings in the Midlands, is now occupied by a building society. The annual diary in **Newark** is full of antiques fairs – at least six are held each year, including the largest antiques fair in Western Europe. There has been a substantial amount of new housebuilding, including 1,000 new houses at Farndon where small two-bedroom houses sell at £104,000 and one-bedroom apartments at £80,000. Along the newly developed waterfront, overlooking the marina, a two-bedroom apartment could cost £155,000.

'The annual diary in Newark is full of antiques fairs – at least six are held each year, including the largest antiques fair in Western Europe**'**

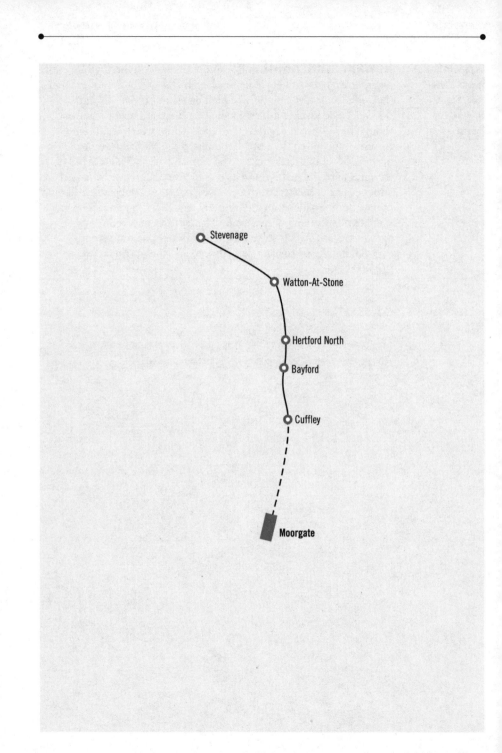

Stevenage

Watton-At-Stone

Hertford North

Bayford

Cuffley

Moorgate

Journey: 39 min
Season: £1480
Peak: 6 per hr
Off-peak: 3 per hr

CUFFLEY is prime commuter country, much of it built in stockbroker Tudor style on what was once a wooded hillside. Though the character of the houses is intensely suburban, the village is still surrounded by proper farmland. Some of the large bungalows in their ample gardens have had new houses squeezed in beside them. Others, most oddly, have been converted into houses by having extra storeys added on top. There is no council housing to speak of. Two-bedroom flats can be bought for around £170,000; three-bedroom semis around £325,000. In the Ridgeway, mansions backing on to woodland can cost well over £1m.

The village has a high proportion of commuters and elderly residents, and young families are moving in. The local residents and conservationists are a vociferous force, opposing the building of a golf course on nearby farmland a few years ago and, more recently, the opening of a branch of Tesco. The village has enough shops to provide practically two of everything. It also has its own primary school. Older children go to Potters Bar. Leisure activities include the Cuffley Players and an operatic society, plus a football club and bowls, a floral arts club, Brownies and Guides. There is a tennis club and public courts are available.

Journey: 44 min
Season: £1940
Peak: 2 per hr
Off-peak: 3 per hr

BAYFORD is significantly more rural than Cuffley. It is set quietly in the heart of the Broxbourne woods, which are full of footpaths and bridleways, and is not so overburdened with modern development. The older Georgian houses have a pleasing presence as a result. The village is rather spread out. It has both a pond and an open space, which it treats as a green, and a cricket field with a cricket pavilion built with Lottery money. There is a pub, the Bakers Arms, but no post office or shop, and

'Bayford is set quietly in the heart of the Broxbourne woods, which are full of footpaths and bridleways'

most people stock up from Waitrose or Tesco in Hertford. The village has its own mixed infants and junior school, but older children go out of the village. Every two years villagers open their gardens to the public, with the admission charges going towards local amenities.

Together with its neighbours – **Brickendon**, **Little Berkhamsted**, **Epping Green** and **Bayfordbury** – Bayford exudes wealth and charm, and there is little point harbouring any ambition to live here unless you're looking in the £400,000 bracket. Three-bedroom cottages start at £325,000 and houses at £500,000. Detached houses sell for £1.5m–£3m. Brickendon is little more than a tiny hamlet set around a green, half a mile's walk from Bayford. Little Berkhamsted is delightfully wooded and has some lovely weatherboarded cottages opposite the church. Bayfordbury is perhaps not so exclusive since it has the B158 running through it.

Journey: 48 min
Season: £2200
(also valid at
Hertford East)
Peak: 6 per hr
Off-peak: 3 per hr

HERTFORD NORTH Hertford is a surprisingly small, old-fashioned county town, protected by a quilt of green belt at the junction of the Rivers Beane, Lea and Mimram. It is possible to take a boat south to the sea from here by negotiating a series of locks. Much of the town centre is a conservation area, charmingly provincial considering its proximity to London. Independent traders and specialist shops, including Botsford & Sons ironmongers, provide variety and a farmers' market is held once a month. There is a county court, county hospital and all the other public buildings you would expect of an

Period country house in Hertfordshire

administrative centre, the 1939 County Hall on its hilltop being the most ostentatious.

Hertford Town Council organises the annual fun day at Hertford Castle, in addition to an annual music festival, a garden festival and a Christmas gala. Other prominent social groups include the Company of Players, based at the Little Theatre, and the Dramatic and Operatic Society, which organises the annual theatre week. There are also choral and art societies, and a symphony orchestra. There is quite a sporting fraternity too, with a cricket club, canoe club, Hertford Football Club, the Old Hertfordians Rugby Club, and fishing in streams made famous by Izaak Walton in *The Compleat Angler*.

Hertford is generally more expensive than other nearby towns, partly because of its status as county town. Commuters have a good choice of routes into London. The Moorgate/Kings Cross trains from Hertford North provide easy changes to the London Underground at Finsbury Park or Highbury & Islington. Or, if you prefer, there are trains to Liverpool Street from Hertford East (page 54), which connect with the Underground at Seven Sisters and Tottenham Hale. So many people scuttle through the short cuts converging on Hertford North station in the morning that there is a prescribed route known locally as the Commuter Trail. Not many of these commuters live in the area behind the station, which is dominated by council estates, but there are plenty of good streets within walking distance.

'People are often so completely fixated on Bengeo that they will consider living nowhere else'

At the cheaper end of the market, modern town houses can be bought for around £325,000 to £350,000. For middle-range, three- and four-bedroom houses with generous gardens you should look in the Fordwich area. Here you will find semis at around £450,000; detached houses around £750,000. For more extravagant housing see High Molewood and Great Molewood, where large detached houses and chalet bungalows are spread along unmade private roads surrounded by woodland. Five bedrooms, two bathrooms and four reception rooms in Thirties' architectural style might cost around £600,000. The smartest suburb to the north is **Bengeo**. People moving to Hertford are often so completely fixated on Bengeo that they will consider living nowhere else. It has a parade of shops and a good prep school. A five-bedroom house in half an acre of garden will cost well over £1.5m.

However great the appeal of Bengeo for commuters, it is the south side of town which locals consider to be the more desirable. The large

Victorian and Edwardian houses of Queen's Road and Highfield Road, enlivened by the occasional architectural curio, sell at over £600,000 for four bedrooms, £750,000 for five bedrooms.

In the centre of Hertford, upwardly mobile young couples are attracted to the riverside, where terraced cottages were originally built for mill or malt workers. Folly Island has been mercilessly gentrified, regardless of the shortage of parking places, and tiny two-bedroom houses with small gardens now cost around £225,000. The second bedroom tends only to be cot-sized, so those with growing families have to think of moving on.

Outside Hertford, **Hertingfordbury** is probably one of the most exclusive villages in the area. The thriller writer Frederick Forsyth has a house here. The village has no more than 50 or so houses, in addition to a cricket pitch and two pubs, a church and a bridge over the Mimram. Its quaintness sends prices for tiny cottages over £275,000 and detached houses start at £1m.

'Outside Hertford, Hertingfordbury is probably one of the most exclusive villages in the area'

Journey: 54 min
Season: £2400
Peak: 2 per hr
Off-peak: 1 per hr

WATTON-AT-STONE is daubing its pretty face with new development. The main street is where the older properties are – yellow and red brick houses, jettied timber and plaster. But most of the rest of the village is new, and building has been more or less constant throughout the last decade. A five-bedroom period house in the main street might cost around £500,000; a four-bedroom modern detached around £400,000. One of the developments has been to convert an old salmon-smoking factory into mews houses.

'One of the pubs has the old pudding stone outside from which the village derives its name'

The village combines the best of both worlds by being intensely rural (and horsey), and yet close enough to London for theatre and other trips. There is cricket, football and the bonus of tennis on floodlit courts, plus three pubs – one of which has the old pudding stone outside from which the village derives its name – a youth club, a flower club and other village societies. It has the Heath Mount private infant and junior schools as well the village nursery and primary. This is one of the villages to benefit from Lottery funding for a new community hall. The spring which gave the village the other half of its name ('wat', meaning watery) and which gave it brief prominence as a popular spa, dried up long ago. But a hedgerow near the station is supposed to be one of the most ancient in Hertfordshire. Plans to build 93 houses by the railway are waiting for the go-ahead from Hertfordshire County Council.

To Kings Cross	
Journey: 27 min	
Season: £2840	
Peak: 6 per hr	
Off-peak: 4 per hr	

To Moorgate	
Journey: 61 min	
Season: £2840	
Peak: 2 per hr	
Off-peak: 1 per hr	

STEVENAGE See Kings Cross to Newark Northgate line (page 69).

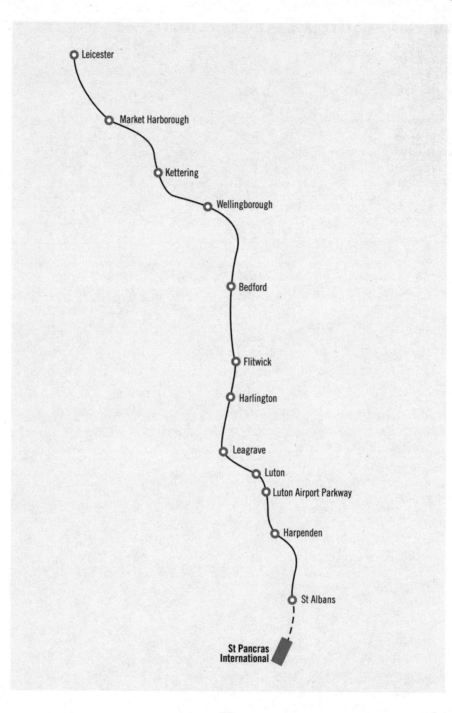

Leicester

Market Harborough

Kettering

Wellingborough

Bedford

Flitwick

Harlington

Leagrave

Luton

Luton Airport Parkway

Harpenden

St Albans

St Pancras International

St Pancras International
> Bedford and Leicester

First Capital Connect Thameslink trains from Bedford continue to Farringdon, City Thameslink, Blackfriars, and London Bridge. Season ticket prices quoted are valid to all these London stations including London Bridge (but not on the Underground) and are printed as to 'London Thameslink'. Beyond Bedford all services are to St Pancras International, and if you wish to travel onwards you have to pay for a Travelcard version (valid on Thameslink and the Underground).

Journey: 19 min
Season: £2680
Peak: 7 per hr
Off-peak: 5 per hr

ST ALBANS Forget the villages around St Albans. The attractions of the town itself, with its medieval centre focused around the cathedral, are such that it has become one of the smartest places to live north of London. Georgian and Edwardian town houses snuggle against quaint old cottages and 15th-century coaching inns. In the cramped but charming streets in the town centre conservation area you could buy a two-up-two-down cottage for around £250,000 to £300,000.

St Albans has excellent communications. It lies roughly equidistant from the M1 and A1, and only a few miles from the M25. The train journey into London is so fast that, in terms of time, it's hardly further from the City than Clapham. In the last two decades some of the country's biggest accountancy firms have moved here, including PwC, Deloitte Touche, KPMG and others.

The shopping centre feels reassuringly traditional with a bi-weekly street market in St Peter's Street and a farmers' market. There are independent shops in George Street and Holywell Hill, and Christopher Place has a variety of smart shops and restaurants, including Carluccio's. The town has several theatres – the Albans Arena, the Maltings, The Sand Pit theatre and the Abbey Theatre, where the formidable local dramatics society, The Company of Ten, performs. There are also frequent concerts and recitals in the Cathedral, and in a converted chapel the Trestles Arts Base hosts exhibitions and performances. The annual St Albans festival of music, theatre and entertainment, organised by the town council, takes place in summer. The selection of private schools is another of St Albans's attractions (see page 98). Lyricist Tim Rice and quantum theorist Stephen Hawking attended St Albans School.

The stylish 15th-, 16th- and 17th-century houses are on Fishpool Street, where a Grade Two listed two-bedroom cottage will sell for £250,000 to £300,000. A two-up-two-down cottage in the heart of town will sell for around £250,000. The main residential area is Marshalswick. Three-bedroom semis here cost £300,000 to £350,000. Large detached houses in Marshal's Drive, with tennis courts, come with price-tags in the region of £1.2m to £2.5m. Marshalswick has its own small shops, library and free car park. Further out of St Albans you will find roads of semi-detached houses where a three-bedroom Fifties' home will cost around £250,000.

For more modern, executive-style houses, the eastern corridor towards Hatfield, around the Hatfield Road, is the place to look. Three-bedroom semis sell for around £380,000 upwards; four- to five-bedroom detached houses will break £450,000.

Villages in the St Albans catchment include **Chiswell Green** – home of the Royal National Rose Society – **Shenley** and **London Colney**, where Samuel Ryder, founder of the Ryder Cup, once lived and where the development of flats at Napsbury Park has proved an attraction.

Journey: 26 min
Season: £2960
Peak: 7 per hr
Off-peak: 5 per hr

HARPENDEN is, if such a thing is possible, even smarter than St Albans. It has two cricket clubs, a leisure centre and an indoor swimming pool. The local amateur dramatics society and Harpenden Operatic Group regularly entertain at the civic hall. There is a Sainsbury's, and plenty of boutiques, gifts and speciality shops. The green runs right through the centre of the village, providing a perfect spot to sit and watch the world go by in summer. Schools for all age ranges – both private and state-run – have a particularly high reputation.

Schools in Hertfordshire

Hertfordshire is well served with good schools. But be aware that many which call themselves comprehensives actually run a selective entry system.

Watford's schools are within reach of people living near Chorleywood. Watford Grammar for Boys and its girls' counterpart are comprehensives with strong academic records. Both are heavily over-subscribed.

Harpenden also has strong schools – St George's co-educational comprehensive, which takes some boarders, Roundwood Park co-educational school, Sir John Lawes mixed comprehensive and The King's School independent day school.

Bishop's Stortford has a good private school in Bishop's Stortford College and three good comprehensives: Bishop's Stortford High, The Hertfordshire and Essex High, and St Mary's Catholic School.

Rich pickings can be had in St Albans, not only with the high-performing St Albans Girls' comprehensive, but also a matching pair of independent schools – St Albans for boys (with girls in the sixth form), and St Albans High for girls. Two more schools worth mentioning include the private St Columba's College for boys and Loreto College Roman Catholic Girls' comprehensive.

Other good comprehensives can be found in Potters Bar, Hemel Hempstead, Hitchin and Sawbridgeworth. Strong private schools include Berkhamsted Collegiate in Berkhamsted, Haberdashers' Aske's for boys and for girls in Borehamwood; Haileybury in Hertford and St Francis College in Letchworth.

16th-century
town house,
St Albans

Some of the most desirable properties are those close to the two golf courses or to the East and West Commons, although The Avenues have almost overtaken them now with the added attraction being that the walk to the station takes only ten minutes. A four- to six-bedroom detached house in The Avenues now tops £2.5m. East Common has its own golf course; West Common is more purely residential. In the area of the Commons you could pay £275,000 for a two-bedroom terrace; up to £1m for a large family house. Properties span various architectural periods from Tudor right through to the present day, and many of them have large gardens with the occasional tennis court and swimming pool. Those with shallower pockets could find a three-bedroom home away from the Commons at around £400,000.

There are some pretty villages within reach, any of which might have been lifted straight from the pages of *Country Life*. **Redbourn**, five miles away, is centred around a classic common and picture-book High Street. It is the site of Hertfordshire's first recorded cricket match in 1666. Small shops and a post office provide for day-to-day needs, and there is an infant and junior school. However, it lies too close to the M1 for its own good and the roar of traffic can be heard. A four-bedroom cottage with half an acre will cost £530,000, while a five-bedroom house in two acres will cost £750,000. Hunt through the jumble of older cottages in the High Street to find something smaller and cheaper. For **Wheathampstead** see **Kings Cross to Newark Northgate** line (page 67).

Kimpton, to the north-east, also has an attractive High Street with small shops, and there are good walks nearby in Gustard Wood. Commuters rub shoulders with long-established locals. Prices are slightly lower than in nearby Wheathampstead. There are plenty of terraced cottages but a modern four-bedroom house will cost £450,000. Children attend the village infant and junior school.

Flamstead, due west, is popular for its conservation area charm and active village social life. A thick blanket of green belt gives it a very rural atmosphere, and in the Flamstead Society it has an influential local history group. The village holds an annual charity Scarecrow Festival in August which creates an outlet for creative and artistic talent. Many of the older-established residents are allotment holders, and the garden show is an important annual event. For the amusement of the young there is a football ground and tennis courts, Brownies and Guides. The village has a general store with a post office, a playgroup and junior school, and there are two old pubs which attract customers from miles around. The cottages are a picturesque mix of brick and flint. A two-bedroom example will cost around £240,000-plus; a larger 17th-century three-bedroom house £300,000-plus.

Journey: 26 min
Season: £3120
Peak: 7 per hr
Off-peak: 5 per hr

LUTON AIRPORT PARKWAY Generous and easy parking arrangements make Luton Airport an attractive alternative to catching the train from Luton proper – anything to avoid stressful morning traffic jams. For Luton main entry see below.

Journey: 24 min
(34 min FCC)
Season: £3240
Peak: 7 per hr
Off-peak: 4 per hr

LUTON spreads its mess of modern housing estates, industrial complexes and shopping streets with little grace. It does still have some industrial pride, however, with major local employers including Whitbread and London Luton Airport, and blue chip companies such as Astra Zeneca have made an entrance. The University of Bedfordshire is located here. Shopping is unfussy and run-of-the-mill, and includes The Mall. Other attractions include an 11-screen cinema, five sports and recreation centres and two swimming pools. Luton Town Football Club play at Kenilworth Road.

There are a few odd enclaves for those who prefer period homes. Along and just off the Old Bedford Road, about half a mile from the centre, are some period villas which have been lavishly restored and sport numerous bathrooms where there were non originally. A four-bedroom home here will cost between £350,000 and £500,000, depending on how much has been spent on it. Throughout the town there are plenty of detached Thirties' houses selling at over £225,000 for three bedrooms; up to £325,000 for four bedrooms or more.

Kensworth, to the south-west, is a popular commuter village. Cottages line the main road, with a recreation ground and village hall to provide the community focal points. You might get a tiny two-bedroom cottage for as little as £175,000. Four to five-bedroom detached houses sell for around £500,000. The village has two general stores, a newsagent, a flower shop and its own infant and junior school. There is also some retirement housing.

To the east and south-east of Luton, just over the border into Hertfordshire, are the small villages of **Breachwood Green**, **Bendish** and **Peter's Green**. Bendish is probably the most stylish, being very tiny with old period cottages. A small two-up two-down cottage will set you back by £180,000 here. Prices at Peter's Green are similar, though the place is so small that you could blink and miss it. Prices drop by about 15 per cent here – a four-bedroom, detached Grade Two listed cottage could cost around £475,000. The village lies directly under the flight path to Luton Airport, and the presence of ex-council properties puts choosy buyers off.

Timber-framed cottages, Dunstable

Journey: 39 min
Season: £3240
Peak: 6 per hr
Off-peak: 4 per hr

LEAGRAVE is hardly distinct from Luton. It has its own small precinct of shopping streets, but otherwise can be considered part of the town. In the centre of Leagrave, two- and three-bedroom pre-war terraced houses sell for between £120,000 and £150,000. On the outskirts you find the occasional new development where two-bed terraces start at around £115,000.

Dunstable, two miles west at the threshold of the Dunstable Downs, is far more captivating. The old town centre is dotted with timber-framed buildings, old coaching inns (Dunstable was an important coaching stop on Watling Street), and some attractive Victorian terraces. It is has a bi-weekly outdoor market and lots of small designer shops, which are good for birthday presents, though for mundane household purchases most people go into Luton. State schools include middle schools and an upper school which also provides adult evening classes. Dunstable has its own leisure centre, swimming pools, a nightclub, and a new theatre, the Grove. The

Downs provide plenty of leisure opportunities, including a golf club and Whipsnade Wild Animal Park, and are a favourite haunt for hang-gliders and kite-fliers. Victorian terraced homes with two or three bedrooms fetch around £160,000 to £190,000. A two- or three-bedroom semi on a modern estate would cost around £170,000; a three- or four-bedroom detached house from £200,000 upwards.

Also in the Luton catchment area is **Houghton Regis**, a former village of about two miles square, not quite swallowed up by encroaching development. Modern estates and Thirties' semis make up the bulk of the property stock, with prices hovering at around £145,000 for three bedrooms. At its heart it has some small quality shops on Bedford Square.

Journey: 45 min

Season: £3320

Peak: 5 per hr

Off-peak: 4 per hr

HARLINGTON, on the very tip of the Chiltern Hills, has an attractive core of timber-framed houses and thatched cottages grouped around the church. They are in a conservation area, and anything with two bedrooms will cost at least £150,000. On the outskirts are two estates built about 30 years ago. Three-bedroom semis are priced at around £180,000 to £240,000; four-bedroom detached houses at £240,000 upwards. A five-bedroom detached house in one and a half acres, with stables, could be about £500,000. A few local shops and a post office serve a population of around 2,300, but the place is hammered by commuter traffic. There is a good infants school, an upper school and a sixth form college. The nearest middle school is at Toddington (see below), a few miles to the south-west. There is quite a strong sporting tradition in the village.

Toddington, which lies just off the M1, has a population of about 5,000 and a range of shops and schools. There are a few elegant houses around the green, and some intriguing old pubs. Toddington Manor was the home of Henrietta Wentworth, mistress of the Duke of Monmouth, the illegitimate son of Charles II. The town has grown paunchy with new development. Property prices are slightly lower than Harlington's, with three-bedroom semis at around £210,000.

Prettier villages in the Harlington area include **Tingrith** and **Milton Bryan**. Both these are hamlets of no more than 40 picture-postcard cottages each, plus the occasional Georgian farmhouse. There are no shops or schools, and both appeal to the better-heeled sort of commuter. Cottages start at around £120,000; family-sized period houses fetch between £200,000 and £500,000.

Journey: 49 min
Season: £3320
Peak: 6 per hr
Off-peak: 4 per hr

FLITWICK Little remains of old **Flitwick**, which was just a cluster of timber-framed houses and brick cottages. New development has entirely changed its character. Much of the new building has been for the benefit of commuters, whose trains come thundering straight through the centre of the town. Apart from the railway, the most noticeable central landmark now is a huge branch of Tesco. Flitwick has three lower schools and one middle school; upper-school children have to travel to Ampthill (see below). For those with surplus energy there is a sports centre with a dance studio, swimming pool and squash courts.

Prices in the modern estates range from £220,000 to £240,000 for a three-bedroom semi; over £250,000 for a four-bedroom detached house. A three-bedroom Victorian house in the centre could be bought for £220,000 to £250,000. Commuters from as far afield as Daventry flood in to street park here and save on the price of a season ticket.

Ampthill, a small Georgian market town with a population of around 7,000, makes Flitwick look like an ugly sister. Its picturesque centre is set around a market square, dotted with antiques shops and other small specialist outlets. It has a Waitrose, schools for children of all ages, and a handsome park of around 160 acres. It is believed that Catherine of Aragon once lived here and received visits from Henry VIII. A three-bedroom peg-tiled estate cottage might be picked up for £250,000; a four-bedroom detached period house from £300,000 to £400,000; or a rare Georgian gem with a bit of land for £600,000.

Steppingley, a tiny village a mile to the west of Flitwick, has little more than 40 Duke of Bedford peg-tiled estate cottages, a cricket

Duke of Bedford cottages, Steppingley

club, pub and a good restaurant. The atmosphere is upmarket and horsey. Prices for two- to three-bedroom cottages are in the region of £150,000 to £200,000. A four-bedroom detached period house will fetch between £300,000 and £600,000. Out of the village along one of the lanes you could expect to pay up to £500,000 for a Georgian farmhouse with a bit of land.

Journey: 40 min
(59 min FCC)
Season: £3600
Peak: 6 per hr
Off-peak: 4 per hr

BEDFORD Though still a market town, **Bedford** has to a certain extent allowed its individuality to become submerged by its own commercial success. Modern office blocks have appeared in the historic centre. Multi-national companies located here include Unilever. The modern Harpur Centre shopping mall is complemented by quality small shops along the High Street, as well as big-name stores, supermarkets and a tri-weekly market. The Bunyan Centre is the place for most sports, and there are three swimming pools, including the Oasis 'beach pool'. The Civic Theatre provides a forum for amateur dramatics, but is upstaged as a venue by the Corn Exchange. The Aspects leisure centre has restaurants, a gym and multi-screen cinema. The town is also a centre of learning, having Bedford College, the University of Bedfordshire and nearby Cranfield University.

Along the embankment by the River Great Ouse, where people stroll in summer and sit to watch the waterfowl, there are some large, tree-shaded Victorian houses – probably the nicest properties in the town. One of these with five to seven bedrooms would cost over £650,000. There are also some purpose-built flats in the same area. The smallest one-bedroom apartment starts at £100,000. A three-bedroom Victorian terraced house nearby would cost £175,000; a three- to four-bedroom semi up to £200,000. For the rest of the town the general rule is that the houses are more modern the further out you go, but prices do not vary much. You can expect to pay around £175,000 for a three-bedroom semi; £200,000 for a three-bedroom detached.

Most of the sought-after villages in the flat countryside around Bedford are to the north. **Oakley**, just over four miles to the north-west, has in its High Street some old brick farmworkers' cottages that once belonged to the Duke of Bedford's estate. You would pay from around £185,000 for one of these with two bedrooms and a long

Schools in Bedfordshire

Bedford's strongest suit is its independent sector, which includes Bedford High and Dame Alice Harpur for girls, Bedford for boys and Bedford Modern (mixed), all of which have pupils bussed into school from a large catchment area.

'The watermill has been restored and once again mills flour'

garden. There is also a good deal of modern development where you would pay about £175,000 for a three-bedroom semi; from £250,000 for a four-bedroom detached. Youngish families mix with the small number of commuters. Village social life revolves around the village hall, cricket and football teams, the gardening club and the two pubs. There is a village store, a post office, primary and middle schools.

Bromham, on the Ouse three miles north-west of Bedford, is a large village with a population of 5,000. Many of the local families have lived here for generations. The limestone cottages in the village centre are surrounded by modern housing and building is still on-going. There is a supermarket, post office, two general stores, a petrol station, hairdresser, fish-and-chip shop, health centre, two pubs and a lower school. Local events include an annual apple day. The watermill has been restored and once again mills flour. Bromham House, an old manor house now used as a venue for weddings, has had its grounds filled with new housing. A three-bedroom semi could be bought for £185,000, a detached four- to five-bedroom house with garden in Bromham House grounds, £500,000.

Biddenham, due west of Bedford, is the favourite village for London commuters. It is close to the town (the station is a brisk 15-minute walk), yet it feels deliciously remote and is set around a classic village green. All this makes it one of the most expensive villages in the area. Properties range from 17th-century thatched cottages to imposing Thirties' houses, plus a few modern developments built with managing directors in mind. Prices range from £150,000 for a two-bedroom cottage to £600,000–£700,000 for a substantial family house. A development of 300 houses has been built with a shop, a cricket field, tennis courts and a community centre as part of the package. Four-bedroom houses here cost £250,000. There is a cricket club and tennis club. The village hall is packed at parish council meetings, and everyone gets involved in local events, including an annual summer show. Conservation issues are policed by the Biddenham Society.

'Biddenham village hall is packed at parish council meetings, and everyone gets involved in local events, including an annual summer show'

Beyond Bedford, all services are to St Pancras International only.

Journey: 56 min
Season: £4840
Peak: 4 per hr
Off-peak: 2 per hr

WELLINGBOROUGH is so plain it defies description yet the

improved train service is bringing in new life blood in the form of commuters. It has a good range of major chain stores, several supermarkets including a Sainsbury's, and a modern shopping mall – the Swansgate Centre. Schooling is good, with three state secondary schools and one private school, Wellingborough School for boys. A night out in Wellingborough used to be mean going to a pub, but the town now has The Castle theatre, an arts complex and the new Waendel Leisure Centre complete with swimming pool.

The town has a mix of Victorian terraced houses, smart newish developments and some not-so-nice council estates. Developments around the railway station are popular as starter homes. A two-bedroom quad (a quarter of a house split into four) will cost £110,000; a three-bedroom semi £150,000–£170,000; a four-bedroom detached just over £190,000. There are some pleasant older properties in Northampton Road, where you could expect to pay over £180,000 for a three-bedroom Thirties' house. For Victoriana, look in Hatton Park where houses cost £200,000 upwards. A four-bedroom modern detached house on one of the better developments – the Gleneagles Estate, for instance – would cost between £210,000 and £250,000.

Rushden, a few miles to the east, is about one-third the size of Wellingborough and rather less attractive, with some charmless early Seventies' architecture and the extra dollop of houses planned which might simply add to the anywhere-land feel. The consolation for house-buyers are some reasonably-priced Victorian terraces, ranging from around £85,000 to £115,000 for two or three bedrooms. A four-bedroom detached modern house will cost over £175,000. Shopping is adequate: there is an Asda on the edge of town and a Waitrose within. The main source of local pride is the sports centre and the splash-leisure pool. There is no cinema since the old picture house was converted into a theatre for amateur dramatics and bingo. Rushden was the birthplace of H.E. Bates, who used Rushden Hall – one of the few historic buildings surviving in the town – as the model for Evensfield in *Love For Lydia*.

A favourite state school is Ferrers School in **Higham Ferrers**, four-and-a-half miles to the east of Wellingborough. The village has now become a town, hardly separated from Rushden, with an attractive High Street lined with period stone

Red-brick and stone cottage, Wellingborough

properties and new developments fanning out on either side. A four-bedroom stone house here will cost over £285,000; a rare, rambling five-bedroom terraced property on the market square, over £450,000. Some of the villages close by are worth looking at too. **Wymington** has a good mix of stone and thatch, with a spread of old farmhouses down the lanes, and **Podington** has a quality of timelessness that is very attractive. You could find a period three-bedroom stone house for around £360,000, a five-bedroom thatched home for around £800,000.

Wollaston, about seven minutes' drive due south of Wellingborough, is centred around a cluster of old cottages, with modern developments, an industrial estate and council housing on the outskirts. The makers of Doc Martens have their headquarters here. It has small shops, a post office and its own primary and secondary schools. The conservation watchdogs of the Wollaston Society have enjoyed some triumphs, including the arrival in 1985 of a bypass to take the strain of the A509. Property prices start at £125,000 for a three-bedroom semi; £210,000 for a four-bedroom detached; and £375,000 for an 18th-century stone cottage. A four-bedroom, double-garaged, detached house overlooking the fields might cost £325,000; a seven-bedroom, 13th-century house in 2 acres recently sold for £1.5m.

'Grendon is a pretty village consisting of 18th-century cottages gathered around the church'

For real village atmosphere you should head south to **Grendon**, about five miles from Wellingborough. This pretty village consists of 18th-century cottages gathered around the church, with some Victorian terraces and a few individual modern properties. Villagers get by with one pub and a good primary school. There is a limited bus service. The population of over 500 includes young families, commuters, and some elderly residents in bungalows. Village life centres around the Church Social Committee, Village Hall Committee, the WI, football and cricket teams. There is an annual church fête and periodic fund-raising ventures which attract considerable support. Expect to pay at least £250,000 for a period cottage; upwards of £140,000 for a two-bed Victorian terrace.

East of Wellingborough is **Raunds**, a small town not to everyone's taste, with a 14th-century manor house and Victorian buildings surrounded by modern estates. Its tightly-knit community of about 8,000 is served by two supermarkets, a post office and smaller shops. Small terraced houses can be bought for £90,000; three-bedroom Victorian semis for £110,000; and modern three-bedroom detached houses for £150,000 upwards.

Also on this side of Wellingborough are **Great** and **Little Addington**. Both are cottagey with some modern development on the wings – mainly four-bedroom detached houses. The two villages share a vicar, a playing field, a youth club and WI, though there is still a certain amount of friendly rivalry which brings people out in summer and

'Green wellies, Land Rovers and waxed jackets are common currency in the Addingtons'

winter for inter-village sporting contests. Another highlight of the social calendar is the annual horticultural society show. There is a Church of England primary school and a playgroup for tots, of which there are a fair number. New housebuilding is seriously restricted here, so prices can only go up. You would have to pay around £250,000 for a three-bedroom stone cottage, possibly thatched; around £300,000 for a modern four-bedroom detached. A five-bedroom stone country house with an acre of land could cost up to £600,000. The area is so seriously horsey that estate agents say that anything with a pony paddock is bound to sell. Green wellies, Land Rovers and waxed jackets are common currency here.

Journey: 63 min
Season: £5364
Peak: 4 per hr
Off-peak: 2 per hr

KETTERING is a no-nonsense East Midlands market town, well supplied with leisure opportunities and good shopping. All the big-name stores are here, including Tesco, Sainsbury's and Marks and Spencer, and the modern Newlands Shopping Centre is useful if not actually inspiring. There is a leisure village and the 180-acre Wicksteed Park is not far away with its fairground theme park. Those addicted to more sedentary pleasures will be pleased to hear that there is a 10-screen cinema.

The town has a few old Georgian terraces in the centre, larger Victorian houses forming a ring around them, and modern estates on the outskirts. You might pick up a two-bedroom Victorian terrace for £90,000, or a three-bedroom Victorian house with original features and a good garden for around £110,000.

The countryside here at last begins to pick itself up off the Bedfordshire plains. It is a mellow, slightly rolling, farmland landscape which draws people from Kettering out into the surrounding, frankly villagey, little market towns. Look at **Rothwell** and **Desborough** to the north, and **Burton Latimer** to the south. All are similar, with Victorian market places, small shops and their own primary and secondary schools. Property prices are similar to those in Kettering. Rothwell is particularly pretty and has a gem of an Elizabethan market hall. The centre is a designated conservation area, and it has the benefit of a state secondary school, Montsaye. A two-up-two-down terrace will cost £85,000; a three-bedroom terrace £100,000; a three-bedroom semi £125,000 to £135,000; a four-bedroom detached £150,000.

One of the more notable smaller villages is **Geddington**, four miles north of Kettering, with a population of around 1,400. A medieval bridge crosses the River Ise here, with a forested hillside providing an attractive green backdrop. There are three pubs, a village hall, post office and primary school, and bowls, tennis and cricket clubs. At its heart is a cluster of old cottages, though new housing has forced itself in and there are some Victorian terraces too. For a two-bedroom terraced house or a small cottage you would have to pay upwards of £160,000. Closer to Kettering on this side is the tiny village of **Weekley**. There are possibly no more than 150 people living here altogether, many of them from old farming families, some of them elderly (the old vicarage is now a residential home). Among the thatched cottages there is a pretty thatched post office and Jessica's Tea Shop, which is much photographed. There is no school or pub, but the tea shop, village hall and church provide venues for coffee mornings, sports club meetings and choirs. Weekley is a quiet, compact, well-heeled and tight-knit village where a cottage – should you be lucky enough to find one for sale – would cost around £210,000.

**Journey: 60 min
(70 min peak)
Season: £6228
Peak: 3 per hr
Off-peak: 2 per hr**

MARKET HARBOROUGH
People grow very fond of Market Harborough, home of the first Liberty Bodice, with its distinctive half-timbered Old Grammar School on stilts in the centre, now used for public functions. The population is a manageable 19,000. Georgian offices and shops are still in place in the town centre. Local firms include the Harboro Rubber Company and there are three business parks on the outskirts. St Mary's Place shopping centre in the old cattle market has a Sainsbury's and an indoor market. A farmers' market is held once a month and an antiques market takes place every week. There is a leisure centre and swimming pool, a 100-seat theatre large enough for local productions, but no cinema.

‘People grow very fond of Market Harborough, home of the first Liberty Bodice’

Some of the nicest properties are the large Victorian villas along the Northampton Road, where three-bedroom houses start at £230,000. There are also some rather gracious tree-lined avenues in which mature Thirties' semis and detached houses are likely to cost £200,000 to £350,000. Victoria Avenue (actually a cul-de-sac) and Lubenham Hill, are both popular.

North of Market Harborough you enter the wide-open, rolling countryside of the Welland Valley, where villages of thatch and stone are connected by unhurried roads. This is serious hunting country – Quorn territory. Life in The Langtons – **Church Langton**, **Tur Langton**, **West Langton**, **East Langton** and **Thorpe Langton** – revolves around horses

---

Schools in Leicestershire, Rutland and Lincolnshire

Leicester itself has The Beauchamp College, a co-educational comprehensive with a reputation for being both liberal and achieving good results, and two independent schools – Leicester (mixed) and the High School for Girls. Soar Valley College comprehensive also does well in the school league tables. Dominant mixed public schools in the area, mostly boarding, include Uppingham and Oakham.

Lincolnshire is known for its good grammar schools in towns such as Boston, Bourne, Castor, Grantham, Gainsborough and Spalding.

and farming. Church Langton is the largest of this idyllic clutch of villages and West Langton the smallest, though they are all really little more than hamlets, clusters of stone and thatched cottages. All except West Langton and Tur Langton have a pub. Church Langton has the only primary school. Prices vary according to how much land comes with the house and the quality of the views, but you could reckon on paying over £250,000 for a three-bedroom stone cottage; up to £500,000 for four bedrooms and an acre of land on a hilltop.

Another gem is **Foxton**. It lies about two-and-a-half miles north-west of Market Harborough on the Grand Union Canal. Its famous series of locks – ten altogether in two flights rising through 75ft – and an inclined plane boat lift (the subject of a restoration plan) are a great attraction to tourists in the summer. The village itself is pretty, with old stone and thatched cottages and only a few ex-council houses. Swingbridge Street is possibly the nicest. The population is a friendly mix of young families, commuters and farmers. There is a village hall, infant and junior schools and three pubs. A three-bedroom detached cottage will cost £200,000, rising to around £450,000 if it has an acre or two of land. Ex-council houses fetch around £160,000 to £200,000. It is worth noting that in the villages to the north of Market Harborough you might still find old manor houses which make very compact, manageable homes. For six or seven bedrooms, a few acres of land and stabling, you would pay around £700,000 to £1m.

Close to Foxton is **Gumley**, a tiny one-street village on a hill. There is a pub but no shop or school. Many of the villagers own horses and have farming interests. Property rarely comes on the market and price depends on the view. You might find a two-bedroom Victorian brick cottage for £170,000, or a modern four-bedroom house for £280,000 to £300,000.

Journey: 69 min
(78 min peak)
Season: £7252
Peak: 5 per hr
Off-peak: 4 per hr

LEICESTER This gutsy, modern Midlands city is not likely to woo the heart of too many London commuters though it is very conveniently placed close to the M69, the M6 and the M1. Its prosperity was built on hosiery, then on the mass production of boots and shoes, and more recently on engineering and computing. The city has cleverly married public and private spending to good effect, and private developers have turned old warehouses and factories into fashionable lofts and flats. For instance, in the old Pick Building where army uniforms were made, a one-bedroom apartment can be bought for around £110,000, two bedrooms for £160,000. There is a student population, for both Leicester and De Montfort universities are here, and the fact that 35 per cent of the population is non-white means it is culturally fabulously varied. This is the land of steam, antiques and agricultural fairs, but also now a land of many cultures, where the Caribbean Festival in August attracts 10,000 people and the Hindu celebrations of Diwali and Navratri eclipse those anywhere else in Europe. The Leicester covered market is reknowned for its cheeses and pies. The Golden Mile on Belgrave Road attracts shoppers from all over the world in search of silks, saris, jewellery and spices. Leisure here means sport. For participants the city has bowling rinks, BMX and skate facilities, tennis courts, cricket and football pitches, swimming pools and leisure centres. For spectators there are Leicester City FC, Leicestershire County Cricket Club and the indomitable Tigers – Leicester Rugby Football Club.

Highfields, the red light district that has been cleaned up, is generally avoided. So are some of the ugly council estates, though these offer cheap housing – three-bedroom semis at £110,000 to £120,000. Just to the south of the city is the comparative comfort of **Stoneygate**, where there are large Victorian and Edwardian villas, some of which have been converted into flats. A three-bedroom Victorian house here will cost £275,000; a five-bedroom detached £400,000. Prices are similar in **Oadby**, which also has its share of older streets and a gentle mix of new housing.

There are some very pretty villages nearby in the Charnwood Forest and up the Wreake Valley, though perhaps some of the most unspoilt stone villages lie slightly out of reach towards Oakham. To the east is classic hunting country, where the Fernie hunt borders with the Quorn. **Hoby** in the Wreake valley is particularly charming. In this and any of the villages close by, a four-bedroom detached period house might cost £300,000 to £500,000, while the smaller two-bedroom variety will cost £130,000 to £200,000. In the Charnwood Forest you come close to the old coal-mining area of Coalville and granite quarrying area of Mountsorrel, but the forest itself is completely unspoilt and fiercely protected. Prices of small cottages in **Quorn** are similar to those in the Wreake Valley, but large period properties with six to eight bedrooms and one and a half acres of land can be priced at £750,000 to £850,000.

'The Golden Mile on Belgrave Road attracts shoppers from all over the world in search of silks, saris, jewellery and spices'

'To the east is classic hunting country, where the Fernie hunt borders with the Quorn'

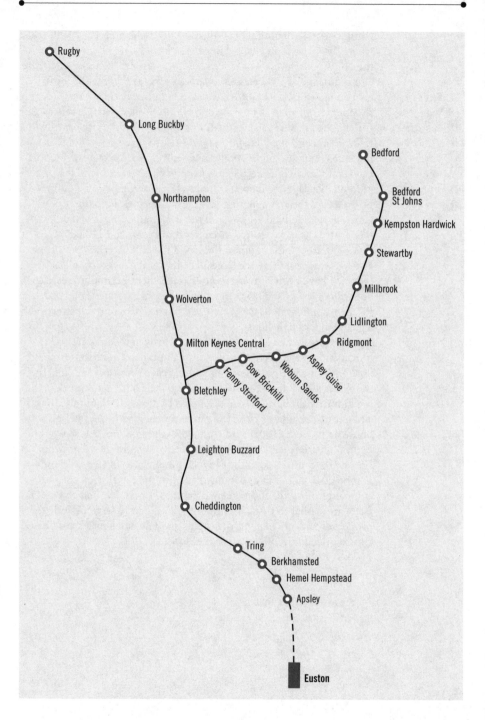

Rugby

Long Buckby

Northampton

Bedford

Bedford St Johns

Kempston Hardwick

Stewartby

Millbrook

Wolverton

Lidlington

Milton Keynes Central

Ridgmont

Aspley Guise

Bow Brickhill

Woburn Sands

Fenny Stratford

Bletchley

Leighton Buzzard

Cheddington

Tring

Berkhamsted

Hemel Hempstead

Apsley

Euston

Journey: 30 min
Season: £2796
Peak: 2 per hr
Off-peak: 2 per hr

APSLEY is well-liked for its sense of identity. It has Victorian two-bedroom terraces at around £230,000 within walking distance of the station and a large waterside development set round a marina on the canal where a swish two-bedroom apartment costs £210,000. Plans to build 325 new homes on nearby green belt have been given the go-ahead despite local opposition. **Boxmoor** is also worth looking at as a refuge from the modernity of Hemel Hempstead, to which it is now annexed. It still has a few canalside cottages. You can buy older two- or three-bedroom cottages for around £235,000, or spend from £370,000 to £800,000 on a smart modern detached house with four bedrooms. Sunday afternoon walks might take you close to Watford to Cassiobury Park beside the Grand Union Canal, which leads into Whippendell Woods – 160 acres of beech, oak and hornbeam.

Bovingdon, to the south-west, is another antidote to Hemel Hempstead. The centre still has a village feel to it, with a green and a good medieval hall house. House prices are 15 per cent higher than in Hemel Hempstead, though there has been a lot of modern development. The market, held on Saturdays on the site of the old Bovingdon airfield, has more than 500 stalls, selling everything from home-made pies to hand-sewn clothes. 'To tell you the truth, Bovingdon is a bit of a nothing place but people who live there think they live in a village,' is how one local cynic described it.

Journey: 27 min
Season: £2924
Peak: 4 per hr
Off-peak: 4 per hr

HEMEL HEMPSTEAD may not be to everyone's taste, just pre-dating Stevenage as a New Town, but it is very conveniently placed. The M1 and M25 both pass very close to it, the train to London takes less than half and hour, and Heathrow is 40 minutes away by car. It still has rough Hertfordshire meadows on three sides. After all, the idea which underpinned the New Town concept was that people could combine the pleasures of town and country, and escape the overcrowded conditions of London. Now the town is undergoing a £360m regeneration project to provide more housing and shopping, due for completion in 2013. In the meantime, facilities include a shopping centre, a sports centre, a newly rebuilt ski slope, and an eight-screen cinema.

The old town grew up around the Norman church, with Regency and Victorian villas springing up along the Marlowes to take advantage of the distant views to the Chilterns. A two-bedroom cottage in the old town will cost £250,000. To the east you come to the sought-after area of **Leverstock Green**, where the housing is mostly post-Fifties. A four-bedroom detached home would cost between £390,000 and £450,000; a three-bedroom semi £280,000 to £340,000. There are also some very large houses set in half-acre plots in Longdean Park that fetch over £650,000. Ex-local authority housing tends to sell for a good deal less than private housing, so a two-bedroom house might be had for over £160,000.

The New Town has an all-dancing shopping centre with all the chain stores anyone could need. British Telecom is located here and the British Standards Institute also has offices in Hemel Hempstead.

Potten End, to the north west, is a dispersed Chiltern village with a green and the Martins Pond pub. It borders on beautiful National Trust land that stretches along the spine of the Chilterns from Ivinghoe Beacon to Berkhamsted. You can buy a Thirties' detached house with a tile-hung bay window in a quiet suburban road for around £575,000. Old cottages, however, are thin on the ground. A substantial house with five bedrooms and half an acre of garden might fetch £800,000 or more.

Chipperfield is expensive too, though the centre has long-since been ribboned with developments built to accommodate fugitives from Watford. It is redeemed by its wooded common webbed with footpaths, and by the old village centre where the green is faced by an inn, the church and some little brick cottages. A four-bedroom detached house (most of the houses are this size or larger) would cost £585,000.

> *Potten End borders on beautiful National Trust land that stretches along the spine of the Chilterns from Ivinghoe Beacon to Berkhamsted*

Journey: 31 min
Season: £3068
Peak: 4 per hr
Off-peak: 4 per hr

BERKHAMSTED is a prosperous old market town wedged in the valley bottom, with the railway and canal running through some of the best countryside close to London. A general market on Saturdays, a farmers' market once a month and a flower-seller in the High Street provide constant charm and colour. English Heritage looks after the castle, where Chaucer was clerk of works. It is now little more than a few fingers of flint, but an increasing source of wonder to historians who have been studying fresh excavations. People are attracted to the town by the thickly wooded common, towpath walks along the Grand Union Canal, and Berkhamsted Collegiate School, which includes Graham Greene among its alumni.

On the steep valley slopes to the south are shoals of Victorian and Edwardian houses with large gardens, while the centre of town is packed with Victorian terraces. You can get a three-bedroom, 19th-century terraced house for around £430,000 within walking distance of the station. Canalside flats right in the centre sell for £250,000 to £275,000 for two bedrooms. Detached three-bedroom houses built in the Sixties and Seventies cost £450,000 to £650,000. The large, individually designed, secluded houses in private roads run extravagantly from £800,000 to £1.2m.

A bypass came to the rescue in the Nineties, removing much of the traffic from the heart of the town. The busy shopping centre has all the chain stores, a variety of restaurants and two fitness centres. The art deco Rex Cinema has been named 'Britain's most beautiful cinema'. There is a sports centre, and a golf course on Berkhamsted Common, the rest of which is mostly owned by the National Trust.

Little Gaddesden, to the north, is very desirable, perched on a ridge 600ft high in the Chiltern Hills. Most of the large houses and cottages face directly on to the beechwoods and heathland of the vast Ashridge Estate, which is classified as an Area of Oustanding Natural Beauty. Physically, the village is strung out in a linear settlement pattern; socially it is rather cliquey. You would pay £600,000 for a four-bedroom, Thirties' detached cottage in three-quarters of an acre. There is a Church of England primary school, a church half a mile outside the village, and a village hall that hosts all the usual coffee mornings and clubs. The big house has been converted into a business school.

Close by is **Aldbury**, a film-set village of thatched and timber-framed cottages clustered around a large pond, with stocks and whipping post. Even the smallest cottage here costs at least £300,000 and will usually sell by word of mouth. There is a general store and post office, two pubs – the Greyhound Inn and the Valiant Trooper – and a golf course. Sightseers come to admire the village's good looks.

'The Rothschilds lived at Tring Park and used to be seen driving around in traps pulled by zebras'

Average: 36 min
Season: £3292
Peak: 4 per hr
Off-peak: 3 per hr

TRING station is one-and-a-half miles outside the town in a hamlet called simply **Tring Station**. The Rothschilds lived at Tring Park, and their stamp is everywhere. They gave open spaces, provided cottages, and in 1905 built the stockbroker-style, half-timbered Rose & Crown Inn. They also founded what is now known as the Natural History Museum at Tring, full of stuffed bears, sloths and other exotics typical of this eccentric family who used to be seen driving around in traps drawn by zebras. Today Tring performs the dual role of commuter dormitory and market town.

There are plenty of Victorian houses and new estates. A two-bedroom flat might cost £180,000; a two-bedroom Victorian cottage £215,000 to £265,000; a three-bedroom semi £269,000 to £375,000; a four-bedroom detached from £450,000. Tring does have a shopping

Three-bedroom cottage, near Tring

centre, though people tend to use Aylesbury, Hemel Hempstead or Milton Keynes for more serious shopping. There is a farmers' market on alternate Saturdays. The Tring Nature Reserve's four reservoirs, used to store water in the 18th century, attract flocks of wintering ducks and are a Site of Special Scientific Interest.

Two-and-a-half miles further north of Tring Station is **Ivinghoe** – a pretty village close to Ivinghoe Beacon from which you can gaze across to the chalk-hill white lion of Whipsnade Wild Animal Park. The centre of the village makes a pretty picture out of the older houses sitting sleepily on two sides of the green and the handsome watermill.

Journey: 41 min
Season: £3300
Peak: 2 per hr
Off-peak: 1 per hr

CHEDDINGTON is a quiet little village, best known for the fact that the Great Train Robbery took place at the railway bridge just outside. Prices are similar to Tring's and slightly higher than Leighton Buzzard's. You could buy a four-bedroom detached house for £400,000 upwards; a three-bedroom Victorian semi for £285,000 upwards; or a substantial Georgian farmhouse for around £850,000.

Journey: 34 min
Season: £3308
Peak: 3 per hr
Off-peak: 4 per hr

LEIGHTON BUZZARD has swallowed whole the smaller town of **Linslade** on the west of the River Ouzel, which is where the station is located. It is prime commuterland. Leighton Buzzard proper is an old market town with drunken timber and brick buildings, a twice-weekly market and a monthly farmers' market. The smartest roads to live in are Plantation Road (known as Bedfordshire's most beautiful mile) and Heath Road, studded with trees and a mix of Victorian and modern houses. Prices range between £200,000 for a two-bedroom semi to £700,000 for a large family house. In other parts of the town the standard price for a modern four-bedroom detached is £350,000. The town is well-padded in green belt.

Around the station in Linslade, which is more leafy than Leighton Buzzard itself, are Victorian terraces where two-bedroom houses sell for around £155,000, and three- to four-bedroom houses for around £175,000 to £220,000. There are two recently built estates, Billington Park and Sandhills. Billington Park has soaked up the grounds of a former RAF base and two-bedroom houses here cost around £160,000 while three-bedrooms cost around £185,000 to £230,000. At Sandhills a three-bedroom semi is £180,000 to £215,000.

Soulbury, two miles west, is one of the best examples of an open field village in north Buckinghamshire, and its proximity to the station makes it a favourite with commuters. It is on a bus route to Leighton Buzzard and a school bus route to Aylesbury. The half-timbered and thatched houses around the green and church overlook the Ouzel valley. Other cottages are spread out between fields embroidered with footpaths, and there are a few modern properties at the village margin. Houses rarely come on the market, and when they do they are expensive and have gained in value since the completion of a bypass. A period three-bedroom cottage would fetch up to £300,000; a five-bedroom detached around £550,000.

Further west in the Vale of Aylesbury is **Stewkley**, possibly the longest village in England, stretching a mile either side of St Michael's, its remarkably fine Norman church. Between 1912 and 1914 the suffragette Sylvia Pankhurst and her mother lived here in a 16th-century cottage. The village has a reputation for being rather superior and closed to outsiders. A substantial four-bedroom house would cost over £500,000; an ex-council house with three bedrooms over £200,000.

For a less rarefied atmosphere you could look southward to **Wing**, a busy, no-frills village with several shops, including one general store with a post office, a hairdresser and beauty salon, a fish-and-chip shop and two doctor's surgeries. Ascott House, bought by the Rothschilds in 1874, is close by, and village employment and activities have tended to revolve around the estate. Apart from the black-and-white estate cottages, there are rows of late-Victorian brick terraced cottages, plus the occasional thatched house and the usual modern estates on the fringe. A two-up-two-down Victorian terrace might cost £155,000 to £175,000; a three-bedroom Seventies' semi £250,000; four-bedrooms £350,000.

The village has a highly rated primary school, a secondary school, several football teams and a thriving adult education centre (upholstery and painting classes are particularly popular). The large green has footpaths and swings. The drawback is that the village is beginning to feel hemmed in by Milton Keynes and Leighton Buzzard. It is also used as a rat-run by commuters dashing for the Leighton Buzzard trains, though there is talk of a bypass.

One of the most beautiful villages in the area is **Mentmore** – a charming collection of mock-Tudor houses on top of a hill in old Rothschild country. The large village green is ringed with lime trees and offers breathtaking views in every direction. The big house is Grade One listed Mentmore Towers, which caused a furore in 1974 when it was offered to the government and turned down; the contents were sold and important works of art left the country. It has since

'Between 1912 and 1914 the suffragette Sylvia Pankhurst and her mother lived at Stewkley in a 16th-century cottage'

been used as a location for Hollywood movies, including *Batman Begins*, and is now in the process of being converted into a luxury hotel. A modest two-bedroom cottage on the crest of the hill in Mentmore village would cost over £240,000; a country house with a few acres £1.5m to £2m.

Journey: 41 min
Season: £3332
Peak: 4 per hr
Off-peak: 3 per hr

BLETCHLEY is the largest of the three towns gobbled up by Milton Keynes and is home to Bletchley Park, the wartime code-breaking centre, which is now open to the public. The town has a good shopping centre and an open-air general market is held three times a week. 'The funny thing about it is that at the heart of it you will find a 16th-century thatched cottage with an acre of garden,' says one local estate agent. 'Where else can you find an acre of garden in the centre of town?' Bletchley has been developed in waves, reflecting the repeated housing booms of the 19th and 20th centuries, starting with the thatched cottages, then grids of Victorian terraces followed by classic double bay-fronted Thirties' houses built by Tranfield, some of which still have their sunburst stained glass. People tend to stay put once they arrive and few quality houses come on the market. The average price for a three-bed semi is £150,000 to £190,000.

Nearly 40 per cent of the town is council housing, which is why it tends to be looked down upon by some of its neighbours. The ex-council houses offer good value, however, with large three-bedroom semis selling for around £140,000. In the last building wave are the houses of the Eighties' boom – typical mix-and match styles, with one-bedroom flats, small and large houses all mixed up together. A one-bedroom house costs just over £115,000; a four-bedroom detached with a garage over £220,000.

Padbury, to the west, is the classic chocolate-box village with half-timbered and thatched cottages, and a green swathed in leafy trees. The farms around were once owned by All Souls' College, Oxford. It has a butcher, but the future of the sub-post office hangs in the balance. There are tennis courts, a sports field and pavilion, and a village hall. Despite all this, old villagers complain that it is not the place it used to be, there has been such an influx of commuters and weekenders. Among the attractions for incomers is a highly-regarded local school for five- to nine-year-olds. People will wait years to get a house in Padbury and pay £185,000 for a very ordinary three-bedroom semi.

Neighbouring **Adstock** has timber, brick and thatched cottages built along narrow lanes giving it a cosy, compact feeling, and there is a popular local pub, the Thatched Inn. A six-bedroom cottage with exposed beams and inglenook fireplace might sell for £650,000. For a vibrant village life, try **Thornborough**. This is a long, thin village with a church, pub and green (with pond), which is the scene of a great number of village events. There are fêtes and a sports day, followed by a barbecue in the evening. The Thornborough Sports Club caters for athletes and road runners and is a bit of a social hub. The primary school takes children up to eight years old and there is a post office which opens three days a week. When it rains the stream across the road swells and people come out to paddle. There are ducks, which are none too fussy about where they lay their eggs; some of the drakes have been known to end up in village freezers. A circular five-mile walk around Thornborough watermill and the old canal is a favourite Sunday afternoon stroll. A five-bedroom detached house might cost up to £600,000; a three-bedroom 18th-century stone-and-slate semi-detached cottage £325,000.

> Branch line to Bedford via Fenny Stratford, Bow Brickhill, Woburn Sands, Aspley Guise, Ridgmont, Lidlington, Millbrook, Stewartby, Kempston Hardwick and Bedford St Johns

No through trains.
Trains from
Bedford to
Bletchley, 1 per hr
Journey (from
Aspley Guise):
64 min
Season: £3952
(via Bletchley);
£3680 (via
Bedford)

The Marston Vale line is the only remaining section of the former Oxford to Cambridge line. It is only 16 miles long, but is extremely busy since it serves villages that lack good local bus services and is heavily used by children on the school-run to Bedford. Commuters can change at Bedford for St Pancras International, or they can go to Bletchley and change for Euston, which is most people's preferred choice. None of the stations along the line has a car park, nor are they manned. Information is tannoyed from Bletchley to the individual platforms, and tickets are bought from the guard on the train. Season tickets to Euston or St Pancras International are available from Bletchley or Bedford. There are plans to extend the line to Milton Keynes Central.

People living in the eastern suburbs of Milton Keynes (see page 122) tend to use the first two stations, **Fenny Stratford** and **Bow Brickhill**, rather than drive to Milton Keynes Central. Fenny Stratford is mainly Victorian, and you would have to pay over £160,000 for a three-bedroom house here. Bow Brickhill sprawls along a steep hillside reputed to have been a favourite haunt of Dick Turpin. Woodland has been cleared to make way for golf courses. It is an old village, with a beautician and a pub, The Wheatsheaf, but lies on a very busy road. Property is varied, from two-up-two-downs selling at around £190,000, to four-bedroom Sixties' houses from £300,000.

House style in the South Midlands

The least attractive part of the region is Bedfordshire. It is blanketed in clay, which has been made into huge quantities of yellow and orangey-red bricks over the years. Industrial farming has done its worst, and the clay-clogged hedgeless fields only rarely erupt into pretty village scenes. Northamptonshire has long been underrated by London commuters, though it is peppered with lovely limestone houses. Near Collyweston the houses are roofed in stone slates, with gabled bay windows and double stone chimney-stacks.

The stone turns pale and grey as you travel east. Pantiles for the roofs were brought from eastern ports up the rivers Welland, Nene and Ouse.

Woburn Sands has its own distinct identity, with a small High Street for day-to-day needs, and wonderful walks within five minutes of the centre in the Duke of Bedford's woodlands. There are several boutiques, restaurants, a butcher, doctor's surgery and medical centre, tennis courts, a cricket ground and a lower and middle school. In the new Parklands development, half a mile from the town centre, you could buy a three-bedroom semi from £235,000, or a four-bedroom detached house from £300,000. A four-bedroom Victorian villa in town could fetch up to £575,000. Local activities include football teams, bowls and village fairs. **Aspley Heath** (within reach of Woburn Sands station) is where people from Woburn Sands aspire to move, since it has spacious houses set in large gardens with good views. It is known locally as millionaires' row, but you might sneak into a four-bedroom cottage along here for £500,000.

'Aspley Heath is known locally as millionaires' row, but you might sneak into a four-bedroom cottage here for £500,000'

Woburn itself (also within reach of Woburn Sands station) is a beautifully preserved Georgian town, best known for its proximity to Woburn Abbey and popular with golfers. It has a brasserie, several antiques shops and restaurants. Very few houses are freehold since the older they are the more likely they are to be tied to the estate. A two-bedroom period cottage in need of refurbishment could cost £270,000. The occasional smart, modern, four-bedroom house might come on the market for around £690,000; or you might find an ex-council, three-bedroom semi for around £250,000. Woburn gets cluttered in summer with tourists visiting the Abbey and its Wild Animal Kingdom. There is a monthly farmers' market.

For a sedate, select and expensive village, you would look at **Aspley Guise**. Middle-class Victorians regarded it as an 'inland Bournemouth', but modern estate agents like to describe it as 'the Darling Buds of May of Milton Keynes'. It is very traditional. People smile and say good morning to each other, and they bother to keep the village tidy. There is a hotel, and the railway station is tiny. People pay a lot to live here and then stay a long time. A two-bedroom Victorian semi would cost £200,000; a modern four-bedroom house from £400,000. The finest house in the village is Aspley House, believed to have been built by an assistant to Wren, or perhaps even by Wren himself.

Eversholt (within reach of Aspley Guise), on the other side of the Woburn Estate, is typical of the Duke of Bedford's estate in that the rows of cottages have no front doors. It is said that the Duchess didn't like to see people gossiping. A four- bedroom barn conversion would cost over £1m.

Ridgmont is a typical Bedfordshire estate village with cottages built in two styles. There are two-up-two-downs with leaded lights that might sell for £250,000, or three-bedroom detached cottages built in the distinctive red brick of the late 19th century for about £300,000. A large period four-bedroom house on a quiet lane could cost £475,000. The newly completed bypass has reduced through traffic by 80 per cent.

Lidlington is another estate village where the Duke of Bedford sought to muzzle the gossips by building houses without front doors. It has a general store and two pubs. Villagers have voiced strong opposition to a proposed eco town on farmland nearby. Property prices are similar to those in **Millbrook**, which is little more than an old hamlet built for farm workers, with a pub and a golf course. The wooded valley near the church is supposed to have inspired Bunyan's Valley of the Shadow of Death in *Pilgrim's Progress*. A two-bedroom cottage with a courtyard garden might be bought for £170,000; the odd four-bedroom modern house, built to plug the gaps, might fetch £300,000 or more.

Stewartby was built as a model village in the Twenties by the Stewart family, owners of the local brickworks, as a gesture of concern for their employees. The village was extended in the Thirties and Fifties, and a worked-out quarry was flooded to create a lake for watersports within a landscaped country park. The village is the proposed location for a vast freshwater aquarium to be built by the National Institute into the Research of Aquatic Habitats (NIRAH). A three-bedroom semi here would sell for around £210,000; a two-bedroom house for £165,000. **Kempston Hardwick**, a request stop next along the line, is given mainly to light industry and has very little housing.

At **Bedford St Johns** you have reached the southern suburb of Bedford and the nursery slopes of the local housing market. Here first-timers can start out with a three-bedroom Victorian terrace at over £120,000, or a semi from £150,000. Something newly-built with two bedrooms and a garage starts at £140,000, with three it rises to £170,000. For Bedford itself, see page 104.

‘Stewartby was built as a model village in the Twenties by the Stewart family, owners of the local brickworks, as a gesture of concern for their employees’

> Continuation of main line

Journey: 35 min
Season: £3848
Peak: 4 per hr
Off-peak: 4 per hr

MILTON KEYNES CENTRAL The train service to **Milton Keynes** station is so good that it has a vast catchment area stretching all the way to **Daventry** (see page 126). It has some of the newest rolling stock, makes an effort with punctuality, and the trains run so frequently that you hardly need bother with the timetable. Parking, however, is fairly chaotic, with vehicles silting up the side roads rather than paying for the privilege of the multi-storey car park.

To enjoy Milton Keynes properly, you need to think American. The grid pattern of wide boulevards in the centre, with one of the largest covered shopping malls in the country (three miles of shopfronts and 230 stores), plus the sea of car parking, can make you feel as if the whole world has been turned into a supermarket. But the place is thoughtfully planned and very convenient, and the huge shopping area is about to undergo a £10m makeover. The 22,000-acre site, which includes Bletchley, Stony Stratford, Wolverton and 13 former villages, was conceived as a New Town in 1967 and was scheduled to contain a population of 250,000. It is expected to double in size over the next 20 years with 50,000 new homes.

Housing is arranged in segments, with a mix of starter homes, three- and four-bedroom houses and retirement flats in each one, ensuring a full range of age groups and incomes. There are a large number of commuters, but many people are employed locally too – major companies, including Abbey, Mercedes, Argos and BP, have moved here. The Open University and the University Centre Milton Keynes give it academic prowess, and the £19.6m Lottery-funded theatre and art gallery creates a cultural life. Because the town is so young, the population is young with it.

Milton Keynes prides itself on offering cheaper housing combined with a fast commute to couples who cannot afford to live in London, but who want to maintain their jobs in the capital. English Partnerships is running a first-time buyers' initiative in Milton Keynes, assisting with up to 50 per cent of the purchase price. Much emphasis in the design of new housing has been put on energy-saving. Not all the housing is new, however. There are still places where you can find old thatched cottages (and new thatched houses, too, for that matter).

The sports centres are as new and ambitious as you would expect. The Stantonbury Campus offers indoor and outdoor leisure on a large scale. For watersports there is Willen Lake, and winter sports enthusiasts have Xscape, the UK's biggest indoor real snow ski slopes. The Great Ouse skirts the northern edge of the town, as do the Ouzel and the Grand Union Canal. There are also several man-made lakes providing habitats for wildlife. North of the city centre is Linford

Wood, a remnant of an ancient forest now laced with footpaths, bridleways, picnic sites and two wildlife reserves.

Areas are considered upmarket or downmarket according to how closely together the houses are built, and how spacious they are. Perhaps one of the most desirable is **Woughton-on-the-Green**, where the plots are large, houses are traditionally built, and the cheapest three-bedroom semi would cost over £225,000. The **Bancroft Park** area is distinctive because the houses are built around a cleft in the landscape where an old ruin has been used to create a park. A three-bed detached house here would cost around £220,000. **Willen** is also popular because it has a lake and a sense of space. Many of the houses have been built by the owners themselves and a smart five-bedroom home might sell for around £500,000; a detached three-bedroom house for £260,000 to £300,000. In a typical mixed estate like **Bradwell**, a two-bedroom late Victorian cottage would cost £150,000; a two-bedroom new house slightly less.

One of the nicest villages is **Weston Underwood**, built in greyish Cotswold stone (it lies in the northern part of the same ridge of oolite that gives the Cotswolds its character) and dating mostly from the 17th and 18th century. Weston Underwood is entered through stone gates topped with pineapples. This designated conservation area remained in the ownership of the Throckmorton family until the 1920s, when it was sold. The green, overlooked by the house once occupied by the poet William Cowper, is decorated with trees and roses, and is the place to buy cream teas during August. The Cowpers Oak pub has opened a farm shop selling local produce.

A Georgian three-bedroom house in the centre of the village would cost around £350,000, rising to £500,000-plus for a larger property; an ex-council, three-bedroom, Thirties' semi on the edge of the village would cost around £220,000. There are a few new houses, but villagers fight tooth-and-nail against development. Their cause is helped by the watermeadows around the Ouse, which make much of it unsuitable for building.

Community spirit is strong, and is expressed through the fruit, vegetable and flower shows. There are walks through the woods at Salcey Forest. 'Village people try to get to know new people, but the big problem is that many of them are mortgaged so heavily that they are both working and we don't see a great deal of them,' says one of the older inhabitants.

> **'**Village people try to get to know new people, but many of them are mortgaged so heavily that they are both working and we don't see a great deal of them**'**

California-style home, Milton Keynes

The local shopping centre is at **Olney** – popular because it is as traditional as Newport Pagnell (see below) but more rural. It has a weekly market and a farmers' market once a month. Property prices tend to be 10 per cent higher than Milton Keynes. In the market square is the red-brick William Cowper museum, occupying another house in which the poet once lived. The town is famous for its pancake race, run every Shrove Tuesday from the market place to the church. The winning housewife gets a silver cup and a kiss from the verger.

Ravenstone, three miles west, is as pretty, expensive and exclusive as Weston Underwood. The village green sprouts stone houses. **Stoke Goldington** is the biggest in this clutch of villages, with new housing stitched in between the old. Another handsome stone village is **Emberton**, with 170 acres of country park and lakes along the River Ouse. Houses in these villages sell so easily that the owners often dispose of them privately. This entire belt is very convenient for railway users, and only a short drive from the M1.

Five miles north of Milton Keynes is **Castlethorpe**. This is an attractive stone village peppered with modern houses, but it is affected by the railway line running through it. A two- to three-bedroom cottage might cost £160,000 to £190,000; a four-bedroom detached house around £300,000 to £350,000.

To the north-east of Milton Keynes is **Newport Pagnell**, on the Rivers Ouse and Lovat. It has changed over the years from a lace-making town to an industrial and commercial centre. But it has managed not to become forbidding, and modern buildings are sandwiched quietly between the old Georgian houses. The cinema has been turned into a shopping arcade. A two-bedroom house in a Victorian terrace in the centre of town will cost around £170,000. The most popular road is Lakes Lane, where the houses back on to the common. A three-bedroom semi here will cost £250,000 or more. There are also some huge six-bedroom houses that could fetch up to £400,000. Green Park is the most popular of the new estates. A modern, four-bedroom detached house with a double garage will up to £350,000.

People living in the villages to the north of Milton Keynes might use Wolverton station as an alternative to Milton Keynes Central.

Journey: 50 min
Season: £3848
Peak: 3 per hr
Off-peak: 2 per hr

WOLVERTON Stony Stratford is now part of Milton Keynes, but still retains many original 18th-century buildings and seduces buyers quite shamelessly. As a quaint old market town, with a market square just off the High Street, it has quite a different character to the modernity which has swallowed it. The Old George Hotel presents a wobbly, black-and-white profile among the bakers, butchers and building societies that surround it. A Twenties' semi with three bedrooms might cost £280,000, but a good three-bedroom detached Georgian house would cost up to £375,000. The Milton Keynes western expansion area lies to the south with 6,000 new homes planned.

Wolverton has the local station and is packed with Victorian terraces, some of them reminiscent of *Coronation Street*. It falls within the Milton Keynes northern expansion area, brownfield sites are being regenerated and a glut of new-build means that property prices are relatively cheap. A new four-bedroom detached house would cost £350,000; a three-bedroom detached, £250,000; a period end-of-terrace three-bedroom house, £180,000.

To the west of Milton Keynes is **Upper Weald**, a hamlet of brick and stone. There are no shops, but you might find a small period three-bedroom cottage for £300,000 or more. It lies on the edge of the western expansion area and could effectively become a suburb of Milton Keynes once building is completed. Another place worth mentioning is **Wicken**, for its stone houses and church. A 300-year-old three- to four-bedroom stone cottage might cost around £460,000.

Further afield, on a hilltop in unspoilt countryside, is **Buckingham**, a typical market town where the stalls still appear on Tuesdays and Saturdays and there is a famers' market once a month. It remains a pleasure to walk through its steep narrow streets and admire the old inns and almshouses. You might be able to buy a Victorian detached house with four bedrooms and a large garden for £350,000. There are a few modern estates on the edge of town, of which the most popular is Page Hill. The average price of a four-bedroom detached house here is £290,000. The town is very close to Stowe public school, once the home of the Dukes of Buckingham. The gardens, studded with follies by Vanbrugh, Kent and Gibbs, now belong to the National Trust.

> 'It remains a pleasure to walk through the steep narrow streets of Buckingham and admire the old inns and almshouses'

Journey: 59 min (48 min one peak journey)

Season: £4148

Peak: 3 per hr

Off-peak: 3 per hr

NORTHAMPTON

It has to be said that Northampton is an unprepossessing town with a rugged commercial and light industrial bustle. Historically its prosperity came from the manufacture of boots and shoes, but in recent years it has widely diversified. There is a large brewing industry (the British headquarters of Carlsberg-Tetley), and Barclaycard and Avon Cosmetics have a substantial presence. The 13th-century market square claims to be the largest in England. An open-air market is still held here and a farmers' market takes place once a month. The Grosvenor Centre is a huge shopping mall with all the chain stores. Schools include the highly regarded private Northampton High School for Girls.

Northampton is a government designated expansion zone aiming to build 37,000 new homes and supporting infrastructure and services in the borough by 2021. About 8,000 of these have been built to date, mainly to the south and west of the town. A four-bedroom detached house here costs from £270,000 to £400,000. In the middle of the town, one and two-bedroom apartments in the Centro development cost between £126,000 and £169,000. Victorian workers' terraced properties can be picked up for between £90,000 and £220,000. Larger Edwardian terraces and semis in tree-lined streets sell for £180,000 upwards; Twenties' and Thirties' semis start from around £130,000.

The villages close to Northampton tend to be built of dark brown ironstone with roofs of slate rather than thatch

Northamptonshire has never been as fashionable as other counties north of London – people think of it as rather plain. There is little in the way of black-and-white building, and the villages close to Northampton tend to be built of dark brown ironstone with roofs of slate rather than thatch. To the north-west you will find some cottages built of cob (clay or earth bonded with straw), which require very careful maintenance. To the north-east, towards Kettering and Oundle, you break into a belt of bleached limestone. Being closer to East Anglia, the houses here will sometimes be thatched in Norfolk reed. Or they may have Collyweston slates – which are not slate at all, but slivers of very dense, light-coloured limestone.

Due west is **Daventry**, another small market town. It was once a coaching stop on the road to Holyhead; today it has an international railfreight terminal with links to Europe through the Channel Tunnel. Commuters have long been attracted to it, not only from London but also from Birmingham and Coventry, drawn by the M40 extension. The centre is being redeveloped to include an upmarket shopping complex and canalside apartments, in addition to 5,000 new houses across the town. A glut of new-build has caused the price of a new four-bedroom detached house with garage and garden to fall to around £170,000.

Just to the south-west of Daventry is the village of **Badby**, whose 700-year-old woods are famous for bluebells and beeches. The Knightley Way footpath, which runs for 12 miles to Greens-Norton, touches the western edge of the woods, which are a designated Site of Special Scientific Interest. The village itself is built in stone and slate, though there is the occasional thatched roof. The local thatched pub, The Windmill, is one of three buildings in the village that date from before 1500. There is a primary school and a village hall where the Brownies, Guides, WI and horticultural society meet. Within a mile you can climb to the highest point in Northamptonshire, Arbury Hill, whence you can see the Malvern Hills. Four miles southeast of Daventry is the sizeable village of **Weedon Bec**, which has the frustrating disadvantage of having the railway running

Contrasting terraced houses, Northamptonshire

Schools in Warwickshire, Northamptonshire, Lincolnshire and Peterborough

Rugby has the public school that gave its name to the game. It now takes both girls and boys, boarding and day. It is not to be confused with Rugby High, the academically excellent grammar school for girls, which is down the road in Bilton. Another high-scoring school is Lawrence Sheriff for boys.

Warwickshire has two other high spots, Stratford-upon-Avon and Warwick (both within reach of Leamington Spa station), each with a matching pair of high performing independent schools. Stratford-upon-Avon has the Stratford-upon-Avon Grammar for girls and King Edward VI for boys, while Warwick has King's High for girls and Warwick School for boys, as well as Myton comprehensive as a good local state school.

In Northamptonshire, Northampton itself has a good choice of public and private. The state schools include Guilsborough School, Northampton for boys and Campion School (mixed); the non-selective schools include Bosworth Independent College and Quinton House; the independent schools include Northampton High for girls, Northamptonshire Grammar for both sexes, and Wellingborough, which is co-educational day and boarding.

Oundle has the independent day and boarding Oundle School for boys and girls, and the Prince William co-educational comprehensive, to which children are bussed from all over the region. Good comprehensives include Southfield School for Girls and Bishop Stopford at Kettering.

King's School in Peterborough manages to be a kind of hybrid, because of the cathedral; it is a co-educational comprehensive with a good academic record and boarding facilities for choristers.

Venture into Lincolnshire and you find a host of high performing grammar schools in Grantham and Lincoln and most of the towns throughout the area.

---

through it without a station to compensate. It has a similar range of housing and prices to Long Buckby (see page 128), the next stop down the line. **Harpole** is closer to Northampton, and only just off the M1 at Junction 16. A four-bedroom detached cottage here could cost up to £350,000, though you might pick up a little Victorian semi for £250,000. Just down the road, on the south bank of the River Nene, is **Kislingbury**, a pretty stone village with some thatched roofs. It is relatively unspoilt though there is some new housing. Prices are similar to Harpole. A large five-bedroom detached house costs around £550,000.

If you want town life but find Northampton itself too depressing, then you might consider looking south-west to **Towcester**. It isn't as pretty as Buckingham and it has a large belt of new housing on one flank – a new four-bedroom three-reception-room house can be expected to cost from £250,000. The central focal points are the square and Town Hall. Towcester racecourse and Silverstone circuit are nearby. Off the main street, two- to three-bedroom Victorian terrace houses sell for around £128,000, and a rare large detached Victorian house would fetch £350,000. Plans are at the consultation stage to expand Towcester and build 3,000 homes and a bypass to the south of the town.

Roade is plainer still, offering a mix of traditional Northamptonshire stone, Victorian terraces and Sixties' estates. It is popular with London commuters because they have a choice of stations – Northampton or Milton Keynes – or they could opt to take the car down the M1. Property prices are higher than those in Northampton.

East of Northampton you could look at **Earls Barton**, which has a church with a Saxon tower, thought to be the finest in the country. The village has expanded to become a small town. It has Barkers shoe factory with a shoe museum in the grounds. The fact that it is a whisker away from the A45 makes it very convenient for people working in Northampton or **Wellingborough** (see page 106), where the boys' public school is situated. A small Victorian terraced house would sell for over £130,000; a detached house with four bedrooms would fetch £250,000 or more.

Journey: 95 min
Season: £4180
Peak: 2 per hr
Off-peak: 1 per hr

LONG BUCKBY Having grown up around the railway, canal and A5, the attraction of Long Buckby is good communications rather than charm. With a strong Victorian core and a plethora of Seventies' estates, it stretches for one-and-a-half miles and contains a population of 4,500. There are shops and a post office. A four-bedroom detached house might cost £230,000, but something grander in a landscaped garden could reach £380,000. A Grade Two listed, Regency country house would fetch around £895,000. The cheapest houses are Victorian cottages selling for up to £145,000.

Journey: 50 min (90 min London Midland)
Season: £6304 (all operators); £4600 (LM only)
Peak: 3 per hr (Virgin); 2 per hr (LM)
Off-peak: 2 per hr (Virgin); 2 per hr (LM)

RUGBY has never attracted architectural plaudits but it has managed to develop a certain vigour in the last few years and at night it buzzes with restaurants, nightclubs and bars. There is now a farmers' market once a month. The old industrial base has been replaced with a more commercial one. For rail-users, Rugby offers home-going commuters the fastest journey from London to any destination in this guide: the 82.5 miles take just 47 minutes, an average of 105mph. The journey up to London in the morning, at 50 minutes, is a rather more sedate 100mph. Holders of 'all operator' first class season tickets travelling by Virgin get a free breakfast and free snacks and drinks at other times. Rugby is best known for the boys' public school, used as a model for *Tom Brown's Schooldays*, where the eponymous ball game began in 1823 and whose former pupils include Rupert Brooke and Matthew Arnold. The Rugby Football Museum is opposite the school and Gilberts rugby football manufacturers are still going strong.

Small houses for first-time buyers in the centre of town sell at around £100,000. There is also cheap property in the **Brownsover** area, where you could buy a three-bedroom semi for £130,000. The more upmarket areas are **Hillmorton** and **Bilton**, where you could find a dignified three-bedroom semi for £140,000, or you could pay £200,000 to £300,000 for four bedrooms on a new development. In Bawnmore Road, Bilton, property becomes more expensive, rising to £545,000. In Hillmorton Road there are some substantial five-bedroom Victorian semis for which you could pay up to £430,000.

Living to the south of Rugby is thought to be slightly better than living to the north. Its most salubrious suburb is **Dunchurch**, a village two miles from the centre with a dozen black-and-white timbered houses, as well as large, detached, new four–six bedroom houses which sell for £400,000 to £500,000. There are also some period two-up-two-down cottages that fetch around £180,000. Second best is **Clifton upon Dunsmore**, to the north, which again has a villagey feel to it, though the houses tend to be smaller. A two-bedroom terraced cottage will cost £145,000.

For a proper village you need to look south-east to **Ashby St Ledgers**, one of the last good Northamptonshire thatch-and-stone villages before the more industrial Midlands takes over. It is remarkable in that it was an estate village, built by Lord Wimbourne in 1912 and designed by Lutyens. Development was so tightly controlled that there are only 44 houses in all – the tradition was that two new houses were built every time the lord of the manor died. There is an old barn on the green that serves as the village hall. Since the Wimbournes left, the village has changed hands three times and was bought by the Queen in 2005. There is a strong community spirit among the old villagers and a pub which strains at the seams. The half-timbered gatehouse next to the church is where Robert Catesby, one of the ringleaders of the Gunpowder Plot, is supposed to have met the other conspirators. Houses rarely come on the market, but for the privilege of living here you could expect to pay £300,000 for a Grade Two listed, three-bedroom, thatched terraced cottage.

Birdingbury, south-west of Rugby, is another sought-after village. It has only about 150 houses, most of which are now occupied by commuters rather than the agricultural workers for whom they were built. Houses tend to be a bit more expensive because it is so close to **Leamington Spa** (see page 146). A two-bedroom period cottage might cost around £240,000; a five-bedroom period detached, £600,000. The River Leam meanders through the village, and there is a fishing club. Cricket and football are played at **Marton**, a mile away. The nearest school is at **Leamington Hastings**.

Sheer convenience makes **Kilsby** and **Barby** commuter habitats. Both are beside Junction 17 on the M1, and close to Rugby. Kilsby is unremarkable but has a supply of four-bedroom modern semis selling for around £215,000. A four-bedroom detached period cottage costs around £320,000. Barby is smaller, with a stronger sense of village about it, and has a few old cob houses among the 19th-century and modern brick. A four-bedroom detached house here might sell for £240,000 or more. There are a few shops, a village hall, a school, and a claim to fame in that the MacLaren baby buggy was designed here in the Sixties by Owen MacLaren.

'In Ashby St Ledgers the tradition was that two new houses were built every time the lord of the manor died'

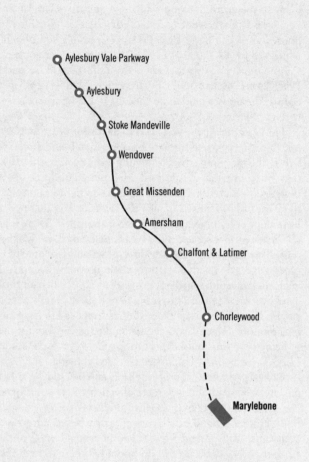

Aylesbury Vale Parkway

Aylesbury

Stoke Mandeville

Wendover

Great Missenden

Amersham

Chalfont & Latimer

Chorleywood

Marylebone

Marylebone

> Aylesbury (via Chorleywood)

Journey: 32 min
(Chiltern Railways);
39 min Metropolitan
Line tube to Baker
Street

Season: £2032*

Peak: 2 per hr
(Chiltern); 4 per hr
(Underground)

Off-peak: 2 per hr
(Chiltern); 4 per hr
(Underground)

*Travelcard
includes all Greater
London tubes, trains
and buses

CHORLEYWOOD The Victorian development of the railways created Chorleywood by making the lovely Chess Valley accessible from London. The M25 dominates and clogs up with traffic, but a scheme to widen the motorway is underway, which should alleviate the jams and make it possible to reach Heathrow in 20 minutes. Commuters tend to strangle the lanes with their parking rather than leave the car in the car park.

Nevertheless, people enjoy the large 250-acre common with its nine-hole golf course and the wonderful views across the valley – so much so that they are willing to pay £300,000 for a two-bedroom cottage, or over £800,000 for a four-bedroom detached period house in what is known as the station estate, a ring of Victorian and Edwardian houses built to take advantage of the first rail link with London. Berks Hill, South Road, Haddon Road and Hillside Road are all highly prized. The gated Loudwater estate once had the highest concentration of millionaires in the country. Prices are cheaper in the ring of Thirties' and Fifties' houses and outer ring of Seventies' and Eighties'. In Chalfont Lane, where large properties on one side of the road are set in a couple of acres, prices start at around £2m; on the opposite side, in half an acre, prices are from £1m. There are a few small flats from £150,000 – a price that in Watford would buy a two-bedroom house – but first-time buyers in Chorleywood are young City types who can afford to start at £200,000. Two riding stables, a business park and local pub have been swept away to provide upmarket housing where two- three-bedroom apartments cost around £500,000.

'The gated Loudwater estate once had the highest concentration of millionaires in the country'

In addition to the easy half-hour journey into London, Chorleywood offers a lively community, which makes good use of the public and club tennis courts, football and cricket pitches, and two village halls. The district beyond the village centre is very scattered. Houses trail up either side of the valley, leaving the shops in the bottom. This is inconvenient for elderly pedestrians, though there is a shuttle-bus service. Big shopping is done in Amersham and at the three-times-a-week market in Watford. Local schools retain a very high standard and reputation.

Journey: 34 min (Chiltern Railways); 43 min Metropolitan Line tube to Baker Street

Season: £2376*

Peak: 2 per hr (Chiltern); 4 per hr (Underground)

Off-peak: 2 per hr (Chiltern); 4 per hr (Underground)

*****Travelcard includes all Greater London tubes, trains and buses**

CHALFONT & LATIMER

Little Chalfont is a mini-town with a station, two schools, a post office, strip of shops, four restaurants, library and a number of very expensive houses in large grounds. 'Too spread out to be matey,' said one resident. Latimer is much prettier, with timbered cottages around a triangular green where a two-bedroom cottage will cost at least £450,000. 'It's the schools you see – the grammar schools are as good as the private,' says one agent. The River Chess, flowing past Latimer House, offers trout fishing. **Chenies**, equally picturesque, was a typical feudal village owned by the Dukes of Bedford for 400 years until 1954. Be prepared to pay £400,000 in either village for even the smallest cottage. A couple of miles north-west of the station is **Ley Hill**, a particularly lively and friendly spot with golf and cricket on the common, two pubs called The Crown and The Swan, and an infant and junior school. There are lots of local activities, including a dog training club, and there is talk of a farmers' market in the future. The wooded countryside surrounding all these villages attracts hearty backpackers who come to enjoy the spectacular walks.

Journey: 39 min (Chiltern Railways); 47 min Metropolitan Line tube to Baker Street

Season: £2720*

Peak: 3 per hr (Chiltern); 3 per hr (Underground)

Off-peak: 2 per hr (Chiltern); 4 per hr (Underground)

*****Travelcard includes all Greater London tubes, trains and buses**

AMERSHAM

The old town of Amersham is anchored by a 17th-century market hall. The High Street, lanes and little courtyards offer a picturesque variety of architectural styles from timber-framed houses to Georgian brick – sometimes just façades on much older buildings. A plethora of old pubs recalls the town's history as a staging post on the coach road from London to Aylesbury, and traffic still comes to a halt in September when the annual charter fair is held. The smallest period cottage can cost from £280,000, with substantial houses up to £1.75m. The new part of the town, Amersham-on-the-Hill, was developed in the early 1900s when the Metropolitan Railway Company brought City merchants and West End traders from Aldgate and Baker Street. As the last stop on the Underground, Amersham was considered the end of commuterland until motorways made distant villages accessible. The more modern housing includes ex-council flats from £170,000, three-bedroom semis from £280,000, and four-bedroom family houses at £450,000. There are cricket, football and hockey clubs, a swimming pool, a film society and several riding stables and pony clubs. People often move here to take advantage of the local grammar schools – Dr Challoner's for boys in Amersham, and Dr Challoner's High for girls in Little Chalfont. **Chesham Bois** (the name derives from the Boyes family, owners of the manor in 1276, rather than the surrounding woods) feels itself to be set apart from the rest. It has six schools, a well-managed common, a village shop and a powerful community heartbeat. The houses stand well apart from each other, some in an acre of land. Prices soar to £1.1m or more.

Chesham, only a short drive away, is also on the Metropolitan line. The town is beguiling, cupped by the Chiltern Hills and brushed by the River Chess which flows, with an accompanying riverside walk, through beech woods, past watercress beds and a trout farm. The shopping is good, with standard supermarkets and multiple stores, but also speciality shops, including a saddler, French baker and music shop. Sainsbury's brought with it The Elgiva Theatre as lucrative planning gain. Many of the shops front ancient buildings, some half-timbered 16th-century, others brick-and-plaster.

Journey: 46 min
Season: £2460
Peak: 4 per hr
Off-peak: 2 per hr

GREAT MISSENDEN

The narrow main street lined with houses and shops from the 15th to 19th centuries gives **Great Missenden** an intimate air and makes it an attractive small centre within easy reach of central London. It is also just a short stroll from the surrounding woods. High Street shops provide for day-to-day needs. Apart from a private tennis club there is little entertainment for the young in terms of youth clubs and cinemas. But it attracts buyers from Beaconsfield and Gerrards Cross who feel displaced by changes in their own neighbourhoods and come in search of old-fashioned peace and quiet. This is Roald Dahl territory – he is buried in the cemetery and the Roald Dahl Museum Story Centre is dedicated to him. A few born-and-bred residents live in the town centre, where 19th-century cottage conversions with two or three bedrooms cost up to £525,000. There is a good deal of later development within walking distance of the centre. Prices range from £270,000 for a three-bedroom semi to £375,000 for a newly built three-bedroom detached. There are also some handsome Edwardian houses set in mature grounds at around £1m. For a Thirties' four-bedroom house in a couple of acres you might expect to pay £1m to £3.25m.

'The Lee has some of the grandest houses ever set around a tiny village green and a picturesque pub'

The surrounding villages have a pecking order headed by **The Lee**, a secluded community in the leafy uplands above Great Missenden. It has some of the grandest houses ever set around a tiny village green and a picturesque pub. The rambling manor was for many years owned by the Liberty family, who did much to preserve the village. It is a conservation area so new development is frowned upon. There is 'a little new money, but they keep the properties as they should'. The area is favoured by captains of industry, writers and actors distinguished enough to need shelter from the public gaze. There is nothing under £400,000 here, and the average is £725,000 for a four-bedroom cottage.

Next in line is **Lee Common** (these villages are sometimes satirically nicknamed Lee Posh and Lee Common), separated from Lee by the Liberty Estate parkland where village shows and fêtes take place. The houses tend to be smaller, built for workers on the Liberty Estate, but it benefits from having a village shop and local primary school. A four-bedroom, semi-detached 19th-century cottage would cost around £450,000. For Thirties' houses overlooking green-belt farmland, look at **South Heath**. It has a sub-post office-cum-stores, and a likely price-tag of £625,000 for a four-bedroom bungalow.

Journey: 52 min
Season: £2680
Peak: 4 per hr
Off-peak: 2 per hr

WENDOVER The beautiful National Trust countryside of the Chilterns attracts a lot of walkers to **Wendover**. The tables outside the bistro cafés make a picturesque setting for a refreshment stop. Part of the Icknield Way, Europe's oldest highway, runs through the broad High Street, which is cobbled and tree-lined and offers lively shops, restaurants, banks, a post office and a library. There are many period houses, from Georgian all the way back to the enchanting thatch-and-timber row of Coldharbour Cottages, said to have been a gift from Henry VIII to Anne Boleyn. Infilling has been carefully done and blends well with the mature buildings. A three-bedroom semi costs around £235,000; a new five-bedroom house, £600,000. There is a first, middle and secondary school in the town and three golf courses in the neighbourhood, plus tennis, bowls and squash clubs, church societies and handsome old inns to gather in. Yet the town safeguards privacy by being too big for everyone to know everyone else's business.

At the turn of the century **Weston Turville**, north-west of Wendover, was breeding Aylesbury ducks for the London market and making straw plait for the Luton hat industry. Its older properties are on the eastern edge of the village, but they are well outnumbered by the modern developments. Family houses range from three-bedroom semis at £249,000 to four-bedroom detached houses at £455,000 or more. There is a small parade of shops, two good pubs, tennis courts and golf. The village has a combined first and middle school; older children go to grammar and secondary schools in Wendover or Aylesbury.

Journey: 56 min	
Season: £2760	
Peak: 4 per hr	
Off-peak: 2 per hr	

STOKE MANDEVILLE is little more than a suburb of Aylesbury. It has a general store, several pubs, a sports club and hotel, and a combined first and middle school, but is largely dominated by the world-famous hospital and a lot of Thirties' houses. These sell from £249,000 for a three-bedroom semi to £294,000 or more for a four-bedroom detached house with grounds.

Aylesbury	
Journey: 60 min	
Season: £3200	
Peak: 4 per hr	
Off-peak: 2 per hr	
*Some services go via Princes Risborough	

Aylesbury Vale Parkway	
Journey: 65 min	
Season: £3440	
Peak: 2 per hr	
Off-peak: 1 per hr	

AYLESBURY Commercial development has overshadowed a good deal of Aylesbury's ancient past. Its heart was cut out in the Sixties to make way for office blocks, and large council estates were built on the north side to accommodate London overspill. As if that was not enough, 17,000 new dwellings are due to be built by 2026, increasing the population from 60,000 to 100,000. The payback is that lots of money and energy are being poured into the town, revitalising the shops, creating a new civic centre and theatre, and improving public transport. A new station, **Aylesbury Vale Parkway**, has opened on the north side of the town to serve a 4,000-home development and the villages nearby. It links into Marylebone via Amersham and Harrow. Commuters prefer to live in the surrounding villages and farmhouses are the popular choice. For those who want something more modern, a three-bedroom semi goes for £149,000, a two-bedroom terraced house for £130,000, a one-bedroom modern apartment for £125,000. Aylesbury Grammar School for boys and High School for girls, and Sir Henry Floyd Grammar School have excellent reputations; and there is an unusually good selection of hospitals in the area. There is a big shopping mall, six-screen cinema, a regular farmers' market, a swimming pool, and the county museum with a special Roald Dahl exhibition.

Most of the surrounding villages have had their share of new developments but **Bishopstone** is still rural in nature despite the busy roads. A spacious, five-bedroom detached house costs £525,000. **Dinton** is blissfully peaceful and still has buildings made of witchert, proper grass verges and no street lamps at night. The future of Dinton Hall, where Cromwell's sword was once kept, has been a local hot potato for years – at one time it was to become a hotel with two golf courses – but it is now safely in private hands again.

To the north-west of Aylesbury, **Quainton** has all the ingredients of the chocolate-box rural idyll – pretty thatched cottages, a broad village green and a ruined medieval market cross, a restored windmill and a group of 17th-century almshouses with dormers and Dutch gables. Discriminating buyers will pay a premium to live here (it is in the catchment of Aylesbury Grammar). Prices range from £190,000 for a two-bedroom cottage to £450,000 upwards for a modern four-bedroom detached. It is a horsey area.

'Dinton is blissfully peaceful and still has buildings made of witchert, proper grass verges and no street lamps at night'

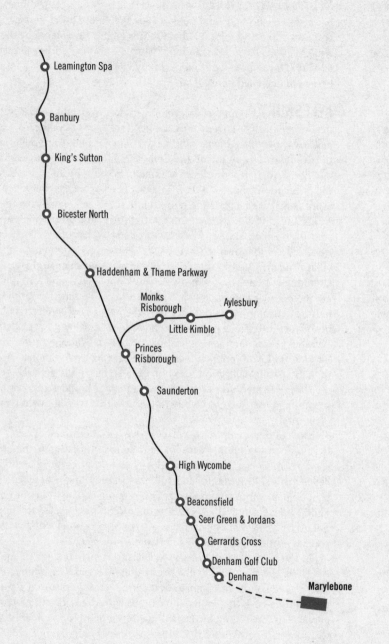

Leamington Spa

Banbury

King's Sutton

Bicester North

Haddenham & Thame Parkway

Monks
Risborough

Aylesbury

Little Kimble

Princes
Risborough

Saunderton

High Wycombe

Beaconsfield

Seer Green & Jordans

Gerrards Cross

Denham Golf Club

Denham

Marylebone

> Leamington Spa

DENHAM AND DENHAM GOLF CLUB If Denham had come straight out of the scenery department of the old Denham studios it couldn't be more picturesque. Only 18 miles from London, it is a patch of rural peace – village hall, small green and a stream winding past wisteria-clad old brick. It would be perfect but for the pub visitors whose motors clog the lanes, accounting for the village's sobriquet as 'the prettiest car park in Buckinghamshire'. Several of the houses are well hidden behind high walls and wooded gardens, so the area is perfect ambassadorial territory and a retreat for distinguished performers in both courtroom proper and courtroom drama. A three-bedroom semi will command £329,000. Larger houses go for £1.75m up to £5m. The other Denhams – **Higher, New** and **Denham Green** (which has a post office) – are simply a few streets of Thirties' semis and bungalows, and Fifties' houses, where a three-bedroom semi can be had for £299,000. Denham Golf Club is little more than a railway halt for the club.

The area is a retreat for distinguished performers in both courtroom proper and courtroom drama

Denham	
Journey:	28 min
Season:	£1760
Peak:	3 per hr
Off-peak:	2 per hr

Denham Golf Club	
Journey:	30 min
Season:	£1760
Peak:	1 per hr
Off-peak:	1 per hr

Journey:	25 min
Season:	£2040
Peak:	5 per hr
Off-peak:	4 per hr

GERRARDS CROSS Easy access to London by rail and road – M40, M25 and M4 all within spitting distance – has given the area around **Gerrards Cross** a reputation for being one of the most expensive in the country. Definitely not for the first-time buyer, this is classic stockbroker belt with tree-lined roads and grand Victorian and Edwardian houses in half an acre or so for up to £2.5m. There are some modern infills but these, too, are big and luxurious. Five-bedroom detached houses go for £800,000 to £2m. Locals have fought and lost a battle to stop Tesco elbowing its way in – they feared the loss of their much-loved butcher and patisserie. There is an M&S, an excellent book shop and fashion boutiques specialising in the super-thin. The population of commuters takes off early, leaving the centre to its small-town trading, and the common to dog-walkers treading the paths once haunted by highwaymen. Properties south-east of the town should be visited several times in different parts of the day as noise from the motorways can be a problem in some roads. Golf and tennis are the main sports. Both private and secondary schools have high standards and are well liked.

South of Gerrards Cross is the village of **Fulmer**, with its wonderful foodie pub The Black Horse, infant school and well-kept gardens. A Grade Two listed, two-bedroom detached cottage set in generous gardens costs £650,000. Further west is **Hedgerley**, which has two shops and a pub, a strong community spirit, summer fête and active conservation group. The lanes are lined with three- to four-bedroom detached houses with large gardens, selling at around £695,000. Lots of walks can be had from the back door here.

Journey: 37 min
Season: £2396
Peak: 2 per hr
Off-peak: 2 per hr

SEER GREEN & JORDANS Seer Green's old rural character has been changed by the Sixties' Manor Farm Estate estate where three- and four-bedroom semi-detached and detached houses sell for £275,000 to £450,000. In the rural setting of Long Grove, one of the finest private roads in the area, properties change hands for up to £4m. The village school is highly regarded. **Penn**, to the west, is a long straggling village with a green surrounded by Georgian houses and 17th-century cottages in timber or brick. Views over the surrounding beech woods are magnificent. William Penn lived here, a leading light in the Quaker Society of Friends. In the neighbouring village, **Jordans**, the Quaker connection continues with a barn built with timbers from the *Mayflower*. The village once hit the headlines because of the peculiarly English problem of cricket balls flying into gardens close to the cricket ground. This is a very cliquey area. Houses range in date from the 16th century to the 1940s, and are at a premium. A five-bedroom detached will command £885,000 here. Hopeful buyers

"Jordans is distinguished for the peculiarly English problem of cricket balls flying into gardens close to the cricket ground"

Part 16th-century property, Beaconsfield

need to be in the know to hear about a sale and estate agents count themselves lucky to get hold of a property here. The charming village centre was designed by Fred Rowntree in 1919, with gabled brick houses set well back from a central green planted with silver birch and poplar. There is the bonus of a good primary school.

Journey: 30 min
Season: £2440
Peak: 5 per hr
Off-peak: 5 per hr

BEACONSFIELD has a dual personality and a dual population. The old town grew at the crossroads of the coaching routes to Windsor and Oxford and is centred on a broad square and a pleasant green. Local people house-hunt in the Old Town for 17th- and 18th-century cottages, priced at £345,000 for a three-bedroom terraced home. Commuters prefer the convenience of the new town that has developed near the station since the 1920s. The average cost of a four-bedroom detached house is £645,000. Typical buyers include professionals and growing families, and young City strivers who move on up the scale to houses costing £2m to £4m. A good prep school and state schools with high reputations add to the attractions, but what used to be a strong community spirit is struggling to stay alive. It revives most energetically on 10 May for the annual fair. The Old Town has a posh furniture store, two jewellers and the Loch Fyne fish restaurant and there is a very popular Tuesday market and monthly farmers' market.

Journey: 33 min
Season: £2760
Peak: 5 per hr
Off-peak: 5 per hr

HIGH WYCOMBE has left behind the wool and furniture industries upon which it was founded in order to embrace modern industries. The result is a myriad of housing from large Victorian piles to Thirties' semis and modern houses which fan out on either side of the valley within a spit of the M40. But the feeling is that it became overblown in the Eighties and that a 'knock-down rather than expand' policy was a better one. One- and two-bedroom maisonettes start at £110,000, and there are plenty of starter homes for first-time buyers in the £130,000 bracket. At the upper end of the scale, a four-bedroom detached will cost £645,000. The smart places to be are on the fringes of the town in **Downley, Daws Hill** and **Bourne End**. There is a variety of schools with excellent reputations – Wycombe High and Wycombe Abbey public school for girls, John Hampden and the Royal Grammar for boys. Shopping opportunities have expanded greatly with the opening of the Eden scheme in the middle of town, which also includes a 12-screen cinema, bowling alley and restaurants. The Swan Theatre attracts celebrity acts and pre-London runs.

The surrounding countryside is very picturesque and often features in films and TV dramas, such as the BBC's *Little Dorrit* and *Vicar of Dibley*. Sought-after villages are to the west and include **Lane End**, which has a pretty, cottagey High Street with a pond, and **Stokenchurch**, where 18th-century brick-and-flint houses start at

£200,000 for two bedrooms. Both villages have basic shops and a post office, and a range of modern housing from £180,000 for two-bedroom cottages to £350,000 for a family detached. Farms and smallholdings in this area can run into millions of pounds.

Journey: 43 min
Season: £2920
Peak: 2 per hr
Off-peak: 1 per hr

SAUNDERTON
Though Saunderton itself is not much more than a station surrounded by small housing estates, it is the most convenient station for some of the prettiest villages in the region. To the west, in an area of outstanding natural beauty, is **Bledlow**. A compact collection of thatched cottages with a few modern arrivals, it dozes beneath Wain Hill, site of one of the two huge turf-cut crosses in the county. No further building is allowed at present in the village, because of its conservation status. There is a village hall and a pub, but no post office or shop. Young residents take their children a mile down the road to Longwick junior or to secondary school in Princes Risborough. Nearby **Lacey Green** is a sprawling village with a popular school, and an ancient windmill run by The Chiltern Society. Life is convivial and centres around the two pubs and busy village hall. A lot of new housing overshadows the few cottages, and the whole area is less cottagey than you might expect. If you can find something small with two bedrooms it will cost £200,000, but property in general here does not come up very often. Many houses are large, detached and swimming in ample grounds. A restored, period four-bedroom house would cost £750,000 to £850,000. The window dressing to look for is the superb view over the Vale of Aylesbury. Unlike other areas, where houses in outlying districts cost more than they do in town centres, prices in the villages around here vary little from those in Princes Risborough.

Journey: 43 min
Season: £2960
Peak: 4 per hr
Off-peak: 3 per hr

Converted barn, near Princes Risborough

PRINCES RISBOROUGH
is a pleasant market town with the relaxed feel of an overgrown village. The High Street is an attractive place to shop and stroll, but it is abandoned for the city each day by at least half the population. A market is held here every Thursday and a farmers' market once a month, and under the small Market House greengrocer's set up their stalls on Saturdays. The annual town festival in July is the highlight of the summer calendar. Human-scale architecture is here in plenty – no large

modern estates, just a few mellow 16th- and 17th-century houses set along little roads and cul-de-sacs. There are some Victorian terraced homes, not always in the best locations, costing from £215,000. Thirties' to Seventies' detached family houses cost from £300,000 for four bedrooms. Local schools take children through from toddler to late-teens, and local clubs include tennis and bowls. The most prestigious area is **Whiteleaf**, right on the flank of the Chilterns. It has a few cottages and a pub and a whole regiment of expensive houses with large grounds and paddocks, for which you should expect to pay at least £950,000. These tend to be owned by business people who belong to the local golf and cricket clubs.

> Line to Aylesbury

Journey: 61 min
Season: £3040
Peak: 2 per hr (a few by changing at Princes Risborough)
Off-peak: 1 per hr (changing at Princes Risborough)

MONKS RISBOROUGH No longer separated from Princes Risborough but rather a suburb of it, Monks Risborough has a few relics of its medieval past and some pretty cottages, but now consists mainly of Sixties' and Seventies' semis and plenty of bungalows which attract retired people. An estate bungalow starts from around £230,000; a roomy three-bedroom semi around £260,000.

Journey: 65 min
Season: £3060
Peak: 2 per hr (a few by changing at Princes Risborough)
Off-peak: 1 per hr (changing at Princes Risborough)

LITTLE KIMBLE Many of the villages in this area sprawl rather than huddle, and Little Kimble is typical. Its straggling lanes contain a mix of properties from a few listed 17th- and 18th-century cottages to 1900s and modern houses. The station house itself is a private dwelling. Prices for average-sized houses can be around 10 per cent above those in Princes Risborough. A three-bedroom detached stable conversion could cost around £455,000, and very occasionally houses with large grounds and paddocks come on the market (Kimble races is an annual event). Although there is no focal point there is a pub, an Indian restaurant and a village hall. With only 800 on the electoral roll, most locals would be able to call 'I spy strangers' when prospective buyers come knocking. Local activities include the WI, a Pilates club and a horticultural society which knows where to look for the rare wild orchids which bloom on the old rifle range. There is also the British Legion. Walks in the area take in Chequers and Ellesborough church, where successive prime ministers have offered the occasional photo opportunity. All Saints' Church at Little Kimble is renowned for its 14th-century wall paintings.

In Little Kimble the horticultural society knows where to look for rare wild orchids

AYLESBURY See **Marylebone to Aylesbury** line (page 135).

> Continuation of main line

Journey: 50 min
Season: £3200
Peak: 3 per hr
Off-peak: 2 or 3 per hr

HADDENHAM & THAME PARKWAY Whichever way you look at it, Haddenham is a pretty big village or a big pretty village, now split into two, the old and the new. The Sheerstock estate of two-, three-, four- and five-bedroom houses, priced from £200,000 to £450,000, is the new. The southern end is the old. Here the green and duck pond make an acknowledged beauty spot popular with television crews filming *Midsomer Murders* and Agatha Christie dramas. Here and there are walls made of witchert (the Saxon word for white earth) topped rather surprisingly with Spanish tiles, enclosing little lanes leading to attractive Georgian and Victorian houses. A Grade Two listed, detached cottage with a large garden costs £585,000. This is a great place for people to retire to. Otherwise, social life is divided into an energetic tennis-playing set who live on the new side, the old Haddenham agricultural and arts set, and new people form the social sandwich filling. Lots of residents commute to London on the M40. There are plenty of local sports, arts and activity clubs, and a village hall where it all happens.

'Haddenham is an acknowledged beauty spot, popular with television crews filming Midsomer Murders and Agatha Christie dramas'

Thame is distinguished by an unusually wide high street, which the annual fair turns into a medieval parade ground against a backdrop of houses from the 15th century to the present. There are plenty of three- and four-bedroom houses at around £300,000 to £600,000. It has three primary schools and good sporting facilities – football, rugby, squash and snooker – and a sports and arts centre. Some commuters prefer to drive to Princes Risborough for the better choice of early and late trains into London.

West of the A418, between Thame and Aylesbury, are three sought-after villages. **Cuddington**, which has a history of being elected best-kept village in Buckinghamshire, has a green and lots of old thatch. Three-bedroom semis start at £300,000. **Chearsley** has a green, pub, shop and church, but no longer a school. There is a pretty set of

Schools in Buckinghamshire

If they can afford the house prices, London parents in search of better state education will often find themselves looking at Buckinghamshire, which still retains its grammar schools. Remember, though, that they are highly selective.

Aylesbury has Aylesbury Grammar for boys, Aylesbury High for girls, and Sir Henry Floyd for both sexes. High Wycombe has a clutch of good schools: Wycombe High for girls, the Royal Grammar School (a day school for boys with some boarding), John Hampden High for boys and Wycombe Abbey girls school, which occupies a Gothic mansion in 160 acres.

Beaconsfield has Beaconsfield High (a grammar school for girls) and Amersham has one grammar for each sex – Dr Challoner's for boys and Dr Challoner's High for girls. At Marlow, the proximity of the Thames has encouraged Sir William Borlase's co-educational grammar to develop a strong rowing tradition. Other high-performing schools include Burnham Grammar, Chesham High in Chesham and the public school Stowe.

thatched cottages and prices are high. **Long Crendon** is considered to be the *crème de la crème* of the area. Once the centre of the needle-making industry, it has a picturesque High Street running off the market square, an attractive green, a primary school and several interesting pubs. It is the sort of place that everyone dreams of calling home, and properties here attract a 10 to 20 per cent price premium. The majority of people who live here work in Oxford.

Journey: 55 min

Season: £3500

Peak: 3 per hr

Off-peak: 2 or 3 per hr

BICESTER NORTH
Bicester has a long history – Bicester With Whaddon Chase Hunt dates back to the 1700s. Despite having an old market square (or triangle) and some 16th-century gabled houses, it stopped being a period piece when the army depot was established in 1941. The town is mainly regarded as a modern provider of very large housing estates with an edge-of-town factory-outlet shopping centre, but the sense of community is maintained with annual celebrations such as a carnival in July. The town centre itself is due to undergo a transformation, including more pedestrianisation, additional shops and a library. One-bedroom starter homes are priced at around £130,000; two-bedroom houses around £185,000.

Villages to the west of Bicester – **Steeple Aston** (see page 175) and the **Bartons** (**Middle** and **Steeple**) – have returned to rural tranquillity following the decommissioning of the USAF base at Upper Heyford, but now fear that large quantities of new housing will fill the gap. The District Council is opposing development due to the historic nature of the site. Meanwhile, the stone-built village of **Kirtlington**, where Christopher Wren's father is buried, has retained is popularity because of its polo park and stud farm. It has a village green with a pond, a post office stores, a couple of pubs and a junior school. New developments here are stone-built in cottage style to blend with the older houses. The larger four-bedroom detached properties cost £300,000 to £400,000. Small houses start at £250,000. An 18th-century cottage with two bedrooms would be likely to fetch more. 'People move here and don't move out again,' says one local.

Villages to the north of Bicester are good value. For the price of a three-bedroom house closer to Oxford, you will get four bedrooms in **Stratton Audley** – Stratton meaning enclosure on a Roman road, and Audley from the family who built the 14th-century moated castle. It is a tiny village where the houses group around the central green, but fears are mounting that the buffer which keeps it separate from Bicester – the land owned by RAF Bicester – will be sold off and used for new development. For £420,000 you could buy a substantial four-bedroom stone period house. Prices are about the same in **Stoke Lyne**, a similarly quiet Chiltern village set in undulating countryside where people are said to keep to themselves.

143

Just over the county border is **Marsh Gibbon**, with houses built of local stone rather than the brick and timber more usual in Buckinghamshire. A sprinkling of low-cost housing has been built here for sale to local families. The result is a busy little place with a village pond, a primary school and a younger than average age profile. A four-bedroom detached house might be found for £480,000.

Launton, back in Oxfordshire, is growing rapidly into a dormitory of Bicester, though the intervening railway and bypass prevents its being swallowed completely. It has a mix of old and young in both population and property. There are quite a few modern bungalows and new estates where a two-bedroom semi would cost around £185,000. Young children go the local primary. Their older brothers and sisters, in common with those from all the surrounding villages, attend secondary school or sixth form college in Bicester.

Journey: 80 min
Season: £4120*
Peak: 1 every 2 hrs
Off-peak: 1 every 2 hrs
* Also valid to Paddington (see Paddington to Oxford and Evesham line, page 175)

KING'S SUTTON A few London commuters travel regularly from

King's Sutton. Others prefer to drive to Bicester, which has a more frequent service. The majority of local residents work in Banbury or Oxford. Apart from the village green, which is dotted with thatched cottages and 18th-century stone houses, the property mix is almost exactly 50 per cent old stone houses, 50 per cent council brick, which residents say makes for a good community. They take advantage of the opportunities to get together through the Playing Fields Association, small tennis club and two churches. There are three village shops, one with a post office, and three pubs. Children go to

Local stone ex-weaver's cottage, Deddington

the local primary school, then to Middleton Cheney Secondary. Despite the fact that several farms and barns have been sold off for conversion, there is still a farming presence. A stone-built four-bedroom house costs £320,000; a two-bedroom cottage with a garden £200,000.

Neighbouring **Charlton** is a one-street village with a popular pub. Pleasant stone houses cost from £500,000 for a Grade Two listed four-bedroom cottage with walled garden. **Aynho** has pretty cottages, too, plus one or two Georgian houses priced at around £450,000 for four bedrooms. Both Aynho and **Souldern** have been badly affected by noise from the M40, but those who don't mind say the A41 was bad enough anyway. There are some big properties around here, hidden away in a couple of acres, and for £620,000 you could find something quite special.

Deddington, a couple of miles south-west of King's Sutton, was equal in importance to Banbury until the canals and railways bypassed it. It is officially a town, but its atmosphere is villagey and it is most sought-after. Houses and small shops gather around the spacious market place, where a thriving, award-winning farmers' market is held on Saturdays. Side roads are lined with honey-coloured stone houses and cottages, many of them Grade Two listed. A busy social life revolves around the primary school, the church, a variety of clubs from football, bowls and badminton to yoga and nature conservation, and there are a number of cottage businesses. Residents work locally as surveyors, accountants and solicitors, and the area is also popular with pilots flying from Heathrow and Birmingham. 'They put a pin in the map between the two and seem to hit Deddington,' says one local. Commuters have tended to drive to Milton Keynes, half-an-hour's train journey from London, but now that the Banbury line is so much better they don't need to. Otherwise, the M40 is close enough for convenience and has de-stressed the A423 between Oxford and Banbury. Prices range from £265,000 for a two-bedroom, double-fronted period cottage to £400,000 for a four-bedroom mid-terraced cottage near the village centre.

'Deddington is officially a town, but its atmosphere is villagey and it is most sought-after'

For train information, see overleaf

BANBURY has spent a lot of time burying its past in order to make way for a bright new future which is now bursting upon it, complete with a revamped shopping centre, new industries and improved rail links. House prices shot up to Oxford and Home Counties levels when the M40 arrived and its strategic position half-way between Birmingham and London could be cashed in. Commercial business parks and light industry lie to the east, Silverstone is 15 miles away, Eddie Jordan's Jordan Grand Prix is 10 miles away and the Benetton racing team is based nearby at Enstone. The older part of the town is

Journey: 72 min
Season: £4120*
Peak: 4 per hr
Off-peak: 2 or
3 per hr
* Also valid to
Paddington via
Oxford, but there
are hardly any
through trains and
the journey,
changing at Oxford,
takes 20 min longer
than to Marylebone

late-Victorian or early-Edwardian, but most properties are post-war. Small semis sell from £150,000, but on the more prestigious western side large Sixties' houses in landscaped gardens command £400,000. Parking at the station is easy enough.

The M40 has also had a mixed effect on the villages within five miles of Banbury. To the north-west, **Warmington**, which is very picturesque, **Shotteswell** and **Mollington** have all been adversely affected by noise; but **Wroxton**, a charming village with winding lanes, thatched cottages, grassy verges and a duck pond, has been made more accessible without suffering any serious damage. Just off the A422 to Stratford-upon-Avon (handy for a shot of Shakespeare), it preserves its tranquillity and yet is only a few minutes' drive from the motorway. It has a school and a couple of pubs, but no shop – people nip over to Horley or do their main supermarket shopping in Banbury. A small semi-detached brick-and-stone cottage with two bedrooms will cost about £279,000; a Grade Two listed, 17th-century thatched cottage of a similar size, £400,000.

On the whole, commuting professionals tend to prefer **Bloxham**, with the result that prices here are slightly higher than in neighbouring villages. There are several 16th- and 17th-century examples built in the local ironstone and buried down pretty lanes. The village has a parade of shops, a public school and good state schools. A couple of small estates of modern houses have brought more cars that clog the centre.

Shenington, too, is a popular and pretty village, full of lovely old golden stone houses. The presence of a rubbish tip not far away does deter some house-hunters, although most residents feel it is not a problem. There is also a neighbouring airfield where noisy go-karting is held, but this happens only a few times a year. The pub has seats outside on the verge of the green, and the primary school is a high-flyer. The charming cottages nearby fetch around £240,000 for three bedrooms, while larger four-bedroom stone conversions go for around £510,000.

Sibford Ferris, a little further south, has delightful mullioned houses with broad grass verges and a mellow blend of stone and thatch. It also has a village shop and post office and a well-respected Quaker school. Two-bedroom terraced houses cost £240,000. The price for a five-bedroom period house is about £535,000.

Journey: 90 min
Season: £5380*
Peak: 2 per hr
Off-peak: 2 or
3 per hr
* Also valid to
Paddington via
Oxford, but there
are hardly any
through trains and
the journey,
changing at Oxford,
takes 20 min longer
than to Marylebone

LEAMINGTON SPA The journey to Leamington Spa is much

quicker than it used to be, making it a viable commuter's haunt. In the past the people who chose to live in this spacious spa town, with its Georgian and Victorian houses and attractive riverside walks, often came because of the development of light industry between Leamington and Warwick. The delightful Royal Pump Rooms, where rich and poor once took baths and needle showers, have been restored as an arts centre, and the town now teems with designer boutiques. One of the nicest parts of the town is the tree-lined Beverley Road, offering a mix of Fifties' and Sixties' detached houses which sell from around £300,000, unmodernised, up to £425,000, restored. Northumberland Road is the most prestigious street, in which the price for a good-sized Twenties' house is £500,000, rising to £980,000 for the best.

Those who are willing to drive across five miles of farming landscape to Leamington station settle in **Harbury**, a lively village with a good community of mixed ages and a cosy, clustered centre near the church and pubs, with frills of modern housing around it. Small modern houses start at £240,000; larger period cottages go for £560,000.

Neighbouring **Bishop's Itchington** is known in estate agency terms as Harbury's poor relation – a three-bedroom end-of-terrace here goes for £162,000; a detached house for £229,000. **Bishop's Tachbrook** has a little row of shops, but the few thatched houses are well outnumbered by Sixties' and Seventies' red-brick estates. A three-bedroom semi will be in the region of £190,000; a semi-detached timber-framed cottage with three bedrooms costs £375,000. The higher price reflects the bonus of easy access to the extended M40, which tends to attract young professionals.

The delightful Royal Pump Rooms, where rich and poor once took baths and needle showers, have been restored as an arts centre

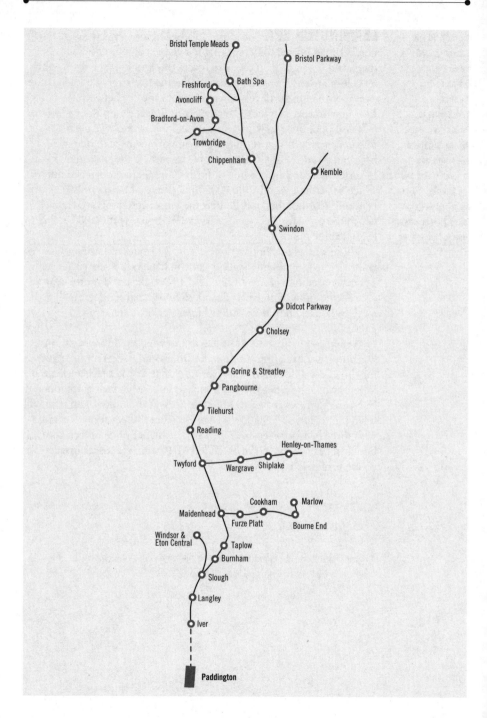

> Reading and Bristol

Journey: 29 min
Season: £1716
Peak: 2 per hr
Off-peak: 2 per hr

IVER This is a lovely village of 16th- and 17th-century cottages clustered around the church, with tree-covered lanes and Iver Heath nearby. Train frequency has improved, but people often use Slough where there are five trains an hour to London. A country cottage with two bedrooms and a small garden will cost £240,000, rising with the amount of land. There are one or two blocks of exclusive flats where you will pay around £180,000 to £270,000 for two bedrooms.

Journey: 32 min
Season: £1924
Peak: 4 per hr
Off-peak: 2 per hr

LANGLEY is really an extension of Slough, with lots of new housing developments. At its heart is the very popular 15th-century pub, the Red Lion, a Norman church and a rare 17th-century church library. The 17th-century almshouses provide a monastic touch. Houses range from £240,000 to £300,000 for a three-bedroom semi on a new estate, to £450,000 for a four-bedroom detached.

Journey: 18 min
Season: £2064
Peak: 5 per hr
Off-peak: 4 per hr

SLOUGH The huge trading estate – supposedly the largest in Europe – is the backbone of Slough, but it doesn't make it pretty to look at. Efforts have been made to improve the quality of life, and work is beginning on an ambitious £400m Heart of Slough redevelopment plan, which will provide a new Creative Hub, piazza and amphitheatre, as well as 1,500 new homes. The twin peaks of shopping are contained in the Observatory and the Queensmere shopping malls, while The Village has the specialist shops. There is also a leisure centre and a sports centre, a 10-screen cinema and an ice-rink. It is a great mix of council housing and private modern estates. New apartments in the town centre include Barratt Homes' Aspects Court, and the Mosaic development near the station where a one-bedroom flat costs about £135,000. Windsor Meadows is particularly sought-after by airline staff because it is ideal for the M4 and Heathrow. A one-bedroom studio starts at around £100,000. A small Victorian two-bedroom terraced house would cost £190,000; a larger three-storey town house might fetch £310,000. The large immigrant population has settled in certain areas, particularly Chalvey.

The train service to Paddington is astonishingly good – of the four off-peak trains an hour, two are now non-stop. The station has a pavilioned roof reminiscent of a French château, and there is good parking.

Watch out for the Heathrow flight paths in this area. **Colnbrook**, two miles east, is affected by low-flying planes, but has a good old pub called The Ostrich Inn and you can pick up a listed, detached four-bedroom barn conversion for £850,000. At the bottom end of the market, you could get a studio flat for £100,000. Two miles north, the landscape becomes suddenly rural and a village such as **Stoke Poges** feels very out-of-the-way. The poet Thomas Gray is supposed to have written his famous *Elegy* in the garden graveyard of the 13th-century St Giles Church, where he is buried. Stoke Poges is a cheaper version of Gerrards Cross, with a small parade of shops and a population peppered with both elderly and young stockbroker types. You might pay £550,000 to £650,000 for a four-bedroom period house in one of its tree-lined avenues. At the lower end of the market you could buy a three-bedroom house on one of the small Sixties' estates for £350,000.

Modern estate houses, south Buckinghamshire

It's the kind of place where a couple of decades ago you could have built a new house in your garden and still have had an acre to spare. Sunday afternoon walks are taken at Langley Park and Black Park.

> Branch line to **Windsor** and **Eton Central**

Journey: 26 min
Season: £2256
Peak: 3 per hr
Off-peak: 3 per hr
*£2512 for both
Windsor & Eton
Central to
Paddington and Eton
Riverside to
Waterloo (see
page 195)

No through trains. Change at Slough. See also Windsor & Eton Riverside on the **Waterloo to Reading** line (page 195).

> Continuation of main line

Journey: 36 min
Season: £2200
Peak: 4 per hr
Off-peak: 2 per hr

BURNHAM has quite a few modern shops, but still manages to cling on to some of its 15th- and 16th-century charm. The centre is quaint and busy with a cobbler, two butchers and a baker. A three-bedroom period detached house might cost £430,000. North Burnham is the place to be. It leads to Burnham Beeches with its huge pollarded beeches and winding lanes. Here a house with five bedrooms in an acre of land will cost around £1m. The area attracts successful stockbrokers, bankers and the odd television presenter.

The northern flank offers some classic Buckinghamshire villages. **Farnham Royal** and **Farnham Common** are strung between Beaconsfield and Slough. Huge houses set in several acres cost £1.3m to £3m. Horse-riding is the popular pastime for wives left at home while their husbands are in the City. Both these little villages are right on top of Burnham Beeches.

For less expensive housing you have to look at somewhere like **Cippenham**, where Barratt is building an ever-expanding community of new homes. It has a Asda and other stores and everything from one-bedroom starter homes for £120,000 to three-bedroom detached homes for £270,000 to £320,000.

The station is used by those who work on the Slough Trading Estate, as well as commuters to London. It has only a small car park.

Journey: 40 min
Season: £2340
Peak: 2 per hr
Off-peak: 2 per hr

TAPLOW This is where you start to find wonderful riverside villages with modest-sized yachts moored to the banks and anglers hunched beneath their green umbrellas. Taplow has lots of old cottages and a church built in 1911 with a distinctive copper spire. You can see Cliveden House, formerly the home of Lady Astor, in the distance on the cliffs above the river. Enormous houses with gardens running down to the Thames go for well over £1m, though in the village itself there are modern three-bedroom houses from £230,000. There are also lots of flats; a one-bedroom modern apartment will fetch £125,000. People who live here might prefer to go to Maidenhead or Slough to pick up the faster train service and park the car more easily.

In Taplow there are enormous houses with gardens running down to the Thames that go for well over £1m

Journey: 44 min
Season: £2432
Peak: 4 per hr
Off-peak: 4 per hr

MAIDENHEAD is an old Thameside town with an ancient heart, small shops, a pedestrianised High Street and a farmers' market twice a month. Facilities include a multiplex cinema, health club and restaurants. Just outside the centre you will find grids of reasonably pleasant turn-of-the-century terraced houses. Those with two bedrooms sell for up to £250,000. The modern developments are on the south-western outskirts, where three-bedroom semis cost up to £300,000. The most sought-after areas, such as Maidenhead Bridge and Boulter's Lock, are close to the river. Here the houses are large, detached late-Victorian, with big gardens and wealthy owners who can afford to pay £800,000 to £1.3m for four bedrooms. A short walk along the Thames is Brunel's Sounding Arch, a remarkably long brick viaduct built in 1838.

Bray, scarcely two miles out of Maidenhead, is a tiny picturesque village on the lip of the Thames and one of the costliest places to live even in this expensive area. It combines closeness to London with a good train service. The narrow irregular streets are lined with timber-framed and Georgian houses. A two-bedroom village house will cost £300,000. The Fisheries offers huge mansions in a woodland setting with a river frontage and prices from £5m upwards.

Remarkably, there are two Michelin three-star restaurants in Bray – the Roux brothers' famous Waterside Inn and Heston Blumenthal's Fat Duck. There is a clutch of resident television stars so the mere act of buying a pint in one of the two pubs can bring you up against Rolf Harris, and joining the local cricket team is likely to attract the interest of Michael Parkinson. The village has a post office and hair salon, and a hockey club and tennis court.

Just outside the village is Bray Studios, where the Hammer House of Horror films were made and short television dramas are still produced. Tourist coaches tend to drive straight through the village because there is no tea-room, although tea is served in the church hall on Sunday afternoons in summer. There are a few modern estates, but they are well-hidden.

Bray is a conservation area and regular regional and national winner of the Britain in Bloom competition. If you want to build anything new, or change the exterior of your house, you can expect heavy opposition. The risk of flooding in the area has been reduced by the construction of the Jubilee River, a large drainage ditch between Maidenhead and Eton.

Edwardian house, near Maidenhead

Heading south you come to the attractive village of **Holyport** set around a large green with a pond overlooked by two of the four local pubs. This is the site of the annual village fair in early June. Cricket on the green has been stopped because too many windows were broken, but enthusiastic cricketers continue to play on their own ground elsewhere in the village. Holyport has some huge Tudor and Georgian houses, and small former estate cottages. A house with half an acre might cost £1m. The village is too spread out to have a strong sense of community, but there is an active preservation society. There is some council housing, a few new private estates, a handful of shops and a primary school.

To the west is **Littlewick Green**, where the houses are built around the cricket pitch and the pub is called The Cricketers. This and neighbouring villages attract a lot of commuters – people running private businesses and staff from Heathrow. Another pretty village, still within the two- to three-mile belt around Maidenhead, is **Pinkneys Green**. It has some huge old houses that sell for over £800,000, and the National Trust house Maidenhead Thicket. The first Girl Guide troop was formed here by Olave Baden-Powell in 1910. Another village worth considering is **White Waltham**. It is very rural, has a thriving primary school, a small airfield, and an active cricket club. Detached estate houses sell at £600,000 to £900,000. Then there is **Hurley** on the Thames, with a lock, a 12th-century pub and a working boatyard. A period two-bedroom cottage might cost around £495,000, a five-bedroom Twenties' manor house £2m.

> Branch line to Marlow via Furze Platt, Cookham and Bourne End

There are no through trains to Paddington from Marlow. There is one through train per hour from Bourne End, peak only; otherwise change at Maidenhead.

Journey: 69 min*
Season: £2768*
Peak: 2 per hr
Off-peak: 1 per hr
* From Marlow, changing at Maidenhead

The service connecting these stations to Maidenhead is nicknamed the Marlow Donkey: it is very short and slow. The line follows the river and lifts its head out of the valleys to give good views. The area is close enough to London for people to commute by car, either on the M40 or on the M4.

Furze Platt station was built in 1937 to serve north Maidenhead, which had been taken over by light industrial development. A spread of new housing has followed in its wake over the last 25 years. At **Cookham** you are in prize countryside now grazed by commuters and television celebrities, swags of it owned by the National Trust. The

Schools in Berkshire

Ascot has a clutch of girls' private schools – St Mary's School Ascot, which is Roman Catholic, Hurst Lodge, Marist Convent and St George's. For boys the dominant school is Eton, at Windsor, which can count 19 former prime ministers among its old boys. There is also Pangbourne boarding and day school for girls and boys, which has a strong naval tradition, and Wellington at Crowthorne for boys (girls in the sixth) with a strong army tradition. In Maidenhead there is Newland Girls' comprehensive.

Reading has Reading School, an unusual state day school for boys (some boarders) with a working week that extends into Saturday morning. For girls there are two independent schools – Queen Anne's boarding and day and The Abbey – as well as Kendrick Girls' Grammar. For boys there is Bradfield College public school and the Roman Catholic boys' school, The Oratory.

Co-educational private schools include Leighton Park and Reading Blue Coat School (mostly boys). Little Heath at Tilehurst is a good co-educational comprehensive. Further out towards Thatcham, girls can attend Downe House (boarding and day), where first-year pupils spend a term at a château in the Dordogne.

Cookham Society actively opposes inappropriate development. The snob address is Cookham Dean, up on the common, where house prices start at £300,000 for a two-bedroom semi and go on to £3m or more for a large riverside house. Cookham Village is old and lovely, with chic restaurants and boutiques in the High Street. Stanley Spencer lived here, and the Spencer Gallery shows some of his works. There is a general store and an excellent butcher. The Cookham Rise area was expanded in the Fifties, close to the brick and flint station building. A three-bedroom semi here costs around £300,000; or you might find a small cottage at around £320,000. Three- and four-bedroom houses in Stanley Homes's small Hatch Gardens development cost from £400,000 upwards. The riverside towpath provides walks and rides for ponies, but if you want to swim or go to the gym, the nearest leisure centre is at Maidenhead.

The river village of **Bourne End** is just as expensive, and much of the social life revolves around sailing. The Upper Thames Sailing Club is here and the Bourne End Marina is top notch. A two-bedroom wooden chalet on Wharf Lane, with mooring, costs about £675,000; a new three-bedroom house in a nearby gated estate, £700,000. A more substantial, secluded riverside home, typical of the area, with six bedrooms, a boathouse and half an acre running down to the river, would sell for £2.7m to £3.2m. A large proportion of the population commutes, but they tend to drive to Beaconsfield (see page 139) and get the train to Marylebone rather than suffer the Marlow Donkey.

Marlow is also prime commuter country. Its ancient High Street stretches down to the river and has a proper fishmonger, chocolatier, a twice weekly market and a monthly farmers' market. Burford County Combined School is a high-performer in the league tables. A two-bedroom Victorian cottage would fetch over £300,000; a three-bedroom terrace around £300,000; a three-bedroom Edwardian house £650,000. Large houses on the river rarely come up for sale and cost at least £2m. The west side of town is considered better than the east. At Marlow Bottom, two miles from the centre, is a huge modern estate with detached houses selling from £395,000. Since it is on the Berkshire, Buckinghamshire and Oxfordshire borders, parents can choose the local education policy that suits them. At nearby **Bisham** is the famous Compleat Angler restaurant and the Marlow Rowing Club, together with some very pretty Tudor cottages, but it is rather spoilt by the heavy through-traffic into Marlow. The parish council has bought an orchard for people to play in and have picnics. Bisham Abbey is home to the National Sports Centre.

> Continuation of main line

Journey: 52 min
Season: £2852
Peak: 3 per hr
Off-peak: 4 per hr

TWYFORD is a typical small town surrounded by countryside. It has all the essential shops and is referred to locally as 'the village'. There are rows of Victorian terraces close to the station. Two-bedroom houses here sell for £190,000, three bedrooms go for around £240,000. The huge, tightly-packed new estate has starter homes at £170,000, up to four-bedroom detached houses at £500,000 upwards. The older, more established and expensive part of the town is **Ruscombe**, with prices ranging from £350,000 to £800,000.

Waltham St Lawrence is two miles away, trapped in a rural world of its own. The price of this, in the form of a detached house with land, is over £850,000; a three-bedroom cottage costs from £500,000. Charming black-and-white cottages mix with modern houses. The village owns its pub, The Bell, and a general store with a part-time post office. There is a good primary school within walking distance, as well as Brownies, playgroups, a cricket club and a silver band. The cricket team plays at **Shurlock Row**, which is rather smaller and pretty, with a pond at the end of the main street. It has a much-respected butcher and two pubs, the Royal Oak and the White Hart. Prices are slightly lower than in Waltham St Lawrence.

For cheaper properties you have to look at the dense modern housing at **Woodley**, built on the aerodrome used by Douglas Bader. Here a three-bedroom detached house might cost over £280,000. At **Charvil**, a popular commuter dormitory, a modern three-bedroom terrace could be had from £240,000 upwards.

‘The village owns its pub, The Bell, and a general store with a part-time post office’

> Branch line to Henley-on-Thames via Wargrave and Shiplake

Journey: 64 min*
Season: £2984
Peak: 1 or 2 per hr
Off-peak: 1 or 2 per hr
* From Henley-on-Thames, changing at Twyford. There are 2 through trains to Paddington in the peak period (journey time 46 minutes). For all other services, change at Twyford

Wargrave lies on a charming stretch of the Thames, and its narrow streets, trees and Georgian timber-framed houses on the river make it a rather prestigious place to live. Paul Daniels has a mansion nearby. But flooding is a hazard here – the 2007 regatta was cancelled because of it. You could get something with three bedrooms on a modern estate for between £325,000 and £450,000, but good secluded houses start at £650,000 and go well over the £1m mark. **Shiplake** is similarly expensive and exclusive. It has a number of new developments on which four- to five-bedroom detached houses cost from £750,000 to £1m.

The rowing regatta, held during the first week in July, has put **Henley-on-Thames** on the map. The first inter-university boat race was held here in 1829, and by 1839 it had become a recognised annual event, the story of which is told in the River and Rowing Museum. The hordes of people who come to drink Pimms in the pink-and-white marquees give the town an annual seizure. Though it remains pretty and rural, straddling the river by way of a lovely stone bridge, it has been affected by the influx of money. Two supermarkets have joined the good mix of small shops already here. The battle to keep the old cinema (complete with organ rising up out of the floor) was lost and it is now a three-screen complex. The organ moved to the Town Hall where it is used for concerts. Two-bedroom Victorian cottages sell for around £275,000; larger terraced houses with no parking sell for around £350,000. Anything large with a river frontage would have a starting price of over £1m. Commuters often opt for flats with views of the river – two bedrooms might cost £400,000.

'The hordes of people who come to drink Pimms in the pink-and-white marquees give Henley an annual seizure'

Hambledon, four miles away, is also worth looking at, if only to admire the cluster of houses around the huge chestnut tree with the village pump beneath. Film location hunters love it. The village has a church, general store and post office, cobbled pavements and a pretty little stream running through. Properties rarely come on the market. A small cottage with no rear garden or parking might be picked up for £350,000.

Riverside residence, Henley-on-Thames

> Continuation of main line

Journey: 29 min

Season: £3492*

Peak: 10 per hr

Off-peak: 9 per hr

*****Also valid to**

Waterloo

READING is a significant shopping and business centre and a university town. It has a farmers' market twice a month. Its prosperity used to be based on beer (Courage), bulbs (Suttons) and biscuits (Huntley & Palmer), but now it has a much higher profile as the gateway to 'silicon valley'. Seven out of 10 American IT firms have bases here, including Microsoft and Oracle. The train service to London is superb – about one every 7 minutes in the peak and only a little less frequent off-peak – as it is one of the busiest rail interchanges in the country (see also **Waterloo to Reading**, page 207). Reading is also the terminus of the Kennet and Avon canal, which offers some marvellous walks to the west.

Different areas cater for different tastes. On the Thames, **Caversham Heights** has a mix of detached houses, flat conversions and modern apartments, and is very residential. The most expensive address is The Warren, up on a hill with river views. A two-bedroom flat in an Edwardian conversion with a mooring and garden sloping down to the river would sell for around £290,000. A large, five-bedroom Edwardian house in three-quarters of an acre costs about £895,000. **Lower Caversham** offers mainly Victorian terraced housing with some modern infilling. A three-bedroom terrace would cost £190,000; a modern two-bedroom flat on the river, £340,000. **Caversham Park** village is made up of town houses built a couple of decades ago. Prices tend to hover between £200,000 and £300,000, which makes it attractive to young families and first-time buyers. **Emmer Green** is very Thirties, with a lot of open land and golf courses. A three-bedroom semi here would cost around £230,000.

West and east Reading are cosmopolitan, and prices are slightly lower. A one-bedroom flat would cost £110,000; a three-bedroom Victorian house up to £220,000. To the south is **Lower Earley** (see page 206) and to the west **Tilehurst** (see page 158), both with their own railway stations. A three-bedroom semi costs from £200,000 to £300,000. **Whiteknights Road**, where the university is situated, has large Edwardian houses that sell from £350,000 to £500,000.

The popular villages nearby include **Pangbourne**, **Goring** and **Streatley** (see page 158). **Sonning Common**, just inside Oxfordshire, is not beautiful in itself, but it lies in a sleepy and countrified area. It has a swag of shops, a bank and a vet. A two-bedroom detached bungalow might be bought for £250,000 upwards. Most of the villages to the south of Reading are not particularly outstanding in any way.

Journey: 70 min (47 min by changing at Reading) Season: £3492 Peak: 2 per hr Off-peak: 2 per hr	**TILEHURST** is a western suburb of Reading. A three-bedroom semi costs between £175,000 and £310,000.

PANGBOURNE, just five miles off the M4, is a riverside commuter haven where the Thames meets the Pang. This is where Kenneth Grahame, author of *Wind In The Willows,* lived and where the buffoons in Jerome K. Jerome's *Three Men in a Boat* stopped off. Canoeists and boating tourists now cavort in the shallows. Its discreet Georgian charm, with its square, weir and meadow, has developed a certain hustle as the population has swollen to 2,500. Local people say it is so busy that you can't cross the road in the rush hour, yet during the rest of the day it is so quiet you can lie down in it. There are old-fashioned shops, including a butcher and baker, as well as an organic supermarket, restaurants and take-aways. Pangbourne, the co-educational public school, stands on Pangbourne Hill. Prices are high. A modern semi in Kennedy Drive would cost from £220,000; a Victorian terrace, £250,000 to £275,000; a period detached house around £475,000 and more. Flats with river views will fetch £200,000 to £265,000. Much larger houses go for anything between £750,000 and £1.5m.

(Journey: 74 min (51 min by changing at Reading) Season: £3492 Peak: 2 per hr Off-peak: 2 per hr)

GORING & STREATLEY sandwich the Thames between them. Both are expensive and pretty, with enough shops to make life manageable. A Victorian semi with three bedrooms will cost £350,000 upwards. Streatley doesn't have the frill of modern housing on its outskirts that Goring has, and it has the Swan on the towpath, which is a seductive hotel.

(Journey: 79 min (56 min by changing at Reading) Season: £3492 Peak: 2 per hr Off-peak: 2 per hr)

CHOLSEY is sprawly, so the prices here are lower. Its main feature, a pretty village green edged with listed cottages, has to face down the parade of modern shops on the other side. The shops and post office are useful and there is a good primary school. The parish magazine carries six pages of clubs and activities to join, including the busy horticultural society, the Cholsey Silver band, and the Cholsey and Wallingford Steam Railway, which is run by volunteers. Agatha Christie is buried here. A three-bedroom house on a modern development would cost from £200,000.

(Journey: 84 min (61 mins by changing at Reading) Season: £3492 Peak: 2 per hr Off-peak: 2 per hr)

Journey: 45 min

Season: £3996

Peak: 6 per hr

Off-peak: 3 per hr

DIDCOT PARKWAY Didcot itself lacks any romance. It has about

25,000 residents and is soaking up new housing like a sponge with 3,300 homes, as well as schools and sports facilities, due to be built before 2018. Recent improvements to the town centre have included a shopping centre, Sainsbury's, five-screen cinema, Centrepiece theatre and the £7.4m Cornerstone arts centre. The most attractive part is **Northbourne**, which is old Didcot and still very beautiful. **East Hagbourne**, just outside, is distinctly special, displaying all the architectural eclecticism of the area – timber frame, thatch, zig-zag brickwork – clustered around the old village cross by the church. **West Hagbourne** is similar, but quieter, with a village pond. Both are popular with staff at the Atomic Research Station at Harwell who can afford to pay from £500,000 for a three-bedroom 17th-century cottage. The tranquillity of the Hagbournes is under threat from plans to build a bypass south of Didcot.

Perhaps the village with the most charm and vigour is **Blewbury**, set against the Downs. The village has pretty old inns, a football club, a cricket green, brass band, church choir and a dramatic society. Once you get off the B4017 the prices are high. A four-bedroom Victorian cottage with garden and annexe, costs around £700,000; a four-bedroom modern house on a small new development, £435,000. The asking price for a new five-bedroom eco-home, with ground-source heating and rainwater reservoir, is £635,000. **East Hendred**, to the west, is a typical Downland village peppered with thatch and timber. It is close to the ancient Ridgeway, which enables you to walk at a giddy height for miles in either direction. 'It's very horsey and a bit arty-crafty,' is how one local resident describes it. **Harwell**, by comparison, is plainer with plenty of workmanlike Victorian houses. A three-bedroom semi-detached cottage here can be had for £330,000; four-bedroom modern houses cost up to £480,000.

The combination of riverside with proximity to London makes some of these villages obvious film-star territory. **Shillingford**, on a bridge over the Thames, and **Warborough** both reek of money. **Wallingford** has a pretty shopping centre with a bookshop and lots of Georgian houses. Riverfront houses cost from £500,000 into the millions; in the side streets a Victorian three-bedroom terrace will cost £250,000. The town is the fictional Cawston in the television drama *Midsomer Murders*.

> '**East Hendred is close to the ancient Ridgeway, which enables you to walk at a giddy height for miles in either direction**'

16th-century thatched cottage, Blewbury

Journey: 61 min
Season: £6848
Peak: 5 per hr
Off-peak: 4 per hr

SWINDON itself is architecturally brutal though wonderfully convenient for commuting, since the Inter-City trains take a last breath here before sprinting on to the West Country. Big businesses such as Motorola, Honda and the Nationwide have their headquarters here. Professionals, bank managers and the wealthier shopkeepers huddle together in the **Old Town**, in Victorian and Edwardian houses on the south side of Bath Road. A three-bedroom terrace at the cheaper end of the market here would cost £155,000. Four bedrooms in a more expensive road would fetch £300,000. **Lawn**, near the lake and nature walks of Coate Water Park, is also sought-after. Thirties' style, five-bedroom detached houses with gardens cost £370,000, new homes about £600,000. Residents are hotly opposing plans for 1,800 dwellings and industrial estates near the water park. **Broome Manor**, with its golf course and a mix of modern Georgian, Regency and ranch-style houses selling at £540,000, evokes the atmosphere of Dallas.

'People tend to flee Swindon for the chalk villages of the Marlborough Downs or the Vale of the White Horse'

People tend to flee Swindon for the chalk villages of the Marlborough Downs or the Vale of the White Horse. The east is more popular, with villages such as **Liddington**, **Wanborough**, **Bishopstone** and **Aldbourne**. These are cohesive, and tend to have primary schools, huge churches and pubs that are still free houses. A four-bedroom house could be bought for between £350,000 and £450,000 depending on position. Ex-council properties sell at around £150,000. Although the villages are only just off the M4, they are seriously horsey and have some prime hacking country right on the doorstep. A walk across the Berkshire Downs connects us to the past as surely as any history book. The white horse is at **Uffington**, against the Ridgeway near Dragon Hill, where St George is supposed to have killed the dragon. It is worth remembering that the further east you go from Swindon, and the nearer you get to **Hungerford** or **Faringdon**, the more attractive the villages and the higher the prices.

Country house, Swindon area

The National Trust owns much of the land to the north of Swindon, including the villages of **Coleshill** and **Buscot**. Here the infant Thames is hardly more than a stream running beneath the willows. **Lechlade** is idyllically pretty with a good collection of Georgian houses, but it fills with boating people in the summer and, being 10 miles from Swindon, is a bit of a slog to reach at the end of a hard day. The stone for St Paul's Cathedral was loaded here.

House style in the West

The great prize in the west is the Cotswolds, where the houses around the upper Thames, the Cherwell, the Evenlode, the Windrush and the Colne rivers are built quite literally out of the landscape. They lie in the great belt of yellowy grey oolite which, when cut and dressed, makes each village street look as natural as an outcrop of stone.

Even the most humble cottages have a kind a churchy grandeur given to the them by the stone, and a decorativeness associated with wealth, including mullioned windows, arched doorways and drip-stones. The real money was made from the sheep dotted across the hillsides and the woollen industry of the 14th and 15th centuries. The roofs, usually made with layers of stone slates and gabled windows to let the light into the top rooms, give that distinctive rhythm which brings tourists by the coachload to admire the scene.

South of Oxford you enter brick country, but there is also some clunch, taken from the Berkshire Downs, and around Aylesbury there is a chalk and clay mixture known as witchert. Many of the houses have lost the thatch they once had – a steep pitched roof is often a clue to the fact that a house was once thatched. Flora Thompson's *Lark Rise To Candleford* is perhaps the best description there is of cottage life in this area at the end of the 19th century.

West of Swindon you reach the great sweeps of the chalk uplands with their ancient barrows, stone circles and white horses cut into the hillsides.

Eventually you come to the toffee-coloured stone of Bath, turned into the gracious 18th-century crescents and squares that make the city so attractive.

Fairford is a thriving community, with shops, active local societies and a church with 500-year-old stained glass windows. A small Cotswold house with two bedrooms might sell for about £190,000. The old gravel pits at **Whelford** are popular with watersports enthusiasts.

Villagers driving into central Swindon from the west have to contend with the volume of traffic. **Wootton Bassett** is a large market town with a good range of local shops, including a delicatessen. Nearby Hackpen Hill has a white horse on its flank. There is a weekly market – once so disorganised that an early photograph shows a large cow emerging from a solicitor's office – and a farmers' market takes place once a month. You can buy studio apartments for £98,000 and ordinary little three-bedroom semis for £170,000 to £200,000.

The **Somerfords** (**Little** and **Great**, divided by the River Avon), are popular because they border the Cotswolds and are closer to the prettiness of **Malmesbury** and its beautiful 12th-century abbey ruins than to the dead weight of Swindon. Great Somerford has a combined shop and post office. They have lots of local societies, from under-fives to the Somerford Stagers amateur dramatics group. Great Somerford also has a primary school. An interest in horses is a useful social passport. The Vale of the White Horse Hunt is on the doorstep, there is polo at Cirencester Park and endless bridleways and footpaths criss-cross the Cotswolds. The price of a new detached house with four bedrooms, two bathrooms and a double garage is £400,000 to £460,000.

Brinkworth has lots of good points, including its foodie pub, the Three Crowns, a gardening club and a quilting group called The Bramble Patchers. Set on a ridge, with wide-angle views, the village is notable for its extraordinary length – stretching to just over four miles. A period house with four bedrooms here will cost £375,000 to £425,000. Slightly to the east is **Lydiard Millicent**, with a pub and a green-belt buffer zone to insulate it from Swindon. A new, four-bedroom detached house might cost £300,000. **Purton Stoke**, which has a pub and a village street that tapers into open countryside, is much nicer than its overblown neighbour **Purton**. A four-bedroom Victorian house at Purton Stoke might have a price tag of £450,000; a two-bedroom, brick semi-detached cottage, £280,000.

To the south there are a very few villages scattered in the sweeping chalk hills between Swindon and **Marlborough**, which actually lies closer to Pewsey station (see page 188).

> Line to **Kemble**

Journey: 79 min
(97 min changing at
Swindon)

Season: £7268

Peak: 1 per hr

Off-peak: 1 per hr
(one hour through
and the next
changing at
Swindon)

KEMBLE is a very pretty Cotswold village, often commended in best-kept village competitions in Gloucestershire. Planning controls are tight, so that even the council houses are built in local stone. The village has a school and a general store-cum-post office, though most people do their major shopping in Cirencester. The abiding local interest is reflected in the biannual flower and vegetable shows. Three-bedroom former estate-workers' cottages sell for around £250,000, Victorian railway cottages for more. At King's Orchard, a 10-minute walk from the station, a new, four-bedroom semi costs from £275,000, or from £340,000 for a detached. Larger farmhouses can cost £600,000, to £1.35m for a five-bedroom coach house. 'Location and rarity is everything,' says one local agent.

To the east is a belt of desirable villages, all close to Cirencester and two good comprehensive schools. **Poole Keynes**, was little more than a farming hamlet with a medieval priory until the Sixties imposed modern housing. **Somerford Keynes** also has a lot of modern development, but is socially very active. It has a pub, the Bakers Arms, and local clubs include bridge and mothers and toddlers. Prices of luxurious new eco-houses on the lakeside Lower Mill Estate vary from £350,000 to £1m. **Ashton Keynes** has a primary school, garage, two shops and some lovely period houses close to the river. As you approach from South Cerney you will see some beautiful 17th-century cottages on the other side of the bridge. A large farmhouse in the countryside nearby would cost up to £975,000, while smaller houses are on a par with the rest of the area. **South Cerney** is close to the Cotswold Water Park – a collection of flooded gravel pits offering water-skiing, sailing and fishing. A converted barn with four bedrooms in this area would cost around £700,000. The village is marred slightly by the large quarry with its constant lorry traffic.

Schools in Gloucestershire

There are highly selective grammar schools here for those who excel, but also good comprehensives and private schools. Villages between Cheltenham, Cirencester and Stroud are surrounded by choice. Cheltenham has the heavily oversubscribed Pate's Grammar for boys and girls, Balcarras comprehensive, and strong private schools, including Cheltenham Ladies' College, Cheltenham College for boys and girls, and Dean Close for both sexes. Stroud has two grammars – Stroud High for girls and Marling for boys. Westonbirt independent for girls is to the south near Tetbury.

Cirencester has Rendcomb College independent school for boys and girls.

Other good comprehensives are in Chipping Campden, Bourton-on-the-Water and Fairford.

About six miles from Kemble, but well worth the journey, is **Down Ampney**, the most charming of the Ampneys (the others being **Ampney St Peter**, **Ampney Crucis** and **Ampney St Mary**), famous as the birthplace of Ralph Vaughan Williams and much admired for its beautiful, gabled manor house, Down Ampney Hall. A tiny two-bedroom semi will cost £250,000; a modern stone family house £345,000. The larger country houses sell for £2m upwards.

> Line to Bristol Parkway

Journey: 90 min
Season: £9192*
Peak: 2 per hr
Off-peak: 2 per hr
* Also valid at
Bristol Temple
Meads

BRISTOL PARKWAY The villages near here are perfect for commuters because the station is easy to reach and parking is plentiful. It also lies at the centre of a motorway network that can speed you north, south, east or west and link you with the major commercial centres of Wales as well as with Birmingham, Swindon and London. It is possible for a couple to live here and for one partner to work in Exeter and the other in London. It offers countryside, yet Bristol is on the doorstep. The station is on a spur that goes direct from Swindon, so you can be whisked to London in under an hour and a half.

It is possible for one partner to work in Exeter and the other in London

Only six minutes from the station are the pricey villages of **Almondsbury** and **Awkley**. They are out of earshot of all the motorways, and an old stone house with four bedrooms might typically cost £425,000. Hortham Village, a new development of Barratt and Bryant homes on the eastern fringes of Almondsbury, offers a range of houses from three-bedroom terraces at around £210,000 to four-bedroom detached town houses at £420,000. Though the villages are out of the way, they are seen as useful locations because of the second Severn Crossing, linked to Junction 17 of the M5. **Hambrook** is also a village with instant appeal despite being within earshot of the M4 and M32. It has a couple of pubs, a hotel and Hambrook Common at its centre. Four-bedroom houses easily creep up into the £400,000 range.

Also within six minutes of the station is **Stoke Gifford** – almost an ex-village (with a serious rush-hour problem) now that it has attracted big companies such as Hewlett Packard and AXA Sun Life, and the Ministry of Defence. The village-proper is packed with old cottages, with those in Mead Road tending to be more expensive than the rest. A three-bedroom cottage will sell at around £245,000. A four-bedroom modern detached house will fetch £250,000 to £350,000. The most sought-after roads are Touchstone Avenue and Fabian Drive, where a four-bedroom detached house costs around £249,000. A new pre-school and nursery has opened to cope with the commuter influx.

It is impossible to ignore the lake of housing at **Bradley Stoke** on Stoke Gifford's doorstep, billed as the largest development in Western Europe. Builders took over a decade to construct about 11,000 houses, with primary schools, sports centres, pubs and supermarkets. A new shopping centre was added in 2008. Housing is pick-and-mix, with one-bedroom flats being sold for £110,000, three-bedroom houses at £160,000 to £240,000, and four bedrooms at £220,000 to £300,000.

'Iron Acton has a village green where girls dance around the maypole in spring'

Much care was taken at Bradley Stoke to avoid the monotony of earlier new development grafted on to **Chipping Sodbury**. The core remains a lovely old Cotswold town with a typically wide main street flanked with houses in Georgian brick and Cotswold stone. A farmers' market takes place twice a month. A 17th-century three-bedroom cottage would cost around £330,000 to £500,000 for four bedrooms. The nearby villages of **Winterbourne, Frampton Cotterell** and **Coalpit Heath** blend one into the other, offering a mixture of old and new with a few working farms in the outlying areas. At the bottom of the market you could buy a three-bedroom ex-council house for £170,000. At the top end you could pay £450,000 or more for a four- to five-bedroom period cottage in half an acre. Residents at Frampton Cotterell are opposing a plan for 220 Barratt Homes on a Greenfield site in the village. **Iron Acton** is also very pretty, with a village green where girls dance round the maypole in the spring, and two pubs.

If you are looking for a house around here it is worth remembering that in the area between Bristol and Wotton-under-Edge prices are affected by people who commute into Bristol. As you proceed beyond **Thornbury**, prices start to drop. On a bad day from this part, the journey to Bristol Parkway station could take 15 minutes, which many might consider too much.

> Continuation of main line

Journey: 77 min
Season: £7616
Peak: 2 per hr
Off peak: 2 per hr

'At one time Box housed the workers building the Great Western Railway; now it harbours the occasional rock star'

CHIPPENHAM is a town that has been busy rediscovering its old heritage – paving the old market square with York stone, bringing back market day and introducing a farmers' market, re-erecting the Butter Cross and cherishing its Roman remains. It has all the basic shops anyone would need, including Emery Gate, a new classical-style pedestrian shopping mall in Bath stone on the banks of the River Avon. It is a place for small family firms, with a business park on the western outskirts.

The set-piece village of **Castle Combe**, five miles away, is known as the prettiest village in England. In the 1960s, the arched bridge over the Bye brook and little stone cottages with steeply pitched roofs were transformed to serve as a seaport for the film of *Dr Dolittle*. It is a bit of a goldfish bowl for tourists, but at least the visitors are expected to leave their cars behind at the top of the village. Residents become very attached and properties rarely come on the market. A thatched cottage could cost from £475,000. The pubs – the Castle Inn and the White Hart – make it convivial. Children go to Bybrook Valley primary school in a neighbouring village.

Far quieter and just as pretty is **Biddestone**, slightly closer to Chippenham, which has a classic village centre with stone houses, duck pond, pubs and a recreation ground for football and cricket. An older three-bedroom detached cottage will cost around £440,000. To the north-east is **East Tytherton**, which is very small, has attractive stone houses and is close enough to the M4 to be favoured by those who prefer the car to the train. **Bremhill**, too, is a charming village with a pub. A former resident, the vicar and poet Canon Bowles, kept the bells around the necks of his sheep tuned to thirds and fifths, and was a favourite visitor at Bowood House a few miles to the south. A cottagey three-bedroom semi would sell at £250,000 to £300,000.

People prefer **Corsham**, which has a Cotswold stone heart and a delicatessen proudly selling local produce. The Heritage Centre concerns itself with the wool trade and stone quarrying. A three-bedroom stone house on the historic High Street sells for around £375,000. A Grade Two listed house with five bedrooms, garden and orchard would cost £895,000. On the two new developments prices range from £200,000 for a three-bedroom semi to £350,000 for a five-bedroom detached. Further towards Bath on the A4 is **Box**. At one time it housed the workers building the Great Western Railway for Brunel; now it harbours the occasional rock star and is considered ideal by those who want to be within easy reach of Bath, but also close to Chippenham railway station. Peter Gabriel's Real World Studios are here. The village has a butcher, chemist and hairdresser,

Schools in Bristol, Bath and Somerset

Good independent schools for girls in the Bristol area include Badminton for boarding and day, Clifton High, The Red Maids' School day and boarding, Redland High and Colston's Girls'. Other independent schools include Bristol Cathedral School (mixed), Queen Elizabeth's Hospital day and boarding school (boys), Clifton College (mixed) day and boarding, Bristol Grammar day school and Colston's Collegiate. Good comprehensives include Ashton Park, Cotham and St Mary Redcliff.

Bath also has its share of educational successes, including Norton Hill comprehensive, and three co-educational independents – King Edward's, Kingswood and Prior Park Roman Catholic College. There is also the Royal High, an independent day and boarding school for girls.

North of Bristol, Cheltenham has an embarrassment of riches when it comes to private schools (see Schools in Gloucestershire, p163). Good comprehensives are to be found in Chipping Campden and Wotton-under-Edge.

and one primary school. There are lots of local activities and the village fête, known as the Box Revels, usually lasts for a week. Two-bedroom stone cottages start from £160,000; larger houses will top the £500,000 mark. Local interests manage to be both horsey and cultural, and also sporting. Here you are in rugby country – thanks to the proliferation of boys' public schools and the huge success of Bath Rugby Club.

Marshfield, west of Chippenham on the A420, has a shop, butcher, doctor, and pet and garden supplies. A four-bedroom terraced house on the High Street, in what was once the last staging post to Bath, would cost around £410,000. This long grey-stone street is dominated by the church tower and has some little almshouses dating from 1625.

Very few local sons and daughters can afford to buy homes in the villages they grew up in. First-time buyers are eased out into small towns such as **Calne**, a former woollen town where the site of a Victorian bacon factory in the centre has been put down to grass. A farmers' market is held once a month. Two-bedroom flats cost from £110,000; an 18th-century, Grade Two listed, three-bedroom beamed house will weigh in at £365,000. **Compton Basset** has been made a conservation area because of its delightful chalk-stone cottages and 12th- and 13th-century church. A stock of surplus Ministry of Defence houses that are eagerly snapped up by younger buyers is known as Lower Compton.

Other villages worth looking at include **Cherhill** (pronounced *Cheryl*), towards Marlborough, which stands beside a huge Iron Age camp and white horse, and has its own primary school. Modern three-bedroom houses start at £200,000. **Heddington** is a small village with infant and primary schools and a Buddhist meditation centre, The Pagoda. It is very upmarket; a modern five-bedroom family house would sell for around £390,000. Another sought-after cluster of properties is at **Charlcutt**. The houses have breathtaking views of the countryside for 20 miles in all directions. Something with five bedrooms and a double garage will cost about £400,000. Although **Sandy Lane** straddles the A342, it is very beautiful and has some very lovely thatched houses. A two-bedroom cottage here might go for £325,000. Its population is mainly retired, and the residents tend to grow high beech hedges to guard their privacy. It is short of local activity, but contains a great deal of wealth. One London commuter from here prefers to travel by helicopter rather than by train. Unfortunately, the village is used as a short cut by motorists heading off the M4 for Southampton.

South of Chippenham the showcase village is **Lacock**, but the jumble of timbered houses in the gorgeous twisted streets around the Abbey are all in the hands of the National Trust. On the fringe a three-bedroom detached house costs around £395,000 or one of the four Huf Haus modern eco-houses starts at £1.15m. Part-time commuters might choose to live in some of the wonderful villages further south in the Avon valley, which are also served by the Melksham branch line to Bath (see below).

> Branch line to Trowbridge, via Freshford, Avoncliff and Bradford-on-Avon

Journey: 112 min*
Season: £7768 (all routes); £6184 (via Salisbury into Waterloo only)
Peak: 2 per hr
Off-peak: 2 per hr
* From Bradford-on-Avon. There are no through trains to Paddington. You must change at either Bath Spa or Westbury. There are through trains to Waterloo but only 3 a day and off-peak (143 min).

FRESHFORD is favoured by retiring Bathonians. It is a strong little community, with its own shop and local railway station. Local trains drop you quickly into Bath, so there is no problem with parking the car and the season ticket price is the same as that from Bath.

Bradford-on-Avon is so expensive that it vies with **Bath**. Indeed, it is built of the same limestone as Bath, on hills falling so steeply towards the Avon that the winding paths between the houses give one the feeling of being in a Greek village. Across the arched stone bridge, and open to the public, is one of the biggest tithe barns in the country. Bradford attracts many tourists who come in summer to wander the river and old shopping streets, have tea, buy second-hand books, and browse the craft shops. It has a good swimming pool, rowing and sailing clubs, and an annual arts festival. There are marvellous walks along the Kennet and Avon Canal.

The attraction of owning a house overlooking the tessellated rooftops of weavers' cottages, miniature 18th-century homes and narrow gardens bulging with hollyhocks is difficult to quantify. There is a definite ex-military and ex-naval presence here. Larger houses sell for hundreds of thousands of pounds, but it is occasionally possible to find a period three-bedroom terrace house on four floors, with a tiny garden, at around £290,000. On the outer roads, three-bedroom ex-council houses in reconstructed stone will sell for £180,000 upwards. Towards the higher end of the market on the edge of town you could get a four-bedroom Victorian stone semi with outbuildings, in over half an acre, for around £600,000.

Broughton Gifford is much quieter, set in deep countryside with a village green faced by Gifford Hall, a 1688 village house. **Steeple Ashton**, like Bradford-on-Avon, was built on the profits of the wool industry. It has a prize-winning village shop run by the villagers, a church with no steeple and a swag of new housing. A Grade Two listed, four-bedroom cottage will cost around £490,000. Nearby is **Keevil**, a collection of rather exclusive cottages with a stone manor house and a thriving primary school. A five-bedroom half-timbered house with large garden and outhouses would cost £570,000.

> Continuation of main line

Journey: 89 min
Season: £7768
Peak: 2 per hr
Off-peak: 2 per hr

BATH SPA People have been known to move into **Bath** and out again within a couple of years – not everyone finds it easy to break into the social circles that centre on its elegant 18th-century squares and crescents. Its attractions are manifold: beautiful parks, specialist shops, some of them rather exclusive, and restaurants where the prices compete with Mayfair. The beauty of commuting from Bath, apart from its physical splendour, is that you can live within walking distance of the station. Indeed you *have* to, otherwise the combined traffic and parking problems will sour your temper before the day has even begun.

'It is possible to live outside the city in one of the villages, but driving into Bath is a problem'

The social hubs include the much-acclaimed international festival in June; the Theatre Royal, which is the starting point for many West End plays; Bath Rugby Club; and the Pump Rooms, where balls are regularly held. The stresses and strains of life can be soothed in the mineral-rich waters of Thermae Bath Spa where the rooftop pool is open year-round. Old Bathonians are extremely tight-knit. Public schools include King Edward's School, Kingswood School for boys and girls, Monkton Combe for boys and girls, and Prior Park College, which is a Catholic school for both sexes.

The sought-after areas are the two hills to the north and south of the river. **Sion Hill** to the north is a sudden slope looking south over the city. This is where all the major crescents were built, including the Royal, for prominent figures in elegant 18th-century society. Very few of these houses are left intact, most have been split into flats. A top floor, two-bedroom flat in Royal Crescent, would go on the market at around £600,000. Between the roads full of architectural gems you will find a mixed bag of houses, though nowhere are prices cheap. A five-bedroom Victorian bay-fronted semi in a quiet road might sell for £600,000 or more.

To the south of the river is **Bathwick Hill**, with Widcombe and Lyncombe Hills, where a sister spa to the famous central spa was found in the late 18th century. The architecture is equally fine, but the views from the houses are rather more rural than those from Sion Hill. Both attract businessmen, professionals and culture vultures, but people attach fiercely to their particular hill and would never swap.

Living in the centre of Bath only became fashionable again in the early Eighties. For decades previously the Georgian architecture was not cherished, and the buildings had blackened and become gloomy. In the late Seventies you could buy a complete Georgian town house in The Circus for £7,000. By 2000 it was worth £1m and now you will pay £3.7m to £4m for one. There is a tendency for the houses to have tiny gardens because they were designed in the belief that people would take their recreation in the parks. If you own a house in a square, you will often have the right to buy a key to the central garden.

Elsewhere, a modest house close to the canal with a small garden, two reception rooms and two bedrooms might be found for £285,000. Three-bedroom ex-council houses sell for £180,000 to £220,000.

It is possible to live outside the city in one of the villages, but driving into Bath is a problem. Parking adds an expensive premium to the season ticket, and traffic wardens are vigilant. To the south is the old Somerset coal mining area, still with the occasional slag heap on the horizon. **Peasedown St John**, an early mining town, has been rediscovered and is now a popular commuter haven.

Norton St Philip, however, has conservation status. It was built in local stone from the profits of the wool industry, and has some small modern cul-de-sacs stitched unobtrusively into the whole. It is known for its pub, The George Inn, which is one of the best preserved medieval inns in the country. Pepys paid a visit with his wife in 1668, dined on 10 shillings and noted a plaque in the church to twin ladies who had only one stomach between them. **Hinton Charterhouse** is similarly unspoilt, with a shop and post office and the 13th-century ruins of

Georgian town house, Bath

Hinton Priory close by. The countryside is full of similar villages that you chance upon as you dip in and out of the valleys. But farming patterns are changing and in **Wellow** the local farmer no longer herds his cattle through the village at dawn and dusk. He has turned to arable and the barns have become houses. A small three-bedroom cottage will cost £350,000 at least. There are a lot of retired people, but also young families who use the primary school. Many people own horses, and there is a Trekking Centre that caters mostly for weekenders.

To the west are the villages served by the Bradford-on-Avon branch line (see page 167). To the north is another magical stretch of countryside where time seems to have turned everything to stone. **Charlcombe**, **Swainswick** and **Woolley** lie in a U-shaped valley in a landscape which is almost Welsh, and which at its northen end becomes positively austere. It is expensive. In Woolley even a two-bedroom cottage would sell for £180,000 to £210,000; a four-bedroom house for over £500,000. To the east of the A46 is another stretch of villages which have that haphazard, ancient quality, including **St Catherine** and **Northend**. **Batheaston** is a favourite with commuters and the retired. Yet it manages to be a working village with post office, general store, garden centre and farmshop, and a large council estate. It has at least 142 listed buildings, which the Batheaston Society does its best to preserve, and has been rescued from heavy traffic by a bypass. You could also look at **Bathford**, which has a village shop, busy village school and playgroup. However, the breathtaking views across the watermeadows to the city may be ruined if a proposal to build a park-and-ride scheme for 1,300 cars on the meadows is given the go-ahead. Further north towards the M4, in villages such as **Upper Wraxhall** and **North Wraxhall**, prices drop considerably, but you become a little separated from the spirit, social life and interests of Bath.

Journey: 102 min
Season: £9192*
Peak: 2 per hr
Off-peak: 2 per hr
* Also valid at
Bristol Parkway

BRISTOL TEMPLE MEADS Commuting from **Bristol** is never easy. Parking is difficult, and the station is hard to get at, being surrounded by sreets of terraces and subject to a major regeneration scheme. There are huge traffic problems. The M32 regularly clogs into four-mile tailbacks, and there is no integrated public transport system to relieve the pressure in a city where a lot of major companies – Lloyds TSB and British Aerospace, for example – have their headquarters. The retail landscape has been transformed with the opening in 2008 of Cabot Circus, an ultra-modern mall under an eye-catching curved glass roof, with Harvey Nichols at its heart. Culturally, it is a rich city, with the Bristol Old Vic, the theatre school, and various pubs providing fringe theatre. The Tobacco

Factory is a popular venue, staging Shakespeare in the round, comedy and music. The Hippodrome attracts the ballet and opera companies. Colston Hall is the rock venue, and the Watershed arts and media centre in the docks shows the arty films. Another big local interest is expressed through Bristol Rugby Club. The well-known public schools include Bristol Cathedral School, Bristol Grammar School, Colston's School and Queen Elizabeth's Hospital.

Clifton and **Clifton Village** are Bristol's Olympian heights, where the mix of Georgian, Regency and Victorian is very special and very expensive. Some of the houses are so large, with eight or nine bedrooms, that they have been divided into flats for upwardly mobile couples who will pay up to £325,000 for something stylish with two bedrooms, marble fireplaces, balcony, ceiling mouldings and a drawing room with shutters. In Cliftonville, many of the 10-bedroom Victorian mansions overlooking The Downs have been converted into offices. It has good independent schools – Clifton High School and Clifton College. A four-storey Victorian house here would cost around £800,000 to £1m. A four-bedroom Victorian terrace in Cliftonwood would cost £425,000 to £500,000.

House prices in the rest of the city have been playing catch-up with remarkable speed. An alternative to Clifton is **Redland**, which has a mix of Georgian, Victorian and Thirties, popular with families. The closer to the city centre you get, the more you feel the presence of students from Bristol University. A two-bedroom first floor flat in a Victorian terrace in Redland, close to Clifton Downs, would be priced at around £200,000. A mid-terrace, three-bedroom Edwardian house, or a charming four-bedroom town house, could be had for £500,000.

Bristol **Harbourside** is worth considering if you haven't got a family. Huge new wharfside developments are interspersed between old warehouse conversions. Isambard Kingdom Brunel's old stamping ground around the Floating Harbour is now busy with bars and cafés. One-bedroom flats cost around £130,000 with a view. Three-bedroom town houses, with or without a view, start from £390,000.

Waterfront apartments, Bristol

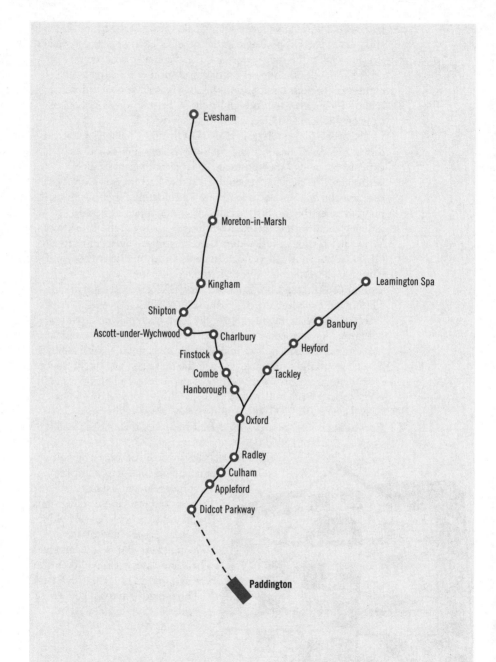

Evesham

Moreton-in-Marsh

Kingham

Shipton

Ascott-under-Wychwood

Charlbury

Finstock

Combe

Hanborough

Leamington Spa

Banbury

Heyford

Tackley

Oxford

Radley

Culham

Appleford

Didcot Parkway

Paddington

Paddington
> Oxford and Evesham

For stations between Paddington and Didcot Parkway, see **Paddington to Reading and Bristol** line, page 149

Journey (from Radley): 62 min, changing at Didcot Parkway

Season ticket (all three stations): £3996

There are 2 through trains per hr in the peaks, and hourly off-peak, but it saves 30–40 min changing at Didcot Parkway or Reading

APPLEFORD, CULHAM AND RADLEY Appleford is little more than a halt with a string of bungalows threaded to the railway line beside a good pub. **Long Wittenham** is a village in two halves, old and new, and is convenient for those who want to use The European School at **Culham**, which was established for the children of people working at the research station there. **Radley** has more trains serving it than the other two halts, but it is a bit betwixt and between to be really sought-after. Its main feature is Radley College, the boys' public school.

'Travelling on an Oxford train can be a bit like attending a literary tea party'

Journey: 57 min

Season: £3996

Peak: 3 per hr

Off-peak: 2 per hr

OXFORD can seem insufferably cliquey to some, but if you belong in some way to the publishing, university, hospital or industrial scenes then it is not too much of a problem. It is, however, very unfriendly towards the car and as it is virtually impossible to drive into the centre, drivers slip round the ring road to find the right point of entry. Plans to further pedestrianise the city centre and re-route the traffic are at the consultation stage. Travelling on the Oxford train can be a bit like attending a literary tea party. As well as the city's obvious beauty, its schools are a great attraction to outsiders. Public schools abound: Magdalen College School, St Edward's and Radley College just outside for boys, and Oxford High and Headington School for girls. Prices in Oxford have simply blossomed in recent years.

The nicer bread-and-butter houses for those making a start in Oxford lie in **Osney** or **Jericho**, both within walking distance of the station. Osney is almost moated by a combination of the Thames and the canal. Two-bedroom Victorian houses here sell for up to £280,000; three-bedrooms houses for £320,000. Prices in Jericho are slightly higher, though the houses are small. Another area to consider is **Grandpont**, where a Victorian house with three bedrooms would fetch from £350,000.

For many, the only area to live is North Oxford, which is peppered with academics and successful professionals. It mushroomed in the 19th century after it was suddenly decided that dons should be allowed to marry. Huge Victorian houses on wide, tree-lined roads provided them with new homes, which now sell at around £900,000 to £2.7m. There are just not enough of them to meet demand. Houses get smaller and slightly cheaper towards **Summertown**, where Cherwell comprehensive is a much-respected school, as is the St Philip and St James' first school. You could buy a family house here for around £550,000. **Wolvercote** village, a little further out, is particularly lovely, with The Trout Inn backing on to Port Meadow. Cheaper little brick-and-tile houses sell at around £250,000.

'For many the only area to live is North Oxford, which is peppered with academics and successful professionals'

Headington is popular with staff working at the hospital, but it is the wrong side of Oxford for the station. Coaches heading for London (Victoria) stop here and many commuters use these instead. **Old Headington** and **Old Marston** are both charming old villages with crooked lanes and stone cottages that have been absorbed by the suburbs. Inhabitants tend to be rather rarefied. Pretty cottages in either might sell for £375,000 to £500,000. Oxford's equivalent of a stockbroker belt – large detached houses with the occasional tennis court or pony paddock – lies outside at **Hinksey**, **Cumnor** and **Boars Hill**. A Thirties' house with six bedrooms, four bathrooms, lofts, outbuildings, double garage and large gardens could be bought for around £2.1m on Boars Hill.

Schools in Oxfordshire

Private schools tend to grab the limelight here, though there are some notable comprehensives. The latter include The Cherwell in Oxford, Lord Williams' at Thame and John Mason at Abingdon; also look at Faringdon, Burford, Kidlington, Witney, Wallingford and Didcot Girls' at Didcot.

Oxford is the real educational powerhouse, with a clutch of independent schools. Girls' schools include Oxford High (day), Headington and Wychwood for day and boarding. Boys have

Magdalen College School and St Edwards for both day and boarding.

Abingdon is the other bright spot. Here you find Radley College, high in the public school firmament, for which you need to put your son's name down at birth, and Abingdon independent boys' day and boarding school, both keen on rowing. For girls there is the independent School of St Helen and Katherine and Our Lady's Convent. Other girls' independents around Oxfordshire include Tudor Hall at Banbury and St Mary's at Wantage.

> Extension to Tackley and Heyford

Tackley and Heyford have only a few services in the peak to Paddington and even changing at Oxford there are gaps exceeding 2 hrs off-peak.

Season: £3996 from either station

Since Oxford is so strangled by traffic and efforts to drive to the station are likely to be stressful, **Tackley** and **Heyford** come into their own with their local trains. **Steeple Aston**, a grey stone-walled village above the Cherwell, is definitely worth looking at. It has a village shop and post office, a choral society, football club and the Steeple Aston Players, who put on productions of plays written by local people. Commuters generally try to join in. The area is seriously horsey. A three-bedroom period cottage can be bought for up to £400,000. Residents are concerned about plans to build 1,000 homes on the former American Air Force Base at **Upper Heyford**, the subject of an ongoing public enquiry. **Hopcroft's Holt** nearby is where the French highwayman Claude Duval clattered about on his horse.

'The Steeple Aston Players put on productions of plays written by local people'

Then there are the **Tews** (**Great**, **Little** and **Duns**). Great Tew is particularly prized because it was a celebrated time-warp village (due to a neglectful previous owner it almost missed out on the 20th century). The combination of stone and thatch, post office and village stores, punctuated by greens and clumps of ornamental trees, has seduced location hunters for historical film dramas. Even the overhead cables have been buried to keep the time-forgot atmosphere. Residents are not antiques, however, and plenty of newcomers have arrived. A tiny two-bedroom cottage will cost £260,000.

For **Banbury** and **Leamington Spa**, see Marylebone to Leamington Spa, pages 145–146. It is possible to reach Paddington via the Oxford branch, but the direct route to Marylebone is much quicker.

> Line from Oxford to Evesham

This line takes you to what many people think is the most beautiful side of Oxford to live, where villages of golden stone rise up from the fields. The skip-hop service to **Charlbury**, **Kingham** and **Moreton-in-Marsh** (better served than **Hanborough**, **Combe**, **Finstock**, **Ascott-under-Wychwood** and **Skipton**, which are sandwiched in between them) has become more frequent in recent years. There are now many more through trains that run from Evesham to Paddington and stop at these three stations. Otherwise you have to get the local train and change at Oxford.

Journey: 80 min

Season: £5236

Peak: 1 or 2 per hr

Off-peak: 1 per hr with some gaps

CHARLBURY
This area is a tapestry of extraordinarily lovely villages. You have to watch for those that are under the Oxford influence and hence more expensive than those further afield. **Charlbury** is very elegant and has a few business units in the stables of Cornbury Park, Lord Rotherwick's estate. There is a farmers' market every quarter. Modern three-bedroom boxes cost from £250,000, or tasteful four-bedroom modern cottages from £475,000. It is just too far from Oxford to be really expensive, or to appeal to the young, who say they can find nothing to do there.

Woodstock, which in Elizabethan times was the glove-making capital of the area, is slightly more expensive – its old stone houses lie closer to Oxford and it is only two miles from **Combe** station. In summer it swarms with visitors who browse through it on their way to Blenheim Palace, eat at the Bear Hotel and walk along the banks of the River Glyme. **Bladon**, just apart from it, is more remarkable still. Its collection of ancient cottages is crowned by the elegant 15th-century chimneys of the old malthouse, and it is scarcely a mile from **Hanborough** station. Sir Winston Churchill is buried here.

One of the best-liked small towns west of Oxford is **Witney**, which is rather less rarefied than some of the villages that surround it. Its fortunes were built on the blanket industry, which employed the waters of the Windrush and the wool from local sheep. It is a refreshing mix of old and new property, with greens at either end, raised pavements studded with limes, and modern shopfronts

Cotswold house near Moreton-in-Marsh

elbowing in between their Georgian neighbours. The central market place and the old covered butter cross give it a strong heart, and a farmers' market is held once a month. Though it is only three miles from **Finstock** station, a lot of commuters from here choose to drive. The town is just off the A40, which links easily to the M40. There are rows of old blanket workers' cottages at around £250,000 each. The huge housing estate of Deer Park has mushroomed on the western flank, with a two-bedroom terraced home selling for £155,000 and a four-bedroom detached for £285,000. To the east, on the 1,200-house Madley Park estate, prices range from £140,000 for a one-bedroom flat to £300,000-plus for a four-bedroom detached.

Journey: 90 min
Season: £5576
Peak: 1 or 2 per hr
Off-peak: 1 per hr
with some gaps

KINGHAM was declared England's Favourite Village by *Country Life* magazine in 2007 for its charm, beauty and setting – it is surrounded by the winding lanes, streams and meadows of the Evenlode Valley. Kingham and all the villages around it are cut in fudge-coloured stone, with the occasional outcrop of council houses at the edge. People tolerate the longer commute to London from here because it is just out of reach of the Oxford influence and therefore cheaper. A handsome four-bedroom stone house could be bought for around £475,000; three bedrooms for £399,000; a smaller terraced property for around £250,000.

The **Wychwoods** (**Milton-Under, Shipton-Under** and **Ascott-Under**) are closer to Oxford and slightly more expensive. Ascott-Under-Wychwood has its own station, served by regional trains running from Evesham to Oxford. Many people moving to the area will aim for the catchment of the popular Burford comprehensive school. A stone house with beamed ceilings, mullioned windows with leaded lights, Tudor fireplaces and five to six bedrooms might sell for around £795,000.

Bourton-on-the-Water, though a model Cotswold village with its own model village, pushes commuter tolerance a little since it is about 10 miles from Kingham station. But with it come the **Slaughters** (**Lower** and **Upper**), the Lower set upon a stream that wriggles through little stone bridges and the Upper being right on the banks of the Windrush. Locals tend to be farmers, retired couples or craftsmen who don't mind being miles from anywhere. The nearest shopping centre is **Chipping Norton**, an old market town, with a farmers' market, where the huge Bliss tweed mill was restored to provide flats and houses alongside a leisure centre (priced at between £275,000 for a two-bedroom flat and £475,000 for a three-bedroom flat, plus service charges). It has a reputation for being wet and windy and locals say it qualified for extra coal rations in the war because it was the coldest place in the region. The White Hart Hotel in the town centre has been converted into apartments costing around £240,000 for two bedrooms.

'Locals say Chipping Norton qualified for extra coal rations in the war because it was the coldest place in the region'

Journey: 101 min
Season: £6188
Peak: 1 or 2 per hr
Off-peak: 1 per hr
with some gaps

MORETON-IN-MARSH
The perfection of towns such as Moreton-in-Marsh and **Stow-on-the-Wold** has meant torture by tourism. They seethe in summer and subside in winter. 'The only people who live here are old dears in unmodernised houses who freeze every winter, or those involved in the tourist industry, or the very rich who can spend the hundreds of thousands necessary to buy one of the lovely big country houses,' says one local resident. A little mid-17th-century cottage with three bedrooms would hit the market with an asking price of around £325,000. Large country houses can run into millions.

'The perfection of towns such as Moreton-in-Marsh and Stow-on-the-Wold has meant torture by tourism'

Terraced
cottages,
Broadway

In Stow-on-the-Wold antiques dealers have a dominating presence, but there is a butcher, bakery, organic shop, chemist, a Tesco and a monthly farmer's market. A two-bedroom cottage could cost £220,000 to £285,000, a three-bedroom terrace on a new development £300,000.

Broadway and **Chipping Campden** are both beautiful towns, built mainly of stone. Chipping Campden attracts elderly people retiring from Birmingham, and brims with local activities. The Chipping Campden Society looks after the historic buildings, many of which were built by affluent wool merchants in the 14th and 15th centuries. There are drama and football clubs, two primary schools and a comprehensive that brings in children from surrounding villages by the coachload.

Journey: 122 min
Season: £6660
Peak: 1 or 2 per hr
Off-peak: 1 per hr
with some gaps

EVESHAM
Though not a great many people would choose to commute daily from Evesham, many might consider part-time commuting. Its tree-lined walks, lawns along the Avon and some wonderful old buildings give it obvious charm. It also has two golf clubs. Property prices are lower here than up in the Cotswolds. A three-bedroom Victorian terrace might sell for £180,000; a three-bedroom modern detached house on an estate for £230,000.

Two-bedroom cottages can be found in the surrounding villages for £225,000, with older four-bedroom detached houses at over £400,000.

The Pershore side is particularly pretty, with picturesque black-and-white villages such as **Charlton**, **Cropthorne** and **Fladbury** (where the celebrated canoe club has sent members to the Olympics). Fladbury tends to attract Birmingham rather than London commuters. The three new housing developments draw a constant flow of people. It has an award-winning butcher, a sports pavilion for football and cricket enthusiasts, and a church primary school for five- to eight-year-olds. The middle school is in the neighbouring village of Pinvin, and secondary students tend to go to Pershore High School. Further north of Evesham is another black-and-white village, **Norton**. It was once ruined by traffic on the A435, but has now been rescued with a bypass. The **Lenches** (**Church** and **Atch**) are also popular on this northern flank.

For truly grand landscape you should look to the west, in the villages beneath Bredon Hill. The **Combertons** (**Little** and **Great**) are especially lovely. **Great Comberton** has a heady mix of half-timbered farmhouses and thatched cottages, while Little Comberton has a village dovecote with walls over one metre thick and more than 500 nesting holes. The red-brick dovecote in Great Comberton is even bigger, with 1,425 nesting holes.

'For truly grand landscape you should look to the west, in the villages beneath Bredon Hill. The Combertons are especially lovely'

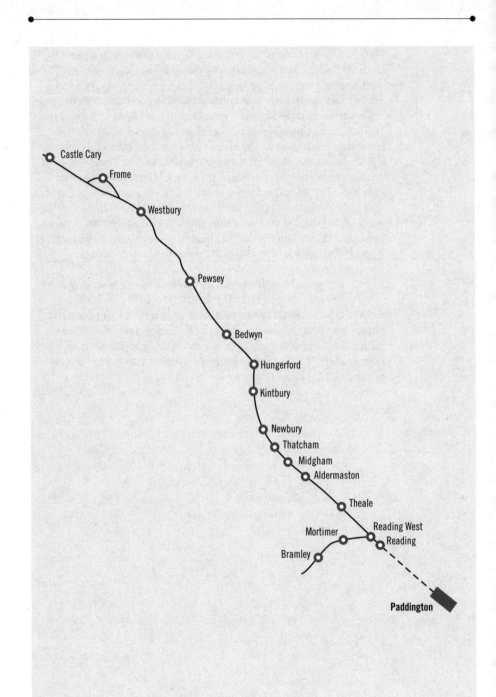

Castle Cary
Frome
Westbury
Pewsey
Bedwyn
Hungerford
Kintbury
Newbury
Thatcham
Midgham
Aldermaston
Theale
Reading West
Mortimer
Reading
Bramley
Paddington

Paddington
> Castle Cary

For stations between Paddington and Reading, see **Paddington to Bristol** line, page 149.

Journey: 42 min
Season: £3492
Peak: 3 through
trains, but, 4 per hr
changing at Reading
Off-peak: 3 per hr
changing at Reading

READING WEST Reading offers fast trains and lies within striking distance of beautiful countryside. For a full description, see page 157.

> Branch line to Mortimer and Bramley

Journey: 49 min*
Season: £3492*
Trains to Reading
(there are no
through trains): 2
per hr peak and off-
peak
* From Mortimer. It
is possible to go via
Basingstoke to
Waterloo in the
other direction as
well, by buying a
season from
Basingstoke to
London (also £3492)

MORTIMER is the smaller and more rural of the two villages and offers a minibus service to the station, which is a boon for commuters. A four-bedroom Victorian family house sells for £500,000 to £675,000; a two-bedroom terraced house for £220,000. A new three-bedroom, detached Bryant Homes' house, on roads with names such as Asparagus Close or Strawberry Fields, will cost about £299,000.

Bramley is a dormitory village that grew up around the railway in the mid-1890s and has had to swallow a lot of new houses in the last few years. It has a baker and a post-office-cum-store. A three-bedroom modern semi will cost £230,000; a larger four-bedroom detached, £350,000. A public outcry failed to prevent Wimpey building 270 homes on a former Ministry of Defence site on the south-eastern fringes of Bramley. Here prices range from £190,000 for a two-bedroom semi to £450,000 for a five-bedroom detached.

'Reading offers fast trains and lies within striking distance of beautiful countryside'

> Continuation of main line

Journey: 41 min
Season: £3492
Peak: 3 per hr
(some by changing
at Reading)
Off-peak: 2 per hr
(one by changing at
Reading)

THEALE Since getting into **Reading** is a nightmare, many people prefer to use **Theale** station instead. It marks the beginning of the Berkshire farming belt beyond Reading, yet is more accessible and gets the fast trains. The council has spent a large amount of money on restoring the town's Victorian image, reinstating cobbles and period lamp posts. Most of the main street, which has a baker, greengrocer and a few offices, is included within a conservation area.

Theale has accumulated large modern housing estates and an industrial area to the south. A huge business park employs 10,000 people and accommodates major companies such as Vodafone, Thorn EMI and Walkers Crisps. Another is planned, together with a new hotel. A new two-bedroom house is likely to cost around £175,000; three bedrooms £190,000. A four-bedroom house (they are in short supply) could command £350,000. Consent has been given for a 350-home 'Lakeside' development, despite objections from the local council and environmentalists. Some say Theale's name came from its brewery, which made 'the ale'.

Journey: 54 min
Season: £3492
Peak: 2 per hr
changing at Reading
Off-peak: 1 per hr
changing at Reading

ALDERMASTON is a very pretty village on the Kennet and Avon Canal, with a main street of red brick and timber houses sandwiched between Elizabethan cottages. To outsiders, however, it is best remembered as the starting point for the Ban the Bomb marches, chosen by protesters because of its proximity to the Atomic Weapons Research Establishment. Despite the traffic that thunders through it on the A340 to Basingstoke, the village has been well preserved and a relief road is planned. Until recently Aldermaston was an estate village and every third year, on 13th December, a candle auction is still held to determine the rent charged for a small piece of land known as Church Acre – the end of the bidding is signalled by the extinction of a candle flame. Aldermaston Manor Hotel was once the big house, set in ample grounds. There is a parish hall, village green, store and post office. Bowls and cricket are played.

The station itself is useful for shuttle services into Reading, whence fast trains to Paddington are plentiful. Newcomers to the village grazing the Wimpey estate at Aldermaston Wharf for purchases will find that a four-bedroom detached house can cost £475,000. They should also be aware that Aldermaston was just one of the towns and villages in Berkshire affected by flooding in 2007.

‘To outsiders, Aldermaston is best remembered as the starting point for the Ban the Bomb marches**’**

Journey: 58 min
Season: £3492
Peak: 2 per hr
changing at Reading
Off-peak: 1 per hr
changing at Reading

MIDGHAM station is actually in Woolhampton, but was renamed Midgham station in 1873 because of the likelihood of confusion with Wolverhampton. Most people drive to Thatcham, because there is only a handful of parking spaces at Midgham station. It is a linear village, 'big in land but not in people' is how one resident puts it. There is a good food-lover's pub called The Coach & Horses. You could buy a four-bedroom detached modern house for around £545,000.

Woolhampton's main street has half-timbered houses along one side and modern equivalents along the other, built when the road was widened in 1931, with the River Kennet as a focal high point. The A4 and the railway thunder through, making it too noisy to hear people speak. There are several shops, a post office, five pubs, and a fine watermill. A four-bedroom timber-framed cottage on the A4 recently struggled to sell at £425,000.

Journey: 50 min
Season: £3492
Peak: 3 per hr
(some by changing at Reading)
Off-peak: 1 per hr
(one by changing at Reading)

THATCHAM The old village of Thatcham, with a green at its centre, has swollen with new developments in the last couple of decades and more is yet to come. It has become a town, good for secondary shopping, but Reading or Newbury (only two miles away) offer much more. Various developers are busy building 880 new homes on former Ministry of Defence land south of the town centre, near the station. Among Redrow's selection of flats and houses, a three-storey, four-bedroom home costs £250,000, or £350,000 for five bedrooms. The most sought-after development is Dunston Park, within easy reach of the station and an established stamping grounds for professional couples and young families. Four-bedroom houses cost around £260,000 to £400,000. South Thatcham is less popular and sometimes less savoury (being close to the sewage works), so prices are lower. 'Such a shame about the poo farm,' says one agent. But lower prices mean good value and the average price for a four-bedroom house here is around £230,000.

❝If you are not careful at Thatcham you can be stuck in your car at the crossing waiting for your own train to whoosh by❞

The snag about Thatcham is that you have to negotiate the level-crossing to reach the station. 'If you are not careful, you can be stuck in your car at the crossing waiting for your own train to whoosh by,' says one exasperated commuter.

Cold Ash, a little over a mile away, is particularly popular, straggling fetchingly down a hill into the Kennet valley. It has about 4,000 residents, a community hall, a shop-cum-post office and some modern infilling. Property here sells quickly. A Victorian, semi-detached four-bedroom cottage will cost £350,000.

The village of **Bucklebury** nearby, in an Area of Outstanding Natural Beauty, has some pretty cottages and a large common criss-crossed with footpaths. The Blade Bone Inn has a copper-plated mammoth's shoulder bone on display, hence the name. Bradfield, the boys' public school, is close. A period cottage will cost from £400,000 to £900,000, but anything larger with land attached will top £1m. There is a curious little 17th-century painting of a fly and sundial in the local church, with the body and legs on one side of the glass and the wings on the other, *Tempus fugit* (time flies).

Journey: 49 min

Season: £3800

Peak: 3 per hr (some by changing at Reading)

Off-peak: 2 per hr (one by changing at Reading)

NEWBURY is a prosperous former market town with a good train service to London, and attracts commuters like bees to a honeypot. It has a mass of pretty downland villages (*Watership Down* country) within reach and is positioned on the edge of the so-called 'Silicon Valley'. The centre is mostly 17th- and 18th-century with a good range of shops, including an old-fashioned pork butcher and pie-maker, and the Kennet & Avon canal provides scenic richness. Many people feel that new buildings have erased all sense of the brick-and-tile traditional country town. Vodafone has a massive presence – it was once spread between 48 office buildings, but has since moved to a huge new headquarters north of town. 'Fifty years ago I can remember cattle and sheep being driven in, and the circus arriving by train and walking through the town. It's hard to imagine any of that now,' says one old resident.

A great mix of people are attracted to Newbury. Computer companies have brought in the upwardly-mobiles; the racecourse (which has its own weatherboarded train station) attracts the punters; the much-contested bypass has been joined by a new underpass running north–south along the A34 to speed traffic further. Builders are busy catering for demand. Close to the centre you could find a three-bedroom restored Victorian house for around £275,000; spacious flat conversions in period buildings go for £350,000 to £400,000. A standard executive house sells for £400,000 to £500,000. In Garden Close Lane or Tydehams, large houses built in the early 20th century in private grounds will sell for £700,000 upwards.

The once quiet night life has burgeoned as bars, nightclubs and health clubs have proliferated. There is a recreation centre and a swimming pool, and two golf courses with a hotel and spa have been built at **Donnington**, just outside. The controversial bypass cuts a swathe straight across Enborne Chase, a beautiful unspoilt belt of land south of the town.

Villagers from as far to the north-west as **Lambourn**, and from **Hurstbourne Tarrant** in the south, use Newbury station. The National Hunt racehorse training centre is at Lambourn and there are more than 2,000 horses in Lambourn and **Upper Lambourn** together, both busy working villages. Stable-hands work from about seven in the morning until midday, when they rush to the village to shop before starting work again at about four o'clock. Lambourn itself has a few general stores, a farm shop, butcher, post office, saddler and an Indian restaurant. Upper Lambourn has very little other than a pub. A three-bedroom semi will cost £210,000. You need a car if you live here, though buses to Newbury and Swindon are becoming more frequent and there is a call-a-bus service to Hungerford station (see page 187). Strings of 20 to 30 horses exercising in the narrow lanes across the rolling chalk hills can frustrate commuters driving to the station to catch the early morning trains, though gardeners love the manure they provide.

Eastbury, on the River Lambourn two miles closer to Newbury, is a lovely, slightly more expensive village with a good pub, The Plough. Houses are built on the riverbanks, cleverly planted with shrubs and bulbs. It is a popular place to retire. A five-bedroom Grade Two listed cottage with barn recently sold for £950,000; a period three-bedroom cottage would cost up to £395,000; a Sixties' four-bedroom bungalow, £445,000. In neighbouring **East Garston** you will find another enchanting village of thatched houses, with three stables, a shop-cum-post-office and similar house prices.

Further east are two more good chalk villages, **West** and **East Ilsley**, just off the A34. East Ilsley, slightly cheaper of the two, has a central square with a pond, and has resisted new developments apart from some sheltered housing for the elderly. Village life has changed dramatically over the years. This used to be the site of a twice-yearly sheep fair (the greatest sheep market in England after Smithfield, they say) and there were 13 pubs, but today only three remain. Undaunted by the demise of the local post office, the residents have pulled together to launch their own community shop-cum-post office. The village has all the walks that the nearby Downs can offer, including the Ridgeway, along which Neolithic and Bronze Age man once commuted. West Ilsley is the pretty cousin, with a church at its heart, a village green, cricket pitch and pavilion, a pub and a good collection of cottages. Its social life tends to be dominated by the horse-racing fraternity. A four-bedroom period house in the centre of the village would sell for around £500,000.

Stanford Dingley, set in the valley of the River Pang a good six miles to the north-east, is thought to be one of Berkshire's most beautiful villages. It has a classic mellow red-brick Georgian rectory, a 13th-century church screened by chestnut trees, and two old inns, The Bull and The Boot. At The Bull a game known as Ring The Bull is played, in which a ring

'Strings of racehorses in the narrow lanes can frustrate commuters driving to the station'

Chalet-style house, Newbury

dangling from the ceiling has to be swung on to a horn. 'We're an active village,' says the parish clerk. 'We have barn dancing and hold summer fêtes, usually in someone's garden.' The River Pang runs through some of the gardens, providing the original setting for the annual tug-of-war during which the losers traditionally fell in, but damage to the banks has caused the event to be moved. Houses rarely come on the market because people tend to stay put. A house with three or four bedrooms might be bought £450,000.

Yattendon, just north of the M4, has a picture-book village square surrounded by black-and-white 17th-century homes, backed up by Cromwellian red-brick houses. The partly moated manor house, the church, rectory and malt house, all look immaculately cared for. Robert Graves's ashes are in the churchyard. The village has a general store and post office, butcher, hairdresser, smithy, The Royal Oak Hotel and a restaurant. Socially it remains fairly feudal. There are tennis courts and a cricket pitch. The village fête is the main annual event. A three-bedroom period cottage costs around £475,000; a modern family home with four or five bedrooms and half an acre will fetch £800,000.

Two miles to the north of Newbury is the village of **Bagnor**. It is scattered charmingly around a tributary of the Lambourn and remains fairly unspoilt, with a green and a pub, The Blackbird. The Watermill, a little theatre with restaurant, attracts good productions and was recently saved after a £3m appeal. **Leckhampstead** also has a star quality setting, high above the Wantage to Newbury road, and wears its thatched cottages proudly around the small green.

Heading south you come to **Highclere** on the main Andover road, where houses range from £380,000 for four bedrooms to £550,000 for the same in a period cottage with half an acre. **Ecchinswell**, immortalised in Richard Adams's novel *Watership Down*, is a handsome neighbour, where a period three-bedroom cottage will cost around £450,000.

KINTBURY is an unremarkable and yet endearingly compact place, named by one newspaper as one of the top ten most sought-after villages in 2007. It sits on the Kennet and Avon canal deep in agricultural Berkshire, where its position attracts an element of tourism. There is a full range of house types and prices, from new developments for first-time buyers to executive detached houses. Locals fear that too many commuters – who don't join in village activities – are moving in and sending prices 'through the roof'. Anything with three bedrooms costs more than £200,000 and even a starter home can cost £190,000. Two miles away is **Inkpen**, a village strung out so thinly that you can't locate its centre (six hamlets have

Kintbury locals fear that too many commuters – who don't join in village activities – are moving in

Journey: 63min
Season: £3892
Peak: 2 per hr
(some by changing at Reading)
Off-peak: 2 per hr
(one by changing at Reading)

merged imperceptibly over the centuries). It is worth looking at, however, because of its position in the shadow of the Berkshire Downs. Steep winding lanes carry you hundreds of feet up to magical windy walks, and panoramic views from the gibbet on Walbury Hill.

HUNGERFORD Being just off the M4, Hungerford is a favourite starting-place for house-hunters in the area. It is on the twee side of pretty, with a pleasant wide High Street stretching down to the Kennet and Avon Canal and the River Kennet. The tea and trinket shops of tourism are combined with upmarket interior design shops and day-today needs. It is the local antiques capital, and has an antiques arcade that is open on Sundays. Cattle graze the 180-acre common – bestowed by John of Gaunt in the 14th century – which gives way to chalk downs and wooded hills beyond.

Journey: 67 min
Season: £3980
Peak: 2 per hr
Off-peak: 1 per hr

The community is close and tightly knit. As one villager says: 'We have a cracking cricket team, a football team, choir, theatre club, band, good nursery school and so on. People get involved here. All the time something is happening, making it all tick.' Ancient rituals are still observed. On the first Tuesday after Easter the Tutti men tour the town extracting kisses from all the women in return for oranges. There is an arts festival and in December there is a pre-Christmas Victorian Extravaganza.

Tutti men tour the town extracting kisses from all the women in exchange for oranges

On the High Street you can buy two-bedroom terraced houses for £225,000 to £260,000. A larger four-storey Georgian house would start at £550,000. Standard four-bedroom houses on modern developments can be had for £230,000. Pressure on housing is a sensitive issue here; plans to build 500 new houses were abandoned after every single person present voted against the plan at a public meeting.

The train service is good enough until about eight o'clock in the morning. After that the number of London trains dwindles to about one every hour or hour-and-a-half.

Black-and-white period houses, Hungerford area

Within easy reach of Hungerford is the village of **Chilton Foliat**, a set-piece combination of brick, slate and thatch, with one shop and a pub. A five-bedroom thatched cottage on the main street would fetch £995,000. **Little Bedwyn**, on the Kennet and Avon canal, is lovely too. It has an outstanding 18th-century farmhouse in chequered brickwork, with a rare octagonal game larder. The farmyard, with timber and brick barns, is right in the village centre. A three-bedroom terraced period cottage will cost £435,000.

Journey: 73 min
Season: £3996
Peak: 2 per hr
(some by changing
at Reading)
Off-peak: 1 per hr

BEDWYN Above Bedwyn lie the great Saxon defensive ramparts of Chisbury Camp. Down by the Kennet and Avon canal towpath is the 1812 Crofton Pumping Station, which houses the two oldest steam engines in the world that are still doing the job for which they were designed: to raise the water level in the canal. A large four-bedroom Fifties' house with a good garden in **Great Bedwyn** will cost around £550,000.

Journey: 67 min
Season: £5000
Peak: 1 or 2 per hr
Off-peak: 1 every
2 or 3 hrs

PEWSEY Daily commuters have risen dramatically in number – at least 100 hop on regularly now. The trains that serve Pewsey are mostly Inter-City services from the west. There are special commuter trains each morning and evening, otherwise it is always possible to get a train to Newbury and change.

Pewsey is a pretty agricultural town between Salisbury Plain and the Marlborough Downs. Some of the shops are still roofed in thatch, and a statue of Alfred the Great stands in the centre, overlooking the young River Avon and its resident ducks. It has a few supermarkets, an estate agent, bank, bakery and so on, and its own comprehensive school, playing fields and sports centre. The old hospital has been converted and the grounds filled with new houses. One of Wiltshire's six white horses was cut into the chalk hillside in 1785 and provides a potent local landmark.

Starter homes with two bedrooms cost £175,000 and will let at £530 a month. At the new Coopers Court development of 100 homes, a four-bedroom detached house will sell for £365,000. A five-bedroom Grade Two listed thatched cottage in need of renovation will cost rather more at £675,000.

The pretty villages nearby in this Area of Outstanding Natural Beauty include **Manningford Bruce**, two miles away, where thatched cottages cluster around the church and there is a post office. A three-bedroom cottage with orchard and paddock costs around £695,000; a Seventies' four-bedroom semi, £355,000. A few miles to the north-west you come to **Stanton St Bernard**. The Pewsey Vale Riding Centre is here, and there are plenty of weekend cottages and larger country houses. A six-bedroom neo-Georgian mansion with indoor swimming pool and views of the Alton White Horse was recently on the market at £875m.

Urchfont, though 10 miles from the station, is also extremely popular. It contains all the ingredients of the ideal village – thatched cottages, a couple of good pubs, 16th- and 17th-century houses around the greens, one of which is next to the church and has a duck pond. There is also a William and Mary manor house. A rose-covered, 18th-century, three-bedroom cottage off the green will cost £290,000.

One of the advantages of living to the west is that you are within reach of **Devizes**, which is so attractive that it is a treat to go shopping there. The market square is surrounded by houses that are older than their Georgian facades. The town has good small butchers and bakers, a Morrisons and a Tesco, and a new shopping centre is planned. Markets abound, with an outdoor market on Thursday, antiques on Tuesday, a farmers' market once a month and an indoor market from Thursday to Saturday. A small period terraced house will cost around £125,000; a three-bedroom period property £200,000 to £230,000. On the numerous new estates, prices start at £130,000 for a two-bedroom coach house and rise to £400,000 for four bedrooms. The Kennet and Avon Canal has a flight of locks, 29 over a two-mile stretch, rising 237ft to the town.

Less than three miles to the east of Pewsey is **Wootton Rivers**, where you pay a premium for prettiness. A two-bedroom thatched cottage here costs £475,000. There is only one street, running up from the bridge over the Kennet and Avon Canal, and a delightful pub called The Royal Oak. Along the towpath are the restored lock and lock-house. The character of the place is so rural that even the churchyard seems merely an interruption in the farming landscape. The church itself is distinguished by a wooden belfry containing an unusual clock with a broomstick for a pendulum. Just to the north, for those in search of sylvan solitude, are the 4,500 acres of Savernake Forest.

East Grafton, a few miles further east towards Hungerford, offers slightly larger houses. A four-bedroom period house with land and pool would command £850,000; a three-bedroom semi-detached cottage £299,000. The A338 runs through it, but it keeps away from the village proper, where there is a large green and a Victorian church edged with thatched cottages.

To the north is **Marlborough**, the old halt for 18th-century stage coaches on the run from London to Bath. Today the town is dominated by the boys' public school (it now takes girls) and the tea rooms where they buy their sticky buns. Marlborough is an extremely popular place to live – it is close enough to the M4 at Swindon, it has a good range of small specialist shops (though Pizza Express and Caffè Uno have arrived) and it is surrounded by spectacular countryside.

Georgian houses are the most sought-after, though there are plenty of half-timbered houses hidden down the small back lanes off the broad High Street. Two-bedroom Victorian terraced cottages sell at around £230,000; detached houses on newish estates £285,000 to £350,000; while an eight-bedroom Fifties' country house in landscaped gardens recently went on the market at £1.55m. There is a jazz festival each summer and a fair in October, but there is no

'Marlborough is an extremely popular place to live – it is close to the M4 and is surrounded by spectacular countryside'

cinema. The church is strong. There is a choral society and a railway society that has restored the old railway track to Swindon as a cycle path. The Scouts and Cubs have taken it upon themselves to clean the chalk outlines of the white horses in the area.

Journey: 87 min
Season: £7768 – but buy one from Castle Cary, which, at £6596, is a lot cheaper
Peak: 1 or 2 per hr
Off-peak: 1 every 1 or 2 hrs

WESTBURY
was once a charming small town, with Georgian houses grouped around the market place and church, and a wonderful Victorian swimming pool, but it has been swamped by new housing. There are a few shops – a butcher, greengrocer, bank and supermarket with post office. Two-bedroom starter homes can be bought for £117,000, and small three-bedroom semis for £140,000. High above Westbury stands the oldest white horse in Wiltshire, believed to have commemorated King Alfred's victory over the Danes in the ninth century.

Bratton, a couple of miles to the east, offers sleepy lanes where a small stream runs past some of the old cottages tucked into the hedgerows. The village has a store and a school. A beautiful four-bedroom Georgian estate cottage would sell for around £695,000; a three-bedroom end-of-terrace for £270,000. **Edington** is similar, though more remote with a nice pub called The Lamb. This area is rather far from any large town so prices tend to be lower and commuting is rigorous. A thatched cottage might cost £249,000 upwards.

Journey: 107 min
Season: £7880 – but buy one from Castle Cary which, at £6596, is a lot cheaper
Peak: 1 per hr (one through train, change at Westbury on others)
Off-peak: 1 every 2 hrs (changing at Westbury)

FROME
isn't quite in the best countryside close to Bath, nevertheless it has a distinctive character with lots of stone buildings set on the steep eastern hillsides of the Mendips. The old market place still features in the daily life of the town, with an outdoor charter market (Wednesdays and Saturdays), country market (Thursdays) and monthly farmers' market. The shopping centre is unimaginative, but does include a Marks and Spencer. There is a cinema and the much admired Black Swan arts centre. The narrow, twisted streets are worth

Late-Victorian house, near Frome

walking through just to enjoy – the most famous is Cheap Street, which is cobbled and has a watercourse running down the centre.

An old terraced cottage with three bedrooms will cost from £155,000 in the conservation area just off the centre. New conversions in an old brewery start at £115,000 for one bedroom, and £145,000 for two.

To the west and south-west are several villages that teeter on the edges of the old stone quarries. When you look, bear in mind that there are plans to expand the quarries at **Whatley** (one of the largest in the UK) and **Leigh on Mendip**. Three miles north is **Lullington**, a very pretty hamlet with a green and a church, where an old stone house with four bedrooms might be had for £450,000.

Journey: 98 min

Season: £6596

Peak: 1 per hr

Off-peak: 1 every 2 hrs

CASTLE CARY

This is long-haul commuting, but people do it. Parking at the station is easy, and you can pick up the trains pelting back and forth to the Devon seaside. Castle Cary sits on the last few ripples of the Mendips before the relentless flatlands of the Somerset Levels. The town owes much of its prosperity to agriculture and the horse-hair weaving trade. There is still a weaver in the town, though the hair is now imported from China. The remains of the old motte-and-bailey castle that gave the town its name are still here. A small market is held on Tuesdays and a farmer's market once a month.

The mellow, golden local stone is what makes people fall in love with the place. There are a few traditional shops, good private schools nearby, a thatched hotel called The George and a notable rectory just outside at **Ansford**, which was once the home of the Reverend James Woodforde, author of *Diary of A Country Parson*. New developments have arrived to the north and more are in the pipeline. A two-bedroom flat can be bought for around £140,000, a three-bedroom terraced house for around £200,000, while a four-bedroom period house and garden will cost £400,000 to £500,000.

Commuters necessarily have to live very close to the station because of the length of the journey. A clutch of places within a five-mile belt include the stone villages of **North** and **South Cadbury**, and **Yarlington**, which is a good agricultural working village with a mix of modern and old houses, priced very similarly to those in Castle Cary. To the north-west is **Ditcheat**, also a good working village. This is dairy country – rich, green and undulating – where much of the milk goes to butter and cheese-making factories.

'Castle Cary sits on the last few ripples of the Mendips before the relentless flatlands of the Somerset levels**'**

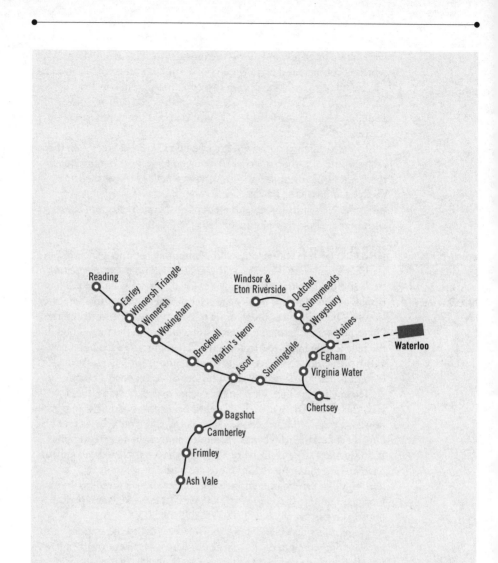

Journey: 35 min
Season : £2000
Peak: 6 per hr
Off-peak: 4 per hr

STAINES has been an important communications point ever since the Romans established a river crossing here on their route from London to the west. Not all subsequent bridges have lasted so well – three of them had collapsed by the end of the 18th century. The present one, opened by William IV in 1832, survives despite the heavy traffic from the A30 and M25. A surprisingly small station car park, accommodating only 50 or so cars, means that the surrounding roads are clogged by all-day parkers. Commuters often prefer to travel from other stations if they can. There is a wide range of housing. Large developments offer flats and houses from £130,000 for a studio, £200,000 for a two-bedroom flat, around £280,000 for a three-bedroom semi and £400,000 to £450,000 for a four-bedroom detached. Staines is one of Surrey's three main shopping centres. It keeps up to date – the huge Elmsleigh shopping centre opened in 2005 and is augmented by arts entertainment venues, including a 10-screen Warner Brothers multiplex, health club and restaurants. The street market is on Wednesdays and Saturdays. The riverside is full of potential and the small roads leading off Laleham Road to the water are sought-after. There is a sailing and a rowing club and along the riverside there are apartments, lawns, walks and moorings. A terraced house with two bedrooms and a patio could cost £390,000.

'Three bridges at Staines had collapsed by the end of the 18th century'

    Laleham, on the way to Shepperton, is the most favoured village, spread along a sizeable stretch of riverside. It has its own cricket club and a few basics – a Spar, an antiques shop and three pubs – and what one local called a 'cliquey atmosphere but a nice clique. Everyone gets on well'. In the predominantly Victorian village centre, three bedroom semis can be bought for £350,000 to £450,000, a large four-bedroom detached house would cost £560,000.

'A cliquey atmosphere, but a nice clique. Everyone gets on well'

> Spur to Windsor & Eton Riverside via Wraysbury, Sunnymeads and Datchet

Journey: 47 min
Season: £2200
Peak: 2 per hr
Off-peak: 1 per hr

WRAYSBURY spreads itself rather wantonly and has several distinguishing characteristics, including two stations – Sunnymeads, only a mile away (see below), still counts as Wraysbury – and three miles of water frontage. It is surrounded by gravel pits, which have been landscaped into 60 acres of lakes, providing sanctuaries for wildlife and a magnet for birdwatchers and sailing clubs. Until recently 80 per cent of the houses were detached and individually built, though as a relatively new village it was rather looked down upon in its early days. Some of the roads are privately maintained by the residents, many of whom work at Heathrow which sends planes straight overhead. The M4 skirts the village without spoiling it, and counts as a convenience rather than a drawback. Wraysbury at one time was a weekend retreat for Londoners and there were many riverside shanties. These have given way to houses in the £650,000 to £1m bracket. There is a sprinkling of pre-Georgian cottages, a few Edwardian and Victorian terraces and some substantial small mansions. Modern three- and four-bedroom houses on a Persimmon development will cost from £350,000, with two-bedroom apartments starting at £230,000. Surrounding green belt should provide protection against future development. There is a handful of local shops, including a pharmacy which makes its own aromatherapy remedies, a post office, two pubs and a village green. One of the major features of life in Wraysbury is the number and quality of the local societies. These offer every option from cricket and fishing to history, drama, country & western and jazz – all well attended and well organised. Opposite the village is the island where Magna Carta is believed to have been signed.

Opposite the village is the island where the Magna Carta is believed to have been signed

Journey: 50 min
Season: £2260
Peak: 2 per hr
Off-peak: 1 per hr

SUNNYMEADS Wraysbury's second station is at Sunnymeads, on the boundary between Wraysbury and **Horton**, which is a rural village with a green, one shop and two pubs, both listed. It has proud historical connections with John Milton, who wrote some of his poems here, and with the Bowes-Lyon family. The local forge built the equestrian statue of George III, known as the Copper Horse, which stands on Snow Hill in Windsor Great Park. The snag is that the village lies directly in the line of most flights approaching Heathrow airport. The mix of properties ranges from a handful of listed houses to ex-council semis. (A new block of apartments on the green has been designed to resemble the old offices that once stood on the site, with flats selling at around £190,000 for two bedrooms.)

A two-bedroom apartment in Old Mill Place, Wraysbury, with views of the River Colne costs £240,000. Bell's Lane is a leafy haven where a five-bedroom detached house would sell at around £635,000.

Journey: 53 min
Season: £2284
Peak: 2 per hr
Off-peak: 2 per hr

DATCHET Only a mile from Windsor, **Datchet** has avoided being overshadowed and retains a village personality. Physically it is compact and shaped like a letter H with two cross-bars. The left of the H is on the river (one of the ports of call in Jerome K. Jerome's *Three Men in a Boat*); the right is on the village green and the two cross-bars are High Street and Queens Road. The railway runs up the middle, regularly halting traffic at the level crossing (including Government ministers complete with police outriders on their way to see the Queen).

Most of the houses here were in the upper price bracket until a couple of decades ago when new estates aimed at first-time buyers began to appear. Studios and one-bedroom terraced houses cost between £90,000 and £140,000. Elsewhere, Victorian three-bedroom semis are from £450,000 to £600,000; detached houses with 150ft gardens and 45ft frontages are from £635,000. Southlea Road is desirable and has some large 18th-century houses at £1m or more.

Datchet has always attracted London commuters and there is a large station car park. The other strong connection is with Heathrow: both ground-staff and aircrew favour the village for its pleasant atmosphere and easy access to the airport. Datchet's charms have also attracted its share of past and present celebrities, including Sir William Herschel, the astronomer, Sir Robert Watson-Watt, the inventor of radar, and now a clutch of ageing showbiz personalities. There is a post office, two pubs, a library, a Montessori, local primary and secondary schools. On the second Thursday of each month there is a village market, selling home-made and home-grown foods and handicrafts. There is a local golf club (the course acts as a flood plain when the river rises), a water-ski club, cricket (sometimes the village musters a showbiz eleven), sailing and a boatyard on the river which does daily hire. The strong community spirit is reflected in the monthly newsletter, *The Datchet Chat*.

For train
information, see
overleaf

WINDSOR & ETON RIVERSIDE Windsor & Eton Riverside is Windsor's second station, a slower route to London than the shuttle from Windsor & Eton Central to Slough (which picks up the Inter-City service from London to Paddington). Commuters from both stations benefit from Windsor's attractive mix of quaint old streets below the castle, smart new shops – everything from old family businesses to chain stores and a branch of Fenwick's – and a monthly farmers' market. It also has the 4,800 acres of Windsor Great Park

Journey: 56 min
Season: £2320*
Peak: 2 per hr
Off-peak: 2 per hr
* £2512 for both
Windsor & Eton
Riverside to
Waterloo and Eton
Central to
Paddington
(see page 150)

close by. Georgian houses cloak Castle Hill, and pepper the centre of the town, which is composed mainly of Victorian terraces. A small cottage in need of improvement will start at £270,000; a three-bedroom house within walking distance of the town centre £400,000 to £475,000 and half as much again if very charming. The west and south of Windsor evolved in the Thirties and Fifties and semis now cost over £295,000. Development is restricted by Crown lands and green belt. At Imperial Park, a large estate on old Haileybury School grounds, apartments sell for £275,000, three-bedroom homes start at £575,000 and six-bedroom detached houses cost £1.25m.

The most fashionable locations are in the Golden Triangle around St Leonard's Hill, King's Road, Adelaide Square and Bolton Avenue. Newish four- to five-bedroom houses at King's Keep on Bolton Avenue sell for an average £684,000. In Clarence Crescent, another desirable road, Victorian four-bedroom houses start at £1.5m. The Guild Hall in the High Street includes a marvellous piece of architectural deception by Christopher Wren. When the town councillors saw his plans in 1687, they apparently demanded more columns to support the upper floor (and their own combined weight). Wren obliged, up to a point. The new columns all end slightly short of the ceiling.

Eton is full of antiques shops, restaurants, and schoolboys in wing collars and tailcoats

Old Windsor, south-east of the town, was described in the *Domesday Book* as the third largest town in Berkshire. It had a wooden Saxon palace, which deteriorated after William built his castle and the town was reduced to a village. Today, Old Windsor it is a small town with parades of shops, a post office, a bank and a convenient bus service into Windsor for major shopping. Large detached houses, some with river frontages, are a main feature of the market. The Friary is the road to aim for, where Victorian houses and modern infills in good-sized grounds cost £600,000 to £1m. The main road is fringed with Twenties'-built houses from £270,000, one or two large enough to

Dutch-style family house, near Egham

satisfy those who want a private estate close to London. These are the choice cuts in estate agents' windows, with price tags over £1m. Elton John occupies one. Two large housing estates provide less expensive homes, priced lower than their equivalents in Windsor where communications are better. Those who choose Old Windsor do so for its more rural atmosphere, fishing, boating, and lively community spirit with plenty of sporting and social opportunities.

The Windsor Farm Shop, in converted potting sheds on the edge of Home Park, sells products from the royal farms, Duchy of Cornwall and local specialist suppliers.

Eton is full of antiques shops, restaurants and schoolboys in wing collars and tailcoats. Inevitably, there is something of an us-and-them atmosphere. A two-bedroom Victorian cottage on the High Street could cost £325,000. Swanky luxury apartments have appeared at Eton Riverside, with one-bedroom flats from £330,000 and penthouses selling at up to £1m.

>Continuation of main line

Journey: 41 min
Season: £2120
Peak: 5 per hr
Off-peak: 4 per hr

EGHAM Although Egham technically is a small town it retains an unhurried atmosphere from its village past. The presence of Royal Holloway (London University's out-of-city campus college) means there are well-patronised bars, bistros and pubs, and a hungry market for student accommodation. Parents buy-to-let to students here. Among the new estates, first-time buyers can buy one-bedroom flats from £170,000. Two-bedroom Victorian semis in the town centre start at £240,000. The town has a good mix of local shopping, including a butcher and a baker whose families have been serving the community for more than 100 years. There are plenty of sports and social clubs, and an active historical society.

To the west, **Englefield Green** is a prestigious address thought by some as rather twee. It comes with a green, traditional pubs and a little high street of shops including a baker. A two-bedroom terraced cottage will cost £250,000. To the south is **Thorpe**, a village bisected by the M25. Despite this apparent handicap, houses here are 15 per cent or so more expensive than their equivalents in Egham. The smallest two-bedroom Victorian semi will cost around £295,000, and there is a preponderance of large houses in spacious plots. A four-bedroom detached house built in the Sixties or Seventies will fetch up to £500,000. There is a theme park just outside the village, but the traffic to it does not pass through the village itself.

Journey: 45 min
Season: £2280
Peak: 5 per hr
Off-peak: 4 per hr

VIRGINIA WATER Brushed by the M25, Virginia Water has seen two enormous new developments in recent years: Virginia Park and St Anne's Park. They are both super-luxurious gated estates, each with a communal pool, gym, Jacuzzi and tennis courts to suit the new rich. Their very presence has pushed prices up. A two-bedroom flat here will cost £350,000 (compared to £225,000 in the village). A five-bedroom detached house with a double garage will cost upwards of £1m. The grand estate lifestyle all began with the Wentworth Estate, built around the famous golf course by a speculative developer named Tarrant in the Twenties. Celebrities flourish in its prosperous atmosphere – the pantheon of names has included Russ Abbott, Bruce Forsyth, Nanette Newman and Bryan Forbes. A five-bedroom family house on the Wentworth Estate will start at £3m and can easily reach £10m. Similar houses in half an acre in Lower Wentworth, which does not overlook the golf course, will fetch £2m. The atmosphere is quiet and rural – the first breath of real countryside outside London – but there is little sign of rural hardship. There are two parades of specialist shops, boutiques, a delicatessen and several excellent preparatory schools. Less expensive houses are few in number. For a two-bedroom Sixties' semi you would pay around £290,000 – which represents a small premium over the next most prestigious area, Sunningdale. The stretch of water that gives the area its name is a great ornamental lake created in the 18th century by the Duke of Cumberland. He also built the nearby Fort Belvedere, later the home of Edward VIII where the abdication was signed.

> Line to Chertsey

Journey: 76 min
(52 min changing at Weybridge)
Season: £2280
Peak: 2 per hr plus another 2 per hr changing at Weybridge
Off-peak: 2 per hr

CHERTSEY is reaping the commercial benefit of lying just inside the M25 – an arbitrary boundary chosen by many London companies relocating their head offices. Developments have sprouted in recent years to cope with the expansion. Very little remains of the famous Benedictine Abbey founded in 666 – Henry VIII ordered the stones to be used in the rebuilding of his palace at Oatlands Park – but the handsome, seven-arched 18th-century bridge is still a landmark. There is a good selection of period properties that, foot for foot, offer better value than up-market Weybridge. Next to the park and woods of St Ann's Hill there are large detached houses with price tags rising above £1.25m. Abbey Road is an equally prestigious address. Grove Road, by the football club, offers more affordable Victorian houses, which cost between £250,000 and £400,000 for three bedrooms. First-time buyers will find a wealth of one-bedroom modern flats at £160,000. Good schools include Sir William Perkins' girls' independent. There is a highly regarded hospital, St Peter's.

Lyne and **Longcross** are the most sought-after villages in the area, graced with large detached houses (it costs 15–25 per cent more to buy into them). Bungalows in large garden plots cost £350,000 to £450,000; a four-bedroom detached house with 100ft garden costs about £550,000. The villages lack properties of real character but the agricultural smells and lack of a bus service are still enough to make country-lovers feel at home.

> Continuation of main line

Journey: 51 min
Season: £2640
Peak: 4 per hr
Off-peak: 2 per hr

SUNNINGDALE The development of the Southern Railway at the turn of the century made Sunningdale accessible to London businessmen who wanted to build country mansions with golf and racing on their doorsteps. Several of these minor palaces still survive intact, but many were demolished in the Thirties and Sixties to make way for new development. Others have been converted into flats. It is a village of two parts – the old village around the church, and the busier shopping area near the station. Part of it lay within Surrey until 1991, when the whole was switched into Berkshire. The most sought-after houses are in Titlarks Hill (where Gary Lineker lives), leading to the golf course, and in Ridgemount and Priory Roads. Large new-build houses in half to one acre sell for between £2m and £3.75m; a ten-year-old mini mansion could cost £5.95m. Kenneth Branagh has completely rebuilt a house here. Sunningdale is not exclusively a playground for the rich. In the old village there are three-bedroom Victorian semis for between £350,000 and £450,000. Think twice before buying a house too close to the A30. When the M25 or M3 get clogged the traffic pours on to the other through roads and jams these, too. There is a good choice of state and private schools. Sport is plentiful but rather exclusive. There are two top polo clubs, and golf at Wentworth and Sunningdale, which has the oldest golf club for women in the country.

'Sunningdale offers country mansions with golf and horse-racing right on their doorsteps'

Sunninghill to the west is a large parish covering several communities, none of which has retained its original atmosphere. The area known as **Cheapside** is small and sweet with The Thatched Tavern that is memorable for its good food. Sunninghill has a busy High Street with 50 or so shops, but its identity problem is not helped by the fact that Ascot station (see page 200) is in Sunninghill, and most people prefer it to Sunninghill station. East-west trains stop at Ascot, and the car park has been considerably extended. Plentiful late 19th- and early 20th-century houses sell to London commuters or to those with jobs or businesses in Camberley or Heathrow. You would pay between £350,000 and £450,000 for a two- or three-bedroom semi. The church is busy, as is the dramatics society, The Quince Players.

A couple of miles south of Sunninghill is **Windlesham**. It a village with a stout heart, which has fended off new development and obtained lottery money to refurbish the amateur Windlesham Club and Theatre. Semis can be bought for £350,000 to £400,000. Yet it flirts with the rich and famous, too. His Highness Sheik Mohammed Bin Rashid Al Maktoum, Crown Prince of Dubai, owns a palatial residence here; Brian May, Queen guitarist, both lives and has a recording studio here; and the Duchess of York famously let Ruby

Wax into her rented house here (and showed Ruby her T-shirt shelves and fridge), but she has since moved on. A five- or six-bedroom Thirties' house, standing in one or two acres in Westwood Road, will fetch between £3m and £6m.

Journey: 54 min
Season: £2784
Peak: 4 per hr
Off-peak: 2 per hr

ASCOT Strangers expect Ascot to be a glamorous place to live, because of its high racing and fashion profile. They are often surprised by its lack of real character. Its main attraction is the racecourse, which was laid out in 1711 for Queen Anne. The shopping centre consists of rows of small exclusive retailers. A farmers' market is held on the third Sunday in the month. The level of wealth, however, can almost be measured by the height of the hedges – and they are lofty here. Racehorse owners (those who own part-share of a horse rather than whole stables) pay a premium for four- to five-bedroom detached houses in Coronation Road and Kier Park. A new-build six-bedroom house on five acres would cost £2.65m; a period house with five bedrooms and an annexe, needing a little work, could be snaffled for £1m. You effectively buy into a rich man's playground – close to Windsor and Heathrow Airport, with golf at Hawthorn Hill and Wentworth, racing at Ascot and Windsor, polo at Smiths Lawn and the Royal Berkshire Polo Club, and boating and sailing on the Thames. For the very rich there are some sizeable mansions. Not more than a mile away is Ascot Place and its several hundred acres, which changed hands for £20m and is now being converted into luxury apartments, where two bedrooms with underground parking cost £550,000. There are slightly smaller fry, though. In South Ascot there are Victorian railway workers' cottages as well as larger Victorian semis that sell at £550,000 for four bedrooms. Property at Grand Regency Heights, a major new development facing the racecourse, sells at prices between £265,000 and £600,000. Royal Ascot golf club is in the centre of the racecourse. There are also opportunities for squash, tennis and cricket.

'The level of wealth can almost be measured by the height of the hedges'

North Ascot is quite different in character from the Ascot that surrounds the racecourse. Concentrated building began here in the 1880s and has been spreading north and west of the racecourse ever since. A Victorian semi in North Ascot will cost £225,000 to £300,000; three-bedroom semis on infill developments start at around £250,000.

Parts of Ascot are in the parish of **Winkfield**, the largest in the county. It covers nearly 10,000 acres and contains communities described as settlements rather than villages with traditional focal points. Winkfield itself is semi-rural, with some listed buildings and small terraces with modern infill, and a new community hall regularly booked by local clubs and societies (from badminton to dancing).

There is a real worry that it will lose its identity and become 'just a place from which to get to other places'. It has several parks and recreation areas but no village green, though it still has an annual May festival. A small terraced house sells for around £350,000; a four-bedroom house in the desirable Winkfield Row goes for £410,000.

Most of the small communities in this area have their own local societies and, as this is partly green belt, the strongest voices belong to the residents' associations and conservation societies fighting against new development. Golf and polo are the favourite outdoor activities and there are numerous riding establishments. To avoid frightening the horses in the Cranbourne area you need to drive almost permanently in low gear. A good local primary school attracts young families.

> Line to Ash Vale via Bagshot, Camberley and Frimley

Journey: 71 min
Season: £2856*
Peak: 4 per hr
(3 through trains; others changing at Ascot or Ash Vale)
Off-peak: 2 per hr
(1 changing at Ascot plus 1 changing at Ash Vale)
* £2988 if also valid via Ash Vale

BAGSHOT Once a wild heathland frequented by highwaymen (it was the perfect distance from London, reached by coach as dusk settled), Bagshot developed in the mid-19th century and is carefully maintaining its Victorian atmosphere. Lamp-posts are period-style and new developments and refurbishments have to be in keeping. The area thrives because of the many London companies that have relocated here and to nearby Fleet. There is day-to-day shopping, and there are good schools and plenty of opportunities for leisure. Connaught Park, a development on the outskirts, is often known as Terminal 5 because of the high concentration of airport personnel who live here. One-bedroom flats sell for around £135,000; two-bedroom houses for between £175,000 and £220,000. College Ride is highly prized for its gardens backing on to Windsor Forest and a tract of land recently made available by the Crown for public use, which is popular with walkers and bikers. Victorian and Edwardian houses in a good position here start at around £250,000 for two bedrooms. In the small modern development on Heywood Drive, four-bedroom houses sell for £380,000 to £450,000.

'To avoid frightening the horses in the Cranbourne area you need to drive almost permanently in low gear'

Journey: 72 min
Season: £2880
Peak: 4 per hr
(3 through trains;
others changing at
Ascot or Ash Vale)
Off-peak: 4 per hr
(2 changing at Ascot
plus 2 changing at
Ash Vale)

CAMBERLEY Before the mid-19th century when the Royal Military Academy was established at Sandhurst, Camberley simply did not exist. Large houses with between 6 and 12 bedrooms were built for officers, with more modest developments and shops following between 1880 and 1910. At first there were two areas, Cambridge Town and York Town, named after the two dukes who had been heads of the academy. But when the mail kept going to the university town instead of the military one, the whole area was united under the single name, Camberley. Most of the largest old houses have gone, demolished to make way for new cul-de-sacs. Those that remain will set you back £600,000 to £800,000 for six bedrooms; a modern infill with five bedrooms costs £800,000. There are also some Victorian terraces, which you can buy into for around £295,000. One disadvantage of living in Camberley is traffic noise from the A30 and M3. Attractions include good high street shopping and the Main Square centre by the station, in addition to the Meadows shopping centre on the outskirts. The Camberley Theatre shows films in the auditorium and provides rehearsal space. There are good schools within reach.

For something more rural and desirable, you need to look west of Sandhurst to **Eversley**, where £400,000 will buy three bedrooms; or £895,000 will buy a period house with four bedrooms on half an acre.

Journey: 68 min
Season: £2880
Peak: 3 per hr
(3 through trains;
others changing at
Ascot or Ash Vale)
Off-peak: 2 per hr
(1 changing at Ascot
plus 1 changing at
Ash Vale)

FRIMLEY is too modern to call itself a village. It is a one-high-street sort of a place, with all the basics and is particularly valued for its good schools. Most of the housing is contained on three large estates. Paddock Hill, for example, was built over a decade ago and offers one-bedroom maisonettes at £148,000, three-bedroom semis at £220,000 and Tudor-style four- and five-bedroom houses at £400,000 or more. A lively young population entertains itself at Bagshot's nightclub or at Basingstoke's bowling alley, ice rink and cinema, 20 minutes' drive down the M3. Five minutes from the centre is Frimley Green, which has a very old heart. The roads off the green have a mix of houses built in the Thirties, Seventies and Eighties. Houses with a country feel on the Guildford Road cost £600,000 up to £1m but you can pay much more for a period piece. Commuter parking is limited but most people either walk to the station or drive instead to Farnborough, whence the direct line to Waterloo takes under 40 minutes.

ASH VALE See Alton section of the **Waterloo to Salisbury** line, page 210.

> Continuation of main line

Martin's Heron
Journey: 59 min
Season: £2800
Peak: 2 or 3 per hr
Off-peak: 2 per hr

Bracknell
Journey: 62 min
Season: £2840
Peak: 2 or 3 per hr
Off-peak: 2 per hr

MARTIN'S HERON AND BRACKNELL Nothing in Bracknell today suggests that in the early 19th century it might have been described as 'a small thoroughfare hamlet adorned with many genteel residences and delightful villas'. In 1948 it was incorporated as Berkshire's only New Town, planned for a London overspill of 25,000. It now has more than 52,000 inhabitants, all of whom must have chosen it for convenience rather than charm. The increase in commuter traffic was sufficient to require the building of a second station, Martin's Heron. Property prices are relatively modest given that the journey to London takes less than an hour. One-bedroom flats can be found for £115,000 to £140,000; three-bedroom ex-council houses are resolutely stuck at £175,000 to come under the stamp duty threshold; modern semis on private developments cost between £170,000 and £240,000; four-bedroom detached houses with double garage and garden, £280,000 to £350,000. Unkind critics attach the 'concrete jungle' tag. Yet there is plenty of high-tech industry to keep a large proportion of the young population busy locally, with good sports facilities, every kind of club, a hands-on science exhibition in the Look Out Discovery Centre and a Coral Reef water complex with a pirate ship, water slides and erupting volcano.

Three miles west of Bracknell is **Binfield**, which has outgrown its status as a village to become a suburb of Bracknell. Historically it is notable chiefly for its connection with Alexander Pope, who lived here as a boy in the early 1700s. It is loosely knit with greens, has a few shops including an art shop, curry house, Chinese takeaway, fish-and-chip-shop, some small businesses, the John Nike Sports Complex

Modern two-up-two-down, near Bracknell

(for dry skiing, ice-skating and tobogganing), as well as the redoubtable Binfield Badger Group.

Modern estate housing includes Temple Park, overlooking the golf course, and Foxley Field where prices start at £205,000 for a two-bedroom semi or end-of-terrace, £225,000 for a three-bedroom detached, £400,000-plus for a five-bedroom detached. A community spirit still survives and young mothers, as well as the established older residents, are involved in the two community centres, drama club, Scout, Brownie and Guide groups, and line dancing. The local primary school has a good reputation, with secondary age children moving on to Bracknell and Wokingham.

Journey: 68 min
Season: £2928
Peak: 2 or 3 per hr
Off-peak: 2 per hr

WOKINGHAM Despite centuries of doffing its cap to nearby royals in Windsor Forest, Wokingham was not granted a coat of arms until Coronation year, 1953. A relic of the royal hunt still survives in Nine Mile Ride, which was cut through the forest to enable ladies to follow the chase from their carriages. The town's Millennium effort to plant 200,000 bulbs has meant that every public and private space should be covered in a haze of bluebells each spring.

The old market town has expanded rapidly during the last few decades, swelling its population from 9,000 to around 150,000. Strategically, Wokingham is extremely well-placed, being served by the A329 London to Reading road and by the M4, which links it to Heathrow airport, the West of England and South Wales. Bus services provide links to Reading and Bracknell. The town centre is surrounded by modern residential streets, many of which are still lined with old oaks and other forest trees. On the west side stands the Woosehill development, containing more than 2,000 houses, shops, a school and community and health centres. Most of it went up in the Seventies and Eighties. The mixed estate offers flats and one-, two-, three- and four-bedroom houses at prices ranging from £150,000 to £500,000. A relatively new addition is Keephatch Park, which has five-bedroom detached houses at £500,000 to £550,000 and four-bedroom houses at £350,000 upwards.

Lucas Hospital in Luckley Road, built in 1665 to provide a home for 16 elderly men, is Wokingham's prize Grade One listed building. The hospital is arranged around three sides of a quadrangle, with a chapel filling the right-hand wing. Visitors are admitted by appointment. Elsewhere there are some attractive 16th- and

Nine Mile Ride was cut through the forest to enable ladies to follow the chase from their carriages

Wokingham has some attractive 16th- and 17th-century houses, particularly in Rose Street and Shute End

17th-century houses, particularly in Rose Street and Shute End. An 18th-century three-bedroom house in Rose Street with no garden could cost £400,000, but would be a rare buy.

The most expensive parts of town are in Murdoch and Sturges Roads, just to the south-east of the centre, where prices for large Edwardian houses, with four or five bedrooms and big gardens, start at £1m. Priest Avenue and Rances Lane are also desirable, where three-bedroom houses in large gardens cost £375,000. Cheaper properties built in the Sixties are found around the Mulberry Business Park and along the Finchampstead and Luckley Roads. A three-bedroom bungalow here will cost around £300,000.

In the north, the large Emmbrook development was begun in the Thirties, with additions in the Sixties, Seventies and Eighties. Modest estate-type housing predominates, with prices starting at £200,000 for a two-bedroom terraced house and rising to £400,000 for a four-bedroom, detached chalet-style house.

'Wokingham is a good area for golf fanatics, who have five courses to choose from'

Wokingham is a good area for golf fanatics, who have five courses to choose from. It also has public playing fields, a sports centre, indoor swimming pool and a small theatre. Shops include Tesco, Waitrose and W.H. Smith, and a farmers' market is held on the first Thursday in the month. Four weeks before Christmas the town seizes up for the winter carnival, and each February it turns out for the half marathon, which attracts over 1,750 entrants.

WINNERSH AND WINNERSH TRIANGLE

Winnersh
Journey: 73 min
Season: £3000
Peak: 2 or 3 per hr
Off-peak: 2 per hr

Winnersh Triangle
Journey: 75 min
Season: £3056
Peak: 2 or 3 per hr
Off-peak: 2 per hr

WINNERSH AND WINNERSH TRIANGLE Winnersh has been built on old Windsor Great Forest land, starting in the Twenties and gathering pace in the last three decades. There is a supermarket, a large health club and DIY store for Sunday Black & Decker fiends. The arrival of a 12-screen cinema upset older villagers, who described it as 'a warhorse with neon signs'. The Winnersh Triangle sounds dangerously exotic, but it is not a place where boats disappear without trace – rather it's a large business centre. Traffic-hum from the A329M and M4 is a constant reminder of the quality of the road communications.

'The rhododendron drive to the next village of Barkham largely survives, though it has been hacked about a bit by new development'

The most famous former resident of Winnersh was John Walter II, son of the founder of *The Times*. He built a Georgian mansion called Bearwood, which his son replaced with the present mansion, now a boys' private school. Walter also built the 'model' estate of **Sindlesham** with its church, pub, school, dower house, cottages, farm and now a golf course. The rhododendron drive which he planted to the next village of **Barkham** largely survives, though it has been hacked about a bit by new development. The model estate itself is now part of Winnersh and rather swamped, but Sindlesham manages to charm. Along the Reading Road are some good-value late Sixties' and Seventies' houses. The village is generally cheaper than Wokingham. A three-bedroom terraced house would cost £225,000. There are also some half-timbered houses

To the north lies **Hurst**, a 'proper' village with a duck pond and green, much the nicest on this side of Reading, although skirted by the M4 it can suffer from traffic noise. It has a shop and a butcher, a post office, a primary school and a strong cricket club. The most desirable four-bedroom cottages here sell for £550,000 to £600,000, but there are cheaper properties, too.

Journey: 77 min
Season: £3096
Peak: 2 or 3 per hr
Off-peak: 2 per hr

EARLEY Despite the name – Earley derives from the Anglo-Saxon words for eagle and wood – there is nothing rural on the horizon here. There are three parts to Earley – Maiden Erlegh, Lower Earley and Earley proper. By some calculations Lower Earley is the third biggest housing estate in Europe, clamped to the southern underbelly of Reading, right beside the M4. Prices range upwards from £125,000 for one bedroom to £425,000 for five bedrooms, but some residents describe living here as tough. The provision of facilities has not kept pace with new houses. Old Earley has the oldest and most expensive properties – older in this context meaning late 19th and early 20th century. Prices range from £180,000 for a two- or three-bedroom Victorian terraced house to £300,000 for a three-bedroom semi and £480,000 for a large four-bedroom house. Maiden Erlegh Park is a belt of ancient woodland with a lake, maintained as a community nature reserve.

'The third biggest housing development in Europe is clamped to the southern underbelly of Reading'

The area is nicer than the less appealing parts of Reading, but still rather a suburban sprawl. The centre of Reading is about 15 minutes away by car, and the 'village' – a misnomer if ever there was one – is enlivened by a large hall of residence for students of Reading University, mostly overseas mature students.

Journey: 82 min*
Season: £3492 (also valid to Paddington)
Peak: 2 or 3 per hr
Off-peak: 2 per hr
* Waterloo only. For faster services see Paddington to Bristol line, page 157

READING For Reading main entry, see **Paddington to Reading and Bristol** line, page 157.

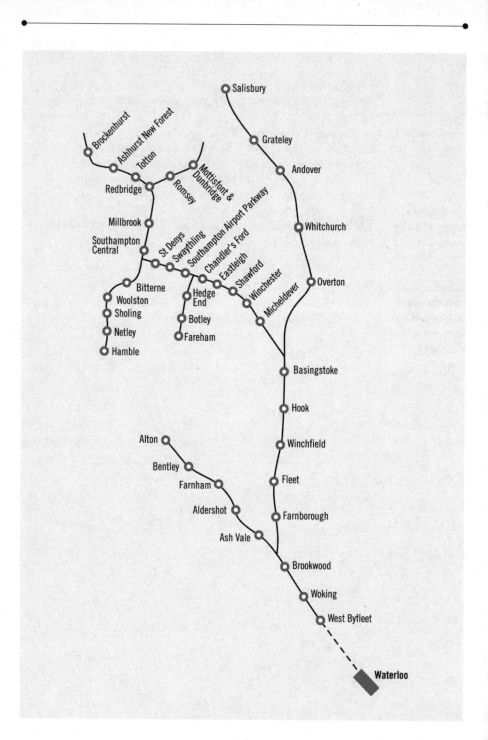

> Salisbury and Southampton

WEST BYFLEET is a large village that has expanded over the years to become inseparable from Woking. Property prices are high because of its proximity to London. A modern three- to four-bedroom town house will be unlikely to cost less than £350,000. An older detached house would be at least £500,000.

Journey: 30 min
Season: £2240
Peak: 4 per hr
Off-peak: 4 per hr

WOKING is a busy commercial town, with a rapidly expanding artistic and cultural life centred on the new museum and gallery, The Lightbox, designed by the creators of the London Eye, which won the Art Fund Prize in 2008. It also has the New Victoria Theatre, the Rhoda McGaw Theatre and six cinema screens. The rail service is frequent, even if available seats may be few, and it is conveniently placed for access to the A3, M3 and M25. The north side of the town is mostly given over to council houses and the south tends to be more sought-after. A neo-Georgian three-bedroom house on a small development would start at around £240,000; a new four-bedroom detached would cost £360,000 upwards. Hook Heath is where the wealthy gather, in mini-mansions on large plots that sell for over £750,000. For lower prices, but a vast range of choice, you could look at Goldsworth Park, where 8,000 homes have been built over the last three decades and a two-bedroom terraced house costs £175,000 to £200,000. New developments by the station come with concierges and private gyms.

Journey: 24 min
Season: £2496
Peak: 12 per hr
Off-peak: 8 per hr

Horsell, on the outskirts and separated by the canal, tends to be slightly more expensive than Woking proper. H.G. Wells lived in Woking for a time, and in *The War of the Worlds* he described the Martians landing on Horsell Common. A Thirties' detached house with three bedrooms would cost from £360,000.

For a vintage Home Counties village there is **Chobham**, two miles to the north-west, no weakling in the Best Kept Village stakes. Lorries have been banned from the High Street, which is very much a conservation area with antiques shops, eateries and a pretty hump-backed bridge over the Bourne brook. Chobham Common is a precious green lung in this part of Surrey, providing wooded bridleways for pony-lovers. People from outside the village run the football and tennis, but the cricket, Brownies, Guides and WI are domestic affairs. The village is very sought-after, so a small period cottage will cost at least £230,000. For a larger period house, perhaps with a paddock, you must expect to pay £900,000.

Journey: 39 min
Season: £2756
Peak: 4 per hr
Off-peak: 4 per hr

BROOKWOOD has the edge on Woking because people prefer the idea of living in a village, no matter how built-up it has become. The strangest fact about the station is that is was built originally to serve the enormous cemetery (created to take 1854 London typhoid victims), not for the convenience of commuters. Small cul-de-sacs of fairly new houses abound. A three-bedroom Thirties' detached house would cost around £295,000.

> Fork to Alton

Journey: 46 min
Season: £2908
Peak: 3 per hr
Off-peak: 2 per hr

ASH VALE is usually considered a rather unfashionable address, though it has the attraction of affordable prices for first-time buyers. It consists mainly of Victorian terraces arranged in grids around the railway station. A two-bedroom terraced house would start at around £175,000.

Journey: 51min
Season: £2940
Peak: 2 per hr
Off-peak: 2 per hr

ALDERSHOT is an army town with a pretty rough feel to it at night. There are 10,000 soldiers and their families. The good thing is that it has terrific sports facilities, including games pitches, gymnastics academy, ski slope and an Olympic-sized swimming pool and as a result has been chosen as the preparation camp for Team GB for the 2012 London Olympics. Victorian terraces went up in Aldershot like mushrooms in a cow pasture. You can buy a two-bedroom terraced house for around £180,000. In the nearby dormitory of Fleet (see page 212), the same house would cost £10,000 more. Aldershot's terraces are surrounded by army married quarters, built in the Thirties and Sixties. Prices rise a little on the Farnham side of town, where a three-bedroom detached house will cost around £350,000. New growth is planned on huge swags of ex-army land.

Journey: 57 min
Season: £3068
Peak: 2 per hr
Off-peak: 2 per hr

FARNHAM is something of a refuge from Aldershot, having a lovely Georgian heart with the castle at its centre. People living anywhere between the two towns will always say they live in Farnham. The south side is more upmarket than the north. It has a country feel, even though it is very well-connected to London by train and the A3. A three-bedroom detached Thirties' house in a quiet road will cost £600,000; a more spacious five-bedroom house over £725,000. There are some modern apartments on the south side, where a three-bedroom unit will cost £250,000 to £375,000. A farmers' market is held once a month.

Journey: 66 min
Season: £3080
Peak: 2 per hr
Off-peak: 1 per hr

BENTLEY is an attractive hamlet, set in the meadows of the River Wey, which has become more sought-after since the bypass put the A31 further east. There are one or two discreet modern estates and a small Charles Church development of large four-bedroom houses with double garages, selling at around £595,000. Smaller, three-bedroom, period terraced cottages may be bought for around £239,000. Jane Austen's brother was once curate of Bentley; Robert Baden-Powell lived in Pax Hill house; and a director of the White Star Shipping line, owners of the *Titanic*, lived at the big house, Jenkyn Place. It is has a primary school and shop and strong sense of community, one reason why it was made the subject of the BBC Radio 4 programme *The Village*. The station is some distance away near Alice Holt forest.

Journey: 70 min
Season: £3200
Peak: 2 per hr
Off-peak: 2 per hr

ALTON is a handsome little market town whose square still fills with stalls every Tuesday. The station building is painted in the old Southern Railway livery of green and cream. The community of 17,000 is essentially a rural one, though it has drawn commuters with the lovely countryside that surrounds it and occasionally been highlighted by agents for its fast growing property prices. You might find a mid-terraced Grade Two listed house with two bedrooms, beams and an inglenook fireplace dating from 1800, for around £195,000. Newer three-storey town houses with three bedrooms start at £360,000. A new development on the fringe of the town has five-bedroom houses from £415,000.

Period five-bedroom thatched houses in the lanes will cost from around £600,000 up to £650,000. One of the most sought-after villages is **Chawton**, a mile away, though the stone-and-thatch cottages only rarely come up for sale.

Chawton's main claim to fame is that Jane Austen lived in a small cottage with her parents and wrote most of her novels here. Her nephew, Edward Knight, lived in the manor house. The cottage is now open to the public.

Old manor house,
Alton area

> Continuation of main line

Journey: 36 min
Season: £2980
Peak: 4 per hr
Off-peak: 3 per hr

FARNBOROUGH It is socially advantageous to have some connection with flying if you live in Farnborough. This is where the Royal Aircraft Establishment was based, and where the Farnborough International Air show is held every other year. The airport has acted like a honeypot to attract aviation-focused businesses. The heart of the town has been ripped out to make way for a shopping centre and a good leisure centre. There are some small Victorian terraces where houses cost around £175,000 each. Further out, the housing is Sixties' vintage: three-bedroom semis at £210,000; four-bedroom detached houses at between £280,000 and £300,000.

Journey: 41 min
Season: £3024
Peak: 4 per hr
Off-peak: 2 per hr

FLEET The train service from Fleet to London is good, and the town is popular with commuters. Another attraction is Fleet Pond, where 133 acres of freshwater lake, woodland, heath and reed beds are fiercely protected by the Fleet Pond Society. Fleet itself divides neatly into quarters, each one conveniently date-stamped. If you have a taste for the Twenties, you'll find a good selection of Arts and Crafts houses with three-bedroom semis around £230,000. If you prefer the architecture of the Fifties and Sixties, closely-packed in leafy roads, then you'll find a range of choice at between £225,000 and £275,000. The other two quarters are modern, built in the last few decades, with many of the three- or four-bedroom houses aimed squarely at that archetypal creature of the Eighties, the yuppy. You could pay £285,000 to £300,000 for four bedrooms; £400,000 to £500,000 for a house with five bedrooms and three or four reception rooms. Creatures of the Nineties and Noughties are here, too – over 2,500 new houses have been built in the last 25 years and another 1,200 are planned. Victorian houses in large gardens can be found in the conservation area to the north of the town.

'Fleet itself divides into quarters, each one conveniently date-stamped'

Journey: 60 min
Season: £3088
Peak: 3 per hr
Off-peak: 2 per hr

WINCHFIELD Around the station there is scarcely a village to speak of. Little more than a mile away, however, is **Hartley Wintney**, practically two centuries removed from Fleet. It has old coaching inns with archways leading into cobbled yards, five village ponds and five village greens with ancient oaks, and the second oldest cricket ground in England. The centre is full of antiques shops and has an art gallery that specialises in English paintings and sculptures. 'Very Hampshire,' says one local. There is a butcher, a bakery, two coffee shops and a market on Wednesday mornings. Social highlights include productions by the local dramatic society, and there are all the usual clubs and societies, including WI, Scouts and Brownies, and a golf course. High prices follow the 17th- and 18th-century architecture; council houses are tucked out of sight. A classic four-bedroom cottage overlooking the cricket ground might cost £650,000. A modern four-bedroom house would be around £400,000, while a two-up, two-down Victorian cottage on the common might be had for £250,000.

Journey: 64 min
Season: £3148
Peak: 3 per hr
Off-peak: 2 per hr

HOOK is modern-day Commuterland as opposed to Metroland, with a major Tesco and hundreds of new houses arranged in estates. A family butcher features among the local shops. The London-bound trains are frequent, and it is very close to Junction 5 of the M3. Four-bedroom detached houses start at around £245,000, rising to £350,000 for one from the up-market builders Charles Church. Annual events include the Hook Fun Run in May. There is a large helicopter base a couple of miles away at RAF Odiham. Thomas Burberry, of raincoat fame, had a house here called Crossways.

Journey: 44 min
Season: £3412 or
£3492 is also valid
into Paddington via
Reading
Peak: 5 per hr
Off-peak: 5 per hr

BASINGSTOKE The station car park is capacious and there is a good selection of fast trains. Some trains start from here, others come through from Bournemouth and Weymouth. Forty years ago **Basingstoke** was a comparatively sleepy market town with a population of 25,000. Now it is a London overspill town with a population of 159,000 and more than 400 companies, including the Automobile Association, IBM, Sony Broadcast and Sun Life Financial of Canada. The shopping centre has all the usual chain stores. Basingstoke Leisure Park has a ten-screen cinema, ten-pin bowling rink, aquadrome, championship-sized ice-rink and golf driving range. The old town is the place for wine bars, pubs and restaurants and The Haymarket Theatre. A farmers' market is held here once a month.

The town offers two-up-two-down Victorian terraces, priced from £170,000, and four-bedroom Thirties' houses at £275,000. In the quiet

*'Watercress
beds are a
particular feature
of the local
countryside'*

of Cliddesdon Road, large, detached, five-bedroom Victorian and Edwardian houses sell for over £600,000. Further out, you come to the council estates. The modern estates are on the outskirts – North Chineham is one of the most popular because it has matured and has a shopping centre with a Tesco superstore. Three-bedroom semis can be bought for £210,000; five-bedroom detached houses for £400,000 upwards. Hatch Warren is similar.

Watercress beds are a particular feature of the countryside. Old Basing, Mapledurwell, St Mary Bourne and Whitchurch all have them. One of the best-known villages, only a short distance from Basingstoke's south-western tentacle, is **Dummer** – a small linear village that found itself besieged by the world's press at the time of Prince Andrew's wedding, being the home of his then parents-in-law. Perhaps because of its exposure it is a rather tight-knit community. A two-bedroom period cottage will cost at least £240,000. A larger Georgian pile with land will cost £750,000.

'Actually Mapledurwell is more Land Rovers. Upton Grey more Range Rovers'

Very close to Basingstoke's eastern flank is **Old Basing**, where old brick cottages are prettily arranged around the church, the River Lodden, and what remains of Basing House. The house was a glamorous Tudor mansion, which became the focus of a two-year siege by the Roundheads during the Civil War and was eventually destroyed. Some of the stone was salvaged and used to build houses in the village. There is a strong village spirit and, says one local, 'the place is alive with horses'. A two-up-two-down period cottage would cost around £230,000. Two villages nearby, **Mapledurwell** and **Upton Grey**, are the stuff of an adman's dream, with Range Rovers carelessly parked outside idyllic thatched cottages. 'Actually Mapledurwell is more Land Rovers, Upton Grey more Range Rovers,' says one insider. Upton Grey has a duck pond, willow trees, some 17th-century cottages, village shop and post office. Prices vary from over £350,000 for a thatched cottage to around £750,000 for a new four-bedroom house.

> Fork to Salisbury

Journey: 61 min
Season: £3496
Peak: 2 per hr
Off-peak: 1 per hr

OVERTON used to be rather pretty and had a defined role as a venue for sheep fairs and silk mills. Now it is where the paper for our banknotes is made. It still retains a certain appeal, though it has become extremely corpulent with new housing estates pushing at its seams. There are some thatched cottages, shops, pubs and restaurants, and a gun shop. A 17th-century, four-bedroom house in the centre will cost around £400,000. Family houses on the new developments cost up to £385,000; large individual houses over £475,000. Winchester Street is the poshest bit.

'On the doorstep is the wonderful rolling chalk downland that envelops the River Test, the landscape used by Richard Adams in *Watership Down*'

Journey: 67 min
Season: £3496
Peak: 2 per hr
Off-peak: 1 per hr

WHITCHURCH is an old silk mill town on the River Test. The mill on Frog Island is now restored and sells extremely expensive bespoke silk lengths. But Whitchurch, too, has grown fleshy with huge council estates and private developments designed for those who made money in the Eighties. At Lynch Hill Park, for instance, large mock-Tudor and mock-Georgian houses are selling in the £300,000 to £350,000 bracket. At the lower end of the market, two-bedroom terraced houses cost around £170,000. To the west of the town, newly-built four-bedroom houses fetch around £350,000. On the doorstep is the wonderful rolling chalk downland that envelops the River Test, the landscape used by Richard Adams in *Watership Down*. An 18th-century brick-and-flint farmhouse in this area would start at £550,000.

Journey: 72 min
Season: £3644
Peak: 2 per hr
Off-peak: 2 per hr

ANDOVER had the stuffing knocked out of it in the Sixties and is now a town of shopping malls and modern housing. It is well-placed for the M3/A303 magic carpet to the West Country and sits plum in the middle of some of Hampshire's prettiest countryside. The new Lights Theatre has given the town a cultural identity, and the theatre at Cricklade College is home to drama and music societies. The arrival of Asda in 2008 brought with it a cinema. In the tapering old market place there is a street market on Thursdays and Saturdays and a farmers' market once a month.

In the few Victorian streets that remain, you might buy a three-bedroom terraced house for around £150,000. Some of the most popular properties are the Twenties' and Thirties' semis, which sell from £180,000 for three bedrooms. The west of the town is where the newest housing is to be found. At Weyhill, for example, you could buy a four-bedroom detached family house for £240,000 to £280,000.

The chalk hills around Andover hold some of the loveliest villages in the country. All those along the Bourne Valley, from **Hurstbourne Tarrant** down to Longparish, have a definite social cachet. Hurstbourne Tarrant sits in the valley bottom with Hurstbourne Hill casting a steep green shadow in the background. Stagecoaches used to change horses here before tackling its merciless incline. William Cobbett visited on his *Rural Rides* – his initials are on a brick in the garden wall of Rookery Farm, where a former owner used to put out plates of food for hungry travellers. Jane Austen's parson brother also lived here and she visited frequently. To move here now you have to pay through the nose: a two-bedroom period cottage could cost £250,000; a four-bedroom period house £400,000 to £500,000.

St Mary Bourne is further east along the sparkling chalk River Bourne, often called the Swift by locals, especially when it is in full spate. The village is a wonderful muddle of brick-and-flint, oak beams, wattle-and-daub and thatch. It has 15 listed buildings and a lovely Norman church. There is a thriving village primary school, five pubs, a village hall and shop, plus all the usual village societies. Some of the local families have lived here for centuries, as an 1842 tithe map has proved. 'Our main worry,' said the parish clerk, 'is that new people moving in want to throw a glass dome over the place and don't want it to change, even though the demands of the village are changing.' A two-bedroom thatched cottage will cost from £220,000; a modern four-bedroom house £400,000 upwards.

Longparish, at the lower end of this exclusive corridor, is indeed a very long parish, threading along three-and-a-half miles of winding lane and the meandering River Test. Some of the field walls and thatched cottages are built of clunch (chalk stone), with modern estates sandwiched in between. The big flints in the fields are known

'The chalk hills around Andover hold some of the loveliest villages in the country'

as 'Hampshire diamonds'; the other white specks are sheep. Property prices are higher than those in St Mary Bourne.

Ludgershall, to the north-west, offers housing even cheaper than Andover's – if you can bear the development going on all around. 'There are hundreds of houses going up. It's out of control,' said one villager. A three-bedroom terraced house built in the Twenties will cost around £140,000; a two-bedroom terraced house around £120,000. Further west are **North Tidworth** and **South Tidworth**, both of which offer outstanding value for money, but have rather transient populations. The army, which has a strong presence in the area, has been shedding staff, with the result that you might pick up a two-bedroom flat for £90,000, or a three-bedroom house for £150,000. **Shipton Bellinger** is very ordinary and again dominated by the army. Three-bedroom semis fetch around £170,000 to £180,000. Closer to Andover itself is the rather more cosy community of **Penton Mewsey**, where you might buy a four-bedroom period house for £400,000 to £480,000.

To the south-west is **Monxton**, with the Pill Hill brook gambolling through it under a small bridge. It is a very compact village with just 79 houses – 31 of which are thatched cottages, many over 300 years old – a small green along the river and a pub. Jujitsu, badminton, line dancing and drama classes take place in the village hall and incomers are welcomed. A small, thatched terraced cottage would cost from £230,000; a four-bedroom modern house over £325,000. **Abbotts Ann**, close by, is also pretty. Its status has risen to rival the villages of the Test or Bourne valleys and it has a village shop with a baker who produces fresh bread daily. You could buy a thatched cottage with three or four bedrooms for £375,000 to £475,000; a four-bedroom detached modern house for about the same.

Stockbridge, further south, has enormous cachet. It lies in breathtakingly lovely countryside and is a great angling centre for some of the best and most expensive fishing in England, along the River Test. The Grosvenor Hotel, with its huge overhanging porch, houses the exclusive Houghton Fishing Club. The wide main street, edged with Tudor and Georgian houses, a superb butcher and other good shops, belies the village's size for there are very few back streets. Stockbridge Down, a mile away, is dotted with ancient earthworks, and up in the hills are the Iron Age forts of Woolbury Camp and Danebury Ring. A two-bedroom period terraced house with a small garden in Stockbridge will cost from £250,000; a more substantial Georgian terraced house around £400,000. Half a dozen new six-bedroom detached houses carry a value of £500,000 or more. An oddity close to Stockbridge is Leckford, an estate village of tied thatched cottages owned since 1928 by the John Lewis Partnership.

'The big flints in the white fields are known as "Hampshire diamonds"; the other white specks are sheep'

The estate is a major local employer and the properties are occupied by working and retired staff. The cottages are painted in the John Lewis trademark green.

Journey: 82 min
Season: £3824
Peak: 2 per hr
Off-peak: 1 per hr

GRATELEY proper is an old-fashioned farming village. Many of the period properties have been in the same families for years and few come on to the market. You could pay £170,000 for a two-bedroom, Victorian, slate-roofed terraced house; over £300,000 for a four-bedroom period house if you were lucky. The Andover side of the village is best. There is a newer area of development around the station, where there are starter homes and council houses. To the south, **Over**, **Middle** and **Nether Wallop** are attractive villages with period properties, but surrounded by a sea of post-war council estates. A four-bedroom, white-washed thatched cottage at Nether Wallop will cost £400,000.

Journey: 89 min
Season: £4152
Peak: 2 per hr
Off-peak: 2 per hr

SALISBURY The city of **Salisbury** is full of visual treats, architectural nooks and crannies, gabled houses, half-timbering and Chilmark stone. Unlike Winchester, which grew out of medieval clutter, it was built on a grid pattern and so has a greater sense of space and order. At the heart of it is the confluence of the rivers Avon and Nadder, spanned by medieval bridges. Another remnant of medieval life is the open-air market on Tuesdays and Saturdays. Shops in the city centre tend to be small and specialised, with Waitrose and Tesco kept out of sight on the edge of town. The Salisbury Playhouse is the main theatrical venue, with the City Hall next door hosting a mix of touring artists and tribute bands. The Salberg provides productions on the fringe and the Arts Centre offers lectures, theatre and film screenings.

The top of the property pyramid in Salisbury is Cathedral Close, once home to the novelist Henry Fielding and the late Prime Minister Sir Edward Heath. It is regarded as one of the most beautiful closes in England, dating from the late 18th century when graves were pushed to one side and houses built for the city's more important residents. The close is perfectly quiet, shut away behind locked gates at night and as expensive as Chelsea or Westminster. A 48-year lease can cost £750,000; a rare freehold could well top £1.5m. There are some good streets near the cathedral, overlooking Queen Elizabeth Gardens, where you might pick up a four-bedroom late-Victorian terraced house with a 60ft garden for £425,000 upwards. A short distance away is Fisherton Island, a small group of detached houses built in the Sixties commanding around £425,000 for four bedrooms. It is also possible to buy into one of the oldest streets in Salisbury, Guilder Lane, where a brick-and-timber cottage with two bedrooms might cost £185,000. Popular schools include Cathedral School, The Godolphin, Bishop Wordsworth's for boys and South Wilts Girls'.

At the lower end of the market are hundreds of late-Victorian terraces fronting directly on to pavements, but beware the parking problem. You might get a two-bedroom terraced house for just over £160,000. In the gentrified streets – identifiable by the hanging baskets – you could pay £170,000, and in St Anne's Street over £300,000. On the city outskirts, areas such as Shady Bower offer flats at around £170,000 and modern four-bedroom houses at £275,000. For a more villagey feel, look to the leafy lanes of Milford, where four-bedroom detached houses fetch around £290,000.

'On the edge of Salisbury Plain, the magic of a country walk might be exploded by a training exercise'

Outside Salisbury, the Wiltshire chalk downlands and the five valleys of the Avon, Wylye, Nadder, Ebble/Chalke and Bourne provide the setting for some very attractive, unspoilt villages. Some are subject to flooding in bad weather. Those to the south tend to be more popular. Those to the north are on the edge of Salisbury Plain, where there is a massive military presence and the magic of a country walk might be exploded by a training exercise.

Penetrating deeply into the south you come to **Fordingbridge**. This is rather far for regular London commuters, but people's fondness for it is such that it acts as a magnet for the villages between it and Salisbury. Its best asset is the River Avon, crossed by a seven-arched medieval bridge and overlooked by a statue of Augustus John, who once lived here. It has shops good enough to meet day-to-day needs, as well as a bookshop, antiques shop and china shop. It is ideally placed for people who like to hack across the New Forest and for anglers with rods on the Avon. There is a real mix of housing, from the often flimsily built, but sought-after houses of the New Forest, for which you could pay £190,000 for two bedrooms, to huge Twenties' set-pieces in 20 acres from £1.2m. Pony paddocks are expensive here. On one of the several modern developments you would pay £230,000 for a three-bedroom detached house; up to £350,000 for four bedrooms.

Nearby is **Breamore**, pronounced 'Bremmer', a typical Wiltshire brick village. 'It's a horsey, hunting, shooting village. Brilliant,' said

Schools in Wiltshire

Salisbury gets all the accolades. The Goldophin is an independent day and boarding school for girls, and there are two grammar schools – Bishop Wordsworth's for boys and South Wilts Girls' – both of which get excellent results. Other strong independent schools include St Mary's School Calne for girls, Dauntsey's in Devizes and Marlborough College in Marlborough, both co-educational.

Good comprehensives include those in Wootton Bassett, Corsham, Sheldon and Malmesbury.

one happy local. Breamore House, home of the Hulse family, is an Elizabethan manor overlooking the Avon valley, open to the public. There is a good choice of period houses, but catching one as it comes on the market is like finding a hen's tooth. Villages slightly to the west within this group – **Rockbourne** and **Martin**, for example – are also very rural and pretty, and a two-bedroom period thatched cottage here will cost £300,000. Rockbourne and **Damerham** operate one of the first federated primary schools in the country, sharing teachers and facilities. Its reputation is good.

Closer to Salisbury's southern edge, yet with the advantage of being close to Fordingbridge, is **Downton**, a village that once depended on lace-making, flour-milling and paper-making. It has an authentically ancient atmosphere, especially in the lovely main street, The Borough. A two-bedroom semi-detached period house in the village will cost £225,000. It is a large village, with a population of 2,500, so it has better amenities than most, including shops, a medical centre, a bank and a library. Villagers usher in the spring with the annual May Cuckoo fair. There is a country market every Friday where local cheeses can be bought.

Even closer in beside the city's watermeadows is **Britford**, a sleepy collection of brick cottages and farmhouses on the River Avon. It has a school and a common, but there are no shops and it has to share its vicar with other villages. Residents have a reputation for being rather reclusive and rarefied, particularly those who occupy the large houses on the lower road along the river bank. A good period house with four bedrooms would cost well over £500,000.

Nearby are **Odstock** and its neighbours **Nunton** and **Bodenham**, where the social life is rather more robust. People who have moved away find themselves drawn back for the annual fête, to join in the river raft races and dance the night away. Odstock has a school and a pub popular with doctors from the nearby hospital. Prices are similar to Britford's.

The Chalke Valley is also a good hunting ground. **Bowerchalke**, though very much a one-road village, occupies a beautiful position in an Area of Oustanding Natural Beauty surrounded by the Downs, just before the countryside tips over into Dorset. It has a mix of brick-and flint, cob and green sandstone, with some modern houses. Everyone knows everyone else. There is no pub and it has lost its battle to keep its shop, but there is a playgroup. Incomers are not always a bad thing, as one villager recalls. 'Everyone used to inter-marry. The IQ of the village was saved by the arrival of the bicycle.' There is a trout farm and a small stream running through, and endless walks. Houses here and in the neighbouring village of **Broad Chalke** are usually easy to sell. A 19th-century two-bedroom cottage will fetch

‘People who have moved away find themselves drawn back for the annual fête, to join in the river raft races and dance the night away’

£275,000; a modern four-bedroom house in vernacular style £400,000. Broad Chalke is right on the Ebble where it meets the Chalke, and it regards itself as the capital of the Chalke valley. It lies between two chalk ridges, Here Path and Ox Drove Road, which both provide challenging walks. There is an ancient pub, and shops include a butcher who makes his own faggots. The village school is still going strong, and there is a doctor's surgery. One of the most successful of its many clubs and societies is the Wilton and District Youth Band. Owners of some swimming pools in the village allow their neighbours to use them. South Street is particularly pretty because of its thatched cottages.

The town of **Wilton**, three miles west of Salisbury, is spoilt by its position on the A30 and A36, though it has a good market square, peppered with antiques shops, and some nice old houses. A two-bedroom cottage could be picked up for around £225,000. This is where the Wilton Carpets are made. Much of the town is owned by the Pembroke estate. The nearby Wilton House, built by the Earl of Pembroke, is open to the public.

The next spoke in the wheel of valleys around Salisbury is the Wylye Valley. The villages here both retain their sense of rural remoteness and yet have easy access to the city along the A36. **Codford St Mary** and **Codford St Peter** are rather strung out along the road and have plenty of modern houses. They have one of the only village theatres in the country. A four-bedroom house would cost between £300,000 and £350,000; a three-bedroom Thirties' semi around £145,000.

Thatched cottage, Chalke Valley

To the north of Salisbury, the Woodford Valley is given particular charm by the River Avon. There is a dearth of smaller cottages so this is not first-timer country. A four-bedroom period family house, possibly with a paddock, is likely to fetch over £600,000. There are people here whose families have lived in the area for centuries; many of the newer arrivals have military connections. **Lower Woodford**, **Middle Woodford** and **Upper Woodford** are all strung out along the river, so there is no strong sense of community. There is a pub and they share a primary school. Heal House, where Charles II sheltered after the Battle of Worcester in 1651, opens its gardens to the public. Lower Woodford has a pub, beside some old thatched chalk cottages. **Great Durnford** also lies in this exclusive belt and is similarly expensive.

Further north, a couple of miles from Stonehenge, is **Amesbury**. This is in the neighbourhood of three army camps – Larkhill, Tidworth and Bulford – and the army personnel help to keep the first-time-buyer market ticking over. A mass of new developments has sprung up alongside the older brick-and-flint cottages, and more growth is likely. The new Solstice Park business development has brought employment to the area. On the modern estates you would pay around £130,000 for a two-bedroom house, £170,000 for a three-bedroom semi, £235,000 for a four-bedroom house. Older three-bedroom cottages fetch around £225,000. There are a handful of select roads, such as Countess and Stonehenge, where large detached houses built in the early part of the 20th century sell for £300,000 to £400,000.

Just to the east of Salisbury is **Laverstock**, separated by the River Bourne. Large riverside houses appeal to the local bank-manager class, and there is a primary and three secondary schools, which have good reputations. A modern detached house with four bedrooms will cost around £300,000.

> Fork from Basingstoke to Southampton

Journey: 66 min
Season: £3520
Peak: 1 or 2 per hr
Off-peak: 1 per hr

MICHELDEVER The countryside really takes over here. **Micheldever** has a good collection of old thatched cottages arranged haphazardly by the Dever brook and around a triangle of grass with a seat and a tree on it, known as the Crease. Duke Street is perhaps the prettiest for terraced cottages: two bedrooms will cost around £250,000 to £300,000. There is an old-fashioned village school, a store and a pub. The station is a couple of miles from the old village, but has had a whole new community spring up around it. There are Fifties' and Sixties' estates and bungalows, where a family-sized house might cost £260,000. The area has been earmarked for new town development. The main road at one end of Micheldever tends to impinge on the rural dream, but most people hear the A33 and M3 only as a low growl on quiet nights.

Journey: 59 min
Season: £3888
Peak: 4 per hr
Off-peak: 4 per hr

WINCHESTER The city's beautifully simple Norman Cathedral and historic Roman streets, narrow alleyways, footpaths and meadows (which inspired John Keats to write some of his most famous poetry, including 'Ode to a Nightingale') give **Winchester** its compelling appeal. Winchester society is a force to be reckoned with. Much of it revolves around a tightly-knit farming set, for whom the sporting weekend is essential. It has several fashionable hunts and shooting estates, and the Houghton Club on the River Test provides some of the best trout fishing in the country. Upmarket and speciality shops can be found around the square and in side streets such as Parchment Street; there is an antiques market in King's Walk. A park-and-ride scheme has eased parking problems. There are lots of pubs and restaurants. Art exhibitions are held at the Guildhall Gallery, the Winchester Gallery, the Heritage Centre and the new City Space; concerts at the Guildhall and in the Cathedral. The Chesil Theatre and John Stripe Theatre are busy with amateur theatrical productions, while the Theatre Royal attracts national and international stars. The Winchester Discovery Centre includes a library.

Little Minster and Great Minster, next to the Cathedral, are two of the best addresses in the country outside London. Close by is Winchester College, the boys' public school founded in 1382 by William of Wykeham, Bishop of Winchester. Tourists are the main drawback – flocking through to see where William the Conqueror claimed his crown, and where King Canute and Jane Austen are buried, they can't help pausing to look at the beautiful 18th-century houses. Small terraced homes in Cannon and Colebrook Streets are also sought-after, though life here can be inconvenienced not only by parking problems, but also by film units seeking period backdrops. A tiny flat-fronted terraced house could cost between £250,000 and £300,000; a larger imposing Georgian house £400,000 to £700,000. At the lower end of the market, two-bedroom Victorian terraced houses fetch between £200,000 and £350,000, rising to £500,000 for three- to four-bedroom semis. The area by the watermeadows in St Cross is popular with young professional families. Here you can buy two-bedroom Victorian terraced houses, or two-bedroom flats in converted houses, for £225,000 to £300,000. Two up-and-coming areas within walking distance of the city centre are Hyde, where you would have to pay £350,000 for a three-bedroom Victorian terrace, and Fulflood, which is slightly cheaper.

Some people prefer the comparative peace of some of the avenues away from the city centre – Chilbolton and Bereweeke Avenues, for example, where houses range from Victorian to Sixties and a four-bedroom detached could be bought for £500,000. Just outside Winchester is a large modern development, Badger Farm. One-bedroom flats here cost £130,000; two-bedroom terraces £160,000; four-bedroom houses £250,000 to £300,000.

The neighbouring villages compete to be the most beautiful and socially spirited. The particularly desirable area to the north-east contains **Itchen Abbas**, a village described by Charles Kingsley in *The Water Babies*. The Pilgrims' Way runs through it, as does the River Itchen. There is a primary school, a foodie pub, a village hall and the usual local societies. A four-bedroom period house here would cost

'Little Minster and Great Minster, next to the Cathedral, are two of the best addresses in the country outside London'

£450,000 to £700,000. For cricket you must follow the river down to **Easton**, another pretty village with a mix of thatch and half-timber, Victorian and modern, with the snarl of the M3 in the distance. **Avington** is also in this select group. Most of its brick-and-flint cottages are protected within a conservation area. Its flagship is Avington Park, a fine Carolean mansion set in ancient parkland with a lake, which is open to the public. You could expect to pay £275,000 for a two-bedroom thatched cottage in any of these villages.

> **'New Alresford attracts day trippers because of the Watercress Line'**

New Alresford attracts day-trippers because of the Watercress Line, an eccentric railway that offers a half-hour return journey through Hampshire farmland, chalk cuttings and hills. Awarded top place by *Country Life* magazine as the South-East's 'Favourite Market Town', Alresford features rows of striking pastel-painted Georgian town houses and quirky upmarket shops. A weekly market is held in Broad Street on Thursdays. Small two- and three-bedroom Georgian terraced houses around the centre can be bought for £350,000. Neighbouring **Old Alresford** has a fine church and village pond. A four-bedroom detached family house costs between £350,000 and £450,000.

To the north-west is **Crawley**, where there are some picturesque thatched cottages by the village duck pond. It has the kind of star quality that earns it regular appearances on scenic calendars. As an old estate village it was planned as a whole, and some of the architecture is flamboyant. You could pay £500,000 for a detached bungalow or £450,000 for a semi-detached period cottage with three bedrooms. A larger detached house with grounds could reach £1m to £2m.

Sparsholt is rural and convivial, and provides the opportunity for walks from the back door into the hills and woodland in Farley Mount

House style in Surrey and Hampshire

A wonderful mixture of styles is packed between the metropolitan hard edges of south-west London and the retirement haven of the south coast. Through the sandy heaths of Surrey, the collectors' items are the houses designed by Edwin Lutyens in gardens by Gertrude Jekyll. Lutyens's architecture combines formality with naturalness, texture with geometry.

Then comes Hampshire, where stockbroker belt meets Georgian good manners and beautiful villages laze in the folds of the chalk valleys around Winchester and Andover. You have to marvel at what can be done with a stone as soft as chalk. Around Petersfield there are farm walls made of clunch (chalk stone). When it is combined with flint and arranged in a chequerboard pattern or horizontal stripes, it turns humble cottages into architectural curios.

Where the chalk gives way to the poor soil of the New Forest, you find a range of brick and timber, brick and flint, thatched and even cob houses. Particularly pretty are the one-and-a-half storey thatched houses or 'bun' cottages, with steep roofs that look as if they have risen like loaves of bread.

The New Forest itself often disappoints. The original houses were small and low, and now would be considered scarcely habitable. Those that still stand have often been changed and extended beyond all recognition. The exceptions lie in wealthier villages such as Beaulieu and Bucklers Hard in the south, where shipbuilders' oak went into the houses. Bungalow-itis is ever-present along the coast, but makes a strangely natural partnership with the old defence fortifications around Southampton.

Park. The village is particularly proud of its church-controlled primary school, though the influx of new home-owners don't always use it. There is a village shop, post office and a hall, funded partly through the efforts of the local community, where country and salsa dancing happens. Property prices are similar in most of the villages throughout this area. Due south of Winchester the M3 has snaked its way across Twyford Down to join the M27, leaving the old M3 a bizarre sight in a conservation area with the old motorway bridge surrounded by grass.

Journey: 75 min
Season: £3896
Peak: 2 per hr
Off-peak: 1 per hr

SHAWFORD is bisected by the M3, so one of the major factors governing prices here is whether properties have been affected by it or not – hundreds of home-owners filed for compensation. You would pay £260,000 for a two-bedroom Victorian or Edwardian terraced house away from the main road – 10 per cent less if it is in the traffic zone. Towards **Compton** there are some huge individual houses, built on large plots, that sell for £1m to £2m, though some of these are affected by the motorway.

Journey: 83 min
Season: £3984
Peak: 2 per hr
Off-peak: 2 per hr

EASTLEIGH strikes a commercial note after Winchester. It was built around the railway, still has a railway works, and has a clutch of companies such as Pirelli, Norwich Union Healthcare and B&Q. It also has the headquarters of the Royal Yachting Association. In the early days the social divisions between railway employees were underlined by their choice of address. Drivers and inspectors lived in the north; everyone else in the south. Today the north is still the better side of town, and properties here sell for slightly more. Its basic stock in trade is a mass of late Victorian terraced houses, fronting the pavement and selling at between £160,000 and £180,000. The new £25m leisure complex includes a nine-screen cinema, bowling centre and restaurants.

Bishopstoke and **Fair Oak** were once older villages, but they now behave more like comparatively prosperous suburbs of Eastleigh. Bishopstoke has modern estates where you might buy a three-bedroom house for less than £200,000, or a four-bedroom detached house with two en-suite bathrooms and double garage for £330,000. Fair Oak is slightly more up-market, with its village square still intact.

Modern development, Chandler's Ford

Journey: 95 min
Season: £4240
Peak: 1 per hr*
Off-peak: 1 per hr*
*Change at
Southampton Airport
Parkway

CHANDLER'S FORD The stockbroker belt is at Chandler's Ford, parts of which consider themselves to be more Winchester than Eastleigh. Much of it is modern. The Hiltingbury area, developed in the Sixties, has three-bedroom semis at between £185,000 and £220,000; three-bedroom detached houses at £280,000. The Oakmount area, which followed in the late Sixties and early Seventies, has two-bedroom maisonettes now costing £120,000 to £140,000 and three-bedroom terraces at £160,000. In the Eighties came Valley Park. You can buy a four-bedroom house for £240,000 here, though you might think they were rather tightly packed.

The expensive side of Chandlers Ford is **Hocombe**, built in the Thirties when little heed was paid to land values. Large four-bedroom houses, with spacious sitting and dining rooms, spread themselves over extensive gardens and change hands at £500,000 to £550,000. This is where the IBM executives from Hursley tend to congregate. Also on the northern side are two good comprehensive schools, Toynbee and Thornden, which take children to GCSE level. Layers of new housing continue to be added, especially now that the M3 slicing past it offers easier access to the rest of the country.

> Fork to Fareham via Hedge End and Botley

It is also worth considering **Hedge End**, **Botley** and **Fareham**, strung below Eastleigh, because they now have direct train services into London. Hedge End can be reached with a journey of 88 minutes (season ticket £3984). While Botley can be reached in 91 minutes (season ticket £3984). Botley has some good 16th- and 17th-century houses and sits at the head of the tidal reach of the Hamble. The National Trust has bagged a few acres along the river to preserve them for the future. Fareham takes 98 minutes (season ticket £3984). Beyond that Gosport looms like an ugly giant.

> Continuation of main line

Journey: 71 min	**SOUTHAMPTON AIRPORT PARKWAY** This station is really here
Season: £4328	for the convenience of Southampton International Airport. The train
Peak: 2 or 3 per hr	service as a result is fast and frequent, but the station car park is
Off-peak: 2 per hr	rather expensive. Many of the houses are close to the railway line. A

three-bedroom Victorian terraced house would cost between £150,000 and £160,000.

Journey: 97 min	**SWAYTHLING** is an area of Victorian terraces and ex-local authority
Season: £4328	housing with prices lower than Eastleigh's. A two-bedroom house
Peak: 2 per hr	might cost £105,000. Many workers from the nearby Ford factory
(1 through plus 1	have their homes here, and it can seem as if nearly all the 19,500
changing at	students from Southampton University have their digs here, too.
Southampton Airport	
Parkway)	
Off-peak: 1 per hr	
changing at	
Southampton Airport	
Parkway	

Journey: 100 min	**ST DENYS** This is one of the older parts of Southampton and a
Season: £4328	happy hunting ground for first-time buyers. Turn-of-the-century
Peak: 2 per hr	terraced houses and semis sell for between £145,000 and £179,000.
(1 through plus 1	
changing at	
Southampton Airport	
Parkway)	
Off-peak: 1 per hr	
changing at	
Southampton Airport	
Parkway	

> Branch line to Hamble via Bitterne, Woolston, Sholing and Netley

Journey: 124 min
(from Hamble)*
Season: £4328
Frequency: 2 per hr
(1 changing at
Fareham and 1 at
Southampton
Central)
* No through trains

BITTERNE, Woolston and Sholing float on the skyline like a sea of chimneypots. This is probably the cheapest part of Southampton, composed mainly of late 19th-century and early 20th-century terraces, but with some Thirties' housing stitched in, too. It lies on the east side of the Itchen River, crossed by a tollbridge that can seem a bit of a bother. A three-bedroom terraced house would cost around £160,000; a three-bedroom Thirties' semi about £185,000, possibly with good views thrown in. Houses backing on to the river cost substantially more.

Netley is given a certain status by its pebbly shoreline on Southampton Water. It leads to the Royal Victoria Country Park – a marvellous place for picnics, and a vantage point for watching the ferries and tankers chugging across to the Fawley oil refinery on the other side of Southampton Water. Netley also has the remains of the Royal Victoria Military Hospital, where Florence Nightingale nursed casualties from the Crimea. Large four-bedroom family houses, built in the early Eighties, might cost around £500,000. More modestly, a small two-bedroom terraced house would fetch around £190,000. Part of the old military hospital has been converted into flats, selling at around £190,000 for two bedrooms.

Hamble (together with the village of Warsash on the other side of the Hamble River) is used as the setting for yachty television series. It is one of the most concentrated yachting centres in the country, positively bristling with marinas and boats for hire. It is very smart, though in spite of all the visible wealth it still retains the atmosphere of a village. There is a green and a church, and a huge common that leads down to the water. It was a working fishing village until 1914. Some pioneering aviation work was also carried out here, and in the Second World War the Americans used it as a base to prepare for the D-Day landings. Property prices can break the £1m barrier, but you could find an ordinary three-bedroom semi for around £300,000.

> Continuation of main line

Journey: 78 min
Season: £4328
Peak: 2 per hr
Off-peak: 2 per hr

SOUTHAMPTON CENTRAL Southampton is a busy modern city that has attracted some sizeable companies, including Price Waterhouse and Skandia Life, and the Marine and Coastguard Agency. Its increasingly aggressive commercial face, unrivalled shopping, strong cultural identity and proximity to the sea and the New Forest are all major assets. Ambitious developments are underway, with street makeovers and a north-south spine to link the centre with the waterfront. The former Pirelli factory site is being transformed into Watermark WestQuay with an IKEA store, and Southampton University's Boldrewood Campus is the location for the Maritime Centre of Excellence.

There are three galleries, including the elegant art deco City Art Gallery, cinemas and nightclubs. The Mayflower Theatre stages West End musicals, ballet and opera, Southampton University's Nuffield Theatre offers a range of productions from Shakespeare to contemporary drama, and the Turner Simms Concert Hall features both classical music and jazz. Rock concerts and other music events are held at the Guildhall.

Southampton Football Club is based at St Mary's and there is first-class cricket at Hampshire's Rosebowl county ground. Participation sports include golf, and tennis, athletics, swimming and diving in a complex at The Quays. Southampton Airport provides flying lessons for those with strong stomachs and the money to match. But the principal leisure activity is still probably sailing. There are clubs, moorings and dinghy schools all along the coast.

Ocean Village is the place for weekending sailors – a mixture of docklands architecture, shopping, cinemas, bars and restaurants, the Port Grimaud of southern England. A two-bedroom apartment with a berth for the boat costs £205,000 or more; a town house might cost £245,000, rising towards £300,000 if it has a berth.

Schools in Hampshire

People move to Winchester just for the schools. Winchester College independent boys' boarding school (with some day-boys) has a formidable academic reputation. Girls have St Swithun's independent boarding and day school. Among the co-educational comprehensives are Perins and Westgate (to GCSE level). Peter Symonds is an excellent sixth-form college.

At Petersfield there is the progressive school Bedales, an independent co-educational day and boarding school, as well as Churcher's College, a co-educational independent day school. At Hook there is the independent Lord Wandsworth (mixed)

boarding and day. At Farnborough there is Salesian College, an independent Roman Catholic school for boys, Farnborough Hill Roman Catholic girls' day school and Farnborough Sixth Form College. Good comprehensives are at Ringwood and Yateley.

Southampton also has some popular schools. King Edward VI is a selective entry co-educational independent; St Anne's is a comprehensive for girls, with priority given to practising Catholics. Portsmouth's best include Portsmouth Grammar mixed school, St John's mixed school and Portsmouth High day school for girls, all independent.

Old Southampton stretches from the historic Bargate, once the main entry into the town, to Town Quay – a good vantage point from which to watch the ocean-going liners sail into port. A weekly Friday market takes place around Bargate, with monthly crafts, antiques and farmers' markets on Saturdays. There are new developments of luxury flats and listed warehouses converted into apartments on the seafront. Inner Avenue is one of the best places to look for older town houses. A two- or three-bedroom house within walking distance of the city centre would cost between £160,000 and £200,000. For cheaper housing you could look at **Shirley**, where a two-bedroom late-Victorian terraced home would fetch £140,000 to £150,000.

Further out from the town centre is **Bassett**. This has become rather chic because of its proximity to Southampton Common, the university and two good schools – King Edward VI independent school and The Atherley independent school for girls. A three-bedroom Thirties' semi here might cost £150,000; a three-bedroom detached house around £300,000 upwards. There are some larger, rather distinctive, four-bedroom houses which sell for over £400,000.

North of Southampton is **Chilworth**, which is considered irredeemably smart. Wealthy businessmen are attracted to the individually built large houses with anything from half an acre to two acres of ground. Smaller three- or four-bedroom houses start at around £500,000, with prices rising above £1m as you enter the mini-mansion market.

'Town Quay is a good vantage point from which to watch the ocean-going liners sail into port**'**

Journey: 87 min
Season: £4328
Peak: 1 per hr*
Off-peak: 1 per hr*
* Change at
Southampton
Central

MILLBROOK A surprising number of people cannot resist living along the coast to the west, or in remote parts of the New Forest, even though it means taking this sweeper service into Southampton. Millbrook, still in the Southampton suburbs, is mainly ex-local authority and a Fifties' three-bedroom terraced house can be picked up for around £160,000.

Journey: 90 min
Season: £4328
Peak: 1 per hr*
Off-peak: 1 per hr*
* Change at
Southampton
Central

REDBRIDGE At **Redbridge** you hit mixed housing estates, where a modern one-bedroom flat might cost around £92,000 and a two- to three-bedroom semi around £150,000.

> Branch Line to Romsey, Mottisfont & Dunbridge

**Journey: 98 min
(from Romsey)
Season: £4356
Frequency: 2 per hr
from Romsey;
1 every hr from
Mottisfont &
Dunbridge***
*** No through trains.
Change at
Southampton
Central,
Southampton Airport
Parkway or
Salisbury**

ROMSEY scores high marks for quality of life. It is a classic English market town with a strong agricultural base. A general market is held three times a week in the Cornmarket and the Hampshire Farmers' Market comes to Romsey every two months, selling local produce. The original market place is overlooked by a statue of Lord Palmerston. The silent simplicity of the Abbey, which is essentially Norman, gives the centre of the town a tremendous architectural and spiritual uplift. It has a lavish leisure centre and small specialist shops, with Southampton near enough for major purchases. It also has its own newspaper, and a theatre, The Plaza, a Thirties' cinema bought by the Romsey Amateur Operatic and Dramatic Society and restored. Another local treasure is the Sir Harold Hillier Gardens, three miles to the north, comprising an outstanding collection of trees and shrubs. Broadlands, once the home of Lord Mountbatten and now occupied by his grandson, Lord Brabourne, is also just outside the town. In the centre of town a restored two-bedroom Victorian terraced house would cost around £230,000. The small farms and older country houses dotted along the Test Valley start at over £650,000 and run into millions.

Michelmersh is a secluded parish nestling below the hilltop church of St Mary's. The settlement, with its designated conservation areas, historical farm buildings and cottages, dates from 985. It overlooks the country's best and most expensive trout fishing on the River Test, still has the famous brickworks making hand-made bricks from local clay, and bursts with community spirit which makes it a much sought-after village. You could buy a four-bedroom house for around £650,000, but prices vary enormously depending on position and age.

Mottisfont is another of the area's wonderful surprises, owned mostly by the National Trust. You will need at least £650,000 to be in the running for one of the handful of houses left in the open market. It is a stopping-off point for ramblers on a trail that runs from Totton, close to Southampton, along the chalk downs to Inkpen Beacon. The National Trust's Mottisfont Abbey, with its gardens of old-fashioned roses beside the River Test, is open to visitors.

'The National Trust's Mottisfont Abbey, with its gardens of old-fashioned roses beside the River Test, is open to visitors'

> Continuation of main line

Journey: 107 min
(95 min changing at
Southampton
Central)

Season: £4376

Peak: 2 per hr
(some changing at
Southampton
Central)

Off-peak: 1 per hr

TOTTON is part of the Southampton sprawl, being joined to the city by a causeway across the River Test. It offers a wide variety of new estates, with four-bedroom, double-garaged, detached houses priced at £340,000 and above. The Woodlands side of Totton, which faces on to the New Forest, is distinctly more up-market. Here you could pay £500,000 for a three-bedroom house with a paddock; £250,000 for a modern bungalow with two double bedrooms.

'Ashurst New Forest station was the closest to Lyndhurst that the powerful local landowners would allow the railway to come'

Journey: 112 min
(98 min changing at
Southampton
Central)

Season: £4376

Peak: 2 per hr
(some changing at
Southampton
Central)

Off-peak: 1 per hr

ASHURST NEW FOREST station was the closest to Lyndhurst that the powerful local landowners would allow the railway to come. Lyndhurst, known as the capital of the New Forest, is exquisitely pretty, but seizes up with tourist traffic in the summer. People come to visit the church, with its stained glass by William Morris and Burne-Jones; to admire Swan Green with its cordon of thatched cottages, and to visit the audio visual centre. The Forestry Commission has its local headquarters here in The Queen's House, a former royal hunting lodge. Lyndhurst has proper shops, including a marvellous butcher and a fruit and veg shop.

Property prices in the New Forest are high, despite the fact that the scarcity of building materials means that the quality of the older houses is often rather poor. Prices in Lyndhurst start at around £190,000 for a two-bedroom terraced house and rise effortlessly to £700,000 in sought-after Pikes Hill Avenue. A newish development in the centre provides cheaper property, with three-bedroom detached houses at around £285,000 and four-bedroom versions around £320,000. An owl and otter park set in 2,000 acres of woodland, is nearby.

'Lyndhurst has proper shops, including a marvellous butcher'

Journey: 93 min
Season: £4624
Peak: 2 per hr
Off-peak: 2 per hr

BROCKENHURST is blessed because it receives the fast trains from Weymouth. They stop here, at Southampton Central, Southampton Airport Parkway and Winchester, then go non-stop to Waterloo. This is a pretty, vibrant village with some gracious old houses set in half an acre or so, for which you might pay £650,000 and more, and some new estates within walking distance of the centre where you could pay £425,000 for four bedrooms. Brockenhurst teems with tourists in the summer.

'Beaulieu is the most exclusive village in the area ... Lymington is an extremely expensive, but rather quaint yachtsman's playground'

Beaulieu, four miles to the east, is the most exclusive village in the area, where people compete for invitations to Lord Montagu's drinks parties. A three-bedroom thatched cottage costs £400,000 upwards; a six-bedroom house with a couple of acres on the Beaulieu River, fit for the occasional stray pop star, sells for several million. The Beaulieu Motor Museum is a great attraction.

The village of **Pilley Bailey**, known locally as Pilley, is a little less expensive. It is small, with a pub, a church and a shop. A two-up-two-down cottage here would fetch around £250,000. The whole of this area is close to the sea, and in particular to **Lymington** – an extremely expensive, but rather quaint yachtsman's playground. A 150-year-old

New Forest Thirties' house

cottage close to the river with three bedrooms will cost £675,000 here. A fast shuttle train links it to Brockenhurst.

As rail services have improved, commuters are now prepared to move even further down the line to **Bournemouth**, attracted by its pine-cloaked valleys, sandy beaches and breezy cliff tops. It is also a commercial success story, attracting big insurance companies to relocate and establishing its name as a major conference centre. The journey to London can be done in 108 minutes, an annual season ticket costs £5,128, and there are three peak trains per hour. Incomers are attracted to the purpose-built leasehold flats in blocks with sea views along the Eastcliff, each of which has its own price hierarchy. A middle-market block will yield a one-bedroom flat from £325,000; two bedrooms for £375,000; three bedrooms £450,000. You will be extremely lucky to find a freehold house facing full frontal to the sea; should such a rarity come on the market, you could expect to pay £650,000 to £700,000 for three bedrooms, a roof terrace and cliff-top access.

'Commuters are now prepared to move even further down the line to Bournemouth'

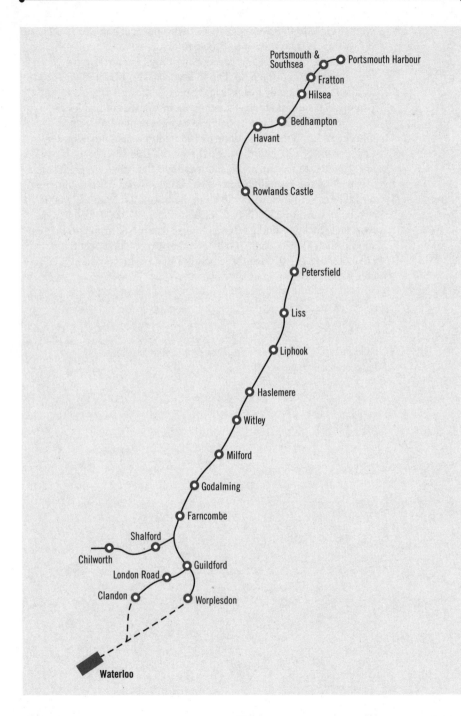

Portsmouth &
Southsea
Portsmouth Harbour
Fratton
Hilsea
Bedhampton
Havant
Rowlands Castle
Petersfield
Liss
Liphook
Haslemere
Witley
Milford
Godalming
Farncombe
Shalford
Chilworth
London Road
Guildford
Clandon
Worplesdon
Waterloo

> Portsmouth

Journey: 33 min
Season: £2560
Peak: 2 or 3 per hr
Off-peak: 1 per hr

WORPLESDON Sandwiched between Woking and Guildford, Worplesdon is a main-road village with the A322 cutting straight through it. The station is at least a mile from the centre, but it is close to some rather nice private roads running off Goose Rye Road. Large Twenties' and Thirties' detached houses here sell for £600,000 upwards. A four- or five-bedroom gabled and dormered house with a detached granny-annexe will fetch around £850,000.

Sutton Green, a mile south-east of the station, is semi-rural. A two-up-two-down turn-of-the-century cottage will cost from £250,000 upwards; a four-bedroom detached house of the same period will be over £600,000. Cottages and converted former agricultural buildings on Richmond Estates' Sutton Place Farm sometimes come on the market for £850,000 to £1m.

Journey: 34 min
Season: £2760*
Peak: 5 per hr
Off-peak: 4 per hr
***** **Also valid via**
London Road
(Guildford), see
page 237

GUILDFORD Even though it is so close to London, Guildford town centre offers rich pickings for shoppers and culture vultures alike. The steep, cobbled, pedestrianised High Street has a wide variety of boutiques and specialist shops, and the Friary shopping mall has all the major chain stores. Architectural highlights include the Guildhall, with its famous 1683 projecting clock, and one of the country's few modern cathedrals, designed by Sir Edward Maufe with a very plain interior. The Yvonne Arnaud Theatre attracts London-bound shows on their way to the West End, The Electric Theatre is a leading studio theatre, and the nine-screen cinema keeps film buffs happy. The Guildford Philharmonic Orchestra is also widely respected. Athletes head for the Spectrum leisure centre, which has an athletics track, an ice-rink, ice hockey and ten-pin bowling.

It is possible to live right in the centre of the town. A limited number of one-bedroom flats over the High Street shops will cost around £150,000; in St Luke's Square (on the former hospital site), good one-bedroom flats sell for around £185,000. There are some streets of old houses around Guildford Museum, near the remains of the 12th-century castle at the bottom of the High Street. Most have been converted to business use, but the occasional three-bedroom terraced property comes up for a premium price of £350,000 upwards. Three-bedroom Victorian and Edwardian houses behind the High Street will fetch up to £350,000.

On the north side of town, in the **Woodbridge Hill** area, are the typical bay-fronted, net-curtained, respectable mind-you-own-business streets of provincial England. The houses are solid, with good-sized rooms, but even though it is convenient for the hospital, the cathedral and the university it isn't the most popular area. A three-bedroom Thirties' detached house will cost around £280,000; a three-bedroom semi £240,000. Cornhill Insurance has its headquarters here. More appealing is **Fairlands**, particularly with the over-60s, where housing built in the Sixties and Seventies has bedded down and matured nicely, and where a good community spirit has evolved around the school, the doctor's surgery and so on. It even has its own free local news magazine. It is a good place to look for a bungalow – three bedrooms cost £280,000. A three-bedroom semi-detached house will cost slightly less.

On the north-eastern fringe is **Burpham**, no longer a village, but a sea of modern houses, designed with enough breathing space to make them palatable. Good primary and secondary schools make this a popular area for families. There are two developments – Weybrook Park and Weyley Farm. A tiny studio costs just under £100,000; a three-bedroom semi £250,000; a large four- or five-bedroom house from £450,000. There are also some large early 20th-century houses with five bedrooms and four reception rooms that sell for over £500,000. Nearby **Merrow** is now a suburb of Guildford with one development, Merrow Park. It has a golf course and leafy private roads where houses built in the Thirties now have the occasional bungalow wedged between them. Both bungalows and houses, with four to five bedrooms, tend to sell in the £600,000 range.

The south of the town is particularly well-heeled and attracts successful local professionals. White Lane has some large houses, built in the Twenties and later, with big gardens and views across to the North Downs. The likely price for one of these would be over £1m. Further to the south-west is Loseley Park, an Elizabethan

Small modern estate house, Guildford area

country house which is open to the public and whose farm produces the well-known dairy products that bear the Loseley name.

A popular village to the south-east is **Cranleigh** (see entry for Ockley on the line to Horsham, page 282). Closer to Guildford's southern flank is **Bramley**, which is well-liked and rather expensive. Its exclusivity is expressed by the presence of a prestige car dealer and well-subscribed golf club. There is a post office, florist and traditional electrical shop. Another attraction is the girls' private school, St Catherine's. A modest three-bedroom semi here will cost £300,000. A four-bedroom detached with a large garden and driveway over £500,000.

> *'Its exclusivity is expressed by the presence of a prestige car dealer and well-subscribed golf course'*

To the north-west of Guildford is **Wood Street**, a large village surrounded by farmland, with an ample village green, church, post office and two pubs. The council housing is discreetly tucked away and there is quite a lot of property built between the Thirties and the Sixties. For £280,000 you might pick up a three-bedroom Edwardian semi, or a more modern three-bedroom detached house with a large garden backing on to fields.

> Waterloo to London Road (Guildford) via Clandon

Journey: 50 min
Season: £2492
Peak: 3 per hr
Off-peak: 2 per hr

CLANDON West Clandon and East Clandon both command very high prices. The station is at West Clandon, a linear village, part of which is protected as a conservation area, part devoted to council housing. Until 1900, East Clandon was solely an estate village attached to Hatchlands Park, a National Trust house with splendid Robert Adam interiors and gardens by Repton and Gertrude Jekyll. It is a very pretty village, with a traditional pub and a tennis court for the exclusive use of village residents. A Fifties' four- or five-bedroom house in either village will cost over £750,000.

Journey: 55 min
Season: £2648
Peak: 3 per hr
Off-peak: 2 per hr

LONDON ROAD (GUILDFORD) London Road is Guildford's second station. For description of Guildford see page 235.

> North Downs line east to **Shalford** and **Chilworth**

Journey: 48 min
Season: £2816
Peak: 2 per hr*
Off-peak: 1 per hr*
* Change at
Guildford

SHALFORD is a one-street village of period houses and cottages with a green. Parking is easier at the small station here than in Guildford. Two-bedroom Victorian terraced houses start at £200,000. Five- or six-bedroom houses can cost £600,000 or more. Shalford Mill, an 18th-century timber-framed and tile-hung watermill on the River Tillingbourne, was given to the National Trust in 1932 by a group of anonymous donors known as 'Ferguson's Gang'.

Journey: 47 min
Season: £3184
Peak: 1 per hr*
Off-peak: 1 every
2 hrs*
* Change at
Guildford

CHILWORTH spreads itself along the A248, a mix of houses and bungalows built in the Thirties and Fifties. Cars tend to park along both sides of the road as few of the houses have garages. The village has its own primary and middle school, good pubs and an old gunpowder factory on the banks of the Tillingbourne. Houses have large gardens and views to St Martha's Hill. A three-bedroom Thirties' semi would cost from £250,000.

> Continuation of main line

Journey: 44 min
Season: £2872
Peak: 3 per hr
Off-peak: 2 per hr

FARNCOMBE is the poor man's Godalming (see below), of which it is now a suburb. It does have its own recognisable centre, graced by the presence opposite the playing field of ten early 17th-century red-brick almshouses, still administered by the Worshipful Company of Carpenters. A four-bedroom Victorian semi-detached house in Farncombe will sell for around £350,000; a Twenties detached three-bedroom house for £300,000; a modern two-bedroom terrace for £220,000 or more.

Journey: 47 min
Season: £2904
Peak: 4 per hr
Off-peak: 2 per hr

GODALMING Forever prosperous, Godalming thrived first on the wool trade, then as a coaching stop on the London to Portsmouth road, now on café culture. Since the 1870s it has been the home of Charterhouse, the co-educational private school. The High Street contains a wonderful collection of 16th-, 17th- and 18th-century buildings, and in the centre is The Pepperpot, a distinctive colonnaded building with a clock tower. Godalming was further distinguished by being the first town to replace gas street lighting with electric. Its shopping is typically small-town, with one or two specialist shops, a Waitrose in the centre and a Sainsbury's on the edge. There are good walks along the River Wey that runs from Godalming Wharf to the Thames at Weybridge, complete with locks and weirs. For autumn colour the place to walk is the National Trust's Winkworth Arboretum. The two most fashionable areas of Godalming are **Busbridge** and

Charterhouse, both with views of the Hog's Back. Busbridge offers an excellent range of primary and secondary schools, including Prior's Field independent school for girls. Its quiet leafy streets are lined with properties spanning every period from Victorian to the Thirties, and a famous water tower converted into an eccentric house. A three-bedroom detached house here will set you back £450,000, though you could pay up to £1m for a large house with half a dozen bedrooms and a capacious garden. Charterhouse is similar. The tail-end of Mark Way is a private road where some of the older houses were built in such enormous acreages that strips of garden were sold off for building plots in the Fifties. A four- or five-bedroom house set in a third of an acre will cost at least £550,000. At the lower end of the market are some two-bedroom terraced houses on small modern developments that sell for around £225,000 to £250,000.

The nearby village of **Dunsfold** is lovely if you can afford it. The houses, some of them dating from the 15th and 16th centuries, are gathered around an open common, with a pub, small shop, nursery school, and church picturesquely set apart on a mound next to a 1,000-year-old yew tree. Even a tiny two-bedroom period farmworker's cottage will fetch over £250,000. Larger houses start at £500,000.

> 'At Dunsfold the church is picturesquely set apart on a mound next to a 1,000-year-old yew tree'

Journey: 50 min
Season: £2928
Peak: 2 per hr
Off-peak: 1 per hr

MILFORD has been carved up by main roads, including the A3, but there are compensations in the surrounding rambling-and-riding countryside. The village sprawls around the church and shops and is renowned for the Secretts Farm shop selling fresh local produce. There is a broad range of properties. You might pay around £200,000 for a two-bedroom ex-council house; £250,000 for a Thirties' three-bedroom semi; £325,000 for a modern three-bedroom semi; £500,000 and over for a four- to five-bedroom Victorian or Edwardian family home.

Elstead, three miles to the west, is more rural, with bracken-covered Surrey commons within walking distance. Sir Edwin Lutyens spent the early part of his career working in the area, which contains a large

Schools in Surrey

Guildford has a highly valued independent boys' day school, Royal Grammar, which creams off the top ten per cent of the ability range in the area. There is a choice of three independent schools for girls – Guildford High day school, St Catherine's day and boarding and Tormead day school. The two co-educational comprehensives of note are Guildford County and George Abbot.

Other good independent schools are scattered throughout the county. They include Charterhouse for boys (girls in the sixth) and Prior's Field for girls

at Godalming; Cranleigh School for boys and girls at Cranleigh; Caterham for both sexes and Woldingham for girls at Caterham; Dunottar Day for girls and Reigate Grammar for both sexes at Reigate; The Royal School for girls at Haslemere; the Lingfield Notre Dame for boys and girls at Lingfield; St John's for boys and sixth-form girls (fully co-educational from 2010) in Leatherhead; Notre Dame Senior for girls at Cobham.

Good comprehensives can be found at Dorking, Weybridge, Esher, Effingham and Epsom.

number of his houses. The 21-acre gardens of Fulbrook House were designed by Gertrude Jekyll. The village has a pretty watermill, now a pub and restaurant, a 12th-century bridge and a green, but the fight is on for traffic calming on the B3001. It is a thriving village with lots of young families. There is a popular primary school, post office and lively sports and social scene with football, cricket and a tennis club. A one-bedroom flat in a converted Edwardian house will cost just over £150,000; a Victorian two-up two-down terrace or a two-bedroom Thirties' semi, £250,000. A large detached house, built in the early part of this century and backing on to the commons, will cost £600,000 upwards.

Journey: 54 min
Season: £2968
Peak: 2 per hr
Off-peak: 1 per hr

WITLEY is spread out over several miles, with housing estates from the various 20th-century building booms linking arms around the half-timbered and tile cottages of the old village centre. You would pay anything from £225,000 for a two-bedroom terraced house to well over £750,000 for an early 20th-century detached property with five bedrooms. Witley Common, 500 acres of National Trust land, is a great local asset. The station is a mile to the south at **Wormley**. This is a quiet residential area where a detached house built in the Twenties, shielded from the road by a bank of trees and a long driveway, is likely to cost over £600,000. On a hilltop eminence is King Edward's private school for boys and girls.

Hambledon, a mile to the east, won the Surrey Village of the Year award in 2008 for the strength of its community activities. It lies in a hollow surrounded by hills and woods. The village has a pretty green with a cricket pavilion and pond. One of the oldest houses, Oakhurst Cottage, is kept by the National Trust as a 16th-century museum. The village school is now a nursery school, the shop has been revived by the community and is staffed by volunteers and part-timers, and the old workhouse has been converted into luxury apartments known as Hambledon Park. Houses rarely come on the market, and the tiniest of cottages would be likely to fetch £300,000. A 17th-century Grade Two listed house with three bedrooms set in half an acre would start at £600,000; grander houses fetch over £1m.

'The green in the centre of Chiddingfold hosts a spectacular bonfire night party with 400 torchbearers'

Chiddingfold, two miles south of Witley station, is also tailored to the traditional image of a perfect English village. The green in the centre hosts a spectacular bonfire night party, with 400 torchbearers, and a summer festival. It is overlooked by the oldest pub in Surrey, the

Crown Inn, and by an 11th-century church. There is a good primary school and a number of thriving community groups. Shops include a chemist, two general stores, a post office, hairdresser and butcher, and a fishmonger calls weekly. In the reign of Elizabeth I there were a dozen glassworks in the village, the profitability of which can be seen in the lovely half-timbered houses of the period. The church is notable both for its Chiddingfold glass windows and for the huge collection of lichens in the churchyard, which is an attraction to botany students from all over the country. The large 16th- and 17th-century houses on the green would break the £1m to £2m barrier if they ever came on to the market. There are a couple of small modern developments where you might buy a four-bedroom, modern detached house for £450,000.

'The huge collection of lichens in the churchyard is an attraction for botany students from all over the country'

Journey: 49 min
Season: £3140
Peak: 5 per hr
Off-peak: 4 per hr

HASLEMERE is rich commuter territory, surrounded by National

Trust land and with a pretty High Street stiff with half-timbered 16th-century buildings. The shops are intimate and intriguing. An attraction is the Haslemere Educational Museum, which contains displays of British birds, geology, zoology, local history and so on – the mummy with one toe exposed is a big hit with schoolchildren. There is a good blend of private and state schools, including the independent Royal School for girls.

There are very few houses in the centre. In Lower Street you might find an artisan's Victorian two-bedroom cottage for £200,000. In Petworth Road a large detached Victorian house with walled gardens will cost £800,000. Ubiquitous Thirties' semis spread outwards from the centre, selling for £250,000 and upwards depending on the street. Three Gates Lane runs off the northern end of the High Street and contains substantial homes with large gardens, which sell from £500,000 to £5m. This is a popular area because it is convenient for the town centre. Alfred Lord Tennyson lived for the last 25 years of his life at Aldworth House, which is still occupied as a family home in Tennyson's Lane. Houses here have views of Blackdown Hill or east to the South Downs. Wonderful walks abound.

Victorian terraces can be found on the Wey Hill side of town, with banks and building societies, small supermarkets and chip shops complementing the large Tesco. A two-bedroom terraced house here will sell for just over £225,000. On the Deepdene estate you might buy a two-bedroom terraced house for £180,000, a three-bedroom semi for £220,000 or a four-bedroom detached house with a garage from £370,000.

North of Haslemere is the 900ft Gibbet Hill which, if you are up to the climb, gives lofty views over the Weald and the North Downs. To the west is the open heathland of Frensham Common with

Frensham Great and Little Ponds. Both have sandy (and rather dirty) beaches. They were created in the 13th century to supply fish to, among others, the Bishop of Winchester.

Between these two beauty-spots lies **Hindhead**, which was once rather fashionable – Sir Arthur Conan Doyle, George Bernard Shaw and Lloyd George lived here. But it has had its nose put out of joint by the A3, which comes to a standstill here quite regularly, though a tunnel is now under construction and due to open in 2011. There are still some huge houses that sit snugly behind their shields of greenery, but there is little point considering them unless you have upwards of £700,000 to spend, though you could buy into a modern development by the A3 for £275,000. Hindhead Common, 1,100 acres of heath and woodland, is a major local attraction.

Though it has a proper little shopping centre, **Grayshott** is still at heart a village. From 1898 to 1901 Flora Thompson, author of the semi-autobiographical *Larkrise to Candleford* trilogy, was assistant postmistress in Grayshott. Among her customers were Arthur Conan Doyle and George Bernard Shaw. Local potter Phil Bates has lived and worked in the village for over 40 years and says 'it's the best village between Waterloo and Portsmouth'. A two-bedroom Victorian house will cost over £220,000; a large Thirties-built house with several acres and a pony paddock around £750,000. **Grayswood**, on the lip of Haslemere, is less exclusive but still in the top drawer. Twenties' and Thirties' detached houses come on to the market priced at around £350,000 for three bedrooms; two-bedroom Victorian semis go for £225,000.

'Local potter Phil Bates says Grayshott "is the best village between Waterloo and Portsmouth"'

'The Surrey/Hampshire boundary looms large in people's minds because there is intense rivalry between the two counties'

Seven miles south, beyond the Blackdown Hill, is **Midhurst**, an old market town on the River Rother whose attractions include Cowdray Park polo ground and a regular farmers' market. There are some very attractive houses. Next to the church, for example, is a Queen Anne terrace with likely price-tags close to £400,000. The parklands of some of the largest houses in the town – Heatherwood, Elmleigh, Guillards Oak and Heathfield Park – have been developed as small housing estates. The average price for a four-bedroom detached house (of which there is a great number) is £350,000. Heathfield Park also has some pseudo-Georgian three-bedroom terraced houses, priced at around £275,000. Another good area is Close Walks Wood. A dozen or so houses have encroached into the woodland and would fetch around £650,000 for four bedrooms. Elsewhere in the town you could find an ordinary three-bedroom late-Victorian terraced house for around £200,000.

Journey: 64 min
Season: £3184
Peak: 2 per hr
Off-peak: 1 per hr

LIPHOOK The Surrey/Hampshire boundary looms large in people's minds because there is intense rivalry between the two counties. Liphook falls just into Hampshire and is surrounded by lovely countryside. It is cheaper than Haslemere because it is further south, but has good access to the A3. The Square, where six roads converge, is a conservation area dominated by the 17th-century Royal Anchor Hotel. There has been considerable development close to the centre of the village in recent years. Shopping is much improved and there is a Sainsbury's Country Store. New apartments, well placed for village amenities, cost from £135,000 to £200,000. A three-bedroom terrace on Loseley Park will cost £200,000; a four-bedroom detached £350,000. Victorian three-bedroom semis in Liphook fetch between £190,000 and £250,000; a five-bedroom house over £400,000

Journey: 71 min
Season: £3288
Peak: 2 per hr
Off-peak: 1 per hr

LISS is sliced in two by the railway and River Rother. It is very mixed and not greatly sought-after, though it does provide a good range of houses. One-bedroom modern flats start at £95,000. Two-bedroom Victorian terraces cost from £210,000; three-bedroom modern detached houses £300,000. There are some large Victorian properties in the more popular Liss Forest area, where a four-bedroom house will cost £400,000 or more. On the outskirts, four- or five-bedroom period houses with a few acres start at around £750,000.

Four miles north-west is **Selborne**, an idyllically pretty village slightly handicapped by a main street too narrow for the volume of traffic. The house of the 18th-century naturalist Gilbert White is an attraction to tourists, as are the beech hanger and meadows (now owned by the National Trust), which he described in his classic book *Natural History and Antiquities of Selborne* in 1789. It also contains an exhibition dedicated to Captain Oates, companion to Captain Scott on his ill-fated expedition to the Antarctic, and his family. The High Street is lined with picturesque brick-and-limestone cottages, some thatched, some early Victorian, though it turns into a line of slow-moving traffic at peak hours, controlled by traffic-calming bumps and pinch points. A small, late 19th-century stone cottage here will sell for around £300,000. A four-bedroom cottage on the hillside, with large grounds and lovely views, could fetch £800,000. There is a small amount of modern housing; the price for four bedrooms and a double garage is around £375,000.

‘The High Street is lined with picturesque brick-and-limestone cottages, some thatched’

Journey: 63 min	
Season: £3412	
Peak: 4 per hr	
Off-peak: 3 per hr	

PETERSFIELD The countryside around Petersfield is largely a designated Area of Outstanding Natural Beauty that is often referred to as Little Switzerland or the Hampshire Alps. This area will make up the western end of the proposed South Downs National Park. A line of beech hangers follows a meandering escarpment from Binstead, just to the the west of Alton, to Petersfield, where it connects with the South Downs and rises to a 900ft peak at Butser Hill. Butser is within the Queen Elizabeth Country Park, four miles south of the town, which is the place for picnics, pony rides and grass skiing.

With this remarkable landscape to hand, and with Winchester and Chichester only half an hour by car, it is not surprising that Petersfield is a very desirable, and hence expensive, place to live. (Beyond Butser Hill to the south, property prices drop rapidly as you move outside commuting range.) Petersfield owed its initial prosperity to wool, leather and its usefulness as a coaching stop on the road to Portsmouth. Its charm comes from the grouping of ancient buildings around The Square, a former market place where a thrice-weekly market, a fortnightly farmers' market and a French food market are held. Running off it is Sheep Street, lined with 16th- and 17th-century houses. A small two-bedroom house here would cost around £250,000. The Spain is a kind of unexplained opening in the original street plan, now containing some good Georgian houses. Petersfield was once a predominantly agricultural town, but is now popular with retired couples as well as with commuters to London and Portsmouth.

Fifties' detached house, Petersfield

Just a short walk from the High Street is a pond and 69 acres of heath. Here there are boats for hire, a cricket pitch and golf course, as well as lonelier spots where you come across Bronze Age burial mounds. Every October The Heath is the scene of the Taro Fair – once a horse fair but now a throng of roundabouts and stalls. The best addresses in town are on The Heath. Imposing Victorian or Edwardian detached houses, with up to eight bedrooms, several reception rooms and a billiards room, sell from £750,000 to over £1m. Typical residents are successful local solicitors and retired naval officers.

On the outskirts are some substantial houses built in the Twenties. Four bedrooms will cost from £500,000. Major new developments have appeared, including town-centre flats which start at £180,000 for one bedroom. Herne Farm is still under construction and offers one-bedroom flats at £150,000, to five-bedroom detached houses at £550,000. The Village, built in the centre of the town, is of 'olde worlde' design and colourfully painted. A three-bedroom house here costs £400,000; four bedrooms £450,000 or more. Stoneham Park, built in the Seventies, has two-bedroom houses at £180,000; four bedrooms from £300,000. The Gallifords is similarly priced.

'A notable feature of village life are the social events at Bedales'

Surrounding Petersfield are some beautiful villages. Two miles north is **Steep**, a trickle of houses across a hillside, which they share with the co-educational private school Bedales. There are dramatic views of the beech woods, to which you can walk by taking a route across the common, past the primary school and up into the hangers. A notable feature of village life are the social events at Bedales, which include plays in the Olivier Theatre, concerts and talks. There is also an art gallery open to the public. You could buy a small period cottage in Steep for around £250,000; a three-bedroom Victorian semi for £400,000; a four- or five-bedroom detached Victorian house for up to £800,000. A one-off, five-bedroom detached modern house with an acre of garden could start at £800,000.

Sheet, one mile north-east of Petersfield, exudes historic charm. An ancient horse chestnut stands on the village green close to the Queen's Head pub, with the church and a terrace of old cottages nearby. Two former mills set off some of the larger houses very nicely. The small village sustains a large primary school, which serves its Thirties' housing estate and the surrounding villages. Prices have risen since the bypass drained away the traffic. A two-bedroom period cottage will cost around £250,000; a three-bedroom Thirties' detached bungalow £300,000 or more. A four-bedroom Georgian house might fetch around £600,000.

To the south-east of Petersfield is **South Harting**, recognisable from a distance by its octagonal copper church spire seen against the backdrop of Linch Down, and beneath it in the graveyard lies the novelist Anthony Trollope. The main street, running uphill to the church, has thatched and timber-frame cottages, hairdresser, post office and carpet shop. There is a primary school and villagers have secured the future of the village shop by owning it outright. A three-bedroom half-timbered cottage in South Harting will cost just over £280,000; a three-storey Georgian house with four bedrooms around £600,000. The village hall is the meeting place for all the local clubs and societies, including the Harting Society, a nursery school and a mothers-and-toddlers group. There is football and cricket on the recreation ground. Uppark, the house restored by the National Trust after it was burnt down, is a mile away up the hill.

To the west is **West Meon**, which suffers from traffic on the A32, and its quieter sister village **East Meon**, both lying in the shadow of the Downs. West Meon has a primary school, a post-office-cum-store, a butcher, clubs and societies. It is a popular paragliding area. A 16th-century, four-bedroom thatched cottage in need of modernisation might cost a little under £500,000; a Seventies-built three-bedroom semi around £275,000. East Meon is the prettier of the two, with the River Meon flowing beneath a sequence of little bridges. There are one or two 14th-century houses, plus some Tudor and Georgian, and a working forge. A four-bedroom Georgian house would cost over £650,000; a newly-built four-bedroom house in The Meadows, £540,000. Leydene Park is a new development a few miles south with giddy views of the coast, tennis courts and five-bedroom detached houses for over £1m.

> 'East Meon is the prettier of the two villages, with the River Meon flowing beneath a sequence of little bridges'

Journey: 87 min
Season: £3608
Peak: 2 per hr
Off-peak: 1 per hr

ROWLANDS CASTLE

has all the appearances of a traditonal English village – a crescent of green at the centre, flanked by cottages, Georgian and Victorian houses. A large country house, Deerleap, stands behind a flint wall opposite, and has in its grounds the remains of the castle that gave the village its name. The place is stiff with money and retired medics and naval officers. There is a long waiting-list of people eager to pay the not inconsiderable fee to join the golf club. The village has its own primary school, shops, five foodie pubs on the green, vet, doctor's surgery, football and cricket pitches, tennis and cricket clubs. Huge detached houses built in the Twenties and Thirties with an acre of garden sell for around £800,000 in Links Lane, which is the smartest address. Bowes Hill is also smart, with four- and five-bedroom houses of the same period priced between £500,000 and £600,000. Nearby is Ditcham Park, the private school for boys and girls, which has a liberal tradition, but is not as fashionable as Bedales. Rowlands Castle is strung between the ancient Forest of Bere and Stansted Park, the family seat of the Earl and Countess of Bessborough, which is open to the public.

Journey: 77 min
Season: £3772
Peak: 4 per hr
Off-peak: 3 per hr

HAVANT, too, is fairly sedate. It lies inland from Langstone Harbour, which is a popular sailing and watersports centre with good moorings and sailing clubs. The town is also well placed to take advantage of the cultural riches offered by Chichester, ten miles to the east. Another major attraction is the old shore path (part of which is the Solent Way) to Warblington and Emsworth, running past Hayling Island and a much-prized area of marsh and mudflats designated as a Site of Special Scientific Interest. The older part of Havant is now masked by modernity, notably by the Meridian shopping centre, with library and multi-storey car park en suite. A short walk away is The Parchment, so called because the modern flats and mews houses here are built on the site of an old parchment-making works. A two-bedroom flat will cost £150,000; a four-bedroom house with two bathrooms £250,000. More up-market areas are Meadowlands and Wade Court, both within half a mile of the town centre. Individually designed detached houses with four and five bedrooms, built in the Twenties and Thirties with plush gardens, sell for between £450,000 and £750,000.

'A major attraction is the old shore path to Warblington and Emsworth running past Hayling Island'

A mile to the east are **Warblington** and **Denvilles**, comforting Thirties' suburbs with new accretions where three-bedroom detached houses with large gardens sell for around £230,000 and humble three-bedroom semis can come as cheap as £175,000. A four-bedroom detached house on a Seventies' estate would fetch between £230,000 and £250,000. Warblington prices may be slightly higher. For sea views look at **Emsworth**, once famed for its oysters, which has foreshore properties with price tags at over £1m. Or cross the causeway to **Hayling Island** where you find unadulterated English seaside with a mix of post-war bungalows and large houses at £120,000 to £1m, with boat yards and sailing clubs at the end of sandy lanes.

Journey: 96 min
Season: £3772
Peak: 3 per hr
(some by changing at Havant)
Off-peak: 2 per hr
(1 by changing at Havant)

BEDHAMPTON is, with Denvilles and Warblington (see above), one of the main residential areas of Havant. It was developed in the Fifties as a series of bungalow estates where something with three bedrooms will now cost £230,000 to £260,000. There are three-bedroom semis for around £220,000 and detached houses for £250,000.

Housing developments cling on to Havant for several miles around, and to the north they don't let go until you get beyond Clanfield. Within this built-up area are former villages such as **Cowplain**, where there are (30- and 40-year-old) well-worn estates and bungalows. A three-bedroom detached house or bungalow on a Sixties' development might cost £200,000 to £215,000. **Denmead** village proper is highly sought-after. It has shops, pubs and a village green. A late 1880s' cottage with three bedrooms and a bit of land could fetch £325,000. There are also plenty of small new developments, popular with young families because of the local school. Prices are higher than those in Waterlooville.

Waterlooville is an established town, around 80 per cent of which was built during the last two to three decades. Off Tempest Avenue, which runs from one end to the other, is a run of cul-de-sacs with mixed housing in each. A studio apartment will cost £65,000, a three-bedroom semi from £155,000, and a four-bedroom detached house £250,000. To the south of Waterlooville is **Purbrook**, where bungalows have crept between the 19th-century houses. A two-bedroom bungalow will cost £190,000, a four- to five- bedroom detached house in The Brow will cost £350,000 to £400,000. There is a well-regarded Roman Catholic secondary school that attracts families.

Journey: 101 min
Season: £3984
Peak: 4 per hr
(some by changing at Havant)
Off-peak: 3 per hr
(1 by changing at Havant)

HILSEA is really north Portsmouth (see below). Streets of houses built in the Thirties fan out around the station. A three-bedroom semi will cost between £160,000 and £200,000.

Journey: 87 min
Season: £3984
Peak: 3 per hr
Off-peak: 3 per hr

FRATTON is the home of Portsmouth Football Club, known to friend and foe alike as Pompey. For the rest it is very Coronation Street, like much of Portsmouth. Flat-fronted two- to three-bedroom terraced houses sell for £105,000.

Portsmouth & Southsea
Journey: 91 min
Season: £3984
Peak: 3 per hr
Off-peak: 3 per hr

Portsmouth Harbour
Journey: 96 min
Season: £3984
Peak: 3 per hr
Off-peak: 2 per hr

PORTSMOUTH & SOUTHSEA AND PORTSMOUTH HARBOUR

The Navy dominates Portsmouth. Along with IBM, the Navy is the biggest local employer, though it can sometimes create a them-and-us feeling in the city – particularly when hordes of American seamen come ashore and head straight for the nightlife in Southsea. The dockyard has been home to the Royal Navy for 500 years, and the fleet is still serviced here. It is not only a good place for spotting modern warships, there is also an impressive collection of historic ships, including HMS *Victory* and the *Mary Rose*, which attracts tourists all year round. On top of the naval traffic are the constant comings and goings of the Cherbourg, Caen, St Malo, Le Havre, Santander and Bilbao ferries into Albert Johnson dock. In the Mountbatten Centre, the city has one of the best leisure centres in southern England, which also doubles as a conference and trade show venue. Portsmouth Grammar School is the local private school that takes both boys and girls.

Portsmouth Harbour station is close to **Old Portsmouth** and the ferry terminal for the Isle of Wight, and a short ferry-ride from Gosport. An 18th-century four- or five-bedroom house in Old Portsmouth would cost £500,000 to £600,000. Quaint little cottages of the same period cost around £325,000. Gun Wharf Quays is a new marina with smart shops, restaurants, a nightclub and Jongleurs comedy club, where a one-bedroom flat costs from £180,000 and a large penthouse up to £1m; four-bedroom modern town houses sell for £400,000. North of Portsmouth Harbour, towards Fareham, is **Port Solent**, a product of the high-earning, fast-living Thatcher years. The marina is the centrepiece, with the surrounding houses, shops, restaurants and sailing school. A two-bedroom flat will cost £260,000; a three-bedroom town house with a berth £320,000.

Throughout the city, first-time buyers compete for two-bedroom Victorian and Edwardian houses, priced at around £120,000. A third bedroom puts the price up to around £155,000. Second-time buyers attracted to newish houses, could look in **Anchorage Park** in the north of the city, where four-bedroom detached houses cost £250,000; a studio, £100,000. Others might prefer to browse among the bay-fronted Victoriana of **North End**, an area undergoing gradual gentrification. A three-bedroom terraced house here would cost around £135,000.

Southsea has more the feel of a seaside resort, with two piers, a shingle beach, permanent funfair, ballroom and the King's Theatre. It is packed with shops, restaurants and pubs. Running back from the seafront are plenty of Victorian and Edwardian houses. You would pay around £250,000 for three bedrooms and £350,000 to £400,000 for four bedrooms. Two- or three-bedroom dockworkers' terraced houses further back from the sea sell for £120,000 to £150,000.

'Buyers might prefer to browse among the bay-fronted Victoriana of North End'

Edwardian family home, Portsmouth

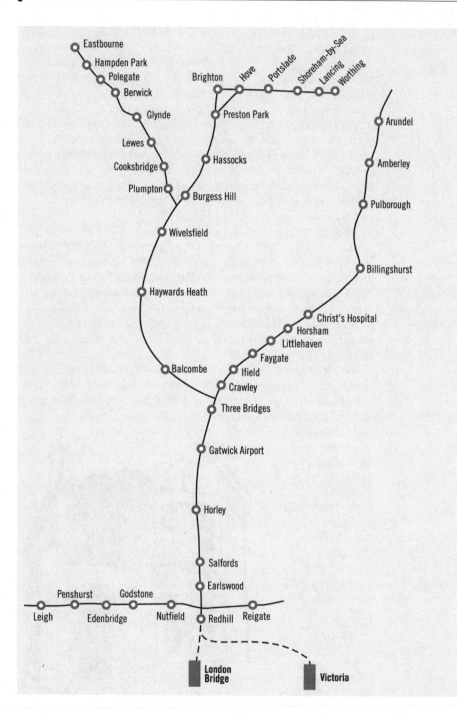

Victoria/London Bridge
> Arundel and Brighton
and on to Eastbourne, Lewes & Worthing

Many peak and all off-peak services from Brighton to London Bridge go on to Blackfriars, City Thameslink, Farringdon and St Pancras International. The season ticket prices quoted for London Bridge from stations on the main line are generally valid across London to St Pancras International (but not on the Underground). These seasons are also available to Victoria. Note that Gatwick Express services may now be used for part of the journey for all stations south of Gatwick at no extra cost.

To Victoria
Journey: 27 min
Season: £2200
Peak: 3 per hr
Off-peak: 2 per hr

To London Bridge
Journey: 31 min
Season: £2200
Peak: 3 per hr
Off-peak: 4 per hr

REDHILL has now outstripped its older neighbour **Reigate** (see page 254), though it only began to sprout in about 1841 when the railway arrived. It is now heavily commercialised. There is a huge shopping centre, The Belfry, anchored around a large Marks & Spencer, The Harlequin theatre and a sports centre, Donyngs, with a sauna, squash and badminton courts, swimming pool and gym.

Redhill is slightly cheaper than Reigate. There is an abundance of good Thirties' semis and detached houses with bay windows and steep cottage-style rooftops. One-bedroom flats cost £110,000 to £135,000, two-bedroom flats £150,000 to £180,000. New developments have sprung up around the station offering two-bedroom apartments from £200,000 to £250,000. You can buy little two-bedroom cottages from around £175,000, three-bedroom terraced houses for £180,000 to £200,000, and three-bedroom semi-detached houses for £200,000 to £250,000. Something more sumptuous, with four or five bedrooms and generous gardens, could be bought for £575,000.

> North Downs line east to Leigh via Nutfield, Godstone, Edenbridge and Penshurst

For train information, see overleaf

NUTFIELD is little more than a ribbon village that has grown up along the A25, with the pedigree of a 13th-century church off the High Street. It offers an active social life, including two cricket clubs and a football club. You can buy a three-bedroom semi for £250,000. A new four-bedroom detached house could cost £350,000 upwards.

To London Bridge
Journey: 37 min
Season: £2160
Peak: 2 per hr
(some by changing at Redhill)
Off-peak: 1 per hr

South Nutfield (where Nutfield station is situated) has a school, an award-winning general store-cum-post office and the local watering hole is the Station Hotel. A turn-of-the-century semi might cost £240,000; a five-bedroom period house with an acre of land, £750,000 upwards. The most exclusive address is The Avenue.

To London Bridge
Journey: 42 min
Season: £2160
Peak: 2 per hr
(some by changing at Redhill)
Off-peak: 1 per hr

GODSTONE is right on the A25 with a one-way traffic system that turns the centre into a bottleneck when the M25 is jammed. It is no longer the rural backwater where William Cobbett spied double violets as large as small pinks, but it still has the neat gardens he admired, the green, the pond and the White Hart Inn where he stayed. A two-bedroom Victorian cottage in a quiet pocket at the centre might be priced at £235,000. A three-storey, four-bedroom cottage overlooking the green might cost £475,000.

To London Bridge
Journey: 49 min
Season: £2284 (also valid Edenbridge Town) or £2908 if also valid via Tonbridge
Peak: 1 per hr (plus 3 per hr changing at Redhill or Tonbridge)
Off-peak: 1 per hr (plus 1 per hr changing at Tonbridge)

EDENBRIDGE has two stations, the other being Edenbridge Town on the Hurst Green to Uckfield line (see page 289). The stations are a mile apart, and the two railway lines hold the worst bit of town in a pincer-grip between them. The area was known as a depository for factories and former council estates, but is improving. The best parts of town are in the north and south. First-time starter flats cost around £140,000; two-bedroom flats from £150,000 to £200,000. Large houses on the golf course built by Rydon Homes are popular and sell at £395,000 to £450,000 for four bedrooms or from £480,000 for five bedrooms.

Although Edenbridge is not one of the gems of Kent, it does have its attractions. It is under an hour from London and the same from the coast. Gatwick is only half-an-hour away, but not so close that aircraft noise is a worry. The town has its fair share of medieval buildings and antiques shops and a string of beautiful half-timbered houses by the River Eden. The Eden Valley Museum in the High Street is housed in a 14th-century farmhouse. The south-eastern portion of the town, towards Hever, is more pleasing, especially where it turns into the hamlet of **Marsh Green**. The south-west end of town, towards Haxted, is also inviting. **Haxted** has a large watermill and the stables next door have been turned into a restaurant, which serves organic salmon and locally reared beef by candlelight, or outside on the terrace by the millpond in summer. On the northern flank of Edenbridge is an industrial estate and a large housing estate, Spitals Cross, where most of the former council homes with thin slit windows and flat roofs are now in private ownership. There are a couple of new developments in this area. Wits say that Edenbridge is a tale of two towns, offering a spectrum of urban blight to rural delight within one-and-a-half miles. There are all the usual sports: cricket, football, tennis, badminton, rugby, hockey and golf.

The villages surrounding Edenbridge are much more scenic than the town itself. They have a number of fine timber-framed houses from the 16th century, built on the proceeds of the iron industry, which collapsed in about 1700.

To London Bridge
Journey: 55 min
Season: £2740 (also valid Edenbridge Town) or £3000 if also valid via Tonbridge
Peak: 1 per hr (plus 3 per hr changing at Redhill or Tonbridge)
Off-peak: 1 per hr (plus 1 per hr changing at Tonbridge)

PENSHURST, nearby, is an attractive, straggly Kentish village with some nice old tile-hung cottages and its own primary school. The heavy influx of commuters here has resulted in a certain them-and-us feeling. Commuters are often referred to as 'invisible parishioners', so slight is their involvement in village activities, but membership of the village football and cricket teams is growing. When Penshurst's general store closed, Lord de L'Isle of Penshurst Place opened up a post office and grocery store in the village garage for the convenience of the elderly. A farmers' market takes place on the first Saturday in the month. Penshurst Place and Hever Castle (see page 289) bring tourists as well as patronage – an irritant in the summer. Activities include amateur dramatics, bridge, dancing and stoolball (a cross between rounders and cricket, played with a round wooden bat). Property is now so expensive that it is beyond the means of local young people. A two-bedroom semi-detached cottage might cost £350,000; a five-bedroom thatched cottage £1.2m; a substantial Queen Anne house over £1.5m.

Chiddingstone is also a show-stopping village. The main street, with Chiddingstone Castle at one end and magnificent half-timbered houses, is owned by the National Trust (the castle made an excellent Toad Hall in a recent film of *The Wind in the Willows*). The Castle Inn is a popular eating place. Prices are on a par with Penshurst.

To London Bridge
Journey: 56 min
Season: £2740 (also valid Edenbridge Town) or £3000 if also valid via Tonbridge
Peak: 1 per hr (plus 3 per hr changing at Redhill or Tonbridge)
Off-peak: 1 per hr (plus 1 per hr changing at Tonbridge)

LEIGH (pronounced *Lie*) is very much a dormitory village. It has a huge green canopied with conker trees, and traditional tile-hung and weatherboarded Kentish houses. There is a post office stores and a hairdresser. The primary school flourishes, and organised activities range from the mothers-and-toddlers group to the cricket club. Leigh is popular with London solicitors and bankers, which explains the arrival of a new development of executive houses. A five-bedroom period property with four reception rooms, granny annexe, tennis court and swimming pool would cost £1m or more; a three-bedroom semi £280,000.

> North Downs Line west to Reigate

To Victoria
Journey: 42 min
Season: £2220
Peak: 3 per hr
changing at Redhill
Off-peak: 2 per hr
changing at Redhill

To London Bridge
Journey: 38 min
Season: £2220
Peak: 3 per hr
changing at Redhill
Off-peak: 1 per hr*,
plus 2 per hr
changing at Redhill
* Off-peak through
service extends to
Waterloo East and
Charing Cross

REIGATE is Redhill's older brother, tucked under the North Downs, with rows of quiet residential streets and a shopping centre with a Morrisons supermarket. The town's 18th-century Priory Park has undergone a £6.2m regeneration, adding football pitches, tennis courts and a skate-park. Sunday afternoon walks are taken on Reigate Heath, 130 acres of open space on the edge of the town, where there is a restored windmill that is used as a church. Education is shared with Redhill. There is a Roman Catholic/Church of England co-ed comprehensive called St Bede's (that prepares students for A-levels and Oxbridge entrance), which gets good results. East Surrey College offers HNDs in art and media, and foundation degrees in business.

Reigate has a greater quantity of properties at the top end of the market than Redhill. The most exclusive areas are High Trees Road and just off Reigate Hill. A large family home on Pilgrims Way with ample gardens would cost more than £1.5m. A two-up-two-down in the town centre could be bought for rather less, at £250,000.

'There is a beautiful common at Earlswood with two lakes for boating and fishing'

> Continuation of main line

To London Bridge
Journey: 39 min
Season: £2220
Peak: 2 per hr plus
2 per hr to Victoria,
plus another 2 per
hr to each by
changing at Redhill
Off-peak: 1 per hr

EARLSWOOD It is hard to find a dividing line between **Earlswood** and Redhill. Some of the people who live here work at the nearby East Surrey Hospital. There are also plenty of commuters, travelling to both Croydon and London. The conversion of the Royal Earlswood Hospital into luxury apartments (where two bedrooms cost £175,000 to £200,000) improved the area and there is a beautiful common with two lakes for boating and fishing. A two-bedroom flat would cost from £130,000; a three-bedroom late-Victorian semi from £200,000.

SALFORDS

To London Bridge
Journey: 42 min
Season: £2612
Peak: 2 per hr plus
2 per hr to Victoria,
plus another 2 per
hr to each by
changing at Redhill
Off-peak: 1 per hr

SALFORDS is nice in parts but has the disadvantage of straddling the A23. It has a village shop-cum-post-office, and several newsagents, but people tend to aim for Redhill, Horley or Hookwood for their major shops. There is a primary school, but older children have to bus to Horley or Redhill for secondary schools. Long-suffering parents spend a lot of time chauffeuring their children about because there is not much for them to do in the village itself (the scout group is at neighbouring Sidlow). Helicopters buzz in and out from the nearby aerodrome. A three-bedroom semi with a long garden here might cost £240,000; a two-bedroom bungalow about the same. Larger properties in leafier roads lie to the east.

HORLEY

To Victoria
Journey: 35 min
Season: £2612
Peak: 4 per hr
Off-peak: 1 per hr

To London Bridge
Journey: 46 min
Season: £2612
Peak: 2 per hr
Off-peak: 2 per hr

HORLEY is quite a busy place on the A23, with a population of 22,000. It has a modest pedestrianised high street, and the local comprehensive, Oakwood School, is well-liked. There is a swimming pool at the Horley Anderson Centre, as well as cricket, hockey, bowling and football clubs. Gatwick Airport is a huge local employer. In the sea of Thirties' semis you could pay between £235,000 and £250,000 for three bedrooms. There are also some Victorian terraces where three-bedroom houses start at around £200,000. The modern Langshott estate, with over 700 houses on it, won awards for landscaping and design when it was built. A five-bedroom detached house here would cost over £350,000. Work has started on building 2,000 to 3,000 new homes in the area over the next ten years.

The village of **Charlwood** clings on to its rural image, in spite of the fact that Gatwick Airport is only a few miles away. The government announcement a few years ago that Gatwick would not expand towards it lifted a black cloud, though the parish council remains vigilant. Villagers lovingly nurse the large number of listed buildings, which include a Grade One listed Norman church. The village has a newsagent, which also sells fruit and groceries, a pine shop-cum-café and a kitchen shop. There is a school for the under-sevens. People living here have the choice of commuting either from Horley or from Gatwick, where the service is fast and frequent. A brick-built two-bedroom

Grade Two listed
house,
Charlwood

cottage might be bought for £195,000; a third bedroom puts the price up to around £215,000.

'Local events take place in the Centenary Village Hall, including craft markets and the annual village summer party'

Smallfield, to the north east, has been greatly affected by the development of Gatwick. Aircraft noise can be a problem, and the very presence of an airport has allowed more industrial development than there would otherwise have been. It has a burgeoning population, with a good mix of young and old, yet it is a straggly place. A great bonus has been the opening of the Lottery-funded MUGA (Multi-Use Games Area) for football, basketball and tennis. Shops include a greengrocer, butcher, and hardware store. Local events take place in the Centenary Village Hall, including regular food and craft markets and the annual village summer party. Prices are similar to those in Horley. A three-bedroom semi-detached house near The Plough pub might sell for £220,000 and a detached three-bedroom house for £225,000 to £250,000. Modern four-bedroom detached houses start at £270,000.

GATWICK AIRPORT Gatwick Express trains whistle into London from here in rapid succession, making it a popular choice for commuters in a hurry. People living in the villages to the west might prefer it to stations on the nearer but much slower **Victoria to Waterloo/Horsham** line (page 279).

To Victoria	To London Bridge
Journey: 30 min	Journey: 29 min
Season: £2400 to Victoria only (also valid on Gatwick Express); £2580 also valid to London Bridge	Season: £2580 (also valid Victoria); £2000 London Bridge on Southern only; £2260 London Bridge on First Capital Connect only
Peak: 5 per hr	Peak: 3 per hr
Off-peak: 8 per hr	Off-peak: 4 per hr

'Gatwick Express trains whistle into London in rapid succession'

To Victoria
Journey: 38 min
Season: £2816
Peak: 4 per hr
Off-peak: 3 per hr

THREE BRIDGES Some of the better parts of Crawley such as **Pound Hill** are close to this station. One-bedroom flats in Pound Hill cost about £120,000; three-bedroom detached houses about £210,000 (see Crawley, below). Three Bridges, so called because of the bridges over the River Mole, was a village in its own right before Crawley was first thought of. It contains some Victorian terraces that sprang up around the railway station, but the bulk of it was built in the early Fifties when more than 2,000 houses were put up for 4,800 newcomers. Prices are about the same as those in Crawley.

To London Bridge
Journey: 33 min
Season: £2816 (ALL)
or £2440 on First
Capital Connect only
Peak: 3 per hr
Off-peak: 4 per hr

> Main line from Three Bridges to Arundel

To Victoria
Journey: 44 min
Season: £2764
Peak: 4 per hr
Off-peak: 2 per hr,
plus 2 per hr
changing at Gatwick
Airport

CRAWLEY is fast shaking off its reputation as the dull kid on the block. It was developed as a New Town after the Second World War for people moving out of London. The design was originally anchored around nine neighbourhoods (now there are thirteen), each comprising a shopping parade, primary school, church, pub, community hall and playing fields. The first new-towners moved in during 1949, when Gatwick Airport was no more than a wartime runway on boggy ground on the town's outskirts. Today, jobs at Gatwick Airport are plentiful, and the factory estates and business parks that have grown up around it include every kind of industry from light manufacturing to pharmaceuticals and foodstuffs.

To London Bridge
Journey: 59 min
Season: £2764
Peak: 2 per hr plus
3 per hr changing at
Three Bridges
Off-peak: 2 per hr
plus 2 per hr
changing at Three
Bridges

The Borough Council has been busy re-inventing Crawley in recent years with a massive investment and smart new shops. The town now has a state-of-the-art £37m sports centre, K2, with a 50m pool, climbing wall, athletics track, all-weather pitches, tennis and badminton courts, and is a designated training ground for the 2012 Olympics. Crawley Skate Park is popular with boarders and bikers. A huge investment in education has provided three new secondary schools and the Central Sussex College campus, plus a new library complex. Plans are afoot for a £750m town centre redevelopment due to finish in 2015. Public transport has had a makeover and now a 24-hour bus service enables people to leave the car at home.

People moving to the area would probably choose to live in one of the neighbouring villages, or closer to Three Bridges station. For £160,000 it is possible to get one of the original three-bedroom semis put up at the beginning of the new town. Studio flats start at £70,000 and one-bedroom flats at £110,000. The original neighbourhoods are still identifiable. West Green, for instance, was one of the first, with its rows of brick terraces and some older railway workers' cottages. The less popular neighbourhoods of Broadfield, Bewbush and Langley Green are changing as people buy ex-council properties. There are plans to create a new neighbourhood of 2,500 homes to the west of Crawley.

To Victoria	To London Bridge
Journey: 54 min	Journey: 61 min
Season: £2764	Season: £2764
Peak: 3 per hr, plus 1 per hr changing at Gatwick Airport	Peak: 2 per hr, plus 1 per hr changing at Gatwick Airport
Off-peak: 2 per hr changing at Gatwick Airport	Off-peak: 2 per hr

IFIELD is on the outskirts of Crawley, but it has a conservation area which contains the old village green, St Margaret's Church and the Plough Inn. The old Ifield Watermill on the millpond is open some Sundays in summer and the timber-framed miller's house is now a pub, The Mill House. A larding of new houses was added in 1956. You can buy a three-bedroom Fifties' semi at £175,000 and two-bedroom cottages from £160,000 (£180,000 in the conservation area). A grander period family house overlooking the green might be bought for £500.000.

'The old Ifield Watermill on the millpond is open some Sundays in summer and the timber-framed miller's house is now a pub**'**

To London Bridge
Journey: 65 min
Season: £3144
Peak: 2 per hr
Off-peak: 1 every 4 hrs

FAYGATE Property is a little more expensive in Faygate than in Crawley, because people like the intimacy of scale offered by the village, but in truth the semi-rural atmosphere is negated by the dual carriageway screeching past.

A two-bedroom Victorian semi will cost £220,000; a five-bedroom modern country house £650,000.

House style in Sussex

The tile-hung cottages of Sussex with their hipped roofs, rich timbering and modest proportions, give the most sought-after villages their texture and colour. Set against the drama of the North and South Downs, often tucked into folds or valleys, their russets and terracottas glow in the landscape.

The tiles themselves are hooked over battens, often fastened only every third or fourth course with nothing more than oak pegs. Baking in the kiln caused them to become slightly distorted, so that they form a pleasingly uneven line with small variations in colour. Line them up, row upon row, and you get a kind of decorative architectural needlework. Vary the shapes by introducing diamonds and fishtails, and the humblest of cottages looks as prettily feathered as an exotic bird.

Architectural deceit is something to watch for in this part of the country. For here it was that mathematical tiles were invented – tiles that look like bricks – in the 18th century. The theory is that this was a means of avoiding Brick Taxes, but it may have had more to do with vanity. Brick was *the* fashionable building material of the time. The deceit continues as mathematical tiles often fool modern house buyers who believe them to be brick. The key to their detection is the absence of lintels and arches over windows and doors.

East and West Sussex are also counties that have provided great wealth and pleasure. This is where William the Conqueror built some of the first Norman castles and established the feudal system. Later royals used the seaside towns as their favoured watering holes, hence all the Regency froth and finery of Brighton. The town was transformed by the Prince of Wales in the early 1800s with the addition of squares and crescents.

To Victoria	To London Bridge
Journey: 62 min	Journey: 69 min
Season: £2764	Season: £2764
Peak: 3 per hr, plus	Peak: 2 per hr, plus
1 per hr changing at	1 per hr changing at
Gatwick Airport	Gatwick Airport
Off-peak: 2 per hr	Off-peak: 2 per hr
changing at Gatwick	
Airport	

LITTLEHAVEN was once a separate village, but is now essentially a part of Horsham, with modern estates providing the putty between the two. The older houses are in Rusper Road, where a Thirties', detached three-bedroom house with large garden costs £350,000. But much of the property for sale is modern, with three-bedroom semis priced at around £220,000. Wise advice from one seasoned commuter: 'The station platform is only four carriages long so you have to make sure you're in the right bit of the train or you can't get off.'

‘Architectural deceit is something to watch for in this part of the country … mathematical tiles were invented to look like bricks’

For train information, see overleaf

HORSHAM is a busy little Sussex town that combines its old character as a smugglers' haunt and late 18th-century garrison town with plenty of interesting little shops and local businesses as well as some bigger high-street names. It has a population of 45,000, which is expanding. It is in a marvellous position, with a good train service to London, but with house prices lower than they are across the border in Surrey. Chichester and Guildford are close enough for theatres, though Horsham has its own small theatre, and the sea is 20 miles away over the South Downs. You can go to the races at

To Victoria
Journey: 56 min
Season: £3144
Peak: 4 per hr
Off-peak: 2 per hr,
plus 2 per hr
changing at Gatwick
Airport

To London Bridge
Journey: 69 min
Season: £3144 (also
valid to Victoria)
Peak: 2 per hr, plus
2 per hr changing at
Gatwick Airport
Off-peak: 2 per hr,
plus 2 per hr
changing at Gatwick
Airport

Goodwood, show-jumping at Hickstead, and there are golf clubs at Pulborough, Mannings Heath, Pease Pottage, West Chiltington and Ockley. It also has a public school, Christ's Hospital for boys and girls, where there is a separate railway station (see opposite).

Some of the houses in the town are collector's items. Walk down Pump Alley and into the Causeway, for example, and you find a street that is much as it was 300 years ago. These houses, with bulging walls and uneven roofs, rarely come on to the market. For something more family friendly – a detached five-bedroom house near the station with access to good schools – you could pay £700,000. A small modern two-bedroom house would cost around £175,000. There are council estates to the east and west of the town.

Local villages also maintain strong links with the past. **Slinfold**, to the east, has a mix of older properties, including Tudor and Georgian, many of them listed, as well as Victorian houses. It still has a village shop, a pub and a school. A six-bedroom, three-bathroom period house with country views can set you back £800,000. Closer to Horsham, separated from it by the A24, is **Broadbridge Heath**, which has a sports centre, a Tesco, and Field Place, the birthplace of the poet Percy Shelley, occasionally open to the public.

Further south is **Itchingfield**, which has an intriguing priest's house attached to the tiny church, and **Southwater**, where a village centre redevelopment has created a square with public art, surrounded by shops, a post office and restaurant. Moving west you come to **Nuthurst**, a delightful village with 16th-century houses and a timber-framed inn. A modern-five-bedroom detached house here would cost £500,000. **Lower Beeding** is small and elongated. The big house, Leonardslee, has rhododendron gardens that are open to the public from April to October. The countryside lapses back into heathland here in St Leonard's Forest, which covers 12,000 acres of old Royal hunting ground, once thought to have harboured dragons and to which (within living memory) pigs were driven up from Brighton to snuffle for acorns.

'The countryside lapses back into heathland here in St Leonard's Forest'

To the south-west is **Cowfold**, which has lost some of its character through being a junction for the A272 and the A281, but it is still well-liked. The Farm Shop sells apple wine made by the monks of the nearby Carthusian monastery. A period two-bedroom terraced cottage here might be bought for £170,000.

North of the Forest is **Rusper**, an enchanting village with a church dating from the 13th century, a high street lined with black-and-white timber buildings and two pubs, The Plough and The Star, which are centuries old. A four-bedroom converted former dairy with a barn and paddock could go for more than £1m. On this side of Horsham you have to beware the intermittent noise of aircraft from Gatwick.

To Victoria
Journey: 68 min
Season: £3144
Peak: 2 per hr
Off-peak: 1 per hr

CHRIST'S HOSPITAL, hardly distinct from Horsham, is dominated by the public school, fondly known as CH by local people, which disgorges pupils in their distinctive blue and yellow uniform. Around it has grown a low-level brick settlement, largely 20th century, which looks to neighbouring Southwater for small-time shopping. It is a much sought-after area, with a disproportionately large railway station. A two-bedroom ex-farmer's cottage in need of work might cost £200,000; a three-bedroom semi in good order would be more likely to cost £235,000.

To Victoria
Journey: 75 min
Season: £3284
Peak: 2 per hr
Off-peak: 2 per hr

BILLINGSHURST feels more like a small town than a large village, with some fine 15th-century houses beached on a shore of modern developments, and a new £6m public swimming pool. It is very much divided by the A29, which follows the route of the old Roman road, Stane Street. Commuters love it because it is more intimate than Horsham or Crawley yet has the fast rail links. 'Our looks and intelligence distinguish us from other villages,' says one resident. A Grade Two listed, three-bedroom attached cottage on High Street, with garage, garden and cellar, would cost £275,000.

Wisborough Green, two miles away, is a film-set village, regularly used by movie directors as a backdrop. It has a cricket green that borders the A272, a village shop-cum-post-office and two inns. A lovely 16th-century four-bedroom cottage with seven acres and stabling would be priced at £775,000. You need to remember that stations south of Horsham are much less well served by trains to London.

To Victoria
Journey: 71 min
Season: £3284
Peak: 2 per hr
Off-peak: 2 per hr

PULBOROUGH This is where the Arun valley becomes spellbindingly beautiful, and houses backing on to it are extremely sought-after, though beware flooding. 'The wetlands, the bird sanctuary, the downland walks, make it an absolutely glorious place to live, full of sunny corners,' says one local resident. Local societies do their stuff – Cubs, Brownies, rugby, cricket and plenty of vigorous football. The green-fingered work hard on the allotments and join the horticultural society. The village has two butchers, two supermarkets, a modern village hall and good schools. In the jumble of brick, flint and thatch you might find a 16th-century two-bedroom cottage with inglenook fireplaces for £350,000, or a three-bedroom version for £425,000.

Many of the villages on the felted slopes of the South Downs are lovely. **West Burton** and **Sutton**, for instance, are small and rural, no more than a handful of cottages and a pub. A pretty four-bedroom detached cottage here might cost £700,000. **Nutbourne**, just to the north-east, is another little hamlet with a pub, The Rising Sun, local vineyards. You might find a two-bedroom cottage for £350,000 or a small manor for £1m. Further west you come to what local people tend rather dismissively to call the Surrey part of Sussex – meaning that it is more suburban in character than the wilder countryside to the east. A four-bedroom cottage in manicured **West Chiltington** will cost £550,000 to £600,000. It is close to the shops at **Storrington**, a village that long ago burst its boundaries with new houses, but which offers a reasonable range of shops and the prospect of a Waitrose supermarket in the future. There are two ponds with ducks and swans, and the Elizabethan Parham House, with a romantic walled garden (open from Easter to September). The River Stor has not burst its boundaries since 2000, but ask about flood risk if you are buying a house here. A modern four-bedroom detached house costs from £300,000.

The old timber-framed houses in the tangle of narrow streets around the square attract lots of tourists

The star in the west is **Petworth**, the town that stands at the gates of Petworth House, with hundreds of acres of National Trust land and a house begun by the Duke of Somerset at the end of the 17th century. The old timber-framed houses in the tangle of narrow streets around the square attract lots of tourists in summer, when the large local car park fills up by breakfast-time, much to the annoyance of the local shoppers, although there is an overflow car park. Petworth is also an antiques centre, with more than 30 antiques shops, but it has a butcher, supermarket and hardware store for essentials, as well as a gunsmith for the sporting fraternity. A music festival is held in summer and the annual fair takes place in November. Villagers feel oppressed by the traffic coming through on the A285 and the A272, but it is hoped that a lorry ban being introduced in 2009 will alleviate part of the problem. A 300-year-old, three-storey, part-timbered, four-bedroom terraced town house recently sold here for £450,000. Commuters have the choice of using the faster line into Waterloo from Haslemere, which is ten miles away (see page 241).

Period town house, Petworth

Fittleworth, closer to Pulborough, is a more mixed kind of village where the former council estate is now part of a housing association. It has its own shop, church and inn, a very good primary school and is close to marvellous riding country in Bedham Woods and on the Downs. A four-bedroom house set in 15 acres would cost £1m.

To Victoria

Journey: 87 min

Season: £3284

Peak: 1 per hr

Off-peak: 1 per hr

AMBERLEY is another of the many villages in this area that have hung on to their character, with flint-and-thatch cottages and old-fashioned cottage gardens. Amberley Castle, once the residence of the Bishops of Chichester and dismantled by Parliamentarians during the Civil War, is now a romantic country house hotel. A footpath to one side leads to Amberley Wild Brooks, protected water meadows visited by migrating birds. There is a shop-cum-post-office, a handful of pubs and an open-air Amberley Working Museum with resident craftspeople. The village is protected from heavy traffic on a side road off the B2139. A two-bedroom thatched cottage with an inglenook fireplace could be priced at £400,000; a larger chocolate box cottage at £500,000 to £600,000. House prices remain on the steep side in several other popular villages further from the station, such as **Houghton** and **Bury**.

To Victoria

Journey: 90 min

Season: £3508

Peak: 2 per hr

Off-peak: 2 per hr

ARUNDEL is a busy old town on the River Arun, dominated by its castle, which is often described as Windsor in miniature. The Arundel Castle cricket ground is one of the most attractive in the country and features high-profile touring games. The High Street, climbing steeply between the river and the castle, has plenty of antiques shops, but none of the standard chain stores. There is a butcher, a fine-wines-cum-deli, and a walking-stick shop in an old printing works in Tarrant Street. The outdoor heated lido opens its doors to swimmers in summer. Chichester is only ten miles away, with its attractions for yachtsmen and theatergoers, though Arundel has its own Priory Playhouse for smaller-scale productions. Goodwood racecourse is also ten miles away on the Downs, and there are plenty of golf courses. The sea is four miles away, and there is a good beach at Climping. The River Arun has to be watched; it is tidal, and one of the fastest flowing rivers in the country after the Severn. The Arundel Wetland Centre, founded by Sir Peter Scott, runs special events for children during the school holidays.

You could buy a two-bedroom cottage in the old town for £275,000, but for a building in traditional brick-and-flint, you will have to pay a premium of £300,000 to £325,000. For three-bedroom houses the price jumps to £350,000 to £400,000. People opt either for old Arundel, which climbs up the hill, layer upon layer towards the castle, or they look at the larger Fifties' houses on the slightly cheaper Chichester side. These have big gardens and garages, are within walking distance of the town and are rather more suburban. A four-bedroom house in this neighbourhood will cost about £450,000.

The villages of **Burpham** and **Wepham** lie to the east, on the way up to the top of Harrow Hill where the views are wonderful. Both are

popular, and a modern, detached four-bedroom home would start at
£500,000, rising to £850,000 for a similar sized period house. **Slindon**,
to the west, is the kind of village people wait years for a chance to
move into. Not only because of its beauty, but because the
involvement of the National Trust means that very few houses are still
freehold. A period house with five bedrooms and a small paddock
could cost £750,000.

> Main line from Three Bridges to Brighton

To London Bridge
Journey: 38 min
Season: £3344 (ALL)
or £2440 on First
Capital Connect only
Peak: 2 per hr
Off-peak: 1 per hr

BALCOMBE Its position on a railway line set deep in an Area of
Outstanding Natural Beauty has gilded the house-price lily in
Balcombe. Commuters have a strong presence here. They usually
begin by sending their children to the local nursery and primary
schools, but switch them into the private system later if they can
afford it after buying the house.

The village has a mix of properties and its great good luck is that
the new estates have been planned well enough to avoid any feeling of
claustrophobia. Just off the village centre, Victorian semis with three
bedrooms, three reception rooms and a garden sell for £380,000. A
five-bedroom, swanky new house with six acres outside the village
could fetch over £1m.

Balcombe is described by the parish clerk as 'happy, friendly and
caring'. Strangers are soon spotted by vigilant members of the
Neighbourhood Watch. Among the myriad clubs and activities is a
Care Group which arranges to take people to hospital, collect
prescriptions and so on, and a Christmas Tree Society to aid the
needy. There are societies to cover the needs of every age group from
mixed Cubs to pensioners, plus tennis, cricket, football and
badminton clubs.

The village is close to Ardingly (the last syllable rhymes with eye)
Reservoir where people sail, windsurf and fish at weekends. Mostly
the reservoir is used by students from Ardingly College, the
independent school for boys and girls which sits on the bank. The
hill-ridge village of **Ardingly** is best known for the National Trust's
Wakehurst Place gardens, leased by the Royal Botanic Gardens at
Kew. The three-day agricultural show every June makes it the
agricultural capital of Sussex. The grounds are also used for antiques
shows and Pony Club camps. Ardingly's 100-year-old village hall is
heavily booked with ballet classes, mothers-and-toddlers, playgroups
and horticultural society meetings. A Thirties' semi with three
bedrooms in a quiet cul-de-sac within walking distance of all these
activities sells at £280,000 to £310,000.

To Victoria
Journey: 44 min
Season: £3344
Peak: 6 per hr
Off-peak: 3 per hr

To London Bridge
Journey: 42 min
Season: £3344 (ALL)
or £2900 on First
Capital Connect only
Peak: 3 per hr, plus
2 per hr changing at
East Croydon
Off-peak: 4 per hr

HAYWARDS HEATH This is prime commuter country, close to the M23 and the M25, fed by fast trains to London yet close enough for trips to the sea. Successful local businesspeople and airline pilots from Gatwick also help to put up prices. The town feels hugely superior to Burgess Hill, which is three miles away and probably has slightly better shops, though Haywards Heath has both a Marks & Spencer and a Sainsbury's to boast about and a major town centre regeneration scheme is in the pipeline. Property prices are high. A simple one-bedroom flat will cost around £115,000, rising to between £150,000 and £200,000 for a two-bedroom flat. A modern detached four-bedroom house with two bathrooms is likely to cost around £500,000. Better parts of town are in the conservation areas at Lucastes and Lewes Road. Also popular is Muster Green, where the large Victorian and Edwardian houses have ample gardens around an open space that has much of the character of a village green.

You can throw money at houses in the Haywards Heath area. Villages such as **Wineham** are very popular. Here, a three-bedroom period cottage might cost around £350,000. **Lindfield** has all the ingredients of the perfect village: a high street with plenty of independent shops, tile-hung Sussex houses, five pubs, a junior and primary school, a pond with ducks, a large open common and a historic parish church. There is a wide range of housing from Elizabethan and Georgian to 20th-century, including some ex-council properties. Stockbrokers' houses are slipped into the lanes round about. A Victorian house with four- to five-bedrooms could be bought for £500,000, a three-bedroom Victorian semi with a long garden will cost over £400,000.

Further north still, **Horsted Keynes** is another village that mutated during the Fifties. You drive through the centre thinking how lovely the village green is, then turn a corner and confront a mass of cheap housing. The pretty bit is still very popular and commands higher prices than Haywards Heath. A mid-terrace two-bedroom cottage with a little garden will cost £230,000. About a mile away is the privately run Bluebell Railway, a great delight for steam-train enthusiasts. **Paxhill Park** is popular for its golf course, but lacks a real village spirit.

To the east is **Scaynes Hill**. It has been sliced in two by the A272 but has some dignified Victorian houses and a fine village hall, The Millennium Centre, completed in 2000. A two-bedroom bungalow might be snapped up for £225,000. **Fletching** is tiny, but has a lovely collection of 16th-century houses and a couple of pubs, including The Griffin Inn, a renowned gastro pub (see also page 293).

Less than two miles to the west of Haywards Heath is the tall spire of **Cuckfield** parish church, which German bombers used as a landmark during the Second World War. Beyond it you negotiate a tortuous bend, then climb the beautiful 15th-century high street, lined with medieval cottages. At the brow of the hill the spell is broken and medieval England dissolves into Victorian and modern. A Fifties' three-bedroom semi here could be bought for £225,000 upwards.

'Cuckfield is extremely active and shows its independence in eccentric ways'

Since the village was once a staging post it is well-endowed with pubs; there are five altogether, for a population of 3,000. Cuckfield is extremely active and shows its independence in eccentric ways. A fight with the district council in the late 1960s over the ownership of the playing fields resulted in the village declaring independence and producing its own passports, currency and stamps. It still holds mock elections for a mayor every year, and residents pay one penny to vote. The Independent State of Cuckfield is the eccentrically named local pressure group, which does much charity fund-raising. Cuckfield has its own museum and local beauty spot, New England Wood.

To the west are the more remote hamlets of **Bolney** and **Warninglid**. Both had strong connections with the medieval iron industry. They are rather beautiful and kept scrupulously tidy by their inhabitants. A four-bedroom house with Tudor features will cost £500,000.

WIVELSFIELD

WIVELSFIELD station is actually two-and-a-half-miles away on the edge of Burgess Hill. The village is split, with the older part gathered around the church, and the newer part on the east of the B2112 at Wivelsfield Green. Property prices are similar to those in Burgess Hill (see opposite). People tend to pass through it on their way to Haywards Heath or Lewes. The influx of London and Brighton commuters since the war has doubled the population to over 2,000, but the old village families are still involved in agriculture and Young Farmers' events are well attended. It has a post-office-cum-village store, which stretches to delicatessen food and French bread, a hairdresser, two garages and two pubs. The popular primary school has moved from its Victorian buildings into brand-new premises. There are lovely old tiled cottages in some of the older roads, such as Church Lane. A three-bedroom semi would come to the market with a £270,000 price tag.

To Victoria
Journey: 52 min
Season: £3344
Peak: 3 per hr, plus 2 per hr changing at East Croydon or Haywards Heath
Off-peak: 2 per hr, plus 1 per hr changing at Haywards Heath

To London Bridge
Journey: 49 min
Season: £3344 (ALL) or £2900 on First Capital Connect only
Peak: 2 per hr
Off-peak: 2 per hr, plus 2 per hr changing at Haywards Heath

Unusual tile-hung cottage, Wivelsfield

To Victoria
Journey: 55 min
Season: £3344
Peak: 4 per hr, plus
2 per hr changing at
Haywards Heath
Off-peak: 2 per hr,
plus 1 per hr
changing at
Haywards Heath

To London Bridge
Journey: 52 min
Season: £3344 (ALL)
or £2900 on First
Capital Connect only
Peak: 2 per hr, plus
2 per hr changing at
Haywards Heath
Off-peak: 2 per hr,
plus 1 per hr
changing at
Haywards Heath

BURGESS HILL was an intimate little place until a few decades ago.

In 1951 its population was just 8,000. Since then it has been overwhelmed by new estates built to soak up London overspill. The population has shot up to 29,000 and is still climbing with big companies, including British Oxygen and American Express, having moved in. A relief road and link to the A23 unlocked pockets of building land for thousands more new houses, but a grass buffer to the west of town known as the Green Crescent provides a protective belt of sorts. A planned mixed-use regeneration of the town centre promises larger shops, pedestrian areas, an arts centre and a facelift for the railway station. There is a Waitrose in the town centre and a Tesco on the outskirts. Cultural treats can be had at the cinema and the Burgess Hill Theatre (venue for local dramatic and choral societies), and muscle tone can be developed at the Olympus leisure centre. Secondary schoolchildren go to Oakmeads Community College; the fee-paying alternative for girls is Burgess Hill School.

The town is downmarket of Haywards Heath and probably offers the lowest property prices to be found in this expensive mid-Sussex belt. Two-bedroom houses start at around £170,000; three-bedroom houses at £180,000; four-bedroom houses at £250,000. Silverdale Road, Keymer Road and Folders Lane are where you find the most expensive older houses, with company directors and airline pilots settling at around £450,000. A few very old farmhouses still survive on the former commons.

To Victoria
Journey: 64 min
Season: £3344
Peak: 3 per hr, plus
2 per hr changing at
East Croydon or
Haywards Heath
Off-peak: 1 per hr,
plus 2 per hr
changing at
Haywards Heath

For London Bridge,
see overleaf

HASSOCKS likes to think of itself as a village, but it is actually the

size of a town with a population of 7,000, a high proportion of whom are retired. It snuggles up to **Hurstpierpoint** and **Keymer**, though the people of Hurstpierpoint regard themselves as quite separate. The small shopping parade meets basic needs, but for serious food shopping people go to the Waitrose or Tesco at Burgess Hill. Hassocks is not architecturally distinguished. It grew up around the railway in the 19th century, with new developments appearing in the Thirties and Fifties. But it does sit under the wing of the South Downs, so there are magnificent views of the Jack and Jill windmills on the crest where you can take lonely windblown walks.

You would pay around £300,000 for a three-bedroom modern detached house; £390,000 for a three-bedroom Thirties' detached house with a large garden. A new development of 250 homes is underway. Hassocks has primary and secondary schools, which are thought to be good. There is a Beacon Club for the mid-teens, but not much for older teenagers to do. The Sussex game of stoolball is still played here, kept alive by the Stoolball Association. It is a form of rounders, reputedly invented by milkmaids who wanted a recreational

To London Bridge
Journey: 55 min
Season: £3344 (ALL)
or £2900 on First
Capital Connect only
Peak: 2 per hr, plus
2 per hr changing at
East Croydon or
Haywards Heath
Off-peak: 2 per hr,
plus 1 per hr
changing at
Haywards Heath

use for their three-legged milking stools. There is an amenity association that looks after conservation, plus drama and horticultural societies.

Ditchling, just to the east, is one of the most rarefied spots in this part of Sussex, luxuriating in a dramatic valley beneath the spine of the South Downs, though it is hammered by traffic heading straight through for Brighton. During the 20th century it attracted a succession of artists and calligraphers, originally drawn by a Roman Catholic community founded by the sculptor and typographer Eric Gill, which settled up on the Downs. A Thirties', three-bedroom cottage-style semi might sell for £350,000; a detached Victorian family home with four bedrooms, £700,000. Houses at the cheaper end of the market can stick because people moving to Ditchling want something rather more special. Over the years it has attracted many famous inhabitants, including the actress Dame Ellen Terry and currently Dame Vera Lynn. It has a few basic shops, tea shops, an art gallery, a good primary school and a Museum of Local Life. It is particularly proud of its choral society. Nearby is Ditchling Common, offering nearly 200 acres of walks; and Ditchling Beacon, over 800ft high, where a fire was lit to warn of the approach of the Spanish Armada.

The illustrator Raymond Briggs lives in the nearby hamlet of **Westmeston**, which is also a beautiful quiet retreat at the foot of the Downs. The village pulse can be taken in the Parish Hall where events are held, including the annual flower show, yoga classes and a nursery. The nearest primary school is in Ditchling and there are secondary schools are in Lewes, Chailey and Hassocks. A six-bedroom detached house with indoor swimming pool, annexe, tennis court and two acres of land could cost £1.8m.

Schools in East and West Sussex

The ample arms of the North and South Downs give Sussex schools the most beautiful settings. At Crawley in West Sussex, occupying a 19th-century mansion with a monastery and abbey attached, is Worth School, the independent boarding school for boys. Burgess Hill is an independent day and boarding school for girls.

Haywards Heath offers a choice of popular private and state schools. These include Ardingly, the co-educational boarding and day school, and Warden Park comprehensive. At Horsham, the choice includes the comprehensives Millais for girls and Tanbridge House co-educational, as well as nearby Christ's Hospital independent co-educational boarding school (where the fees are means-related) and Farlington independent girls'

boarding and day school. There are good comprehensives in Chichester.

Brighton has attracted a rash of independent schools. These include the girls' day school Brighton & Hove High, and the independent co-educational day and boarding school Brighton College. Roedean boarding school for girls is nearby, as is Lancing College, boarding and day for boys and girls.

Eastbourne has Moira House independent boarding and day school for girls and Eastbourne College independent boarding and day school for boys (with girls in the sixth), set in wonderful cloisters around a cricket square. Another school highly spoken of in East Sussex is St Leonards-Mayfield, near Crowborough, a girls' independent.

To Victoria	To London Bridge
Journey: 67 min	Journey: 64 min
Season: £3344	Season: £3572 (ALL)
Peak: 3 per hr, plus	or £3120 on First
3 per hr changing at	Capital Connect only
East Croydon or	Peak: 2 per hr, plus
Haywards Heath	2 per hr changing at
Off-peak: 1 per hr,	East Croydon or
plus 2 per hr	Haywards Heath
changing at	Off-peak: 2 per hr,
Haywards Heath	plus 1 per hr
	changing at
	Haywards Heath

PRESTON PARK is a part of Brighton that particularly attracts commuters because of its railway station. A four-bedroom, three-storey Victorian house might cost £450,000. It is much leafier than the Victorian streets of North Laine and West Hill, which are both close to the station in Brighton proper.

To Victoria
Journey: 51 min
Season: £3572
Peak: 4 per hr
Off-peak: 3 per hr

To London Bridge
Journey: 56 min
Season: £3572 (ALL)
or £3120 on First
Capital Connect only
Peak: 1 per hr plus
3 per hr changing at
East Croydon or
Haywards Heath
Off-peak: 4 per hr

BRIGHTON has metamorphosed into London-on-Sea, having developed an increasingly sophisticated and cosmopolitan air, playing up its strengths as a conference centre and weekend retreat. It is short on domestic gardens and garages, but the frivolity of the Royal Pavilion, the beautifully landscaped parks and the backdrop of the Sussex Downs make it an enviable place to live. The Brighton Festival in May is England's biggest arts festival. There is a plethora of restaurants and the Theatre Royal attracts plays on their pre-London tours. There has always been a theatrical crowd in Brighton – Lord Olivier once lived there – attracted by the Regency terraced houses of Montpelier. Big seafront town houses sell at over £1m. Brighton has always been *the* place to have a flat, and the various building booms of the past few decades have provided plenty, in both purpose-built blocks and large converted houses. There is a boating crowd, too, drawn by the marina, which is undergoing a major regeneration to provide more housing and retail space.

Commuters tend to live within walking distance of the railway station, within half a mile of the seafront, though parking is tortuous. There are various interlocking conservation areas that house-hunters might aim for. **North Laine**, **West Hill** and **Clifton** are close to the station, all now gentrified with boutiques and antiques shops. In the Montpelier and Clifton Hill Conservation Area, a three- to four-bedroom Regency house with distant sea views and a sun room sells for around £650,000. Modern two-bedroom apartments near the station can be bought for around £200,000. For the Regency equivalent in Seven Dials, you could pay £300,000. In the New England Quarter, recently developed on a brownfield site to the east of the station, a one-bedroom 'eco' apartment with rooftop allotment costs £200,000.

Millionaires' Row is at **Roedean**, beside the girls' private school and opposite the marina. Large mansions line up to catch the sea breezes and sell for over £1m. A six-bedroom Victorian semi could be bought for £470,000. If you think about buying anything facing the sea, consider the havoc wrought by salt-laden winds on your exterior paintwork.

> Fork from Plumpton to Eastbourne

To Victoria
Journey: 59 min
Season: £3344
Peak: 1 or 2 per hr
(plus 2 per hr
changing at East
Croydon or
Haywards Heath)
Off-peak: 1 every
2 or 3 hrs

PLUMPTON The railway line divides Plumpton into two parts, Plumpton proper and **Plumpton Green**. The latter consists of modern estates close to the railway station, with the National Hunt racecourse to the south. A roomy three-bedroom Victorian semi in need of refurbishment with a large garden could cost £350,000. The old village is anchored to Plumpton Place, a 16th-century moated manor. It has a general store-cum-post office and a primary school, and is the home of Plumpton College, a former agricultural college that still offers predominantly land-based courses. There is wonderful riding over the Downs. The wildflowers on the Downs are prized by honey farmers. **East Chiltington**, with The Jolly Sportsman pub, is deliciously unspoilt. Here you could pay £220,000 for an ex-local authority two-bedroom terraced house, or £1.3m for a seven-bedroom country house with outbuildings and nine acres.

To Victoria
Journey: 63 min
Season: £3344
Peak: 1 or 2 per hr
(plus 2 per hr
changing at East
Croydon or
Haywards Heath)
Off-peak: Nil

COOKSBRIDGE The desirability of Cooksbridge is reduced because it sits on the main road to Lewes and on the railway line, both of which can be noisy. It is more a collection of houses than a village, and prices lag behind a little. A three-bedroom Victorian terraced house could be bought for £185,000; a Georgian, four-bedroom, detached family home for £400,000.

To Victoria
Journey: 68 min
Season: £3572
Peak: 1 or 2 per hr,
plus 3 per hr
changing at
Brighton or
Haywards Heath
Off-peak: 2 per hr,
plus 2 per hr
changing at Brighton

LEWES

LEWES Large parts of Lewes, the county town of Sussex, are still medieval in style, particularly along the main street, which follows the route of an ancient causeway. The passages winding away from it are an irresistible invitation for shoppers to explore. Bookshops, antiques shops and 15th-century timbered cottages lean against colour-washed houses. The Bloomsbury connection (Vanessa Bell and Duncan Grant used to live here, and Virginia Woolf lived at Rodmell, two miles away) has left an arty-crafty atmosphere and the town is always alive with exhibitions and craft shows. It has its own coterie of resident artists, several of whom work in studios at the Star Brewery.

Property is more expensive than in the surrounding areas. A modern two-bedroom terraced house costs £180,000 to £220,000; a two-bedroom character terraced home, over £220,000. It would be likely to have a mean garden or a small courtyard since the town is tight for space, so parking is like playing sardines. The tiny cobbled streets just off the High Street have a particular cachet and houses here do not often come on the market. When they do, you can expect to pay £500,000 for a Victorian or Edwardian semi. There are some bland modern private estates which generate little interest among incomers.

Shopping is adequate. Lewes has Boots, Waitrose and Tesco, and Eastbourne and Brighton are not far away. The local private school is The Old School. The great social occasion of the year is the huge Bonfire Night party, which commemorates the burning not of Guy Fawkes, but of a batch of Protestant martyrs.

‘Rodmell seduced the Bloomsbury Group with its mix of flint-and-thatch and tile-hung cottages, folded into the Ouse valley’

There are some extraordinarily lovely Downland villages around Lewes. **Kingston**, in the south, has a street of distinguished old houses and a modern estate where four-bedroom detached houses sell for around £325,000. A three-bedroom Thirties' semi could cost £420,000. The village is something of an enclave for Sussex university professors. Then there is **Rodmell**, which seduced the Bloomsbury Group with its mix of flint-and-thatch and tile-hung cottages, folded into the Ouse valley. A three-bedroom cottage will cost over £300,000. Neither of these villages has shops, though both have pubs. Any house with views of the Downs sells for 15–20 per cent more.

To the north is **Barcombe**, which has prices to match its beauty. A four-bedroom chalet bungalow just off the High Street might sell for £430,000. It is really a village of three parts. Barcombe Cross has tile-hung houses and shops, a pub and a 16th-century Forge House.

Barcombe Mills, on the River Ouse, is where people go for picnics. A detached four-bedroom family home here could cost over £750,000. Old Barcombe, by St Mary's Church, was abandoned by the population during the plague. **Ringmer** is more of a dormitory to Lewes, where houses sell briskly on the prettiness factor. Three-bedroom semis fetch about £220,000 to £250,000; a large four-bedroom detached farmhouse around £450,000; a three-bedroom barn conversion with four acres, £675,000. The centrepiece is the village green, fringed with old cottages overlooked by the parish church, where cricket is played in the summer.

To Victoria
Journey: 78 min
Season: £3672
Peak: 2 per hr
changing at
Haywards Heath or
Lewes
Off-peak: 1 per hr
changing at Brighton

GLYNDE consists of the big house, Glynde Place, The Trevor Arms pub, a post office and village store, an 18th-century church and a grassy bank that becomes a cloud of daffodils in spring. It has a village hall, football and cricket clubs. Mount Caburn, one of the highest points along the South Downs, looms above. Glyndbourne opera house, which draws the dinner jackets with their picnic hampers between May and August, is on the parish boundary with Ringmer. Much of the local property is in private ownership and leased to villagers.

To Victoria
Journey: 83 min
Season: £3672
Peak: 3 per hr, mostly
changing Haywards
Heath or Lewes
Off-peak: 1 per hr
changing at Brighton

BERWICK is best known for having a church decorated with murals by Duncan Grant and Vanessa Bell in the Forties, which were so vivid that they caused an outcry. Unfortunately it draws coach parties in the summer, as does Drusillas theme park. Houses close to the station were built during the Thirties, many of them offering good views of the Downs and Arlington reservoir. A three-bedroom semi sells at around £220,000; a Thirties' detached four-bedroom house near the station, £320,000.

To Victoria
Journey: 80 min
Season: £3672
Peak: 1 or 2 per hr
(2 per hr by
changing at
Haywards Heath)
Off-peak: 2 per hr,
plus 1 per hr
changing at Brighton

POLEGATE is really the outer rim of Eastbourne. It is a village that billowed during the Thirties and again in the Eighties. The single High Street has everything from a greengrocer to a hairdresser. Thirties' and Fifties' semis sell at £160,000 to £180,000. It is very popular because of the station. A one-bedroom flat can cost £90,000, a two-bedroom flat from £110,000. Polegate sprawls in its egalitarian way towards Hampden Park, and there is no distinct division between the two.

To Victoria
Journey: 86 min
Season: £3672
Peak: 1 or 2 per hr
(2 per hr by
changing at
Haywards Heath)
Off-peak: 2 per hr,
plus 1 per hr
changing at Brighton

HAMPDEN PARK

There are expensive and cheap sides to Hampden Park, which glories in all the variations on the theme of suburban mock-Tudor that you could imagine. In a good area three-bedroom terraced houses sell for £150,000; modern four-bedroom detached houses start at £300,000. There is nothing in the Victorian department. This is where Eastbourne has its industrial estate, and hangar-sized stores such as B&Q and a 24-hour Tesco.

To Victoria
Journey: 86 min
Season: £3672
Peak: 1 or 2 per hr
(2 per hr by
changing at
Haywards Heath)
Off-peak: 2 per hr,
plus 1 per hr
changing at Brighton

EASTBOURNE

is still very much a holiday resort and retirement town. Attractions such as Fort Fun and the Treasure Island theme parks resound in summer to the shrieks of holidaying children, who then make for the beautiful Victorian pier to gorge themselves on ice-cream. Adults can indulge with a trip to the Winter Gardens, Devonshire Park or the Royal Hippodrome Theatres. There are also nightclubs and cinemas. Healthier pursuits include stupendous cliff walks over Beachy Head and those vast switchbacks of chalk, the Seven Sisters.

To live within walking distance of the station you have a choice of Edwardian and Victorian houses, or some Thirties' detached. Prices vary enormously depending on size. You could pay £235,000 for three bedrooms; over £500,000 for a mock-Tudor with five bedrooms. Studios cost £60,000 and one-bedroom flats start at £90,000. One of the most prestigious addresses is The Meads, a conservation area that attracts professionals and couples who have retired early. A five-bedroom semi here might cost £500,000. You can expect to pay a premium price if you want to live near any of the three golf courses – The Royal, The Downs or The Willingdon.

Thirties' Tudor-style house, Eastbourne

> Spur from **Preston Park** to **Worthing**

There are some other stations along this route, but the London trains don't stop at them. For Preston Park, see page 269.

To Victoria
Journey: 66 min
Season: £3572
Peak: 1 or 2 per hr,
plus 2 per hr
changing at Brighton
or Gatwick Airport
Off-peak: 2 per hr,
plus 1 per hr
changing at Brighton

HOVE is much more sedate and 'respectable' than its neighbour Brighton, though the two are now officially joined at the hip by the Brighton and Hove City Council established in 1997. Its image has been that of a haven for the elderly, and indeed it does have plenty of sheltered housing and low-level flats. As part of its campaign to attract a younger set, Hove has built up a sporting image with a big sports complex offering everything from martial arts to synchronised swimming.

Hove suffered in the Thirties when some of its most important houses were demolished and replaced with ten-storey blocks of flats. Nevertheless, there are still some classic, sweeping Regency curves to be found in the Brunswick area, some good Sussex cottages near the seafront, and some fine Victorian and Victorian Gothic houses in The Avenues. Property tends to be cheaper on the outskirts, where the modern estates are situated. A two-bedroom Victorian garden flat just off the seafront could cost £250,000; a Regency balcony flat with sea views £350,000 upwards; three-bedroom family houses start at £260,000 and good family houses away from the sea can hit £1m. The up-market sedate addresses are Tongdean Avenue, Tongdean Road and Dyke Road Avenue, with the new millionaires' row at the west end of town where Norman Cook (aka Fat Boy Slim) and Heather Mills have houses backing on to the beach. A whole house on the seafront will start at £1m.

Georgian terraced house, Hove/Brighton area

'Just as Hove has had a complex about Brighton, so Portslade has one about Hove'

While Sussex County Cricket Club still calls Hove home, Brighton and Hove Albion FC were moved into temporary quarters at the Withdean Stadium in Brighton and are now awaiting the building of their new 22,000-seat stadium at Falmer on the northern outskirts of Brighton. There are two golf clubs, the West Hove and the Brighton and Hove. And there is, of course, the beach. In the last decade this sedate old lady of a town has developed a certain sparkle by acquiring a galaxy of restaurants along Church Road, which are good enough to lure foodies from Brighton and the surrounding area.

To Victoria
Journey: 70 min
Season: £3704
Peak: 1 or 2 per hr
(2 per hr by
changing at East
Croydon or Gatwick
Airport)
Off-peak: 1 per hr,
plus 3 per hr
changing at Hove
or Brighton

PORTSLADE Just as Hove has had something of a complex about Brighton, so Portslade has one about Hove. It might not look particularly impressive as you drive through, but if you turn off the main road you will find some 16th-century flint cottages and a church dating back to 1150. Portslade's recent history is not very distinguished. Two decades ago it was known locally as 'nappy valley', because it offered a mass of housing cheap enough for young couples to buy and breed. Housing is still relatively inexpensive. Two-bedroom terraced houses sell for over £175,000, three-bedroom terraces for £185,000 and three-bedroom Thirties' semis for £195,000 to £225,000.

An old field in the centre makes a green of sorts for people to walk on. Money has been spent on restoring and repaving Portslade's main streets, installing Victorian-style streetlamps and renovating the Victorian redbrick water tower that used to supply an isolation hospital. American Express sponsored the installation of a camera obscura, which gives a wonderful panoramic view of the South Downs.

To Victoria
Journey: 74 min
Season: £3704
Peak: 1 or 2 per hr
(3 per hr by
changing at East
Croydon or Gatwick
Airport)
Off-peak: 2 per hr,
plus 2 per hr
changing at Brighton

SHOREHAM-BY-SEA Shoreham is a Victorian seaport, which still imports up to two million tonnes of cargo each year. The High Street, which has the River Adur running along the bottom of it, has basic shops for day-to-day needs, and the Holmbush Centre has brought Marks & Spencer and Tesco to the town. Shoreham is relatively free from hotels and bed-and-breakfasts and does not feel like a seaside resort. It has a sandy beach at low tide, and a popular pit-stop for wildfowl in the Widewater, a lagoon behind a man-made shingle bank. Shoreham Airport (whence the first commercial flight was made in this country) still runs charter flights and is the base for several flying schools. Across the river on the shingle spit is the site of what was once Bungalow Town – a colony of wooden huts, made largely from disused railway carriages, which were occupied by the London Music Hall fraternity. Some early films were made there, but most of it was destroyed in the Second World War to prevent its use as a beachhead. Commuters gravitate towards Shoreham Beach, North Shoreham and the town centre where two-bedroom ground floor flat

Bay-fronted bungalow, Shoreham-by-Sea

starts at around £160,000. A two-bedroom bungalow with a sun room would fetch £190,000 to £225,000. For a three-bedroom semi in Shoreham Town or Beach, you would have to pay around £260,000. There are two secondary schools and the boys' public school at Lancing is nearby.

Work has started on a regeneration programme for Shoreham Harbour over the next 15 to 20 years to provide 10,000 new homes, 7,000 jobs, and retail and leisure facilities. The beach will be improved, the railway station upgraded, and an extension of the proposed Rapid Transit System will link Shoreham with Brighton, Hove and the Sussex coast.

An extension of the proposed Rapid Transit System will link Shoreham with Brighton, Hove and the Sussex coast

To Victoria

Journey: 78 min

Season: £3704

Peak: 1 or 2 per hr (3 per hr by changing at East Croydon or Gatwick Airport)

Off-peak: 1 per hr, plus 3 per hr changing at Hove or Brighton

LANCING
Old north and south Lancing have blended into one, and new buildings have been added to the quaint High Street. Many people commute to Gatwick and Brighton from here, but few to London. There are just a couple of thatch-and-flint here among the Thirties' terraces and Sixties' and Seventies' housing. A two-bedroom flat on the seafront, with balcony and garage, might cost £130,000, but a period cottage with two bedrooms is likely to be nearer £180,000. A three- to four-bedroom detached house could be bought for between £350,000 and £450,000. Lancing College, the co-educational public school, stands in 550 acres on a spur of the Downs overlooking the sea. There are several primary schools that feed the state secondary school, Boundstone Community College.

To Victoria

Journey: 81 min

Season: £3704

Peak: 1 or 2 per hr

(3 per hr by changing at East Croydon or Gatwick Airport)

Off-peak: 2 per hr, plus 2 per hr changing at Brighton

WORTHING has been increasingly popular with commuters over the last decade, absorbing house hunters displaced by high prices from the Surrey commuter belt, and Brighton and Hove. To be within walking distance of the station and shops you would need to live in one of the Thirties' terraces north of the town centre and obtain a resident's parking permit so that you can park. Spacious Thirties' three-bedroom semis sell for £200,000 to £225,000. Bed and breakfasts are concentrated in the centre, near the four large hotels, nightclubs, theatres and cinema. The shopping centre is surprisingly varied, with specialist shops. So don't imagine a town full of little old ladies in fluffy hats: the largest segment of the population is the 16–44 age group, and the adult education centre is very well subscribed. Big businesses including GlaxoSmithKline have settled here, too. Worthing is proud of the fact that it is the home of bowls and that the UK governing body Bowls England has recently chosen the town for its headquarters. It has also been selected to host the annual summer International Birdman Rally, featuring human flying machines jumping off the end of the pier, which has had to move from Bognor Regis because of fears over pier safety. A seafront regeneration scheme over the next 15 to 20 years promises to put a twinkle in its eye with a new café/restaurant, renovations to the pier and lido, a skate park, playground, paddling pool and putting areas.

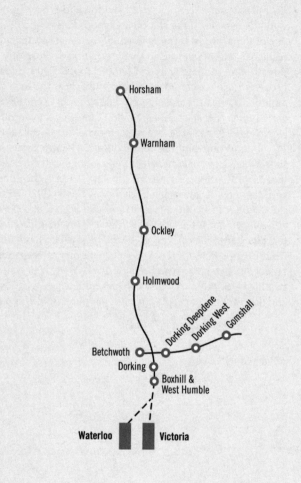

Horsham

Warnham

Ockley

Holmwood

Dorking Deepdene
Dorking West
Gomshall

Betchwoth

Dorking

Boxhill &
West Humble

Waterloo

Victoria

> Horsham

To Victoria
Journey: 50 min
Season: £2012
Peak: 2 per hr (plus
2 per hr to
Waterloo)
Off-peak: 1 per hr

BOXHILL & WEST HUMBLE Just beyond the M25, London suddenly lets go and gives way to one of the best-known beauty-spots in the south-east. Box Hill itself rises to nearly 400ft above the River Mole and affords panoramic views of the surrounding chalk downland and glimpses of the South Downs. It has become very popular in spite of the fact that the approaches to it are given over to caravan sites. Big houses with big gardens attract the interest in **Box Hill** and sell for over £1m, though for many it is more a place to visit, than to live in. A 19th-century, three-bedroom detached cottage could cost £450,000.

West Humble is no more than a handful of houses at the foot of Box Hill. Norbury Park is close by. There are three working farms and Bocketts Farm, a rare breeds farm open to visitors.

To Victoria
Journey: 50 min
Season: £2200
Peak: 2 per hr
Off-peak: 2 per hr

To Waterloo
Journey: 50 min
Season: £2200 (also
valid to Victoria)
Peak: 2 per hr
Off-peak: 2 per hr

DORKING is an ancient market town shot through with antiques shops, some new buildings and a couple of delicatessens. It prides itself on its variety of restaurants, from Thai to French. Reigate Grammar and St John's at Leatherhead are the two popular local public schools. Guildford is close enough for smart shops and the theatre. Denbies is England's largest vineyard, where they run daily tours and have recently opened a guest house. Property prices in the area are fairly constant and the web of villages surrounding Dorking has much to offer. A three-bedroom semi with work to be done sells for £275,000 to £350,000. A period three-bedroom farm cottage would cost £500,000. One-bedroom flats sell for about £140,000.

Five miles west is **Shere**, a village with a stream bubbling through it that is so pretty that British Gas used it to illustrate the rural idyll in an advertising campaign. The square is picturesquely framed with old houses; it has a 12th-century church (used as a location in the film *Bridget Jones' Diary*), several shops, a post office, two pubs, tea rooms and a couple of antiques shops. Social acitivies abound, including a gardening club, youth and old folks' organisations. For the time being it retains its village school. The dramatic society is shared with

Peaselake, which backs on to Hurtwood Common, one of the many Surrey commons that are covered in golden broom and gorse, with shelter-belts of pine. The village has a green with a war memorial and is very leafy. Another popular village is **Abinger Hammer**, which has a green, a working blacksmith and an insatiable passion for cricket. The full Australian team was invited to play here, and the villagers managed to make the return match, too. There is also an annual celebrity match. Men swap their white flannels for green tights when the annual medieval fair comes round to Abinger Common. Opposite the pub is a clock tower from which a little man emerges every hour to strike the bell with a hammer, hence the name of the village.

'The poor soil made it unsuitable for farming, so it became a refuge for smugglers and squatters'

Nearby is **Holmbury St Mary**, which has a green and a post office that opens in the mornings. This was once considered to be one of the most remote places in Surrey. The poor soil made it unsuitable for farming, so it became a refuge for smugglers and squatters and only began to be recognised as a village in the 1850s. It became popular with weekenders who built the first large Victorian houses up on Holmbury Hill, from where there are magnificent views over the Weald. By far the most remote spot here now is **Coldharbour**. Designated an Area of Outstanding Natural Beauty, it clings to the side of the 960ft Leith Hill, from which, on a clear day, you can see the Channel. It is a mountain in the middle of Surrey. The narrow winding roads that lead up to Coldharbour are often cut off in winter. There is a pub, a church and good-neighbourly residents who offer lifts for elderly villagers into Dorking.

To the east is **Brockham**, with 18th-century houses overlooking the green, pubs, a primary school and 16th-century church. You can easily spend £500,000 to £2m on a large house here, but there are some superb smaller ones which start at around £235,000. The main event of the year is the bonfire on Guy Fawkes night, which draws thousands of people from miles around. **Leigh** (pronounced Lye) is also an extremely popular small village with a 16th-century priest's house on the green and a weatherboarded pub. **Newdigate** is tucked right away from the main roads and has an excellent farm shop, a blacksmith and a new estate of executive homes.

'Holmbury St Mary was recognised as a village in the 1850s. It became popular with weekenders who built the first large Victorian houses up on Holmbury Hill, from where there are magnificent views over the Weald'

> North Downs line west to Gomshall via Dorking West

Journey: 58 min
(from Gomshall)
Season: £2944 or
£3184 if also valid
via Guildford
Peak: 3 per hr*
Off-peak: 1 per hr*
* Change at Redhill
or Guildford. There
are no through trains

DORKING DEEPDENE is a good-quality residential area, close to the station yet set in beautiful woodland. It takes its name from the Deepdene Estate, which was owned by the Howard family. Large detached houses in Deepdene Wood sell for £750,000 to £1m, although a six-bedroom Thirties' house recently sold for £2.1m. Three-bedroom semis cost around £225,000 to £250,000. **Dorking West** is partly residential, partly commercial, with new business parks springing up. A small terraced house would cost around £280,000; a semi £300,000 to £350,000. **Gomshall** is an expensive village marred by traffic. A Victorian two-bedroom semi would cost just under £280,000.

> North Downs line east to Betchworth

Journey: 59 min
(from Betchworth)
Season: £2164
Peak: 2 per hr*
Off-peak: 1 per hr*
*Change between
Dorking and Dorking
Deepdene using
footpath link or at
Redhill. There are
no through trains

BETCHWORTH Sitting on the banks of the River Mole, surrounded by the North Downs, **Betchworth** is something of a local beauty spot. It has some 17th-century houses inhabited by retired High Court judges and diplomats who can play golf at nearby Betchworth Park. A four-bedroom detached house is likely to cost £500,000; a two-up-two-down further out at Peeble Hill would start at £300,000. A large manor house close to the centre of the village could fetch £2.5m.

> Continuation of main line

To Victoria
Journey: 59 min
Season: £2292
Peak: 2 per hr
Off-peak: 1 per hr

HOLMWOOD Note that between Dorking and Horsham, the stations of Holmwood, Ockley and Warnham have a poor evening service – the last train leaves Victoria at 7.20pm (though there is one more at 11.26pm). Some villages have been badly affected by the A24 cutting south. **Beare Green** straddles it, and now consists mainly of houses built during the Seventies and Eighties. These sell for less than those in Dorking, of which it is effectively a dormitory. A modern three-bedroom house would start at £300,000. In the older part of Beare Green, around the village pond, a four-bedroom house with a large garden could cost £1.5m. The **Holmwoods** (**North** and **South**) are also staked out along the A24. North Holmwood retains its green and pond, but has been submerged by new housing. The surrounding countryside is lovely, with 600 acres of common for pony treks and long walks. Just to the north is a memorial to Alfred Gwynne Vanderbilt, a member of the American millionaire family, who sacrificed himself by handing his lifejacket to a woman passenger when the *Lusitania* sank in 1915.

To Victoria
Journey: 63 min
Season: £2432
Peak: 2 per hr
Off-peak: 1 per hr

OCKLEY Ockley's prettiness is being spoilt by traffic on the A29, but it has some strong points, including a cricket pitch (visible from the main road), a conventional green with period houses around it, and its own school. The area lies close enough to Guildford for commuters to take advantage of the fast trains into Waterloo (see page 235) as well as the local theatre and shops. Others commuters choose to jump a station by driving to **Clandon** (page 237), where it is easier to park.

Cranleigh, strung between Ockley and Guildford, would meet many people's idea of the perfect small town. This is where the first cottage hospital was established. The main street has a story-book intimacy and, despite a population of 12,000, the town still thinks of itself as a village. Fountain Square has been pedestrianised and a beautiful avenue of maple trees leads to one of the best cricket greens in England. Shops include the well-loved department store Manns, a fishmonger, a bakery, gift and shoe shops, delicatessens and a gun

Modern family house, Horsham area

shop. People travel far and wide to come to Brawlings, the butcher, for its hand-made sausages and other produce. A general market is held every Thursday and a farmers' market once a month. A three-bedroom period cottage might cost between £600,000 and £700,000; a larger old house with three acres and a tennis court could fetch over £750,000. A modern five-bedroom house in the village is on the market for £995,000. The area is wealthy and popular with City executives, owners of successful local companies, TV personalities and ageing rock stars. Cranleigh School is the local boys' public school; the sister school, St Catherine's, is at Bramley near Guildford (see page 237).

To Victoria
Journey: 70 min
Season: £2888
Peak: 2 per hr
Off-peak: 1 per hr

WARNHAM
A sign warning that deer may cross the road is the first thing you see as you approach **Warnham** and its deer park. The old farming community has now been largely replaced by commuters to Guildford, London and Horsham, who are attracted by the green, pubs and old houses. Prices are lower than in Cranleigh. A small semi in need of modernisation might sell for £250,000. Larger detached houses start at around £450,000 and rise to over £1m.

To Victoria
Journey: 56 min
Season: £3144
Peak: 4 per hr
Off-peak: 2 per hr,
plus 2 per hr
changing at Gatwick
Airport

HORSHAM
For Horsham main entry, see **Victoria/London Bridge to Arundel** line, page 259.

To London Bridge
Journey: 69 min
Season: £3144 (also
valid to Victoria)
Peak: 2 per hr, plus
2 per hr changing at
Gatwick Airport
Off-peak: 2 per hr,
plus 2 per hr
changing at Gatwick
Airport

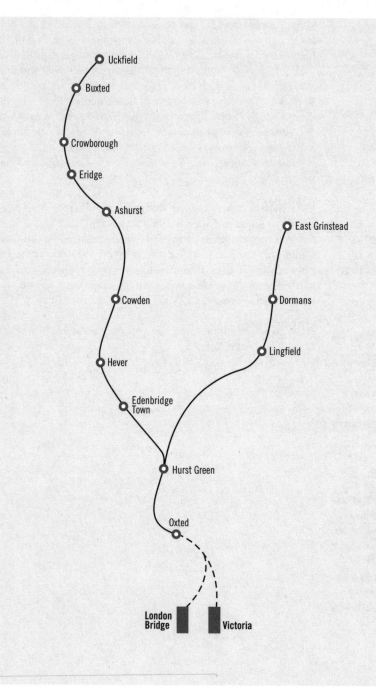

Victoria/London Bridge
> East Grinstead and Uckfield

To Victoria

Journey: 39 min

Season: £1740

Peak: 2 per hr, plus 4 per hr changing at East Croydon

Off-peak: 2 per hr, plus 1 per hr changing at East Croydon

To London Bridge

Journey: 31 min

Season: £1740

Peak: 4 per hr

Off-peak: 1 per hr, plus 2 per hr changing at East Croydon

16th-century cottage, Oxted

OXTED is everything that most people would want a small town to be. It is safe for children and pleasant to live in, but not so pretty that it suffers invasion by tourists. It has a population of around 14,000, and all its vital organs are centralised within walking distance of each another, including the station, cinema, Barn Theatre, shops and Tandridge Leisure Pool (which has a gym). The cinema has a wine bar and gets all the new releases, yet the atmosphere is cosy enough for parents to allow their children to go unaccompanied. The town is also reasonably safe to walk around after dark.

There are two main shopping streets: Station Road West, which is lined with mock-Tudor shops, and Station Road East. Supermarkets include Morrisons and Sainsbury's. Old Oxted is the prettiest part of the town, where the 14th- to 16th-century cottages have pleasantly weathered pantiled roofs. Much of the rest is classic Thirties' development.

A huge number of people commute to London or Croydon; otherwise people work in local shops or in the factories at Hurst Green. The wealthier residents live in the private wooded roads of Rockfield Road, Icehouse Wood and Bluehouse Lane, where large detached houses cost from £650,000 to £875,000.

Nearly all the gardens in the town are large by London standards, most extending to half an acre or more. Even the few modest two-bedroom Victorian terraces, selling at £300,000 to £350,000, have 100ft gardens.

'Teenagers looking for a good night out head for East Grinstead or Croydon, where there are nightclubs. Older funsters go into London for theatres, or to country restaurants'

Teenagers looking for a good night out head for East Grinstead or Croydon, where there are nightclubs. Older funsters go into London for theatres, or to country restaurants. There are golf courses nearby at Tandridge and Limpsfield.

'The Chart is a stretch of common land that tumbles over the edge of the Weald, offering superb views'

Limpsfield and **Limpsfield Chart** are five minutes away by road. Both villages are occupied almost exclusively by newcomers, and both are split by the A25. A car is essential for living here. Limpsfield is olde worlde and expensive, its main street eyecatchingly lined with old stone cottages. There are a few shops, a pub, a very good bookshop and a highly-rated restaurant called The Old Lodge. Limpsfield Chart is also attractively set in National Trust landscape. The Chart is a stretch of common land that tumbles over the edge of the Weald, offering superb views as you head south, and containing remnants of an old Roman road. In spring the woods are carpeted with bluebells. A Grade Two listed two-bedroom cottage costs from £325,000.

The village of **Tandridge** is less expensive, with Sixties' and modern housing added to the mix. Three-bedroom Victorian houses and artisans' cottages cost over £300,000. Tandridge has a pub and a primary school, and has the feel of a proper village even though it is only two miles from the M25. The north is the nicest part, with a lovely church and steeple standing on a little hill. A former vicarage with five bedrooms and 1.5 acres could cost £750,000.

To Victoria
Journey: 41 min
Season: £1740
Peak: 2 per hr, plus
4 per hr changing at
East Croydon
Off-peak: 2 per hr,
plus 1 per hr
changing at East
Croydon

To London Bridge
Journey: 34 min
Season: £1740
Peak: 4 per hr
Off-peak: 1 per hr,
plus 2 per hr
changing at East
Croydon

HURST GREEN is more mundane and sprawly than Oxted, and cheaper. But it is a popular choice for people moving out of London looking for varied house types at low prices. On the Sixties' Home Park estate, for instance, you could buy a two-bedroom house from £200,000, or three bedrooms for £240,000. A four-bedroom, detached Seventies' house on the Waldrens estate would go for £525,000. There is a Wates estate, where one-bedroom starter homes on Barnfield Way cost around £135,000, and a couple of council estates with some ex-council houses for sale. The town is segmented, and some of the segments are much nicer than others. The Green itself is picturesque and is framed by older houses. A four-bedroom house on The Green would cost from £600,000. The advantage residents have here over those in Oxted is that they are more likely to get a seat on the train. A semi-detached three-bedroom house nearby, with 150ft rear garden, could fetch around £250,000. Other parts of Hurst Green harbour the odd factory or two. All the segments have infant and junior schools, churches, post office and shops. Between Hurst Green and Edenbridge lies Staffhurst Wood, famous for its bluebells.

> Fork from **Hurst Green** to **East Grinstead**

To Victoria
Journey: 48 min
Season: £2016
Peak: 2 per hr, plus
2 per hr changing at
East Croydon
Off-peak: 2 per hr

LINGFIELD and Dormansland (see page 288) are glued together by Lingfield racecourse. Lingfield is the larger and older of the two villages, with a population of about 5,000. There has been very little new development, so the marvellous collection of Tudor, Jacobean and Georgian properties remains intact, and many of the buildings are scheduled as ancient monuments. Modern interlopers include the occasional Thirties' house and a small Eighties' estate, including retirement properties.

The area is very popular with people who need to be close to Gatwick airport. Pilots, air hostesses and ground staff live here; so do many business travellers. There are excellent communications. The M25 is only eight minutes' drive away and the M23 is also close by. Lingfield has a typical range of village shops, including two small supermarkets, a post office, a butcher and a baker. Next to the pond at the heart of the village is a strange stone structure roofed with iron bars. This is the so-called 'cage', built in 1473 and thought to have been used as a lock-up for poachers and drunkards.

❛Lingfield's marvellous collection of Tudor, Jacobean and Georgian properties remains intact❜

House prices cover an enormous range, from a two-bedroom flat at £175,000 to a five- or six-bedroom detached family house in a couple of acres for £750,000 to £1m. There is no such thing as a 'typical' Lingfield house to extrapolate average prices from, but a three-bedroom Victorian semi might go for £250,000; a three-bedroom detached for £275,000. A two-bedroom terraced house in a new Argyll Homes development would cost £249,950. Houses at the top end of the market might come with their own equestrian facilities though the racecourse, one of the first in Britain to have an all-weather surface, has not attracted many trainers or jockeys to live in the area. The style is more Pony Club and conspicuous wealth. A Grade Two listed, five-bedroom property in nine acres, with a swimming pool, tennis court and paddocks, could fetch £975,000. The village has a primary school. Older children are bussed to Oxted.

DORMANS Dormansland is slightly smaller than Lingfield, with a population of around 4,000 if you include Dormans Park. It has a post office, a hairdresser, a couple of pubs, a church and a primary school. Houses are largely Victorian with a smattering of modern and small council estates. **Dormans Park**, which is actually closer to the station than Dormansland itself, has a curious history. It grew up when rich Victorians used to come down from London for Lingfield races. A number of little summer houses were built around the Dormans Hotel (now disappeared), where many of them liked to stay. The summer houses grew in grandeur and Dormans Park became the sort of place where the playboys of the time liked to entertain their mistresses. Nearly all the houses are large, detached villas in sizeable plots surrounded by countryside. A five-bedroom affair with an acre of land, a paddock and outbuildings, might sell for £1m. The area is rather secluded and has no local facilities of its own.

To Victoria
Journey: 51 min
Season: £2016
Peak: 2 per hr, plus
2 per hr changing at
East Croydon
Off-peak: 2 per hr

EAST GRINSTEAD The town of East Grinstead itself retains the characteristics of the market town it once was, though it now has a relief road and other modern appendages. It is in two parts – the old town, which includes much of the High Street, and London Road, which contains the new major shops. It is becoming more of an industrial and commercial town, with new offices springing up. East Grinstead draws in people from the surrounding villages for their regular shop, though large or specialist items have to be sought in Croydon or Crawley. A farmers' market is held twice a month in the High Street. The Kings Centre provides a swimming pool and sports complex for hearties, while The Atrium has a nightclub, a pub and

To Victoria
Journey: 55 min
Season: £2016
Peak: 2 per hr, plus
2 per hr changing at
East Croydon
Off-peak: 2 per hr

two cinemas for night owls. The Chequer Mead Art Centre has a 320-seat theatre. One of East Grinstead's attractions to commuters is that its station is at the end of the line, so there is no danger of going to sleep and missing your stop.

There are some pretty, old buildings in the centre of the town, including 14 hall houses in the High Street. Particularly handsome is Sackville College, a Sussex sandstone almshouse with high chimneys, quadrangle and gardens, which has been converted for sheltered housing. Otherwise there is a wide range of housing, mainly on modern estates. Cheap starter homes and flats cost between £100,000 and £120,000. A three-bedroom Sixties' semi would cost £260,000; a larger, modern mock-Georgian four-bedroom house will fetch over £350,000.

Two manor houses outside the town are put to strangely contrasting uses. Saint Hill Manor, to the south, is the headquarters of the Church of Scientology. Gravetye Manor is one of the best small country house hotels and restaurants in Britain. For fishing, sailing and walking there is Weir Wood Reservoir. To the south is Ashdown Forest, where the countryside becomes very beautiful. Here you come up on to the High Weald, where you find some of the last remaining heathland in the south-east.

> Fork from **Hurst Green** to **Uckfield**

Services now go into London Bridge, not Victoria

To London Bridge
Journey: 41 min
Season: £2284 (also
valid at Edenbridge)
Peak: 2 per hr
Off-peak: 1 per hr

EDENBRIDGE TOWN For main entry see **Edenbridge** on the **North Downs** line east from Redhill, page 252.

To London Bridge
Journey: 44 min
Season: £2280
Peak: 2 per hr
Off-peak: 1 per hr

HEVER is one of the area's tourist attractions, popular with visitors en route to Hever Castle, where Henry VIII courted Anne Boleyn. The village is unspoilt and is an extraordinarily small place to command its own railway station. Consequently, a house here will cost around £150,000 more than a similar property in Edenbridge. A modern, chalet-style three-bedroom bungalow would fetch between £300,000 and £400,000; a detached four-bedroom house, £600,000; a period farmhouse with land, £1.5m, if one was to become available as they tend to stay in the same family for 30 years or more. There is no cheap property in Hever, but the least expensive are the former labourers' cottages from the Astor estate. These have been sold and, as the locals put it, 'tweed up' by their new owners. The village has a church, a few houses, a golf course and the Henry VIII pub. Beyond a massive stone gateway you enter the drive to Hever Castle and its strange mock-Tudor village, which is hired out for conferences. In high summer, plays and concerts are held in the Italian gardens; in winter a Christmas Fair raises money for the local church and school.

Hever's Church of England primary school has such a good reputation that it reverses the usual demographic trend. Instead of children being bussed from village to town, children from Edenbridge are brought to Hever. Even so, locals have had to fight to keep the school from being closed. Village life is lively though there are no shops and the nearest post office is three miles away in Edenbridge. Horticultural shows and WI markets are held in the village hall. Although Hever proper is small, the parish has 800 names on the electoral roll and is quite far flung. As there is nothing for teenagers to do, it is probably just as well that the population consists of solicitors, commuters, retired people and minor landed gentry.

To London Bridge
Journey: 48 min
Season: £2280
Peak: 2 per hr
Off-peak: 1 per hr

COWDEN is a very pretty village cushioned amid the quiet leafy lanes that wind through the Weald. Its main street has a curious symmetry, with a housing estate at each end and a pub in the middle, and it contains the village's oldest houses, many of which date back 400 years. Buses do exist here, but you would be seriously inconvenienced without a car. There are no shops. It pays to get on with the neighbours, because the same people are likely to belong to the same societies – the horticultural society, British Legion and WI, among others – and to turn up at the same events. There is no school, and little to occupy teenagers. A period, three-bedroom, end-of-terrace house costs about £415,000; a 16th-century, Grade Two listed, five-bedroom house, about £960,000.

‘Buses do exist, but you would be seriously inconvenienced without a car’

To London Bridge
Journey: 53 min
Season: £2280
Peak: 1 per hr
Off-peak: 1 per hr

ASHURST is very rural and slightly reserved. You may have to spend six months waiting on the platform with the other six passengers at Ashurst station before they get round to acknowledging you. Though the village is very small it has a modern village hall where keep-fit groups, yoga classes, IT tutorials and a pre-school group strut their stuff. Property in Ashurst is more expensive than nearby Eridge (see below), but houses in both villages rarely come up for sale and you'll have to move quickly if you want to buy. There is a bus service of sorts but, as ever in this area, car ownership is essential.

'Groombridge Place was chosen as a location for the film *The Draughtsman's Contract* ... the gardens are open to the public in summer'

The larger villages of **Langton Green** (see page 298) and **Groombridge** are also close to Ashurst. Groombridge straddles the county boundary with the modern dormitory village forging into Sussex and lovely Old Groombridge lingering in Kent. The old part, including the 16th-century terraced cottages, the Crown Inn, facing the triangular green, the 17th-century moated manor house, Groombridge Place, and its 200-acre estate, was marketed in 1992 with an asking price of £3.25m. The big house (chosen by the director Peter Greenaway as a location for his film, *The Draughtsman's Contract*) is now used mostly at weekends. The gardens are open to the public in the summer.

To London Bridge
Journey: 58 min
Season: £2280
Peak: 2 per hr
Off-peak: 1 per hr

ERIDGE is a very small village best known for its huge park, which is scored with footpaths. It has a church, but has lost its store and post office. Much of it was once part of the Abergavenny estate. Some of the old estate cottages occasionally come on to the market.

To London Bridge
Journey: 63 min
Season: £2280
Peak: 2 per hr
Off-peak: 1 per hr

CROWBOROUGH is one of those strange areas which are sedate and suburban to the core, with a serviceable High Street that has Boots, Sainsbury's and Waitrose. A farmers' market is held on the fourth Saturday of every month. The town began as a series of big hilltop hotels built around a golf course. Later it became a popular retirement haven and then, in the early Fifties, came an explosion of housing estates, which turned it into a commuter dormitory with a population of 23,000. There is a leisure centre with swimming pool, badminton and squash.

The Warren is the smartest part of town, built to the north and looking down over Ashdown Forest. Homes in the Warren are mainly detached houses with four or five bedrooms, priced in the £500,000 to £1m bracket. Most of the larger houses once stood in grounds of at least one acre, but have since had smaller houses or flats built around them. This infilling has spoiled the previously rather gracious character of the area.

On the newest estates, a one-bedroom starter home costs £115,000, a three-bedroom house £295,000. Much of the building in and around the town centre is Victorian, and the least attractive streets are those near the station and the industrial estate. Further out are a number of former 16th- and 17th-century farmhouses. Sir Arthur Conan Doyle lived at Hurtis Hill, and when he died in 1930 he was buried in his back garden overlooking Crowborough Common and the golf course. His body was later exhumed and reburied in Minstead Churchyard in the New Forest. The house has since been turned into a residential home for the elderly, Windlesham Manor, but the town still fills up with Sherlock Holmes fans for the annual Conan Doyle festival.

'Crowborough fills up with Sherlock Holmes fans for the annual Conan Doyle festival'

Rotherfield, nearby, has at its core a conservation area studded with listed buildings, antiques shops and Victorian terraces. Prices are 10–15 per cent higher than in Crowborough. A small cottage costs around £285,000.

To London Bridge
Journey: 70 min
Season: £2280
Peak: 2 per hr
Off-peak: 1 per hr

BUXTED is mostly modern, but nevertheless quite attractive. It has a population of around 4,000, and real shops that sell clothes and food rather than antiques. Property prices are slightly higher than those in Uckfield. A Victorian two-bedroom cottage would cost £245,000.

To London Bridge
Journey: 75 min
Season: £2280
Peak: 2 per hr
Off-peak: 1 per hr

UCKFIELD is a rapidly expanding 'strip' town. The population currently stands at around 13,000, but new houses are going up all the time. Older properties are mainly Victorian – a three-bedroom semi of this period will cost between £180,000 and £235,000; a Thirties' property of the same size, £250,000. For a smallish town there are a lot of facilities, including a Somerfield supermarket, leisure centre, cinema, library, bowling green and the nearby Piltdown golf club. A farmers' market is held once a month. Uckfield is surrounded by lovely countryside, ideal for walking or cycling. To the north-west, the country lanes wind into Ashdown Forest. Here there are some rather grand houses with five bedrooms, paddock and enormous garden costing over £1m.

Locals find the train service so slow that many prefer to drive the 12 miles to Haywards Heath for a much shorter journey (page 265). Uckfield used to be a notorious bottleneck on the A22 to Eastbourne until the bypass was constructed. Public car parks in the town are free, which is a mercy for people from the surrounding villages who have very few shops of their own.

The beautiful villages nearby are **Fletching**, **Nutley** and **Barcombe Cross**. Fletching is the most desirable. It has no new estates and is set in the Ashdown Forest, making it ideal for walks and pony rides. This is a village like villages used to be, with a close-knit community and a good centre with beamed pubs. Many of the houses are picture-postcard trim. Three-bedroom properties, some with half an acre of land, sell for around £400,000 to £500,000. The former butcher's shop, in need of work to convert it into a two-bedroom cottage, is priced at £250,000 (see also page 265).

Little Horstead, to the south, is popular with golfers because of its proximity to Horstead Place, a large country estate with hotel and golf complex.

'Fletching is like villages used to be, with a close-knit community and a good centre with beamed pubs'

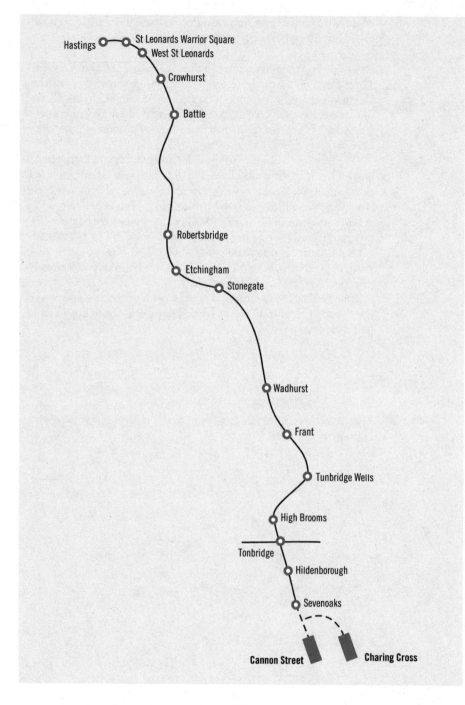

Hastings
St Leonards Warrior Square
West St Leonards
Crowhurst
Battle
Robertsbridge
Etchingham
Stonegate
Wadhurst
Frant
Tunbridge Wells
High Brooms
Tonbridge
Hildenborough
Sevenoaks
Cannon Street
Charing Cross

Charing Cross/Cannon Street
> Hastings

All trains are to Charing Cross, except where specified, and all call at Waterloo East. Most also call at London Bridge. Cannon Street can be reached off-peak by a frequent service of 11 trains per hour from London Bridge. Where through peak-hour services to Cannon Street are shown, these call at London Bridge and so give extra services to Charing Cross by changing.

Journey: 33 min

Season: £2480

Peak: 4 per hr (plus 3 per hr to Cannon Street)

Off-peak: 4 per hr

'A survey showed more cars per head of population than any other town in England'

SEVENOAKS has been a commuter town ever since the railway arrived in 1862. In the later part of the 20th century it developed a reputation for wealth – a survey showed more cars per head of population than any other town in England. The concentration of private schools is another reliable money indicator. There is Sevenoaks School for boys and girls, Walthamstow Hall for girls, and a clutch of prep schools. The childrens' fathers are surveyors, accountants, solicitors and other successful professionals. The shops are good, and there is a Sainsbury's and a Tesco, though many locals prefer shopping at Bluewater or Tunbridge Wells. Outsiders flock into Sevenoaks for the quaint little shops in Dorset Street, Bank Street and Well Court. Other attractions include the Stag Cinema and Stag Theatre, the swimming and sports centres, an abundance of golf courses, and The Vine, the pitch on which the first-ever nationally reported cricket match was played. Sevenoaks Cricket Week happens every July, and if the sound of ball on bat is not music enough to your ears, then there is the Sevenoaks Summer Festival of music, drama and art. Nearby are the wooded walks of the North Downs Way, the lakes and grassland of the Sevenoaks Wildfowl Reserve, and Knole – one of the largest private houses in Britain, set in a vast deer park, where Vita Sackville-West spent her childhood.

Some of the most expensive addresses are on the Wildernesse Estate, where small mansions were developed on two-acre plots during the Thirties. Many of these now have smaller modern houses squeezed in beside them, often bought by what estate agents refer to as New Money. A five- to eight-bedroom house here will cost £2m to £3m with a swimming pool and all the trimmings. The Kippington area is also popular, offering a mix of Victorian, Thirties' and post-war housing priced in £1.5 to £2m. Throughout the town you can buy ordinary four-bedroom family houses of varying periods at prices between £650,000 and £850,000. One of the quaintest old streets is Six Bells Lane, where tiny one-bedroom 18th- and 19th-century cottages cost around £250,000. There is a snag here, however. If the cottages score points for charm, they lose them on parking difficulties. There are more flats in a purpose-built block also overlooking the Vine, where a really spacious three-bedroom apartment with views would cost £300,000 to £400,000.

Journey: 41 min
Season: £2840
Peak: 3 per hr (plus 3 trains to Cannon Street)
Off-peak: 2 per hr

HILDENBOROUGH is something of a poor relation to its wealthy neighbours. It has the occasional shop and garage but no real centre, and the B245 makes it a place to drive through rather than to stop in. For affordable housing, however, it's worth a look. A two-bedroom house will cost around £150,000; three bedrooms £300,000 to £400,000. There is a farmers' market every Tuesday.

Journey: 38 min
Season: £3000
Peak: 5 per hr (plus 3 per hr to Cannon Street)
Off-peak: 6 per hr

TONBRIDGE has none of the glamour of Tunbridge Wells, to which it gave its name, though it does have the remains of a motte-and-bailey castle on the banks of the River Medway in the town centre. It is a busy one-street town with quite a few businesses and small industries. It also has the private Tonbridge School for boys and two grammar schools for girls. A one-bedroom flat in Tonbridge will cost £130,000; a two-bedroom terraced house from £175,000; a three-bedroom detached £250,000 to £300,000.

Journey: 52 min
Season: £3220
Peak: 3 per hr (plus 3 trains to Cannon Street)
Off-peak: 2 per hr

HIGH BROOMS is the industrial face of Tunbridge Wells, dominated by out-of-town retail stores. It consists of a steep hill lined with streets of Victorian terraces, mainly built in brick from the old Tunbridge Wells brick company, whose workers lived here. It is within reach of the more elegant part of town, but property prices are low enough to attract young commuters. A two-bedroom terraced house will cost around £180,000; a three-bedroom semi around £220,000. On the eastern side are Sherwood Park and Home Farm, two areas where new housing estates burgeoned during the Eighties. A two-bedroom flat here will cost £160,000; four bedrooms £300,000.

Journey: 55 min
Season: £3300
Peak: 4 per hr (plus 3 trains to Cannon Street)
Off-peak: 2 per hr

TUNBRIDGE WELLS is to Kent what Bath is to Somerset. The gracious crescents and elaborate terraces, designed by Decimus Burton to serve its image as a fashionable 18th-century watering hole, still give it an air of great prosperity. Beau Nash was master of ceremonies at the wells from 1735, and you can still take a foul-tasting sip from the dipper at the Pantiles. For a more complete re-creation

of the past there is 'A Day At The Wells', one of those sight, sound and smell museums that aim to leave as little as possible to the imagination. Modern Tunbridge Wells caters for recreational tastes of every kind. There are a couple of art galleries, theatres, a cinema, a lively arts centre and two golf courses, as well as a rugby club and Kent County Cricket Ground. It is a shopper's paradise, with a huge range of specialist shops, kitchen shops, chocolate shops, tea-rooms, antiques shops and bespoke jewellers. In the Royal Victoria Shopping Mall you find all the chain stores. There is a farmers' market every Saturday, alternating between the Town Hall and the Pantiles. The town is also rich in good primary and secondary schools.

Undoubtedly one of the best addresses in Tunbridge Wells is Nevill Park, a private road with lodge gates at each end, ten minutes' walk from the station, where large and sumptuous houses dating from the 1800s to the present day overlook the town from a ridge. On one side is the green expanse of Tunbridge Wells Common, on the other is Hungershall Park where a semi-detached house would cost between £1m and £2m and a grandly proportioned villa with seven bedrooms and three reception rooms might cost £3.95m.

You will need a similarly deep pocket if you want to consider one of the 21 exquisitely designed houses by Decimus Burton in Calverley Park. A house here might cost from £1m to £2m, or £3m for an exceptional property. In Calverley Park Crescent, where shops were originally designed into the ground floors beneath heavily-gardened balconies, you could find a home for between £1m and £2m. The imposing private houses built along Mount Ephraim are also sought-after, though 70 per cent of them have been turned into flats. A one-bedroom flat will cost around £175,000 while a three-bedroom house will cost £675,000.

‘You will need a deep pocket if you want to consider one of the exquisitely designed houses by Decimus Burton in Calverley Park’

Stable block conversion, near Tunbridge Wells

Ordinary family houses are to be found in Royal Chase and Culverden Down, behind Mount Ephraim and only a short walk from the station and shops. Many of these were built during the various building booms of the 20th century. A family-sized house here might be bought for £500,000 to £770,000. Buyers of more modest means head east to the tightly-knit area of terraces and semis where a three-bedroom semi with no garage will cost between £190,000 and £235,000.

The reputation of the local schools is another major factor in the town's popularity. They include Skinners, a boys' grammar school; Tunbridge Wells Boys' Grammar; Tunbridge Wells Girls' Grammar; and two comprehensives. All are close to St John's Sports and Indoor Tennis Centre and swimming pool.

'**Tunbridge Wells is surrounded by rich riding country, well provided with bridleways and livery stables**'

Tunbridge Wells is surrounded by rich riding country, well provided with bridleways and livery stables. The Eridge and South Downs Hunt and the Pony Club are both vigorously attended. **Langton Green**, two-and-a-half miles to the west, is a favourite with local businessmen. It has its own village shops, pubs, some old village houses and cottages, plenty of new housing and a popular mixed prep school, Holmwood House. A four-bedroom detached house here will cost between £500,000 and £600,000, but in private roads close to the school prices rise steeply to between £875,000 and £2.5m. A two-bedroom cottage would cost £250,000.

Immediately to the north of Tunbridge Wells is **Pembury**, which has a bypass and offers a large volume of middle-range modern housing. A three-bedroom detached house here would cost around £300,000, but you need to avoid the roads used as peak-time rat runs. For a grand Georgian house on the green at Pembury, you could pay £1.5m. See also Penshurst, Leigh and Chiddingstone on the North Downs line (page 253).

Journey: 63 min
Season: £3300
Peak: 1 per hr (plus 3 trains to Cannon Street)
Off-peak: 1 per hr

FRANT The most striking feature of this hilltop village is its green. Surrounded by superb timber-framed and Georgian houses which now sell for more than £1m a piece, it makes a perfect setting for village cricket. A four-bedroom converted stables on the green would fetch £735,000. The village has its own shop, a bowling green and a well-attended primary school, though the rural idyll is marred slightly by lorries using the village as a cut-through. The station is actually at Bells Yew Green, where for years the stationmaster ran a wellie-warming service for homebound commuters. Post-journey comfort these days is more likely to be found at the Brecknock Arms, just around the corner.

Lamberhurst is definitely a village worth looking at. A by-pass has saved it from the hammering of the A21, but the welcome quiet it provides has pushed up property prices. The village has some good oak-framed houses, antiques shops, a village store-cum-post-office, and a vineyard. Two-bedroom cottages sell for £200,000 or more. A modern four-bedroom house backing on to Lamberhurst golf course would sell for £380,000.

WADHURST is a narrow, busy and attractive village set in an Area of Outstanding Natural Beauty in the High Weald. It is big enough to have around 30 shops, including a couple of banks, butchers, doctors, dentists, solicitors and so on. Lying on the borders of Sussex and Kent, it offers the choice of two different county education systems. Some people choose Wadhurst's own Uplands Community College, which combines the role of comprehensive school with adult education and sports centre. Others shuttle their children into Kent to take advantage of the old-fashioned grammar schools in Tunbridge Wells. Lots of teenagers ride horses and ponies and there is a local livery stable.

A two-bedroom village house, old or new, will cost around £190,000, a luxury two-bedroom flat in one of the small modern developments around £350,000. Three-bedroom terraced houses built in vernacular style fetch £225,000 or more. A decent period house with four bedrooms and a garden will cost around £320,000; something more lavish with five bedrooms, tennis court and swimming pool will be between £750,000 and £1.25m.

Journey: 63 min
Season: £3500
Peak: 1 per hr (plus 3 trains to Cannon Street)
Off-peak: 2 per hr

'On the borders of Sussex and Kent, Wadhurst offers the choice of two different county education systems'

STONEGATE itself is tiny and is becoming increasingly desirable. It is something of a drive-through village with a good primary school and several modern executive developments. Victorian three- to four-bedroom semis sell at around £340,000; four-bedroom Edwardian detached houses at £550,000. Neighbouring **Ticehurst**, is attractively set around a central square in a conservation area. Three horse chestnut trees guard the bus stop in the old village pump shelter. Shops include a village store, baker, butcher, pharmacy and greengrocer. There are also estate agents and a handful of pubs. Ticehurst has its own primary school and a good choice of local societies. It is more out-of-the-way than Wadhurst and prices are about 10 per cent cheaper. A small semi in a cul-de-sac will cost £165,000; a weatherboarded two-bedroom cottage £200,000; a three-bedroom bungalow £165,000; a five-bedroom detached house on a new development, £600,000. A big house in the village will cost from £700,000.

Journey: 74 min
Season: £3520
Peak: 1 per hr (plus 3 trains to Cannon Street)
Off-peak: 1 per hr

Journey: 79 min
Season: £3520
Peak: 1 per hr (plus
3 trains to Cannon
Street)
Off-peak: 1 per hr

ETCHINGHAM is popular because it is reasonably good to look at

and has the convenience of its own railway station. The village winds up the hill from the railway, offering a sprinkling of traditional weatherboarded properties among the 18th-century houses and a Fifties' estate. There is also a modern development opposite the village hall. Etchingham has a general store, post office and a butcher that has been in the same family for generations. There is a much-loved primary school and the Etchingham British Legion Club where people meet for billiards and darts. A small semi in the village might cost around £200,000; a three-bedroom detached house down one of the lanes would be around £250,000 to £350,000.

Burwash is more attractive than Etchingham and is well known for its striking High Street of white weatherboarded and tile-hung houses, tea-rooms, brick footpaths and lime trees. Not so well-known is its warmth and friendliness. Prices are higher than those in Etchingham, for though it is further from the station, it is prettier. On the edge of the village are some five- and six-bedroom modern houses, each one set in half an acre of garden, selling for £600,000 to £800,000. Half a mile away is Bateman's, where Rudyard Kipling lived and wrote *Puck of Pook's Hill*.

'Half a mile away is Bateman's, where Rudyard Kipling lived and wrote *Puck of Pook's Hill*'

To the north-east, back over the border into Kent, is **Hawkhurst**, a village in two halves. Housebuyers would probably avoid the half that contains the junction of two main roads in favour of an area known as The Moor in the neighbouring valley. This has a large village green, playing fields and small shops and cottages. A two-bedroom terraced house will cost around £180,000; a three-bedroom semi, £250,000; a four-bedroom detached modern house, £400,000. A four-bedroom period house in one of the lanes will fetch over £500,000. Both Hawkhurst and its much smaller neighbour, **Sandhurst**, are within the catchment area of Cranbrook School, one of the most highly respected schools in Kent, run on traditional grammar school lines. Hawkhurst is also the setting for Marlborough House private prep school.

Journey: 83 min
Season: £3520
Peak: 1 per hr (plus
3 trains to Cannon
Street)
Off-peak: 1 per hr

ROBERTSBRIDGE Considering the prettiness of the countryside

that surrounds it, **Robertsbridge** is surprisingly unprosperous. There is no major town or city centre close enough to attract regular commuters, and those who come here tend to want escape. Hastings, it has to be said, does not offer bright lights. Robertsbridge's lovely village high street has been relieved of through-traffic by a bypass. It has a sub-post office, part-time bank, butcher, chemist, greengrocer, general store and two hairdressers. A farmers' market is held here once a month. The modern village hall hosts regular meetings of the archaeological society, playgroups and dancing classes. There is also football, stoolball for women and cricket. The Gray-Nicholls factory makes bats out of locally-grown willow (and also the round wooden bats for Sussex stoolball). A three-bedroom cottage will cost £200,000 to £250,000; a three-bedroom modern house, £250,000; a larger country house with extensive grounds, £600,000 to £700,000. A five-bedroom period house, with 10 acres, tennis courts, swimming pool and an annexe, would have a price tag of £3.5m. The village's most famous resident was the late thinker and journalist Malcolm Muggeridge.

Journey: 79 min
Season: £3640
Peak: 1 per hr (plus 3 trains to Cannon Street)
Off-peak: 2 per hr

BATTLE is as self-contained, charming and spirited as any market town in England might have been before the 20th century came along to ruin it. Its most famous asset is the remains of Battle Abbey, on the site of King Harold's defeat by William the Conqueror in 1066. A spectacular bonfire is lit on the playing fields on Guy Fawkes Night, big enough to rival the one in Lewes. The town otherwise has a High Street full of shops and inns, some of them timber-framed or weatherboarded, and there are some nice old tea rooms for connoisseurs of the sticky bun. A farmers' market is held once a month. A first-time buyer could find a two-bedroom period cottage in need of renovation for just under £150,000. Three-bedroom semis come at £235,000; four-bedroom detached houses at £350,000 to £400,000. A six-bedroom period town house close to the High Street could cost up to £1.3m.

In the lanes around Battle are some rather grand houses in the £500,000 to £1m range. A converted oast with twin roundels and seven bedrooms would be likely to fetch in excess of £1.25m. Of the neighbouring villages, **Sedlescombe** is particularly pretty with a traditional village green fringed with brick and tile-hung cottages. It has a post office, tea room, pub, hotel, restaurant, good primary school and societies on every night of the week. Villagers have built a modern village hall. **Catsfield** and **Ninfield** are so popular that most of the house moves involve people already living there. Social trends have been reversed here because a new shop *and* a new pub opened in the last few years. For rural tranquillity there is **Penhurst**, a picturesque hamlet in deep Sussex countryside. Prices in all the villages are roughly similar to those in Battle itself.

Grade Two listed terraced cottage, East Sussex

301

Journey: 95 min
Season: £3660
Peak: 1 per hr (plus 3 trains to Cannon Street)
Off-peak: 1 per hr

CROWHURST

The station makes **Crowhurst** an extremely sought-after village. The electrification of the line was followed by an influx of buyers from outside the area (two-thirds of people looking for property at that time were from London). You can now expect to pay £180,000 for a two-bedroom Victorian cottage; anything from £400,000 to £1m for an older detached house. As you come down the hill from Bexhill you see the remains of the old medieval manor house next to the Norman Church. There are some lovely tile-hung houses and the oldest yew tree in the county – it may have been here to welcome William the Conqueror. Crowhurst has often been voted best-kept village, though the judges have criticised it for the clods of mud left by the herds of cows that plod through for morning and evening milking. The Plough Inn runs an annual pumpkin show, providing plantlets to people on a specific date so that all the competitors start level. The village has a post office, a primary school, clubs, sports groups including tennis and cricket, a horticultural society and a busy drama group. Tesco at Hollington sends a bus to the village each week, and there is a shopping and recreational complex at Glyne Gap, between Bexhill and Hastings. There is also a farmers' market in the village on the first Saturday of the month.

West St Leonards
Journey: 100 min
Season: £3760
Peak: 1 per hr (plus 3 trains to Cannon Street)
Off-peak: 1 per hr
St Leonards Warrior Square
Journey: 90 min
Season: £3840*
Peak: 1 per hr (plus 3 trains to Cannon Street)
Off-peak: 2 per hr
* Also valid to Victoria via Eastbourne, but the journey is half-an-hour longer

WEST ST LEONARDS AND ST LEONARDS WARRIOR SQUARE

Though the stations are only three minutes apart, many trains do stop at both. **St Leonards** was created by James Burton and his son Decimus as stylish early speculative development. It was conceived by them as a dignified residential area, but time has taken its inevitable toll. A string of fish-and-chip shops and restaurants overlook the seafront. Conservationists are beginning to pamper the bits they can such as Victorian Southwater, which has attracted lottery funding. People from South London and Tunbridge Wells tend to move here for the sea air and comparatively low prices – though the serious retirement area is to the west, at Bexhill-on-Sea. Studio flats start at only £40,000, with smarter one-bedroom units at £65,000 to £85,000. A sea view can affect prices in boom time, but in a time of glut it tends not to make much difference. Three-bedroom houses of any period tend to cost between £150,000 and £180,000.

There are also some very large six-bedroom Victorian houses built by James Burton in more salubrious areas such as Upper Maze Hill and The Green. A six-bedroom, four-storey detached house with sea views and in need of restoration would cost around £360,000.

Journey: 93 min

Season: £3840*

Peak: 1 per hr (plus
3 trains to Cannon
Street)

Off-peak: 2 per hr

* Also valid to
Victoria via
Eastbourne, but the
journey is half-an-
hour longer

HASTINGS has never quite caught the limelight in the way that

Brighton has. Much of it has a slightly down-at-heel look, though the population still swells with trippers and holidaymakers during the summer. There are good walks along East Cliff across the gorse-covered valleys to Fairlight. Hastings seafront is much like any other, with a fine pier built in 1872. The Castle ruins now tell the 1066 story in audio-visual style. The White Rock Theatre does a good line in variety shows, concerts and plays, and there is a cinema. The High Street shops and the modern Priory Meadows mall draw shoppers from the neighbouring villages. You can buy fresh fish from fishermen pulling their boats up on to the beach.

Much of the housing is Victorian. Commuters usually prefer to live within walking distance of the station, close enough to the William Parker comprehensive if they have families. A two-bedroom house in this area would cost around £110,000; four bedrooms between £160,000 and £200,000. One-bedroom flats in a converted house come at around £65,000. A view, or even a squint of the sea, will add a small premium. A two-bedroom top floor flat with a sea view will cost around £90,000 to £100,000.

One of the smartest areas is **St Helen's**, close to Alexandra Park, where a three-storey, four-bedroom Victorian house will cost £250,000 to £275,000, and a three-bedroom semi with 100ft garden over £150,000. For modern properties people look to **Parkstone**. A two-bedroom bungalow here will sell for between £160,000 and £175,000; a four-bedroom detached around £210,000. Property prices in other parts of Hastings have fallen steeply and the neighbourhoods have become popular with the disadvantaged. If you don't mind it being in need of repair, you might find a small Victorian house for as little as £100,000. The most expensive area is probably the **Old Town**. Some people find it too claustrophobic, with tourists pressing their noses against the windows in summer, but others find the innate charm of the close ancient streets well worth the extra money. Here you might pay £100,000 to £130,000 for a two-bedroom flat; £250,000 to £300,000 for a four-bedroom Edwardian terrace.

‘Much of
Hastings has a
slightly down-at-
heel look, though
the population
still swells with
holidaymakers
during the
summer’

‘If you don't mind it being in need of repair, you might find a small Victorian house for as little as £100,000’

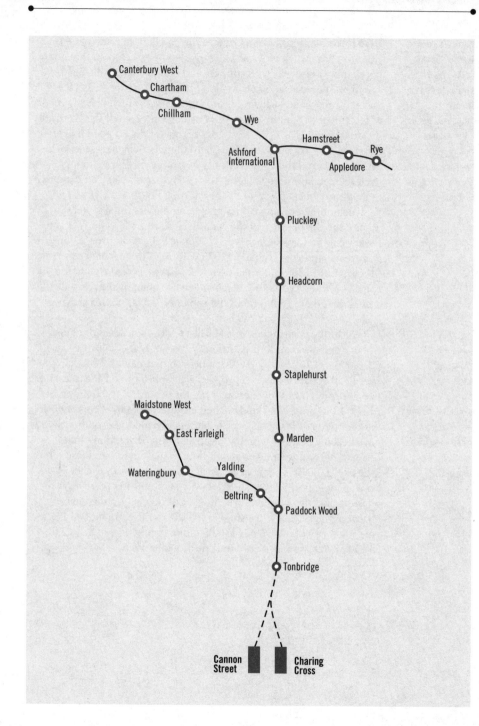

Canterbury West
Chartham
Chillham
Wye
Ashford International
Hamstreet
Appledore
Rye
Pluckley
Headcorn
Staplehurst
Maidstone West
East Farleigh
Marden
Wateringbury
Yalding
Beltring
Paddock Wood
Tonbridge
Cannon Street
Charing Cross

Charing Cross/Cannon Street
> Canterbury
(via Tonbridge and Ashford)

All trains are to Charing Cross, except where specified, and all call at Waterloo East. Most also call at London Bridge. Cannon Street can be reached off-peak by a frequent service of 11 trains per hour from London Bridge. Where through peak-hour services to Cannon Street are shown, these call at London Bridge and so give extra services to Charing Cross by changing.

TONBRIDGE For Tonbridge main entry see **Charing Cross/Cannon Street to Hastings** line, page 296.

Journey: 47 min
Season: £3160
Peak: 3 per hr plus
2 per hr to Cannon
Street
Off-peak: 3 per hr

PADDOCK WOOD Londoners have always been attracted to **Paddock Wood**. Those with happy memories of hop-picking settled here after the Second World War. More recently there has been a steady trickle of suburban refugees from Bromley and Orpington. Paddock Wood now is the centre for the distribution of fruit and vegetables between this area and Europe. It is large enough to support a department store, a Waitrose, a sports and leisure centre and some light industry. Its comprehensive school has a good reputation and doubles as an adult education centre. Three-bedroom semis cost between £200,000 and £245,000. Four-bedroom detached houses cost £250,000 to £425,000. It would be misleading to describe all the property here as cheap, however. The convenience of the journey into London means that a large detached house with extensive gardens can fetch £800,000 upwards.

> Branch line to Maidstone West via Beltring, Yalding, Wateringbury and East Farleigh

For train
information, see
overleaf

Close to **Beltring** station is the Hop Farm Country Park. It contains the largest group of Victorian oast houses in the world, and runs many events and craft fairs throughout the year. Beltring itself is not an identifiable community and has no more than a few houses. Nearby **Laddingford** is a village on the River Teise, a trout stream. It has a good pub, The Chequers, and a clutch of detached and semi-detached houses with generous gardens, which sell from £180,000 upwards.

Journey: 68 min
(from East Farleigh)
Season: £3160
Frequency: 2 per hr*
* Change at
Paddock Wood.
There are no
through trains. It is
also possible to
travel to Charing
Cross via Strood in
the opposite
direction

Yalding is a lovely old village served by winding country lanes. There are several shops, a post office, a working forge, a beautiful 14th-century bridge over the River Beult and a Church of England primary school. A farmers' market is held once a month. The settlement was once one of the main shipment points on the River Medway for cannon from the Wealden iron industry. A three-bedroom house with a handkerchief garden will cost £200,000 upwards; a substantial period property with extensive gardens and grounds, around £725,000.

The prettiness of **Wateringbury** is marred by the busy A26 Tonbridge to Maidstone road, which thumps through it. It has some shops, a post office and a Church of England primary school. You would have to pay over £340,000 for a newly built five-bedroom detached house; over £535,000 for a period detached house with land. The village has a few fine, stone-built Georgian houses and creeping modern development.

East Farleigh is much quieter than Wateringbury (though it is increasingly used as a rat run to Maidstone) and just as attractive with a five-arch 14th-century bridge pinning the centre together. It has a county primary school and a shop-cum-post-office run by villagers from a Portakabin in the pub car park following the loss of their post office in 1995. Small cottages cost at least £155,000. A newly built town house on the river might fetch £250,000; a Grade Two listed, four-bedroom detached house, £400,000.

For **Maidstone**, see **Victoria to Ashford International** line, page 314.

> Continuation of main line

Journey: 61 min
Season: £3280
Peak: 1 per hr (plus
3 trains to Cannon
Street)
Off-peak: 1 per hr

'Goudhurst is a classic English village with half-timbered cottages and a duck pond'

MARDEN has some pretty Kentish weatherboarded houses, genuinely useful shops, including a butcher, fruit and vegetable shop, and a farm shop selling locally sourced produce in what was once the court house and lock-up. There is a post office and a primary school. Two-bedroom bungalows sell for around £180,000. You might find a three-bedroom period cottage for £270,000, but a larger five-bedroom listed farmhouse will fetch £685,000 at least.

Just over four miles to the south is **Goudhurst**. It is set on a hilltop surrounded by orchards, cornfields and hop gardens and has lovely views across the valleys of the Low Weald. This is a classic English village with half-timbered cottages, a duck pond and a church, which is lit spectacularly at night. It is a self-sufficient community with its own primary school, shops and a tea shop for the summer visitors. A three-bedroom mid-terraced house can be bought for £195,000; a period cottage with land, from £480,000. Just over two miles to the south, there is a huge forest known as the Bedgebury Pinetum, which has one of the world's finest collections of conifers.

Journey: 55 min

Season: £3540

Peak: 3 per hr plus
3 per hr to Cannon
Street

Off-peak: 3 per hr

STAPLEHURST has a little light industry and a large Mazda
warehouse by the station. It is a plain village in comparison with some
of the jewels of the Kentish landscape which lie to the south. But the
vibrant community spirit (from a football club to a bellringers'
society) helped it to become Kent Village of the Year in 2003. With
6,000 residents it is large and has its own primary school, five pubs,
two churches and a full range of shops. Three-bedroom semis on
Sixties' estates sell for around £180,000; four-bedroom detached
houses from at least £350,000. Period properties carry the expected
premium, with a three-bedroom cottage selling at over £300,000.

Cranbrook has a special appeal for Londoners concerned about
schooling. Cranbrook School for boys and girls has a reputation
sufficient to add a premium to property prices within its catchment
area, which stretches just over six miles. The school is state-run, but
fees are charged for boarding so parents will sometimes choose to live
outside the area for the cheaper house prices (a £1m house can sell for
£200,000 less beyond the boundary) and pay for their children to
board. Cranbrook is an enchanting town of weatherboarded houses,
with a well-preserved smock mill at one end. A farmer's market takes
places once a month in Vestry Hall, and the nearby Weald Smokery at
Flimwell has won awards for its smoked meat and fish. New houses are
being slipped in all the time. Small two-bedroom houses, old or new,
start from £180,000. Three-bedroom semis cost £190,000 to £215,000;
period farmhouses on the outskirts from £875,000 to over £1.3m.

'Cranbrook is an enchanting town of weatherboarded houses, with a well-preserved smock mill'

A mile up the lanes from Cranbrook is **Sissinghurst** – a pretty one-
street village of weatherboarded and half-timbered houses with a pub
and primary school, close to Sissinghurst Castle (National Trust),
where Vita Sackville-West and her husband Harold Nicolson created
their wonderful gardens. **Benenden** is just over seven miles from
Staplehurst (15 minutes by car) and is popular with commuters. It is a
perfect Kentish village set around a green (cricket is played in
summer) beside the King William IV and The Bull pubs. There is a
handsome range of brick and weatherboarded cottages and old hall
houses close to the parkland of Benenden, the girls' public school. A
detached family house with three acres and an annexe, and in need of
some modernisation, could cost £750,000.

Journey: 67 min

Season: £3580

Peak: 3 per hr plus
3 per hr to Cannon
Street

Off-peak: 2 per hr

HEADCORN is very popular with commuters, not least for its large
station car park. It has an excellent shopping centre, which includes a
Sainsbury's Local, butchers, bakers, a hardware store, haberdashery,
factory outlet shop and a post office, bank and restaurants. Other
assets include a primary school, a monthly farmers' market, village
green, a flower farm and vineyard, an aerodrome and the Lashenden
Air Warfare Museum. Well-heeled commuters pay over £450,000 for

a detached house and good-sized garden on a smart modern development. Medieval timber-frame cottages are silent reminders of the past. A timber-framed farmhouse or barn conversion with swimming pool might cost £925,000 to over £1.9m. Within the village itself, a period four-bedroom house will fetch around £495,000. A three-bedroom detached house right in the centre will cost £250,000.

Smarden, three miles to the east, is a beautiful well-kept village with listed cottages grouped around a 14th–15th-century church. There is a primary school, a post office, a butcher and an art gallery. The mobile library calls once a week. The village teems with activities, including a cricket club and gardening club. It tends to be popular with families. Large, family-sized period properties with perhaps two acres will cost from £600,000 upwards. A Grade Two listed three-bedroom cottage will cost £280,000; a two-up-two-down semi, £175,000.

Biddenden, three miles south of Headcorn, is favoured because of its proximity to Tenterden, a stylish Wealden town that has become something of a local antiques centre. It has a newsagent, butcher, pub and hairdresser. This is where you find Kent's oldest commercial vineyard and can buy locally made ciders, wines and apple juices. An 18-hole international golf course, Chart Hills, designed by Nick Faldo, is nearby. A three-bedroom end-of-terrace house could cost £190,000; a four-bedroom detached house with paddock, £550,000 or more.

Journey: 78 min
Season: £3640
Peak: 2 per hr (plus 3 trains to Cannon Street)
Off-peak: 1 per hr

PLUCKLEY The countryside around **Pluckley** will be familiar to anyone who remembers the television serialisation of H.E. Bates's *Darling Buds Of May*. The influence of the Dering family – previous lords of the manor of Surrenden Dering – is obvious here. Kentish ragstone was used for many of the older houses, most of which have distinctively-arched Dering windows. The village has remained small, with a population of just over 1,000 served by two shops, a hugely admired silversmith, three pubs, one church, and a Church of England primary school. Leisure opportunities include cricket, tennis, and Pluckley Pantomime Unlimited. The smallest two-bedroom semi-detached cottage can fetch £130,000; a four-bedroom detached house, £465,000; a period country house with half an acre and panoramic views, £575,000 or more. Pluckley has the dubious reputation for being the most haunted village in England (*Guinness Book of Records 1998*).

Bethersden, a couple of miles south of the station, is another pretty conservation village of listed weatherboarded and tile-hung houses. It clusters around a post office and general store, a butcher, a church, two pubs and a primary school. A two-bedroom restored brick cottage will cost about £165,000; a four-bedroom period house, £295,000.

<table>
<tr><td>

Journey: 63 min
Season: £3780 (also
valid to Victoria)
Peak: 3 per hr plus
3 per hr to Cannon
Street
Off-peak: 2 per hr
plus 1 per hr to
Cannon Street

</td><td>

ASHFORD INTERNATIONAL For Ashford main entry see **Victoria to Ashford International** line, page 318.

</td></tr>
</table>

Note: in 2009 the service will commence from St Pancras International via the high speed Channel Tunnel route, serving Ashford and stations to the east into Thanet. The season tickets rates quoted for the stations between Ashford and Canterbury West will then change.

> Branch line to Rye via Hamstreet and Appledore

<table>
<tr><td>

To Charing Cross
Journey: 95 min
(from Rye)
Season: £3840 (also
valid to Charing
Cross/Victoria via
Hastings)
Peak: 2 per hr*
Off-peak: 1 per hr*
*There are no
through trains. All
services change at
Ashford
International

</td><td>

HAMSTREET is a large and expanding village, with a green and a duck pond, which has had some of its tranquillity returned thanks to the arrival of a bypass. It was built on land reclaimed from Romney Marsh. It is well served by, among others, a primary school, doctors' surgery, post office counter, pub, supermarket and a hairdresser. A small terraced house might cost £160,000. A four- to five-bedroom house in large grounds will fetch £425,000 or more. Just to the north are Hamstreet Woods, a linked series of five woods in a nature reserve famous for its nightingales.

 Appledore is a delightful village and one of the best places to slip off the main road to enjoy the eerie flat landscape of Romney Marsh just to the east. It has lovely old black-and-white houses and a particularly attractive main street, church and two pubs. The school closed due in part to the incomers' preference for private education and village

</td></tr>
</table>

children are bussed three miles to the primary in Wittersham. The village has an old forge, a bric-a-brac shop, an antiques shop and small general store. The Royal Military Canal, on which Appledore stands, was built in 1804 as part of the nation's defences against possible invasion by Napoleon and was re-fortified during the Second World War. Houses sell quickly here, with buyers always waiting for an opportunity. A semi-detached two-bedroom cottage will cost £180,000 or more; a four-bedroom detached house, £250,000; a seven-bedroom, four-reception-room property with land, over £700,000.

 Rye is regarded as one of the most picturesque towns on the south coast. Two miles into the mouth of the River Rother, it was once a flourishing port huddled behind protective sea walls. Now its steep cobbled streets and Tudor, Stuart and Georgian houses attract hordes

❝Two miles into
the mouth of the
River Rother, Rye
was once a
flourishing port
huddled behind
protective sea
walls❞

of summer tourists. It is an intimate place in which to live – most
people seem to know what everyone else is doing. There are plenty of
shops selling food, antiques and souvenirs, and galleries selling work
by local artists, but going to the cinema means a trip into Hastings. A
farmers' market takes place every Wednesday and a general market on
Thursday. Rye has all the usual clubs and societies, including the Rye
Players, and numerous annual events such as Rye Bay Scallops week in
January the Rye Festival in September. The area has a long tradition of
attracting creative types, such as John Ryan, the creator of *Captain
Pugwash*, and Spike Milligan who had a house nearby (in Udimore.) A
two-bedroom terraced house in Rye will cost £160,000 or more. The
picture-postcard streets include Church Square, Watchbell Street and
Mermaid Street, where a two-bedroom detached cottage with mansard
roof would cost around £230,000. The rail journey is arduous so many
choose to drive to Ashford and hop on the train there.

> Line from Ashford to Canterbury

Journey: 87 min
Season: £3780
Peak: 1 per hr plus
1 train to Cannon
Street
Off-peak: 1 per hr to
Victoria*
* Or change at
Ashford
International for a
faster service to
Charing Cross

WYE is possibly the most sought-after village in the Ashford area. Not
only does it have the station, but it also has the remarkable Bridge
Street in which many of the medieval houses are reached by stone steps.
Their purpose originally was to raise the buildings above the stream
that once ran down the middle. The Great Stour still flows through the
village and is overlooked by the Tickled Trout pub. Houses here sell at
a premium as the countryside around is so beautiful and the area feels
tucked away. A three-bedroom period home with a courtyard garden in
the village centre could cost £295,000.

The village has shops enough for anything you are likely to need.
There are also two banks, a garage, primary school and restaurant. A
farmer's market is held twice a month. London University's Imperial
College has a site at Wye Park and the students introduce an
unusually young, cosmopolitan element. The college stages an annual
rag week and celebrates Bonfire Night with a torchlight procession to
the Crown, a chalk image cut into the Downs. There are good walks
along the North Downs Way, which passes through the village, and in
the Wye Nature Reserve. The latter contains a deep wooded hollow
known as the Devil's Kneading Trough.

For train
information, see
opposite

CHILHAM The central square of 14th- and 15th-century black-and-
white houses in Chilham is an irresistible draw for tourists, film crews
and wealthy house-hunters. The church is known for its roughly
chequered flint tower. The gardens at privately owned Chilham Castle –
a Jacobean mansion with a 12th-century keep – were laid out by the

CHILHAM
Journey: 93 min
Season: £3780
Peak: 1 per hr plus 1 train to Cannon Street
Off-peak: 1 per hr to Victoria*
* Or change at Ashford International for a faster service to Charing Cross

17th-century botanist John Tradescant. The post office and general stores provides a focal point for village life, but otherwise the shops are increasingly geared towards tourists. There is a school and doctors' surgery. Properties rarely come up for sale in Chilham. If you are lucky, you might snatch a family-sized house for £400,000. Near the station, a two-bedroom semi-detached house with garden might come up for sale at £210,000. It is a village with a strong community spirit. There are football, cricket, tennis and angling clubs, and on Spring Bank Holiday the square is closed for the annual Pilgrim's Fayre. Chilham also has the advantage of being only five miles from Canterbury.

Old Wives Lees, a mile to the north, is a cheaper alternative, known to locals as Old Wives Knees. There is plenty of modern development here. A three-bedroom older house might cost £220,000.

CHARTHAM The River Stour, which divides before it enters the village, was for centuries the source of power for the former mills, one of which was converted to paper-making in the 1700s and is still in production. Chartham is not as smart as Chilham. It has a mix of old houses – some of the nicest are by the little green and the 13th-century church – and modern estates built on the sites of old orchards and St Augustine's hospital. A three-bedroom terraced cottage in Chartham would cost around £160,000; a four-bedroom detached house up to £285,000. It is served by its own primary school, a handful of small shops, a general store, and a farmers' market every Thursday afternoon.

Petham, three miles to the south-east, also has a mix of old thatched cottages, Victorian and new houses in a lovely setting. It has a church, a primary school and a garden centre. The new village hall has been built of local materials to resemble Kentish farm buildings. A Grade Two listed, four-bedroom former bakery in the centre of the village costs £475,000; a four-bedroom converted oast house in the countryside nearby costs £365,000.

Journey: 97 min
Season: £3780
Peak: 1 per hr plus 1 train to Cannon Street
Off-peak: 1 per hr to Victoria*
*Or change at Ashford International for a faster service to Charing Cross

Journey: 87 min
Season: £3780 (also valid Canterbury East)
Peak: 1 per hr plus 1 train to Cannon Street
Off-peak: 2 per hr, plus 1 per hr to Victoria (half-an-hour longer)

CANTERBURY WEST For Canterbury main entry see **Charing Cross/Victoria to Canterbury line** via Rochester, page 335.

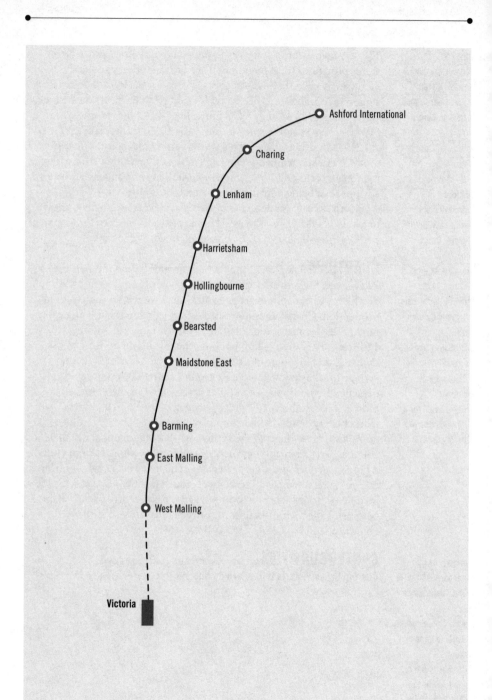

Ashford International

Charing

Lenham

Harrietsham

Hollingbourne

Bearsted

Maidstone East

Barming

East Malling

West Malling

Victoria

> Ashford International

(via Maidstone)

Journey: 50 min
Season: £3080
Peak: 3 per hr
Off-peak: 2 per hr
plus 1 per hr to
Cannon Street

WEST MALLING Considering its proximity to London, **West Malling** is surprisingly unspoilt. The old High Street, in parts Tudor and Georgian, opens out into what was once the market square. There is a Tesco, a highly regarded delicatessen, a bakery, and a store which sells everything from plimsolls to vests. A farmers' market is held once a month. Cake decorating, knitting and sewing are practised in the local craft centre. The village has two primary schools and a 900-year-old abbey. A number of local stalwarts keep the social wheels turning, running the conservation society and fending off new development. The fields that cushion the village from Maidstone are guarded with particular vigilance. The local airfield, an old Second World War fighter station, has been turned over to housing with a business park known as Kings Hill. Four- and five-bedroom houses here range from £250,000 to £600,000. The M20 is close enough to be audible from the nearby woods. A four-bedroom town house in the centre of West Malling is unlikely to cost less than £365,000, though you might pick up a two-bedroom modern box for as little as £150,000.

Journey: 54 min
Season: £3080
Peak: 2 per hr
Off-peak: 1 per hr

EAST MALLING is much smaller than West Malling and its property prices are slightly lower. The old heart is picturesque with a church, pub and village green but ex-council estates tend to dominate. The East Malling Research Station, which develops new fruit varieties, is based in Bradbourne House, a Queen Anne-style mansion. A two-bedroom Victorian terraced cottage might cost £180,000.

Journey: 58 min
Season: £3080
Peak: 2 per hr
Off-peak: 1 per hr

BARMING lies on a beautiful stretch of the River Medway. It was crossed by a wooden bridge built in 1740 until the county council condemned it and had it removed. To outsiders it may seem like a suburb of Maidstone. To those who live here it is very definitely a village. The old centre has been swallowed by new development, yet it is still extremely popular. A two-bedroom terraced cottage will cost from £140,000 to £180,000; a four-bedroom house on a modern development, £350,000 to £400,000. The post office-cum-general store sells everything from wine to plants.

Journey: 58 min

Season: £3160 (also valid at Maidstone West)

Peak: 3 per hr

Off-peak: 2 per hr plus 1 per hr to Cannon Street

MAIDSTONE EAST
Maidstone looms rather brutishly on the Kentish landscape – particularly if you approach it from the pretty southern villages. Nevertheless, it is a friendly and workmanlike hilly town where people manage to have the time to say good morning. Its focus is the River Medway, with the Archbishop's Palace (used as a place of rest on journeys to Canterbury) on the bank. It is a county town rather than a cultural centre. The remains of some 14th-century collegiate buildings are now occupied by Kent Music School. The Maidstone Museum and Bentlif Art Galley are in Chillington House, a 16th-century manor. The Corn Exchange is a cultural focus, too – home of the Hazlitt Theatre and a venue for concerts, dances and conferences. There is a multi-screen cinema in the Lockmeadow Entertainment Centre.

Maidstone has always had a commercial and agricultural bias. In earlier centuries it supplied hops, linen, paper, ragstone and gin to London. Today it is particularly strong on shopping. Fremlin Walk and The Mall offer a host of major high street names. Upmarket specialist shops can be found in the Royal Star Arcade, and designer-shops are set around a courtyard in Starnes Court, a Victorian-style arcade. The Lockmeadow General Market takes place on Tuesdays and Saturdays, carrying on a 700-year-old tradition for markets in the town; a monthly farmers' market is held in County Hall. Mote Park, comprising the former parkland of an old country house, is a popular venue for boating, fishing, football and cycling. For longer walks, the Maidstone Millennium River Park, created in 2001, offers 6 miles of paths trailing the River Medway. The Maidstone Leisure Centre has rock-climbing as well

Detached period house, near Maidstone

House style in Kent

Medieval England is clearly reflected in Kent's many hall houses. They were built with great arched, interlocking timbers, each one carefully notched and marked like a huge rustic modelling kit. Beneath the common roof the entire household would huddle around the central hearth (chimneys didn't appear until the late 16th or early 17th centuries).

Hall houses these days can be hard to recognise because they have been divided up into smaller rooms or had upper floors inserted, but the magisterial timbers soon give them away. You can see beautifully restored examples of early houses at the Weald and Downland Museum at Singleton in West Sussex.

Timber for these old buildings was felled from the great woods that stretched across the Weald (Anglo Saxon for wooded country). The intricate brick- and tilework, made from the local terracotta clays, did not develop until the 17th and 18th centuries, when it was most lavishly applied to the houses of high clergy at Canterbury. Alec Clifton-Taylor described the tile-hanging of Kent in his book, *The Pattern of English Building*: 'A good tile-hung wall is a creation of infinite subtlety, an agglomeration of shallow and slightly irregular convexities, seemingly held in place, under the right conditions of light, by a fine mesh of shadow.'

Weatherboarding is the other familiar sight among these Kentish villages, looking strangely ephemeral for a building material. Cranbrook, built upon the wealth of the Flemish clothworkers who settled here, is like a toy-town made of wood. The clothworkers also left behind them a string of cloth halls and weavers' cottages.

as leisure pools and health-and-fitness equipment. The town has the benefit of four Kentish grammar schools, two for boys and two for girls, plus a MidKent College of Higher and Further Education.

Much of the housing in Maidstone is Victorian. There are terraces of small artisans' cottages where you might pay £130,000 for three bedrooms. The houses get larger as you move further away from the centre. A four-bedroom ragstone house could cost as little as £170,000. The huge Grove Green estate is densely built but popular. You could buy a three-bedroom end-of-terrace for around £175,000, or a four-bedroom detached for £300,000.

To the south-east is **Sutton Valence**, a pretty hilltop village with views over the Weald of Kent. It is marred by the busy A274 running through it, but remains popular because of Sutton Valence School, a private school for girls and boys aged 4 to 18. There is also a local primary. The village revolves around the post office and four pubs, as well as a bookshop, antiques shop and hairdresser. At the centre is an enclave of old houses, some black-and-white half-timbered and some weatherboarded. On the outskirts a good address might cost up to £795,000; a recently renovated, two-bedroom end-of-terrace cottage £225,000. In the churchyard there is a memorial to John Willes, who introduced round-arm bowling to cricket.

Due south of Maidstone, and hardly separate from it, is one of those lovely English villages that everyone would like to call home. **Loose** owes its attraction to its position on the steep valley slope of the fast-flowing Loose stream. Old mills litter the wooded streambanks, which are overlooked by the church and The Chequers pub. The 15th-century half-timbered Wool House is administered by the National Trust and open to the public on written application. The

Loose Viaduct, designed by Thomas Telford in 1830, has helped the village to keep its old-world charm by removing large volumes of traffic. The village has a primary school, a post office-cum-shop and antiques shop. You might find a four- or five-bedroom house for £300,000 to £400,000. On the outskirts a two-bedroom apartment in a Grade Two listed 15th-century manor house could cost £200,000. A three-bedroom waterside apartment in the newly restored and converted Hayle Mill could cost around £400,000.

To the north is **Boxley**, set in an Area of Outstanding Natural Beauty with the North Downs Way and the Pilgrims Way running close by. The village has a good pub, The King's Arms, but no shop. The Channel Tunnel rail-link carves its way close to the village, but trains are hidden by cut-and-cover. To mark the Millennium, at nearby Detling Hill over 20,000 trees were planted to create White Horse Wood, Kent's latest country park.

'The Channel Tunnel rail-link carves its way close to the village, but trains are hidden by cut-and-cover'

Journey: 63 min
Season: £3200
Peak: 2 per hr
Off-peak: 1 per hr plus 1 per hr to Cannon Street

BEARSTED, insulated from Maidstone by a belt of green, is a very popular village, though in recent decades it has become rather bloated with new development. The older part, to the north of the A20, has a core of 17th-century houses around a large green on which is one of the earliest cricket pitches in the county. The poet Edward Thomas lived by the green, close to where the shops now stand – there is a butcher, baker and chemist, a newsagent and three pubs. The infant and junior schools in the area are thought to be excellent. The novelist Baroness Orczy also lived here which is why the Scout troup is known as The Scarlet Pimpernels, after her swashbuckling hero. A three-bedroom cottage near the station could cost £165,000. A family-sized house would reach £350,000 or more.

A disadvantage of Bearsted is that the old and the new sides of the village are rather split, each having its own village hall. Some villagers on the Madginford side, to the south of the Ashford road, feel that the north side grabs the limelight. The new estates to the south have their own supermarket and parade of shops. A modern two-bedroom house is priced at around £165,000.

The first pocket of rural life on Maidstone's eastern flank, but closer to Bearsted, is **Otham**. There is a 900-year-old church, a few ancient half-timbered houses, and a tradition of parish life, which is maintained. A four-bedroom family house might cost you £420,000. The WI hall also does duty as a village hall and nursery school. There are some pretty walks up the valley around the River Len, where you could keep in training for the egg-and-spoon race at the annual fête. In the Len valley is **Downswood**, an area of high-density modern housing estates set in farmland, with four shops, where you might buy a three-bedroom semi for £180,000 or a four-bedroom detached for £250,000.

Journey: 67 min
Season: £3220
Peak: 2 per hr
Off-peak: 1 per hr

HOLLINGBOURNE is one of the prettier villages in this part of

Kent, though it lies in the path of the Channel Tunnel rail-link, which
has been buried underground in order to minimise disturbance. The
High Street is lined with half-timbered houses. A three-bedroom
Georgian terraced town house will cost £205,000; a substantial four-
bedroom detached period house from £775,000. The upper village
clusters around the Elizabethan manor house, with the shops kept in
their place at the lower end. There is also a popular primary school, a
football team and several active clubs and societies. Hollingbourne's
historic church contains the 300-year-old embroidered Culpeper
cloth. The North Downs Way passes through the village and affords
some breathtaking walks.

   This is also the station for Leeds Castle. The castle was built in 1119
in the middle of a lake formed by the River Len, and given by
Edward I to his wife Eleanor of Castile. It was presented to the nation
in 1974 and is now a venue for conferences, open-air concerts, balloon
events and so on. Prices in **Leeds** are similar to those in Hollingbourne.
It merges into the neighbouring village of **Langley**, where there is a
shooting ground and a golf course, and where you can spot deer in the
woodland. A three-bedroom semi will cost around £250,000.

Journey: 71 min
Season: £3340
Peak: 2 per hr
Off-peak: 1 per hr

HARRIETSHAM is split by the A20 and has been heavily developed.

Homeowners can find themselves living with both railway noise and
road noise from the M20. It has a store, post office, an Indian
restaurant, one pub and a Church of England primary school. A
three-bedroom modern semi will cost around £185,000; a four-
bedroom house with a generous garden up to £500,000. Among the
older properties you might stumble across a strange anachronism – a
cottage with a flying freehold on a bedroom in the house next door.

Journey: 74 min
Season: £3340
Peak: 2 per hr
Off-peak: 1 per hr

LENHAM is a large working village with a population of around

3,500. It combines a pretty central market square, surrounded by
Wealden hall houses and Georgian-fronted buildings, with a strong
industrial base on the village edge. In the Seventies the Lenham
Storage Company set up Freightflow, one of Britain's first
international customs depots. This brings a lot of trans-continental
lorries to (but not through) the village. A parish hall has been built on
the outskirts and is regularly used by groups ranging from the
Archaeological Society to the Working Men's Club. There is a
delicatessen, ironmonger, hairdresser and some little antiques shops,
as well as a pub and the Dog & Bear Hotel. A country market is held
in the square once a month. It has its own primary and secondary
schools. Changes in farming methods have led to ramblers often
finding themselves prairie-walking rather than following the ancient

footpaths, but the village's saving grace is that it lies just at the foot of the North Downs, which is a designated Area of Outstanding Natural Beauty. Prices don't vary much in the villages between Maidstone and Ashford. Small cottages start at around £200,000, with prices rising to over £800,000 for the largest period properties. For a three-bedroom semi on a modern estate you would have to pay around £195,000.

Journey: 79 min
Season: £3340
Peak: 2 per hr
Off-peak: 1 per hr

'A modern library has replaced the old pig slaughterhouse'

CHARING At the heart of Charing is the old Archbishop's Palace, once used by Archbishops of Canterbury, but now a private house. The green – a favourite place to sit in summer – overlooks the market place, where a modern library has replaced the old pig slaughterhouse. The main street with its Elizabethan and Georgian-faced houses is a whole town in miniature. It has a butcher, an interiors shop, two grocers, a watchmaker, a post office and a doctor's surgery. Charing likes to be thought of not just as a pretty village, but as a hard-working one, too. A Grade Two listed, three-bedroom terraced cottage in the high street could cost £230,000; a large, family-size period house from £370,000 to £420,000; a modern four-bedroom detached house £330,000. The village has a primary school and a host of clubs and societies. The WI holds a weekly market in part of the Archbishop's Palace.

Note: in 2009 the service will commence from St Pancras International via the high speed Channel Tunnel route, serving Ashford and stations to the east into Thanet. The season tickets rates quoted in the panel, below left, for Ashford International will then change.

Journey: 87 min
Season: £3780 (also valid to Charing Cross)
Peak: 3 per hr
Off-peak: 1 per hr
See also Charing Cross/Victoria to Canterbury West, page 309

ASHFORD INTERNATIONAL People haven't been kind about Ashford since it had to swallow a large amount of post-war development. But as it happens it has got the Eurostar high speed rail-link, which has attracted huge investment. Designated a growth area in the Seventies, thousands of new homes were built. Today it is the fastest growing town in the south-east with a population of 111,000 and plans to build 31,000 new homes by 2031. Park Mall and the newly extended Country Square offer all the major high street stores, including Debenhams. Sainsbury's, Asda, Tesco and the UCL multiplex cinema have set up shop alongside junction 9 of the M20. Sports are catered for at a number of leisure centres, including the Stour Centre for swimming and the Julie Rose stadium for athletics.

Alongside the domestic station used by South Eastern Trains, there is now the International Passenger Station used by Eurostar, with combined traffic of more than 8.5m passengers each year. Lydd's London Ashford Airport is just a few miles away, operating a scheduled service to Le Touquet.

Among the swathes of modern housing a three-bedroom semi with a garage will cost £150,000 to £180,000; a modern four-bedroom detached house £200,000 to £265,000. A two-bedroom period cottage will be over £225,000. Ashford has two good grammar schools, Highworth School for Girls and Norton Knatchbull for boys, and three mixed high schools. Ashford Girls' School is private and takes both boarders and day-pupils.

On the slopes of the North Downs are several tiny hamlets amounting to little more than clusters of houses. **Boughton Aluph** (pronounced Borton Aluf) is rather more substantial. It is centred around a village green on which cricket has been played since 1752. This is flanked on one side by neo-Georgian houses and on the other by the green-painted, corrugated iron village hall, known as the Iron Room. The village has one or two distinguished Elizabethan houses but there is no shop, and the church (a mile away since the village was displaced by the Black Death) is used only in summer. The Stour Music Festival is an annual thrill for lovers of early music. The big house, Eastwell Manor, has become a hotel with a spa and restaurant. A three-bedroom detached chalet bungalow in Boughton Aluph will cost £295,000; a four-bedroom spacious late-Victorian house with large gardens will cost over £695,000.

Challock (pronounced Chollock), also in the north, is similarly priced. The name Challock means 'enclosure of calves'. The village has a considerable number of new houses squeezed between the old, and there are a couple of modern closes. A four-bedroom modern detached house will cost £345,000 or more. Challock is high up on the Downs, 630ft above sea level, and there are some spectacular footpaths and bridleways. The price you pay is that it can be very cold, windy and foggy in winter. The village has a post office-cum-general store, a pub and a The Barn Shop, selling locally grown fruit and vegetables, cheeses, pies, preserves and plants. Each September Challock hosts a Goose Fair to support village projects.

'Challock is high up on the Downs, 630ft above sea level, and there are some spectacular footpaths and bridleways'

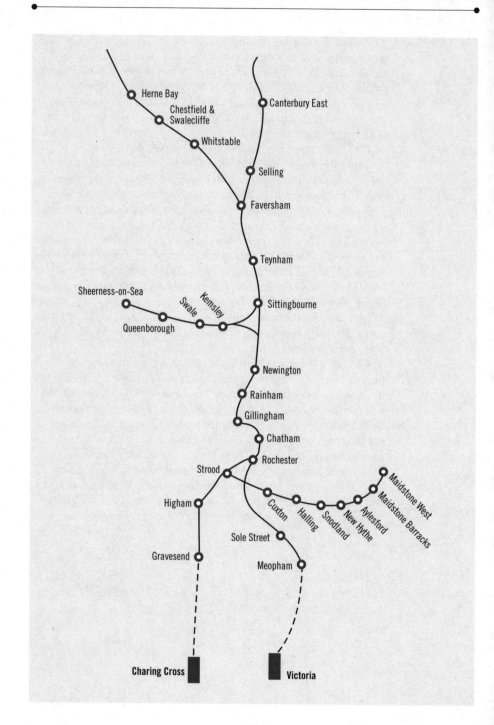

> Herne Bay and Canterbury (via Rochester)

> Line from Victoria to Meopham and Sole Street

Journey: 47 min
Season: £2640 (an 'Earlybird' for trains leaving before 0700 is £2080. Any train home but break of journey not permitted)
Peak: 3 per hr
Off-peak: 2 per hr

MEOPHAM The cricket green at Meopham grabs all the attention, being overlooked by a marvellous wooden windmill, now the headquarters of the parish council. It was built in 1801, reputedly from ships' timbers. The village is long and straggly with a main street dotted with 16th- and 17th-century houses mixed with new. There are six churches, four pubs, three primary schools and a secondary school, as well as a post office, fish-and-chip shop and hardware store. The farmers' market is held once a month in Meopham Fitness and Tennis Centre. You would pay £200,000 for a two-bedroom cottage; £250,000 to £295,000 for a three-bedroom semi-detached.

Journey: 49 min
Season: £2640
Peak: 3 per hr
Off-peak: 2 per hr

SOLE STREET is deceptively small and, because it is very rural, it can be rather expensive. It has a shop known as The Little Shop, and a pub called The Railway. The Tudor Yeoman's House is owned by the National Trust, though you have to make a written request to see it. Houses rarely come on the market. A brick-built semi-detached house with a large garden, within walking distance of the station, would be around £300,000; a four-bedroom modern detached house over £500,000.

Cobham is a pretty north Kent village in an Area of Outstanding Natural Beauty on the crest of a hill. The big house, Cobham Hall, is a girls' boarding school, but the grounds – landscaped by Repton – and the deer park are open to the public in summer. The house is a popular film location and featured in the BBC's adaptation of Charles Dickens's *Bleak House*. The Street has a good range of 18th-century houses, some Victorian and some weatherboarded, as well as a village hall and three pubs, including the Leather Bottle, which Dickens used as a setting in *Pickwick Papers*. There is also a Victorian flint primary school and a general store. A one-bedroom flat in a Victorian terrace will cost upwards of £95,000. A modern, detached five-bedroom house will be at least £450,000.

> Main line from Charing Cross

Journey: 52 min

Season: £2440 (an 'Earlybird' for trains leaving before 0700 is £1860. Any train home but break of journey not permitted)

Peak: 4 per hr plus 3 per hr to Cannon Street

Off-peak: 4 per hr

GRAVESEND For centuries the local economy of Gravesend, London's trade and defensive gateway, has been bound to the River Thames. Many of the traditional riverside industries have closed down, but the paper mills and cement works are still operating and the headquarters of the Port of London Authority and Customs and Excise have moved here. The riverside part of town is heavily atmospheric, with narrow streets and alleyways peppered with old churches, inns and historic fortifications. The best place to watch river traffic ploughing the Thames, and view Essex across the water, is from the Gordon Promenade gardens. The potential of the river is now being realised with redevelopment, parks and new housing.

Efforts to work the London Docklands miracle by replacing old industrial sores with mix-and-match housing have been determined. A vast £150m scheme is planned in the town centre, emphasising Gravesend's heritage and reconnecting the heart of the town with its lifeblood, the River Thames. The Old Town Hall is being transformed to provide a gallery and bistro, and a farmers' market spreads its wares outside the hall once a month. London, Paris, Brussels and Lille are all accessible by fast track via Eurostar from Ebbsfleet International station. There are swathes of Edwardian and Victorian houses, and some handsome Georgian houses. It is a good hunting ground for first-time buyers. A small two-bedroom Victorian house would cost around £130,000 to £140,000. On the river there are some modern developments in which two-bedroom flats with balconies sell from around £170,000. Large Georgian terraced houses with four or five bedrooms can be bought for around £300,000, depending on condition.

Property prices are higher to the south of the town, especially in the Thirties'-built roads around the golf course. A detached house will cost from £200,000 to around £650,000, for which you would also get a very large garden. Another more expensive part of Gravesend is the Windmill Hill conservation area, a mile from the town centre, where some of the houses have giddy river views. A two-bedroom Victorian house would cost at least £160,000. Some of the larger houses have been converted into flats. If you were looking for a house on a decent modern estate, then the answer could be Rivermount, built in the Eighties, where a four-bedroom detached house costs around £250,000 to £260,000, a three-bedroom semi £190,000, and you might get a good view thrown in.

The village of **Shorne**, two miles east, is pretty and old (though with its fair share of new), and very much sought-after since this part of north Kent can seem rather bleak. It is also close to the A2. Snob value adds to the prices of the 15th- and 16th-century timber-framed cottages. You would have to pay £180,000 to £200,000 for a two-bedroom house, £250,000 for a modest three-bedroom house in a terrace. There are a few detached Thirties' houses, valued at around £600,000 to £700,000.

Journey: 59 min

Season: £2600

Peak: 2 per hr plus 2 per hr to Cannon Street

Off-peak: 2 per hr

HIGHAM is mostly a soup of houses built in the Sixties and Seventies with a few older properties thrown in for flavour. A Victorian two-up-two-down will cost around £130,000; a modern three-bedroom semi around £200,000. There is a hairdresser, greengrocer, three pubs and two takeaways. A campaign is underway to save the post office from closure. Gad's Hill Place was Charles Dickens's home from 1856 until the end of his life, and is now an independent girls' school. He left *Edwin Drood* unfinished when he died in 1870.

Journey: 63 min

Season: £2860

Peak: 3 per hr plus 2 per hr to Cannon Street

Off-peak: 2 per hr

STROOD is linked to Rochester by a bridge over the River Medway. Its small High Street has a broader choice of shops than Rochester's, and B&Q, Argos and Matalan draw people from over the water. The houses in the centre are flat-fronted, late-Victorian terraces, which cost around £110,000 for three bedrooms and are attractive to first-time buyers. Close to the station there is a surge of Fifties' housing where a three-bedroom home would also cost around £110,000. In the more sedate Thirties' developments near the fringes of the town, a three-bedroom house would cost around £145,000.

The area is popular for boating. Further out along the Medway estuary, the marina at **Upnor** throngs with hundreds of craft. Developers have catered for the sailors' needs by providing small town houses, costing around £235,000, and semis along the riverbank. The main street is pretty, with old weatherboarded houses. Upnor Castle, now a museum, was built in the mid-16th century to defend Chatham dockyard. The Isle of Grain, which thrusts out like a hammerhead over the mouth of the estuary, bristles with oil terminals and refineries. It is one of the fastest growing container ports in the country. British Gas has 900 acres of land earmarked for future industrial development.

Developers have catered for the sailor's needs by providing small town houses along the riverbank

> Branch line to Maidstone West via Cuxton, Halling, Snodland, New Hythe, Aylesford and Maidstone Barracks

Journey: 83 min (from Aylesford)
Season: £3160 (also valid via Maidstone)
Peak: 2 per hr*
Off-peak: 2 per hr*
* Change at Strood. There are no through trains. Or travel in the opposite direction and change at Maidstone Barracks (footpath to Maidstone East) or at Paddock Wood

CUXTON is one of the Medway villages that boomed with the cement industry during the 19th century. It has an attractive mock-Tudor station with a hand-operated level crossing and an old-fashioned signal box, however the Stategic Rail Authority is thinking of curtailing the service in the future. Some of the houses are Victorian terraces suitable for first-time buyers, selling for around £120,000 for two bedrooms.

On the borders of Cuxton, **Halling** is dominated by the large riverside cement works. This part of north Kent is not very popular, but it does offer the prospect of affordable housing. A detached family house can be bought for £240,000. **Snodland**, too, has been stigmatised by association with the cement industry. Blue Circle and the area around the cement works is plagued by dust and lorries. Snodland has a plain Victorian centre where terraced houses sell for about £130,000. Or you could pay around £160,000 for a three-bedroom semi.

New Hythe is very close to the old Aylesford paper mills, which have now been converted to light industrial use. Victorian and Thirties' semis start at about £140,000. **Aylesford** is marginally more appealing and is thought to offer good value for money. Nearby is a retail park with a Sainsbury's, Comet, Homebase and so on. It has a 14th-century ragstone bridge and some very old houses overlooking the River Medway. These might sell in the region of £140,000 and upwards for two bedrooms. There are also lots of old terraced properties with two or three bedrooms, selling in the £75,000 to £80,000 range. For Maidstone see **Victoria to Ashford International line via Maidstone**, page 314.

Converted oast house

324

> Continuation of main line

To Victoria
Journey: 41 min
Season: £3000
Peak: 3 per hr
Off-peak: 3 per hr

To Charing Cross
Journey: 68 min
Season: £3000 (also
valid to Victoria)
Peak: 2 per hr plus
1 per hr to Cannon
Street
Off-peak: 2 per hr

ROCHESTER Most of this apparently seamless string of north Kent towns looks as if it might have detached itself from the north of England and slipped southwards during the night. Rochester, however, is something of an exception, having sustained a policy of architectural conservation on the back of the Charles Dickens industry – just as in the past it was able to create fine buildings on the back of its maritime trade. The pedestrianised High Street has an intimate villagey atmosphere with tourist shops, gift shops, antiques shops and small businesses packing the narrow streets around it, as well as a monthly farmers' market. It is pleasant to stroll and enjoy some of the older Elizabethan buildings and excellent Georgian houses. The town is stiff with locations used by Dickens in his novels. The Royal Victoria Hotel is The Bull in *Pickwick Papers*; The Bull is The Blue Boar in *Great Expectations*; Miss Haversham's home was loosely based on Restoration House; *Edwin Drood* was set in Rochester. The Charles Dickens Centre at Eastgate House has the reconstructed Swiss chalet workshop in which the author worked while he lived at Gad's Hill. Every year the town dresses itself in 19th-century costume for the summer Dickens Festival and Christmas Dickensian festivities.

One of the most prestigious areas is close to the castle. This was built during the reign of Henry I and has a well-preserved square keep overlooking the river. Nearby are the cathedral, largely 12th-century, and King's School Rochester, the co-educational public school. One of the best places for period properties is St Margaret's Street, where a four-bedroom early Georgian house with garage will fetch £300,000 to £600,000. In the streets just off it, and lying within the same conservation area, are large, five-bedroom Victorian houses, which fetch around £300,000 to £400,000. For less expensive homes you need to travel five or ten minutes out from the centre. Here you will find row upon row of Victorian terraces. They front straight on to the pavement and sell at around £110,000 for two bedrooms. There are a few small estates where you could buy a detached four-bedroom house for about £300,000. One of the most sought-after is River View on Bristol Road, where a detached four-bedroom house with river views could fetch between £500,000 and £600,000. To the south is a large area of Thirties' housing with some bay-fronted terraces and semis, and a few bungalows. The average price for a three-bedroom semi in good condition is about £180,000.

You have to suffer a little to commute from Rochester. The one-way system makes driving to the station difficult, and when you get there it is not easy to park. The area is earmarked for growth, but sites being prepared for new housing have been mothballed for the recession.

'Rochester is stiff with locations used by Dickens in his novels'

To Victoria
Journey: 44 min
Season: £3020
Peak: 3 per hr
Off-peak: 3 per hr

To Charing Cross
Journey: 70 min
Season: £3020 (also valid to Victoria)
Peak: 2 per hr plus 3 per hr to Cannon Street
Off-peak: 2 per hr

CHATHAM

Little flat-fronted Victorian terraces, ideal for first-time buyers at around £100,000, cram the steep hillsides around Chatham dockyards, once the industrial heart of the town. Its first ship was launched in 1586 to join the fleet against the Spanish Armada. Four centuries and 400 Royal Navy ships later, the docks were closed in 1984 and handed over to a trust. The 80-acre site, which contains 47 scheduled monuments, is the most complete Georgian and early Victorian dockyard in the world. Now it is almost as much of an attraction to house-hunters as it is to tourists visiting the several museums located here. You can board a Cold War submarine or a Second World War destroyer, see artefacts from the *Cutty Sark* or walk the quarter-mile long Ropery. Other parts have been converted to residential use with a choice of both restored and new properties. The new developments include one- and two-bedroom flats starting at about £150,000, and town houses modelled on the Georgian officers' terraces, priced at £290,000. Restored properties include 12 houses in a terrace built on five floors between 1722 and 1732. These are the cream of the bunch. Former naval stable blocks have been converted into three-bedroom mews houses selling at about £300,000.

For cheaper modern housing you could look at the Walderslade area, a huge estate with two-bedroom terraces at £125,000 and four-bedroom family houses at £220,000 to £270,000. The Walderslade Woods area is more sought-after and prices can rise to £350,000 for a five-bedroom house.

Schools in Kent

Kent still has some of its old grammar schools, though parents should remember that entry is highly selective.

At Tonbridge there are two grammars for girls and The Judd for boys, as well as the Tonbridge independent boarding and day school for boys.

Tunbridge Wells is full of good schools, including Tunbridge Wells Girls' Grammar, Tunbridge Wells Grammar for boys and The Skinners' School for boys. Kent College Pembury is an independent girls' boarding and day school.

Sevenoaks is rightly proud of Sevenoaks School, an independent co-educational day and boarding school beside Knole Park, and Walthamstow Hall independent day school for girls.

At Cranbrook, close to Staplehurst station, is the Cranbrook co-educational day and boarding grammar school. It is so popular that houses within a five-mile catchment area may carry a premium price. Nearby is Benenden, the girls' public school.

Maidstone has its Girls' Grammar and Maidstone Grammar for boys (girls in the sixth). Girls can also look to Ashford where there is Highworth Grammar for girls, Invicta Grammar and Ashford independent day and boarding school.

King's Canterbury, the independent co-educational day and boarding school, is set in the cathedral precinct and has a strong musical tradition. Its rival is Kent College, an independent, co-educational day and boarding school with its own 90-acre farm. There are also grammars: Simon Langton Boys', Simon Langton Girls' and Barton Court mixed.

Gravesend has Gravesend Girls' Grammar, which does rather better than Gravesend Boys'. Chatham has Chatham Girls' Grammar (boys in the sixth form). Chatham House boys' grammar also performs well in the school league tables. Other good grammar schools can be found in Broadstairs, Sittingbourne and Faversham.

Rochester also has its own cathedral school, mostly for day pupils – King's is co-educational, independent and fiercely no-nonsense. The alternative is Rochester Independent College, a non-selective co-ed. Rochester Girls' Grammar was founded in the 1880s to produce girls 'fit to adorn the homes of England'.

To Victoria

Journey: 48 min

Season: £3020

Peak: 3 per hr

Off-peak: 3 per hr

To Charing Cross

Journey: 74 min

Season: £3020 (also valid to Victoria)

Peak: 2 per hr plus 3 per hr to Cannon Street

Off-peak: 2 per hr

GILLINGHAM is the largest of the Medway towns and commercial

big brother to Chatham, with which it shares the former naval dockyards and depot. The large shopping centre has a pedestrianised High Street with the usual chain stores. There are very good leisure facilities, including an ice rink, leisure centre, leisure pool, indoor bowls and cricket. Gillingham Football Club is currently playing in the second division of the Football League. The dockyard here is ringed by an old Georgian fortification system called the Brompton Lines: one-and-a-half-miles of moats and ramparts overlooked by the Napoleonic Fort Amherst.

Near the town centre, in the tightly-packed Victorian streets, first-time buyers can still pick up small terraced houses for around £110,000 to £120,000. One of the better areas is Darland, a Thirties' estate where four-bedroom detached houses sell for upwards of £220,000.

To Victoria

Journey: 53 min

Season: £3060

Peak: 3 per hr plus 3 per hr to Cannon Street

Off-peak: 4 per hr

RAINHAM is much more suburban in character than either

Gillingham or Chatham, with the atmosphere of a dormitory town. It was once popular with hop-pickers coming down from London. The station is large and the London trains are fast. Housing is a mixed bag, from late-Victorian farmworkers' terraces at £100,000 to £110,000 to Thirties' houses in the Wigmore area, where three-bedroom detached houses sell from £180,000 upwards. Hempstead is another attractive area with an old villagey heart and an outgrowth of new estates: you can pay from £110,000 for a starter home right up to £550,000 for a large detached house. The Riverside Country Park, which extends along the southern shore of the Medway Estuary between Gillingham and Rainham, offers escape from the relentless housing. The park was formed from reclaimed salt marshes and is linked from west to east by the Saxon Shore Way – a coastal footpath that runs 140 miles between Gravesend and Rye.

To Victoria

Journey: 76 min

Season: £3120

Peak: 2 per hr plus 3 trains to Cannon Street

Off-peak: 2 per hr

NEWINGTON The countryside does try to breathe here, but is soon

submerged by Sittingbourne. Newington is thought to be more rural, but in fact it is bisected by the busy A2 and is beginning to merge at one end with Sittingbourne and at the other end with Hartlip. A two-up-two-down terrace will cost about £120,000; a modern three-bedroom semi close to £160,000. Calloways Lane is particularly smart. A large four-bedroom detached house on up to an acre of ground here would sell for £390,000.

'The Saxon Shore Way runs 140 miles between Gravesend and Rye'

Hartlip, a mile or so to the south-west, is more sought-after. It has a villagey feel and is close to the Medway Towns. This is one of the first conveniently placed, attractive villages that you reach on your way out of London through this part of Kent. The conservation area in the village centre encompasses a handful of listed buildings, 15th-century thatched cottages and a fine, half-timbered, pink-and-white house. The rest is brick and weatherboarding, plus some modern houses built in the Eighties. It is a good address. You will have to pay £480,000 or more for a four- or five-bedroom property with a garden. There is a primary school with about 105 pupils, a church, a Methodist chapel and a village hall. The local parish pump is The Rose And Crown – symbolic of Kent's reputation as the Garden of England and its allegiance to the Sovereign. The village is friendly to newcomers and used to commuters. The main worry is that Gillingham might burst at the seams and engulf it.

To Victoria

Journey: 60 min

Season: £3200

Peak: 3 per hr plus 3 per hr to Cannon Street

Off-peak: 4 per hr

SITTINGBOURNE
Like the Medway Towns, Sittingbourne is more affordable for first-time buyers and has grown considerably over the past few years. Much of the town centre looks more like Coronation Street than Kent, with terraces fronting straight on to the pavement. A two- or three-bedroom house here could be bought for between £80,000 and £115,000. Yet it is still only an hour by train from London. The north side of town is the old industrial area, now joined by smart modern developments where prices for a four-bedroom house are between £180,000 and £300,000. On the south side of town, Thirties' detached houses and semis – some of them with good long gardens – sell for £200,000 or more. There are new estates here, too, with three-bedroom terraces at just over £160,000.

The mile-long High Street still displays something of its history as a market town (there is a Friday market) and coaching stop. Pilgrims used to rest here on their way to Canterbury. The Red Lion, the George Inn and Ypres Tavern are still there, and there is evidence of Georgian buildings behind the High Street's modern façades. Plans are taking shape for a proposed town regeneration scheme to provide more shopping and leisure facilities. Sittingbourne was also once a busy harbour town. The muddy Milton Creek running into town from The Swale is lined with warehouses, factories and reedy inlets. Funding is in place for the Milton Creek Gateway Landscape project, which will enable people to walk beside the water. The town's prosperity used to depend on the hugely expanding demand for bricks, paper and cement in the late 19th century. Of these traditional local industries only paper-making remains, the others have been replaced by modern light manufacturing. For recreation there is a huge, multi-million-pound leisure centre, The Swallows.

Restored timber-
framed house,
north Kent

House prices rise a little as you move out to the villages. To the
west is **Stockbury**, which has a pub, green and a farm shop housing the
village shop and post office. It would be difficult to find a property
here for less than £200,000 – for which you might be lucky to get a
two-bedroom bungalow. A four-bedroom house would be nearer the
£380,000 mark. Closer to Sittingbourne is **Borden**. It is quite smart and
attracts executives. Some parts of it are very old indeed; a 13th-
century church is set in the conservation area, which contains some
quaint, white-painted weatherboarded cottages. You would pay from
£130,000 for a semi-detached house. Four-bedroom bungalows start
at around £330,000. Much of the building is in brick, with some
timber-frame and some modern infilling. At the heart of the village is
the Playstool – an old Kentish name for a playing field on two levels.
From the top level you have wonderful views across the countryside.
The main street is called The Street and has a pub. The village has a
high proportion of elderly people as well as a thriving primary school.

'Milstead has a
truly Kentish feel
to it, with leafy
lanes, a church, a
pub and a
thatched cricket
pavilion'

Less than a mile away is **Tunstall**. Prices here are similar to those in
Borden, though the village itself is tiny, with a good primary school,
but no shops. Due south of here is **Milstead**. Opinions and signposts
vary about the correct spelling (several maps and guides, though not
the Ordnance Survey, omit the a), though there is no doubt about its
status as the most sought-after village in the area. It has a truly
Kentish feel to it, with leafy lanes on the slopes of the North Downs
giving on to a church, a pub, a thatched cricket pavilion, a primary
school and old thatched cottages which tend to be occupied by well-
paid professionals. A four-bedroom barn conversion on the outskirts
of the village costs £500,000. The village itself is a conservation area
and the surrounding countryside is a designated Area of Outstanding

Natural Beauty. At the centre there is a tiny green with an old cedar tree growing on it, framed by a row of tile-hung cottages, the church and Milstead Manor. It is a busy place. The cricket attracts people from neighbouring villages. But it is worried about becoming a dormitory village, though there are truly local families who have lived here for years. A car is essential for all those who do not want to have to use the post bus.

> Branch line to Sheerness-on-Sea via Kemsley, Swale and Queenborough

Journey: 110 min
(from Sheerness)

Season: £3200

Peak: 3 per hr*

Off-peak: 2 per hr*

* Change at Sittingbourne. There are no through trains

KEMSLEY was built to house workers from the nearby paper mills and is formally laid out with a central square containing a modern social centre built in Queen Anne style. The area is not greatly sought-after. A four-bedroom detached house with garden costs £230,000. There is also a large new estate on the outskirts where prices are low: three-bedroom semis sell for £160,000 and four-bedroom detached houses for £200,000 or more.

Swale station is in a bleak and remote spot where the only housing to speak of is the occasional farmhouse on the flattest of horizons. It was named after the channel that separates the Isle of Sheppey from the mainland, spanned by the Kingsferry Bridge and newer Sheppey Bridge. The Royal Society for the Protection of Birds' Elmley Marshes Nature Reserve begins here and stretches across the southern part of the island. At **Queenborough**, once again you find the typically north Kentish combination of relentless late-Victorian housing in a harbour setting. The High Street, which provides for local shopping, ends in an esplanade where you can watch the boats using all-tide landing gear. New housing is going up but locals are worried that the infrastructure may not keep pace with it. Two- and three-bedroom Victorian terraced houses sell from about £185,000. The possibility of a new airport on the marshes at Cliff keeps being riased, this time promoted by London mayor Boris Johnson, but is being resisted.

'Sheerness-on-Sea is where Nelson's body was brought in HMS *Victory* after the Battle of Trafalgar in 1805'

Sheerness-on-Sea, at the north-west tip of the Isle of Sheppey, is protected by a massive sea wall above the clean shingle beach, from which there are good views over the Thames estuary. The design of the old dockyards was supervised by Samuel Pepys in his capacity as Secretary to the Navy Board in 1665. This is where Nelson's body was brought in HMS *Victory* after the Battle of Trafalgar in 1805. Today Sheerness has a flourishing cargo port. Most of the town consists of Victorian terraced housing, built for dockyard workers and now selling at around £95,000 for two bedrooms. Ex-council semis sometimes fetch about £120,000. **Minster**, two miles to the east, is more popular. Bungalows here tend to sell for £175,000, three-bedroom semis for £250,000. Established between the wars by speculative developers who sold plots to Londoners who wanted seaside homes, Minster is still growing. There is a community hospital and local shopping. The coast from Minster to Leysdown is a more or less continuous run of caravan sites and chalets.

> Continuation of main line

To Victoria
Journey: 86 min
Season: £3200
Peak: 2 per hr plus
3 trains to Cannon
Street
Off-peak: 2 per hr

TEYNHAM is a sprawling village unromantically sandwiched between the A2 and the railway. It was once ten hamlets, hence its name. Though only a few trains stop here in peak hours, Teynham is very much a commuter village. Most of the houses were built during the Sixties and Seventies. A three-bedroom semi of that vintage will sell for around £170,000. A run of older, turn-of-the-century housing flanking the A2 provides two- or three-bedrooms for around £130,000. Outside the road-rail sandwich lie the hop-fields that supply the Faversham breweries.

To Victoria
Journey: 69 min
Season: £3600
Peak: 3 per hr plus
3 per hr to Cannon
Street
Off-peak: 4 per hr

FAVERSHAM is a hugely popular old market town. The historic Market Place lies within a mainly pedestrianised conservation shopping area, and still has markets on Tuesdays, Fridays and Saturdays. Tudor and Georgian houses exude period charm, and Faversham Creek brings the sights and smells of the river. It was this navigable tidal inlet that earned Faversham its status as one of the Cinque Ports. The warships built here won it the further title of King's Port. There are still some medieval warehouses left on its banks, though today it is the brewing industry that dominates – Shepherd Neame was founded here in 1692 and there are great pubs, including The Chimney Boy, The Bull and The Phoenix. There are barge races in summer and a hop festival in September.

Small, plain terraced houses sell for between £100,000 and £150,000. For more expensive property, the most sought-after streets are West Street and Abbey Street, which contain some of the oldest half-timbered buildings in Kent. They very rarely come on the market, but their current value is probably about £300,000 or more. People looking for new houses and flats should consider the new Whitstable Road development, with prices up to £250,000.

The villages around Faversham benefit from their proximity to such an attractive and popular town. Stretched along a valley bottom to the south-west is **Newnham**. The village is a conservation area with a population of 300, where everyone knows everyone. There are two pubs, the Tapster and the Old George, both serving excellent food. A two-bedroom weatherboarded cottage might fetch £145,000; a four-bedroom detached £295,000 to £330,000. Newnham's big house is an interesting Tudor pile with two chalk fireplaces and decorative plasterwork in the form of tumbling leaves. It is privately owned.

Eastling, a mile from Newnham, has 14th- and 15th-century timbered hall houses and ancient weatherboarded houses scattered along country lanes. The cheapest two-bedroom weatherboarded house would be likely to cost around £150,000; a four- or five-bedroom house with paddocks £400,000 or more. The village has a pub and a church (with a yew tree reputedly over 900 years old), and a primary school with a toddlers' group, but there are no shops. The village has a number of vigorous societies, but the character of the place has changed over the years as commuters have replaced agricultural workers. Two or three miles away is Belmont House, an 18th-century mansion set in fine parkland, which is open to the public.

Boughton village, a couple of miles east, has a charming main street lined with period houses, laced with a few shops and two good pubs. It has a complete cross-section of residents, including quite a few commuters. A modern three-bedroom terrace would sell for £160,000. A larger four- or five-bedroom early Victorian house would be expected to fetch around £300,000.

> Fork from Faversham to Herne Bay

To Victoria
Journey: 81 min
Season: £3600
Peak: 2 per hr plus
3 per hr to Cannon
Street
Off-peak: 2 per hr

WHITSTABLE The sea can be a force to be reckoned with in Whitstable. New sea defences now keep it snug and dry, but in the terrible storm of 1953, waves breached the sea wall and the tide surged miles inland. The oyster industry was severely disrupted then too, though it has been built up again so successfully that the harbour area now contains the largest oyster hatchery in Europe. There is an annual summer oyster festival, and the beginning of the oyster season is marked by the blessing of the sea.

The housing market has slowed recently, though it will continue to have appeal among commuters and second-home hunters. The town centre is full of little Victorian terraces of two-up-two-downs. These now sell for about £165,000. There is also some well-established smart new housing. In the Horsebridge development, a modern, four-bedroom detached house overlooking the sea would cost £250,000 upwards. On the seafront there are some 200-year-old smugglers' and fishermen's cottages with added cutesey value, but they very rarely come on to the market and buyers must move quickly to catch them.

As a resort Whitstable is fairly restrained, though there are the usual seaside amusements and it is popular for yachting and watersports. The rows of weatherboarded fishermen's cottages and old boat-sheds along the shingle beach (there is sand to the east and west) are the subject of a Turner sketch.

'The harbour in Whitstable now contains the largest oyster hatchery in Europe'

Tankerton, on the east side of Whitstable old town, is sedate, slightly more expensive and a popular retirement haven. There is a charming promenade, cliff walks and beach huts. Houses on the seafront sell for between £350,000 and £675,000, and overlook the Tankerton Slopes, a wide grassy verge that runs down to the beach. Extending from the beach is a long shingle spit known as The Street. This is where two tides meet, and at low water you can walk right out along it into the sea. **Seasalter**, to the west, is another retirement area with its own parade of shops and ration of bungalows. In Joy Lane you will find some of the most expensive houses in the area. This is where Somerset Maugham, whose uncle was vicar of Whitstable, learned to ride his bicycle. If you fancy one of the large detached houses he must have wobbled past, you'll need to spend anything from £320,000 upwards. A three-bedroom ex-local authority house will cost around £135,000.

To Victoria
Journey: 85 min
Season: £3600
Peak: 2 per hr plus 3 trains to Cannon Street
Off-peak: 1 per hr

CHESTFIELD & SWALECLIFFE

There is a bit of snob value attached to Chestfield. It is a cut above the seaside tat, thinks of itself as a village and has a private golf club, but is very close to the A299 dual carriageway. There are some very large period houses that sell for over £550,000. Between these are new developments or individually built modern houses on small plots. On the Churchwood Park estate, family houses sell from just under £300,000 to £400,000. The village also has some properties for first-time buyers. Expect to pay around £120,000 for one-bedroom starter homes. Chestfield now spills over into Swalecliffe which has lots of ex-council houses in the £140,000 range. It also has a primary school.

To Victoria
Journey: 86 min
Season: £3600
Peak: 2 per hr plus 3 per hr to Cannon Street
Off-peak: 2 per hr

HERNE BAY

The Victorian seaside resort has spread its tentacles over quite a large area, and the retirement town atmosphere of Herne Bay has been rejuvenated as young buyers arrived from Canterbury. Spacious Victorian and Edwardian houses line the seafront and a flat within one of them will cost around £95,000 or more. Numerous roads lead down to the sea, fitted snugly with two- to three-bedroom terraced houses, which sell at around £140,000; and modern detached houses which rise to £240,000 depending on the views. Herne Bay's long exposed foreshore can be sealed off when there are severe storms; otherwise it is extremely popular with day-trippers, and with sailing and fishing enthusiasts. The seafront has had a

£3.5m makeover, and the pier (the second longest after Southend), which was damaged by storms in 1953 and 1978, is due to get one too. The 1920s' Art Deco bandstand gleams with fresh paint.

One mile inland is the parent village of **Herne**, a collection of pretty white weatherboarded cottages on a hillside with a restored, working, 18th-century smock mill. A mid-terrace cottage here would cost just over £150,000.

Large family house, Herne Bay

> Main line from Faversham to Canterbury East

To Victoria

Journey: 79 min

Season: £3600

Peak: 1 per hr plus 1 per hr changing at Faversham

Off-peak: 1 per hr

SELLING This is a nice position to be in. You are close to the pretty market town of Faversham, near enough to Canterbury for special shopping, and also handy for the sea. The countryside starts to roll south-east of Faversham, and at Perry Wood there is a huge area of unspoilt accessible woodland. The Pulpit, a wooden structure built on the highest point of a mound, offers panoramic views over Kent. There are some very fine half-timbered houses and oasts scattered in the deep lanes around here. A three-bedroom cottage might cost £225,000; a four-bedroom oast conversion £590,000.

To Victoria

Journey: 86 min

Season: £3780 (also valid at Canterbury West)

Peak: 1 per hr plus 1 per hr changing at Faversham

Off-peak: 2 per hr

See also Canterbury West on the Charing Cross/Victoria to Canterbury line, page 311

CANTERBURY EAST

The city of Canterbury charmingly combines modernity and tourism with its medieval heritage. Parts of the centre were bombed in the Second World War and nasty Sixties' infills are now being replaced. Beneath the modern shopping precinct lie Roman mosaics, which are open to the public. The central area is pedestrianised, which makes it a pleasant place to shop, and the new Whitefriars shopping centre has boosted choice. Much of the beautiful medieval city remains in the narrow streets of timber-framed houses around the cathedral, where Thomas Becket was murdered. The most sought-after area is within the city walls, close to the Cathedral and King's co-educational public school. The latter occupies many of the buildings that were formerly part of the monastery attached to the cathedral. Grade Two listed houses here are snapped up quickly. Anything with a garage sells at a premium, as parking in Canterbury can be a nightmare. At the cheaper end of the market, a tiny late-Victorian terraced cottage within the city walls would be likely to fetch between £140,000 and £170,000. An over-supply of smart high-spec flats in the city centre has led to a drop in prices and now they fetch £150,000 to £200,000.

The city margin is ringed with roomy Victorian detached and semi-detached houses. In Ethelbert Road, to the south, haunt of doctors and academics, the houses have as many as ten bedrooms and sell for around £600,000. There are also plenty of modern developments from the Fifties, Sixties and Eighties. An end-of-terrace cottage with two bedrooms within the city walls in the south of the town would cost around £300,000.

The University of Kent, built in the Sixties high on a windy hill just outside the city, attracts a lot of students to the St Stephen's area. Many of the bay-windowed Thirties' semis here are rented – some are bought by the parents of wealthier students. A three-bedroom house could cost around £200,000. Investors and professionals also buy in the area around St Peter's Grove, where a flat-fronted turn-of-the-century house may be picked up for £150,000.

In the countryside around people prefer to look to the south where the landscape is prettier. Two-and-a-half miles south-east is the village of **Bridge**, which is extremely pretty and commensurately expensive. It has a butcher, baker, post office and primary school and offers a mix of late-Victorian and modern houses, but remains compact. A four-bedroom period cottage on the outskirts would cost £430,000. On its eastern side is **Patrixbourne**, which is tiny and pretty and so popular that half-timbered houses and thatched cottages often sell by word of mouth. Period houses here start at £500,000. The Nail Bourne river runs through Patrixbourne, though it fills only after heavy downpours and for most of the year it is dry.

Looking east from Canterbury you find **Wickhambreaux**, a typical Kentish village with a green and an old church on one side, a manor house, and the Little Stour river with a watermill that has been converted into flats. The village once formed part of the Kentish estates of Joan Plantagenet, the Fair Maid of Kent, wife of the Black Prince. There are no shops and a minimal bus service, but the village does have a pub and a Church of England primary school. Two summer fêtes on the green bring the villagers together. There has been little new development for 40 years. A large village house would cost from £700,000. One way of telling old villagers from new is by the name they give to the main street. Incomers rather grandly call it The Street, but to old villagers it is Gutter Street.

At **Stodmarsh**, slightly to the north of Wickambreaux, the landscape becomes very rural, with good views across the Stour valley. Stodmarsh itself is a small village with an excellent pub. Properties rarely come on the market and prices are much the same as in Wickhambreaux and Bridge. The old coal-mining area has been turned into a nature reserve with man-made lakes to attract birds and wildlife.

‘Wickhambreaux once formed part of the Kentish estates of Joan Plantagenet, the Fair Maid of Kent’

Index

M